"THE HIGHER CHRISTIAN LIFE"

SOURCES FOR THE STUDY OF THE HOLINESS, PENTECOSTAL, AND KESWICK MOVEMENTS

A forty-eight-volume facsimile series reprinting extremely rare documents for the study of nineteenth-century religious and social history, the rise of feminism, and the history of the Pentecostal and Charismatic movements

Edited by

Donald W. Dayton
Northern Baptist Theological Seminary

Advisory Editors

D. William Faupel, *Asbury Theological Seminary*
Cecil M. Robeck, Jr., *Fuller Theological Seminary*
Gerald T. Sheppard, *Union Theological Seminary*

A GARLAND SERIES

PENUEL; OR, FACE TO FACE WITH GOD

Edited by
A. McLean
J. W. Eaton

Garland Publishing, Inc.
New York & London
1984

For a complete list of the titles in this series
see the final pages of this volume.

Library of Congress Cataloging in Publication Data
Main entry under title:
PENUEL, OR, FACE TO FACE WITH GOD.

("The Higher Christian life")
Selections from the proceedings of three National
Camp Meetings held at Vineland, N.J., Manheim, Pa.,
and Round Lake, N.Y.
Reprint. Originally published: New York :
W.C. Palmer, 1869.
1. Methodist Church—Sermons.   2. Sermons, American.
3. Camp-meetings—United States.   I. McLean, A.
(Alexander)   II. Eaton, J. W. (Joel W.), 1836?–
III. National Camp-Meeting.   IV. Title: Penuel.
V. Title: Face to face with God.   VI. Series.
BX8333.A1P36   1984   269'.24'0974   84-18862
ISBN 0-8240-6427-5 (alk. paper)

The volumes in this series are printed on
acid-free, 250-year-life paper.

Printed in the United States of America

National Camp Meeting Committee.

J. W. Horn, J. E. Cookman, L. R. Dunn, A. Cookman, R. M. Adams, W. H. Boole, W. L. Gray, G. A. Hubbell, A. McLean, W. B. Osborn, J. Thompson, W. McDonald, J. S. INSKIP, G. Hughes, S. Coleman, G. C. Wells.

Absent members—J. A. Wood, G. C. M. Roberts, W. T. B. Clemm.

PENUEL;

OR,

FACE TO FACE WITH GOD.

EDITED BY

REVS. A. McLEAN AND J. W. EATON,

OFFICIAL REPORTERS OF GEN. CONF. M. E. CHURCH.

"And ye are complete in him."—COL. 2. 10.

NEW YORK:

W. C. PALMER, JR., PUBLISHER,

14 BIBLE HOUSE.

1869.

THE NEW YORK PRINTING COMPANY,
81, 83, and 85 Centre Street,
NEW YORK.

CONTENTS.

Vineland.

CHAPTER I.

BY REV. J. S. INSKIP.

ORIGIN OF NATIONAL CAMP-MEETINGS. Special meetings for holiness, suggested a Camp-Meeting for same purpose. Interview of *Revs. W. B. Osborn* and *J. S. Inskip*. Determination to have Camp-Meeting for this specialty. Call for meeting of the friends of holiness at Philadelphia, and favorable response.

VINELAND UNANIMOUSLY SELECTED. Largest catholicity of spirit cherished, with hope of good to all churches throughout the country. Adoption of title "National Camp-Meeting." Great spiritual fervor, without fanaticism, at Vineland. Conversion of sinners not overlooked, but desired ....

CHAPTER II.

VINELAND—SITUATION.

DEDICATORY REMARKS BY REV. J. S. INSKIP. This Camp-Meeting believed to be of God. All differences and matters not connected with the meeting to be dismissed. Jesus the only theme. Godly seriousness urged. Encampment dedicated.

REMARKS BY REV. B. M. ADAMS. Peculiar feelings in coming to this meeting. Believed would prove an era in Methodism. Depths of hell stirred, but all heaven interested. No time for other than God's work.

REMARKS BY REV. A. E. BALLARD. Idea of the great work of Methodism ; idea of the object of Vineland Camp-Meeting ....

CHAPTER X.

CHAPTER XI.

SERMON OF REV. ALFRED COOKMAN.

CHAPTER XII.

SERMON OF REV. B. POMEROY.

SERMON OF REV. B. W. GORHAM.

CHAPTER XIII.

Manheim.

CHAPTER XIV.

Opening services.

SERMON OF REV. G. C. WELLS.

CHAPTER XV.

SERMON OF REV. CHARLES MUNGER.

" *Sanctify them.*"—JOHN xvii. 17.

SERMON OF REV. R. V. LAWRENCE.

Round Lake.

CHAPTER XXVIII.

SERMON OF REV. W. H. BOOLE.

SERMON OF REV. A. LONGACRE.

CHAPTER XXIX.

SERMON OF REV. L. R. DUNN.

CHAPTER XXX.

SERMON OF REV. WILLIAM BUTLER, D.D.

CHAPTER XXXI.

SERMON OF BISHOP M. SIMPSON, D.D.

CHAPTER XXXII.

EDITOR'S PREFACE.

Of all the thrilling scenes with which the life of the patriarch Jacob is filled, none perhaps is more graphic and certainly none more important than the memorable night spent in prayer and wrestling with his heavenly visitant. Having sent his family and entire retinue "over the brook," he "was left alone; and there wrestled a man with him until the breaking of the day." In the midst of seeming discouragements and denials, he persevered till his victorious faith laid hold of the prize he sought, and the soul-cheering words were uttered, "As a prince hast thou power with God and with men, and hast prevailed."

"Behold, He that keepeth Israel, shall neither slumber nor sleep." "God is the same yesterday, to-day, and forever;" and to the heartfelt cry of His children, "Tell me, I pray Thee, Thy name," shall come the sweet assurance, "God is Love."

In the preparation of this volume it has been the prayerful endeavor to show, that to *every fully consecrated and believing soul*, shall be found other Penuels than that beside the ford Jabbok, and to those who wrestle there it shall be given them to say, "I have seen God face to face, and my life is preserved." May many, as the result of reading this book, have " HOLINESS TO THE LORD " written upon their hearts, and be brought to Jacob's intimate and blessed communion with the Master, both here and hereafter.

Because of the abundance of valuable material, both in sermons and experiences furnished by the three great National Camp-Meetings, it has been found necessary to select only the most excellent and important features, and, in some cases, to omit altogether what otherwise would have been gladly inserted.

In the preparation of PENUEL, indebtedness is acknowledged to various ministerial brethren, to the "Vineland Record," " The Methodist Home Journal," and the " Guide to Holiness."

INTRODUCTION.

BY BISHOP SIMPSON.

A WEEK in the tented grove! A week of Christian conversation, of earnest prayer, and of holy song! How many blissful memories of pure associations and spiritual triumphs linger with us after such a scene! Instruction, exhortation, experience, supplication, and thanksgiving blend their powerful influences on the human heart, giving rise to purer emotions and higher resolutions. Nature seems to wear a more joyous aspect. The hill-tops are bathed in softer light, the variegated landscape has brighter hues, the streams murmur sweeter music, and "all that hath breath" seems to utter a song of praise.

We can scarcely wonder that in ancient times, even amidst the darkness of idolatry, the hill-tops and the groves were favorite places of religious worship. But, as from these summits the "host of heaven" was worshiped, or in the shade of the dense grove adoration was given to some idol, the Jews were commanded to break down the altars and to cut down the groves.

In Northern Europe the strange service of the Druids was held only in the recesses of the forest, apart from the abodes of men. Their priests were supposed, in such places, to pass their time in communion with supernatural powers.

The "Feast of Tabernacles" among the Jews in some respects seems to be the precursor of our camp-meetings. It was held in the heat of summer, immediately after harvest. To it the multitudes gathered from every part of Israel, even "from Dan to

Beersheba." On pain of severe penalty every male was commanded to be present, and to worship for eight days before the Lord. Booths were erected, benches were cut from the palm trees, and in these booths, for eight days, dwelt not only the stranger from distant tribes, but the inhabitant of the city as well, who was required to leave his comfortable abode. This feast was commemorative. Forty years had their fathers spent in the wilderness, dwelling in tents, fed with bread from heaven, and oftentimes drinking of streams, flowing as if from God's own hand, and during all that period their clothes were unworn and their shoes never gave way. This feast indicated man's dependence and God's protection. It was a confession that the harvest just gathered came as certainly from God as the manna which fell from heaven or the water which gushed from the flinty rock. Man turned aside from his daily employments, and, in the midst of Nature's scenery and simplicity, communed with God, looked up into the far deep of the blue sky, and thought of immensity and eternity.

It is also possible that in summer heat, after the exhausting labors of the season, the feast had also a physical design, and was intended to secure perfect rest from toil, and freedom from care, which could not be found in the immediate surroundings of home, and that this rest should be found amidst hallowed thoughts and holy institutions, which would throw a purifying influence over man's social hours. Thus this great gathering from Mount Lebanon to the desert—from the beach of the Mediterranean to the heights beyond Jordan, became an occasion of joy and gladness, as well as a bond of social communion. Here kindred spirits met from every tribe, and thoughts of the one great Father, of His special protecting providence, of their obligations to worship, and of their common brotherhood, bound together more closely the people who were emphatically the family of God.

The early Christians often worshiped by the sea-side, and in seasons of persecution they sought the forest and the cave. The Covenanters of Scotland and the Waldenses, amid their mountain fastnesses, often assembled in the forests, which were made vocal with their songs of praise.

Camp-meetings, as now held, originated in Kentucky and Tennessee about the beginning of the present century. The country was sparsely populated, and houses of worship were few and far between. At communion seasons congregations assembled from a great distance. At one of these occasions an unusual interest was awakened, and, the services being protracted, people came, bringing provisions in wagons, and camped about the church. Other meetings were appointed, wonderful manifestations occurred, and, according to the estimates made at the time, from ten to twenty thousand people sometimes convened. A remarkable outpouring of God's Holy Spirit accompanied these meetings, a strange influence affected the audience, and the whole community was aroused. Infidels and scoffers were not unfrequently awakened, and were made the subjects of Divine power. The excitement began in the Presbyterian Church, but spread rapidly among the Baptists and Methodists. A Presbyterian minister of Kentucky, in a letter dated 1801, to a brother minister in Philadelphia, says:—

"I was lately at a sacramental occasion, and what I saw there exceeds the powers of human language to describe. There were more than one hundred wagons arrived, with families and provisions. Some of them came a hundred miles. A pulpit was erected in the open air, in which a Presbyterian minister preached to eight or ten thousand hearers. Another preached in the Presbyterian church to as many as it would hold. At a little distance there was another congregation of blacks, where one of themselves exhorted, and in a fourth place another congregation of another denomination.

"All the different denominations communicated together, for they were in perfect union. One Sunday there were seven thousand communicants, and it was computed that the several congregations amounted in the whole to twenty thousand persons. The meeting continued from Saturday till Tuesday—above seventy hours—without one minute's intermission. The work of conviction and conversion, of which I was a witness, exceeded, I think, anything heard of since the days of the Apostles. They generally ·fell flat on the ground in an agony of distress. I saw at one time about five hundred lying thus. Some laid but a few minutes, others for hours. When they arose the first words they uttered were, 'Lord, have mercy upon me.' They gradually added more, and, at length, began to exhort. I saw about three hundred of them exhorting at one time—some of them children, who were held up in arms or on the shoulders of men. One little girl, about nine years of age, was put on a man's shoulder, and delivered, I think, a body of divinity. At length, when exhausted, she sank back upon her upholder, upon which a man who stood near affectingly said, 'Poor thing, set her down.' She replied, 'Don't call me poor; I have Christ for my brother, God for my father, and am an heir to a kingdom.'"

For various reasons the Presbyterians ceased to hold these meetings, though they were continued by the Cumberland Presbyterians, whose church had its rise in this excitement. To the spirit of Methodism such occasions were more congenial. In its early history Wesley, Whitefield, and their coadjutors, rejected from the churches, preached to immense multitudes in the open air, and thus many of its proudest conquests were made. Quite possibly their expulsion from the churches was not only made a blessing to the thousands, who otherwise would not have heard them, but it also gave them the habit of conducting religious services in the open air, and to a great degree fostered a taste for such exercises

among their followers. Certainly, without this power of addressing the masses, Methodism would have accomplished comparatively
little among the frontier population.

Finding such gracious results attending these meetings, they
were introduced in a more permanent form, and tents and cottages
were built, people remaining a week or ten days on the encampment. Many supposed that these meetings would be limited to
rural districts, where houses of worship were few and small; but
it was soon discovered that these services might be useful, even in
a crowded population and in the vicinity of large cities, where, by
their peculiar attractions, vast multitudes, who seldom were found
at church, might be induced to attend. In their early introduction
in such localities many went for wicked purposes—to mock and
to interrupt, as well as simply to be amused. Many of these were
arrested by the preaching of the Word, and by the power of the
Spirit were led to consecrate their lives to God. To-day the no-
velty, to some extent, has passed away. Crowds of the very
wicked seldom attend these places. The theatre, the ball-room,
the public garden, the horse-race, and haunts of dissipation attract
these crowds; and for this reason, perhaps, while there is more
order, as well as regularity and solemn service connected with
these meetings, there are fewer instances of those remarkable conversions and wonderful changes which distinguished the earlier
assemblies. Now the camp-ground, neatly arranged, sometimes
beautifully and artistically laid out, with its convenient tents and
bountiful supply of water, and comfortable arrangements for
boarding and lodging, has its attractions for the thoughtful and
sedate. Such meetings will probably become permanent institutions in our land. Among the benefits connected with them a few
may be briefly sketched.

First, they furnish excellent opportunities for recreation and for
the invigoration of health, amidst pure associations and hallowed

thoughts. In summer's heat thousands desire to leave the crowded city or the busy village. Many, worn with the pressure of business, absolutely require an interval of rest. Some may seek the solitude of the forest, to study the forms of Nature or to angle for the speckled trout in the mountain brook. Others seek the sea-side, to bathe in its living waters, or visit watering-places, to mingle in the gay and giddy throng. When a camp is located in a mountainous region, or near the sea-side, all the advantages of a change of air can then be obtained, without the dissipation, late hours, singular habits, and ungodly associations of many of the fashionable assemblies. In their stead there are high and holy thoughts, pure devotion, and motives to a grander life. The current of business thoughts passes away and the heart swells with gratitude and praise to Him who reared the mountain summits in their grandeur, who makes the billows to roll in ceaseless restlessness, and who spreads out the broad landscape in beauty and fertility. Were it but to check the pressure of business, alleviate corroding care, and give the mind a new train of thoughts, such assemblies would be valuable.

Secondly. They favor the Christian association and communion of kindred hearts from distant portions of our land. To be profitable to the highest degree, such meetings ought not to be arranged for any one neighborhood, or for any small section of country. Their aim should be to bring together, from as wide an area as practicable, Christians who may sympathize together. Acquaintances are thus formed or renewed, plans of usefulness are suggested and considered, and Christian effort is increased by the feeling that, though one may be alone in his vicinity, he is part of a large family, and has earnest and active associates scattered throughout the land.

Thirdly. There is an advantage in continued religious thought. Such is the pressure of care and such the tendency of worldly business to occupy the mind, that we seem to need, now and then, to shake off such associations, to rest for a time from our pursuits, and to give a few days to higher thoughts and emotions, that, with intenser interest, the heart may be consecrated to God. Christians, in all ages, have sought, in moments of retirement from the world, for these benefits; or, like our Saviour, they have continued all night in prayer, have gone together to the mountain-top or to the sea-side. Devotion becomes more earnest and intense, the soul seems to gain a higher altitude, broader thoughts flash upon the mind, and, from Nature's holy temples, covered only by the canopy of heaven, the soul seems to mount upward and commune with its God; and from such assemblies Christians oftentimes return to their occupations with their hearts glowing as with celestial fire, ready to speak and act for Jesus as they had never done before. Dr. Young says:—

> " Devotion, when lukewarm, is undevout,
>> But when it glows its heat is struck to heaven ;
> To human hearts her golden harps are strung,
>> High heaven's orchestra chants Amen to man."

Another poet says:—

> " Even as Elias, mounting to the sky,
>> Did cast his mantle to the earth behind;
> So when the heart presents the prayer on high,
>> Exclude the world from traffic with the mind."

The exercises of such a meeting are conducive to these good results. The pulpit or platform, with its company of ministers gathered from surrounding districts; the assembled Christians, from scores of different congregations; the full notes of song that gush out by morning, noon, and night, from thousands of hearts, moved by a spirit of earnest piety; ardent prayer that claims God's blessing, and yearning hearts that look for the fulfilment of God's gracious promises; such agencies often attract the thoughtless, lead to self-examination, and many a Christian is stirred to purposes of higher duty and to efforts full of benevolent aims. There is scarcely a congregation to be found at present throughout our land but numbers among its best members those who have been awakened in these consecrated places, or who have here felt the power of His salvation.

Nor are these meetings confined, in their great results, to one denomination. Though under the control of some one persuasion, many pious people from all denominations attend, and thus a holy influence is spread amid the churches of the land, quickening, exalting, strengthening, for further activity and conquests.

The style of preaching is direct and hortatory. Present results are aimed at; present success is looked for. The pure air gives energy to the preacher and wakefulness to his congregation. The singing is lively, and of such music and song as are known to the multitude. The intervals between the public services are spent, in many tents, in prayer and song and religious conversation, and those who are seeking salvation find earnest friends to aid them, counsellors to instruct them, sympathetic hearts to pray for them, and, under these favorable circumstances, no marvel that vast multitudes are brought under religious influence and turned from ways of wickedness to paths of virtue.

In contrast with many places of folly and many occasions of sin so generally frequented, one may well say :—

> "One day in such a place,
>   Where Thou, my God, art seen,
> Is better than ten thousand days
>   Of pleasurable sin."

PENUEL; OR, FACE TO FACE WITH GOD.

Vineland.

CHAPTER I.

BY REV. J. S. INSKIP.

ORIGIN OF NATIONAL CAMP-MEETINGS—DETERMINATION TO
HOLD ONE—UNANIMOUS SELECTION OF VINELAND AS THE
PLACE.

THE practice of holding special meetings for the promotion of the doctrine and experience of holiness had become more or less prevalent in many of the Christian denominations of our country, when the idea was suggested to the minds of several earnest and devout men that it would be well to hold a *camp-meeting* with that definite end in view. Of the usefulness and benefit of meetings of this character there had been considerable doubt among some truly pious and intelligent Christians. Numerous objections were urged, and every possible endeavor was made to induce those engaged in holding such meetings to abandon them. Sometimes the most uncharitable criticisms were made upon the effect of these meetings, as well as upon the character and designs of those engaged in conducting them. Nevertheless, this method of inducing the churches to seek and obtain the higher life was pursued with increasing vigor and enlarged success. At many of the most popular camp-meetings of the country it was the custom to hold a special meeting for prayer and testimony which was designated " The Holiness Meeting." Some spoke of it reverently, others with distrust, and even sarcastic disapprobation. Still, however, the work went forward. Nor was this strange. There was an unction and a glory attendant upon such gatherings which drew to them multitudes of earnest prayerful believers who cried out day and night, " Create in me a clean heart, O God, and renew within me a right spirit." Then the testimonies given were so clear and direct that it was a privilege to hear them, and crowds thronged to learn from sanctified lips more and more of the wonders of grace. Sinners, as well as cold-hearted professors, were awakened, and many were converted and restored to the Divine favor.

It was thought that if for several days in succession the prayers of the church could be specially directed to this end, much might be done to excite a deeper and wide-spread interest in the all-important question of heart purity. It was also apparent that if the great body of religious professors could be thus aroused, there would be a great extension of the work of God among the unconverted. The activities and efforts of Christianity must ever depend upon the spiritual status of its advocates. What the church will do, as well as the result of what she does, will be mainly governed by what she is. When filled with the spirit of " true holiness," she will put forth the most vigorous and successful efforts to secure the conversion of the ungodly. A sanctified church would soon secure a converted world. The uniform result of genuine holiness has been to awaken a more earnest desire for the progress of the kingdom of Christ, and to increase the faith as well as the endeavors of the church to promote the salvation of sinners.

It was also judged desirable that the people of God from different parts of the country should be brought together and join their faith and prayers in a united effort to get nearer to Christ and obtain a larger measure of the "baptism of fire." By a statement of their experience and a comparison of views, it was hoped that their zeal would be stimulated, and, clothed with a fresh endowment of "power from on high," they would go forth everywhere in the full assurance of God's help and blessing upon the "work of faith and labor of love" to which they had been called. It was conceded by all candid minds that something must be done to excite among professing Christians a deeper interest in this momentous theme. The prevalence of wordliness and formality likewise seemed to call loudly for special effort on the part of those concerned for the extension and ascendancy of evangelical religion.

The persons who finally assumed the responsibility of holding the National Camp-Meeting, of course expected to be misapprehended by many whose good opinion they would very much regret to lose. They were fully aware they would be misunderstood, and perhaps sometimes misrepresented. Their measures and motives they expected would be assailed, and subjected to the most rigid criticism. It was nevertheless understood and agreed among them, that however severe and uncharitable might be the strictures upon their operations, they would make no attempt to respond except in their spirit and manner of life. It was assumed that what they might *say* in their defence would not be of as much weight as they might *be* and *do*. They could richly afford to wait for the matured and more candid judgment that their brethren would render concerning them after time and opportunity should be given for a clearer and more correct view of their real character and designs. True, some of them felt that a life service in the church ought to protect them against intimations of schismatic, fanatical, or disloyal intentions. If, however, a whole life given to the interests of religion should not shield them from such inuendoes, they concluded nothing they could say would be deemed satisfactory by their opponents.

They had no doctrinal novelties to propose to the world. They rather sought and inquired for the " old paths." They desired no modification of church polity, but earnestly hoped for a spiritual revolution by which the whole body of Christian believers might be induced to inscribe on their temples, altars, and banners, " Holiness to the Lord." They looked not so much for the diffusion of a dogmatic idea as for the prevalence of a profound religious experience. Holiness, to their minds, appeared to be more in what men *are* and *do*, than in what they *believe*. No doctrinal " shibboleth " was insisted upon, but it was concluded, that as the Spirit and Word might teach, men should be urged to seek more and more of the " mind that was in Jesus." These facts and considerations will explain why this movement has excited so little controversy. The blessed Holy Spirit has also doubtless guided his servants, so that they have not been decoyed into an attitude in which they would compromise the blessed truth they so much desire shall prevail everywhere, and among all of God's dear children.

It was further understood that in speaking of this glorious theme they would be definite, and as far as practicable adhere to the scriptural terms in which, by Divine authority, it is couched. In taking this position, however, it was not designed at all to reflect upon those who feel at liberty to adopt another course. The *nomenclature* of this question, as set forth in the words of Holy Writ, they deemed sufficiently clear and comprehensive. It was adjudged these were to be preferred to those of human origin and device. Hence the object of the meeting was announced to be the " promotion of HOLINESS." The term was understood to imply "entire sanctification," "perfect love," &c.; and being so freely used in the scriptures, it was supposed would be readily apprehended. Still the endeavor among us has been to avoid adherence to *mere* terms. Terminology, indeed, as such, has been ignored. Facts and ideas, rather than mere words or forms of speech, have attracted attention, and have been made prominent. To elevate the tone of experience more than to correct doctrinal error, has been the object in view. In saying this it is by no means designed to intimate that the doctrinal aspects of this question are unimportant. On the contrary, they are to be urged as fundamental. A people, however, who have had the teachings of Wesley, Fletcher, Watson, Clarke, &c., &c., and have used a hymn-book so full of the doctrine as is ours, and had access to such a biographical literature as we have published, to illustrate this great theme, surely need no argument to assure them that it is the will of

God they should be "sanctified wholly," and "preserved blameless unto the day of his coming." It has
been truly said, this doctrine has ever been peculiar and
prominent in our religious ideas. It may be found in
our hymns, our rituals, our history, our biography, and
all our standard authorities. Hence it was assumed to
be more needful to urge this as a privilege than as a
doctrine—as a phase of religious life to be enjoyed
rather than a creed to be defended.

When they came together for consultation and
prayer, these men found the idea had frequently been
presented to their minds. Still there was some hesi-
tancy to advocate such a measure. Rev. J. A. Wood,
of Wilkesbarre, Pa., for months prior to the time when
the question was settled, had been stirred in spirit, and
had spoken of the matter to others, who also were
moved in the same direction. They had free and
prayerful communication with each other, but could
not for some time see the way quite clear for so
important an undertaking. At length the heart of
Rev. W. B. Osborn, of the New Jersey Conference,
was so full of the matter that he could no longer restrain himself. His mind was so aroused and excited
that he hastened to New York, and coming to the study
of the writer, said with great emphasis: "*I feel that
God would have us hold a holiness camp-meeting.*"
His manner of speaking gave the fullest assurance that
he was persuaded of the truth of his statement. With
unusual emotion he presented his views of the practi-
cability and advantages of such a meeting. To his im-
passioned utterances he received a sympathetic and
cordial response. We knelt together, and in all godly

sincerity implored Divine guidance and help. We prayed, waited, wept, and believed, and the heavenly glory came upon us. It was to our minds no longer a question of doubt that we should hold a camp-meeting for the promotion of holiness. As we arose from the " mercy-seat " we took each other by the hand, and pledged eternal fidelity to God and holiness, and separated with the understanding that at the contemplated camp-meeting there would, by the permission of Providence, be *at least two tents*. We also agreed to invite a number of brethren, who were supposed to be in harmony with our views, to meet, consult, and determine where and when this meeting should be held. Private and personal communication was had with a number of brethren whose position upon this question had long been well defined. A call for a larger meeting was submitted for their consideration, and in due time was issued, inviting those in favor of holding a camp-meeting for the promotion of holiness to meet in the city of Philadelphia, June 13, 1867.

In pursuance of this call a goodly number of brethren from different parts of the country came together at the Methodist Book Rooms. The city of " Brotherly Love " was a fit place for such a gathering. At a glance it could be perceived this company had met " in the name of the Lord." The venerable Dr. Roberts, of Baltimore, was called to the chair, and Rev. J. Thompson, of Philadelphia, was appointed secretary. It was proposed that some time be spent in prayer for the controlling influences of the Holy Comforter. Each one present appeared to be profoundly impressed with the importance and responsibility of the subject in hand.

They moved, therefore, with the greatest solemnity and caution. As one after another led in prayer, the presence of God was more and more sensibly felt. For a time the consciousness of the revelations of the Divine glory and power were almost overwhelming. It was a most extraordinary season—one, indeed, that will never, never be forgotten.

There were many questions to be settled by this meeting. Some of them, it was expected, might be considerably perplexing and difficult. But, under the influence of the mighty and unctuous baptism that came upon all, each embarrassment as it was approached vanished away. It was thought the place of meeting might prove an exciting question; so many came with their minds made up that they had the best position. But a singular unanimity was immediately disclosed when Vineland was named. It was truly wonderful how all preconceived preferences at once were yielded, and the nomination of Vineland was made unanimous. Such, in fact, was the case all through the consultation. It was the most fraternal and religious business meeting any of us ever attended. There was one continued earnest invocation for the light and aid of the Holy Spirit. The considerate and deferential manner of every one who spoke on the occasion was so marked, as to convince all present God had taken the affair into his hands, and would lead us on to victory and success.

In defining the object of the meeting, we found less difficulty than in giving it a name. Upon conferring one with another, we were persuaded the great body of the people and preachers would sympathize with the object of the meeting. We could scarcely believe that any Christian would not be glad to learn that a fresh and earnest endeavor to "spread scriptural holiness over these lands" was about to be inaugurated. Every true disciple of Jesus loves holiness, and aspires to attain and enjoy it. There may be some variation in the method of expressing such aspirations, but all who love the Saviour feel and cherish them. He who does not love holiness can make no just pretensions to love its great Author. Christ is a high priest, "holy, harmless, and undefiled." Heaven is a holy place. God and angels who dwell there are holy. Hence, the consistent Christian ever and earnestly loves and seeks after holiness. To hold a camp-meeting for the specific purpose of promoting holiness, it was concluded therefore, we ultimately would, and must have, the sympathy and prayer of all the "household of faith." While we were fully aware many good people might misunderstand, and hence would misrepresent us, yet the assurance that when fully comprehending our aims they would smile on our efforts, made us bold to proclaim to the world what we designed and hoped to accomplish. We were certain that when correctly apprehended, good men of every name would bid us "God speed." Therefore, we dismissed all care and anxiety on that point.

The unusual character of the meeting required it should be so designated as to be understood. Our object was to put in motion influences that would reach the whole country—all churches, in every part of the land. The largest catholicity of spirit was cherished, and it was therefore resolved to invite all denominations to join at once in the great undertaking before us. There was nothing in our plan and purpose from which any need dissent. Our views of minor points could for the time be set aside, or kept in abeyance. Holding them would not in the slightest degree hinder the most cordial and fraternal action upon the all-important question before us. We could be Presbyterians, Episcopalians, Lutherans, Baptists, Methodists, &c., &c., and yet most heartily fraternize in the glorious work contemplated. How far these anticipations have been realized will be disclosed in subsequent chapters.

The adoption of the title, "NATIONAL CAMP-MEETING," was a happy thought. It was thus distinguished from all other camp-meetings. It was never for a moment designed to interfere with these, except to increase their spirituality and power. The time of holding this meeting was fixed early in the season, in order that those attending it might go to the others in the "fulness of the blessings of the gospel of peace." Preachers and people would thus be prepared for joyous and effective service, whether at camp-meeting or elsewhere. At the first meeting at Vineland there were persons present from all denominations, and from almost every State in the Union. How soon would there be diffused among all sects and parties a catholic and fraternal spirit, if the doctrine and experience of Christian purity were generally prevalent, and how firmly might all these States be joined in national unity and friendship.

The intensification of feeling incident to so large an assembly of fervent spirits can scarcely be conceived, except by those who have had the opportunity of witnessing it. To know to what a point of interest and excitement the mind and heart may be drawn in such circumstances, can be understood only from experience.

It was therefore feared that some over-zealous persons, of whom many are apt to be found on all popular occasions, would be led into extremes which would damage them and the cause with which they would thus unfortunately become associated. The fanaticism of this class has done inconceivable injury to the doctrine. It was apprehended they would be drawn to this great gathering of the people, and accomplish their usual unhappy work. Opposers are eager to seize upon such indiscretions and improprieties of speech and conduct as may be alleged against parties of this character. It is well known that fanaticism is sometimes uncontrollable. In all our deliberations and movements we sought to protect ourselves from this peril. In the main, it must be admitted, we were remarkably successful. To God be all the glory. In some instances, doubtless, expressions have been uttered and views have been maintained for which we would be unwilling that the "National Camp-Meeting" should be responsible. It is, however, occasion of devout thanksgiving to our Heavenly Father that our meeting has been much less disturbed in the way intimated than ordinary camp-meetings frequently are.

In setting forth the fact that the special object of the National Camp-Meeting is to promote the work of holiness among believers, it should also be stated that the conversion of sinners is likewise diligently sought after. Those who take the pains to read this work entire, will see how earnestly and effectively this object has been pursued. The multitude converted at Vineland and Manheim are a most thorough and satisfactory confirmation of the idea that there is an intimate and inseparable connection between the spiritual condition of the church and her success. The work of entire sanctification among believers is always followed by the salvation of sinners. This may readily be explained. The unconverted are fully aware that Christians ought to be holy. They know that it is the privilege and duty of every believer to be sanctified throughout soul, body, and spirit. They read that it is required and enjoined by the Word of God that Christ's followers be wholly consecrated, and love God " with all the heart, with all the soul, with all the mind, and with all the strength." The neglect of such a duty must ever exert a most pernicious influence on the minds of the impenitent, and often completely destroys the effectiveness of all efforts put forth to lead them to God. It is impossible to over-estimate the importance of persuading the Christian church to take higher ground in regard to this momentous question. So far as the "National Camp-Meeting" may contribute to this result, it will answer the purpose for which it was instituted.

CHAPTER II.

THE PARK—DEDICATORY ADDRESS—REV. B. M. ADAMS— REV. A. E. BALLARD.

In the State of New Jersey, thirty miles south of Philadelphia, in the midst of a level country, is situated the pleasant and thriving village of Vineland, a marvel of well-directed energy and sobriety. To her honor be it said that, in obedience to the will of her sovereign and sober people, intoxicating drinks are banished her borders, and indeed from within the limits of the township.

"The Park" is a well-shaded grove of forty acres, most beautiful for situation, where from July 17th to 26th, 1867, was held the first National Camp-Meeting in the annals of Methodism; and, under the arching trees, was a beautiful and extensive "Bower of Prayer," where in the intervals of preaching were held meetings for prayer and the relation of experience.

At the hour announced, many gathered to hear the following

DEDICATORY ADDRESS BY REV. J. S. INSKIP, OF NEW YORK CONFERENCE.

It is evident to me, and it must be to all, that God is present in this place, and the fact of His special presence is to us a clear indication of His approval of this meeting. As for me, I desire no clearer proof of the Divine favor than the evidence of special Divine presence. I am just as sure that this movement is of God, as I should be had it been written as a specific command in God's Word, that the people should assemble on this day in this very place, and for the particular purpose for which they have come; and I confidently believe that the object of our assembling will be accomplished. There are bound up in the religious interests of this extraordinary Camp-Meeting influences which, we trust, shall extend over Christendom.

There are a few suggestions which are now proper to be made. The first is, that all differences should be set aside, and only a spirit of mutual forbearance and brotherly love prevail. We have neither time nor inclination for dispute. Let us dismiss all matters which have no connection with the appropriate exercises of this meeting. The controversialist might perhaps raise objections which I should be unable to answer. I myself have not lost all capacity in this respect, but I have neither time nor disposition for controversy or fault-finding. We have not come here for that purpose, but for the nobler one of holding up a banner that has written upon it, " Holiness to the Lord." Let us point the people to that. Let every sermon aim at it, every exhortation urge it, all prayer embrace it, and the life of every man and woman present exemplify it. This theme we can talk about and never exhaust, and upon it there should be perfect unanimity.

When politics and kindred subjects are discussed, there is always danger of serious disagreement. I remember very well the time when I took more interest in politics than I feel disposed to now, and I very well remember also that disagreement was an essential element in every discussion. Let me propose a subject upon which there can be here no disagreement. Let us talk about JESUS—of him only, and all the time. Let secular matters be kept entirely out of sight—set them all aside! We have left them down yonder in the valley, and have come up to this mountain to worship the Lord our God. Let the world, then, be entirely set aside, and let us all with one soul agree in the desire and prayer to be possessed of the Holy Ghost. This is the blessing which all, I hope, have come here expecting.

In the next place, I would say, Let the meeting be a *serious* one. Godly seriousness, not sadness, will injure no one but will be a power for good if exhibited. Let us then leave all trifling and temporal matters aside, and in all soberness, talk of our experience in the deep things of God, and with all our power each strive for the conversion of others. Thus, seriously intent upon our work, shall God give us abundant success, while His is the power and shall be the glory forever.

At the close of these remarks the encampment was solemnly dedicated to the worship and service of God, which was followed by—

REMARKS OF REV. B. M. ADAMS, OF NEW YORK EAST CONF.

Never before have I gone to a Camp-Meeting with such peculiar feelings as those with which I came to this. For the last two months I have been praying for this meeting. This is the first of the kind ever held, and is yet an experiment; but I trust in God that it will be a sublimely successful experiment, and already do I feel *assured* that this will be so, and that we shall be more than repaid for any sacrifices we may have made in coming hither. My object is to get personally nearer to God, and to help others do the same.

I believe this Camp-Meeting will prove an era in the history of Methodism, and will be a tidal mark of that onward wave for which the Church has been praying and laboring for eighteen centuries. The depths of hell are stirred already against us, and all heaven is interested for us; and if we but do our duty, this meeting will be pre-eminently successful, and all will go away filled with the Holy Ghost. We have no time for mere socialities, but only for God's work. Would that the Lord might fill us with the Spirit now! While we are all in one place, let us be as were the disciples anciently, " *of one accord*," and the blessing will surely come. Oh that, in the name of the Lamb, we might claim it to-day!

The minister in official charge of the meeting then spoke.

REMARKS OF REV. A. E. BALLARD, PRESIDING ELDER IN NEW JERSEY CONFERENCE.

In my conception of Methodism in its inception, in its continuance, and in its development, I have ever considered its object as one—the inception and development of holiness. However much I may or may not have understood it experimentally in time past, yet I so read it and so believe it. My idea of the great work of Methodism now is, to possess holiness in personal experience, and to spread it through the experience of others all over the land. I understand this to be in the fullest, most extensive, and widest sense of all, the true meaning and mission of Methodism. I understand this to be a Methodist Camp-Meeting for the promotion of holiness. Such it was in its inception, and such I trust it will be in its development.

CHAPTER III.

SERMON—TESTIMONIES.

SERMON BY REV. J. W. HORNE, OF NEW YORK EAST
CONFERENCE.

1 *John,* i. 7.—"*And the blood of Jesus Christ his Son cleanseth us
from all sin.*"

THE mere mention of this text ought to arrest the
attention of all, and send through every soul a thrill of
joy. This news is sweeter than the sound of gushing
waters, more precious than tidings of deliverance to the
captive exile, for I am addressing a congregation of
sinners, though doubtless many are sinners saved by the
grace of God.

But we have all been fearfully smitten with sin. We
have been depraved and defiled and made wretched by
it, and are consequently all in danger of perishing
eternally. But if the message which I have to present
to-day be a truthful and an inspired one we need not
despair. Blessed be God, we may be forgiven and
recovered. We may be restored to God, and have
returned to us more than the innocency of childhood,
and be enabled to walk in holiness before Him, who is
alone blessed forever, and who only doeth wondrous
things.

Had I the privilege of going into a hospital, and,

amid the sighs and groans and death agonies of the patients, declare on the highest medical authority that I had a remedy which, if properly applied, would infallibly cure all their diseases, what would you think if some of them, instead of applying the means, should begin to object and to say: "From the nature of the case, from the character of the disease, from the constitution of human nature, from the fact that this disease has been so long in operation, the message that you bring is impossible; we grant you that we might be partially cured, that we might in some measure be cleansed from the loathsomeness of our disease, but it is impossible to be entirely cured." Any person could easily imagine how such would be pitied, and how sad a spectacle it would be to see men become so indolent, physically and mentally, from the effects of the disease which had been preying upon them, that they could not entertain even the possibility of an entire cure. And yet how often the Messenger of the Cross comes before a congregation, from the presence and communion of the Lord of Glory, with such a blessed message from the Word of God as that just read, and instead of thrills of joy and gladness passing through all the congregation, there are some ready to rise up and with most serious aspect begin to say: "From the nature of the case, from the constitution of man, from our position in this life, from the fact that sin has been so long upon us, and left its marks in a manner so abiding, it is a moral impossibility that we should be entirely cured in this life. We may be partially cleansed, but we must carry some remains of this fearful moral leprosy with us to the grave." It is to my mind one of the saddest evidences of human depravity, to think that sin should have obtained such power over us, that we have come to be able to love the chains of our slavery; and when we are told in the Word of God, from the lips of Inspiration, that the blood of Jesus Christ cleanseth from all sin, instead of leaping with joy and gladness to receive the glad announcement, that we should waste a single moment in making objections and in pleading that we must carry the moral leprosy of sin down with us to death.

I propose, looking first to Christ for help, and then to the brethren and sisters for their prevailing prayers, to sustain the utterances of the text by an *argument from analogy;* then to ask and answer the questions, *when* shall the blood of Christ cleanse from all sin, and *how* does the blood of Christ cleanse from all sin; and afterwards, if we have a moment or two to spare, to look at some of the blessings flowing from this cleansing by the blood of Jesus.

And, in the first place, let us take up the argument from analogy.

It is known to you all that the most beautiful and costly garments are liable to become foul and very deeply stained. Are they to be thrown away? must they become useless for ever afterwards? No! There are substances found, which, if properly prepared and applied to such garments, every spot is taken out, every stain is purged, every impurity removed; and behold! though once so foul, now they are as precious and beautiful as ever. Now, would any man say that, in the realm of nature, substances are to be found which remove the foulest and deepest stains, and yet, in the realm of the supernatural, God has made no provision whereby the immortal spirit of his children, stained with sin, can be washed and made whiter than the driven snow? I do not believe it; I never will believe it, in the face of the distinct utterance of God that "Though your sins be as scarlet they shall be as white as snow; though they be red like crimson they shall be as wool."

CLEANSING.

Let us now take another step in this argument. In the Scripture record the water of rivers and pools has, under the presence and blessing of God, been rendered so efficacious as to wash out the most loathsome diseases that have ever cursed human nature. I scarcely need remind you of the case of Naaman, who, cursed with leprosy, would have died in his loathsomeness had he not obeyed the command of the prophet of the Lord, "Go and wash in Jordan seven times." Naaman perhaps expected some grand display of power without the use of any intervening agency, and was only induced to obey after the inquiry of his servant, "If the prophet had bid thee do some great thing, wouldest thou not have done it?" You remember also the pool of Bethesda, for the moving of whose waters the afflicted were accustomed to intently watch. Now my question is this: If the water of rivers and pools, under the presence and blessing of God, could be made to cleanse from the most loathsome diseases to which the human body has ever been subject, shall not the stream of Christ's blood, flowing through all the ages and generations of man's history, have such an efficacy that whosoever shall wash in that blood shall be cleansed from all his guilt? Under the Jewish dispensation the people often became so legally unclean, that if they had dared to enter the congregation of the Lord, they would at once have been smitten with death. The water of purification was prepared, the heifer was taken and sacrificed, her blood poured out, her body burnt to ashes, and with the ashes was mixed pure water, and a man had no sooner taken of this water, or had it sprinkled upon him, than he became cleansed, so that he could enter into the congregation, and enjoy its services. "How much more shall the blood of Christ purge your conscience from dead works to serve the living God!"

So, in the days of Christ's public ministry on earth, when he was despised and rejected of men, a man of sorrows and acquainted with grief, even in these days he had such a power ever present with him, that he was enabled to purify and cleanse the body, soul, and spirit of all who came to him. Now this is my argument: If Jesus, in the days of his humiliation, when despised and rejected of men, before he had paid the price of redemption, before he had freely bought the children of men by the shedding of His precious blood; if even then Jesus had such power and virtue that He could make the vilest clean, I would like to know, now that He is exalted as a Prince and a Saviour to give repentance to Israel and remission of sins, now that God has exalted Him above all thrones and dominions and principalities and powers, can He not cleanse the believing soul from every stain? Yes! It is true that "the blood of Jesus Christ, His Son, cleanseth from all sin." Again, it is admitted by all professing Christians, that the blood of Christ is efficacious in cleansing from sin to some extent. Now if this is so, let me ask from how much can it cleanse, and from how much can it not cleanse? Who can draw the line of demarcation?

HOW?

In answer to the question, how does the blood of Christ cleanse from sin, I would answer, in the first place, not necessarily: It is a work of free grace, and of full and free acceptance. Neither does the blood of Christ cleanse chemically. We are obliged to use figurative language in this as in other cases. We may sing of the "fountain filled with blood," but we know very well there is no such fountain in reality.

Christ's blood takes away sin because it is the blood of atonement, and the blood of atonement becomes the blood of sanctification. "Without the shedding of blood there is no remission of sin." There must first of all be the sacrifice. The blood of Christ satisfied the justice of God, and removed all obstacles, and now that great river of the love and mercy of God, that had become dammed up by sin, by the sacrifice of Christ has been loosed that it may wash out all the stains of the believer, and make his soul whiter than the driven snow. Then, in the second place, the blood of Christ was the price of redemption. Jesus paid down this price of redemption, and by faith in Him we pass out of the family of sin and

Satan, into the family of God. We pass into a title to the privileges and immunities of heaven and eternal life. He is our elder brother, and do you not believe He will sanctify us to the uttermost? Yes! He is able to save to the uttermost all that come unto God through Him. The blood of Jesus Christ, God's son, can cleanse from all sin.

In the next place, the blood of Christ opens the way for the coming of the Holy Ghost, the sanctifier, and we are living under the dispensation of the Spirit.

WHEN?

The next question is: When shall the blood of Christ cleanse from all sin? Is there any specified time in our religious experience when this work is to be done? I answer, No, neither in life nor in the hour of death. The moment of entire sanctification is not necessarily in the hour of death. That would be a strange moment indeed. Death is a mere negation. It has no moral power at all —nothing, in itself, to do with our sanctification.

Another question: Is the work of sanctification a progressive or an instantaneous one? The answer is, sanctification is a progressive work, while *entire* sanctification is the work of but a moment. There is a moment in which the darkness forever ceases; there is a moment in which the dying Adam is dead and the new Adam is all alive, when from centre to circumference the soul is vitalized; there is a moment in which sanctification passes into entire sanctification.

We see then that the instantaneousness of entire

sanctification harmonizes with gradual sanctification. As the moral leprosy of sin spreads its virus through all the system, and men cry out to the great physician, God forbid that they should rest satisfied with a partial cure. The physician is able and willing to effect a complete cure.

GREAT BENEFIT.

But the great benefit of this work is, that in the condition of entire sanctification we are enabled to devote our energies successfully to the great work of lengthening the cords and strengthening the stakes of Zion at home and abroad; and to strive after the building up of saints in their most holy faith. A state of partial sanctification, a chaining down of our attention to the struggle going on in our own spirit, is unfavorable to working for Christ. When the preacher has a consciousness of inward purity, and realizes the power of God in his heart, with what energy and success is he enabled to work!

Again, in a state of entire sanctification we are at liberty to go on to Christian perfection. Entire sanctification is the negative, the being delivered from all sin; Christian perfection is the boundless positive, in the upward paths of which the soul continues to go onward without limit. In the state of entire sanctification the soul can spread its wings and cry, "I fly, I soar, higher, higher up into the infinity of God." The chain which dragged the soul to earth is loosed, the cords which held it are broken, and, like the outward-bound ship, the soul has left the harbor of sin and unrighteousness, has put out to sea, with fair gales and all sail set; and oh! how she speeds along with the fair haven in view, singing as she goes:

> " There I shall bathe my weary soul
>   In seas of heavenly rest;
>   And not a wave of trouble roll
>   Across my peaceful breast."

During the progress of the Camp-Meeting we recorded many

TESTIMONIES,

from which we shall occasionally select.

A BROTHER.—" I have been thinking of one of those wonderful visions of John the Revelator. He saw an angel standing in the midst of the sun. I feel so joyous and happy this morning, with God the fountain of light and life and love all around me, and *all within*, that I stand, like the angel, in the midst of the great Sun of Righteousness. My life is hid with Christ in God."

A BROTHER.—" Fourteen years ago I was converted. For a time I was happy. Then clouds and doubts intervened. I became unstable, and feared I had no root in me. I was quickened again by the Holy Spirit, under the preaching of the Word, and felt my need of a deeper work of grace. I gave myself to prayer, reading of the Scriptures, and earnest seeking after holiness. Light came soon, and I saw that I must be entirely consecrated if I would be happy. '*Be holy*' was the command. I came to this meeting to be blessed. Last night God revealed himself wonderfully, and filled my poor heart with His love; and I can say now that I am all the Lord's, and He is mine."

A SISTER.—"Friends," began a timid lady, "I want you to pray that I may be all the Lord's."—Responses of "Amen;" "Lay all on the altar;" and the verse was sung:

> "Take my poor heart, and let it be
>   Forever closed to all but Thee;
> Seal Thou my breast, and let me wear
>   The pledge of love forever there."

CHAPTER IV.

SERMON BY REV. S. COLEMAN, OF TROY CONFERENCE.

John xv. 1, 2.—*" I am the true vine, and my Father is the hus-bandman. Every branch in me that beareth not fruit, he taketh away : and every branch that beareth fruit, he purgeth it, that it may bring forth more fruit."*

I HAVE often drawn water from this well; and now I am going to try it again, as I feel somewhat thirsty, and the well is one that can never be exhausted. The first thing worthy of notice in the passage is the statement of Christ himself, that He is the true vine and we are the branches. There are deep things in that saying, the first of which is that it implies the great truth that Christ is the author of our being, the author of the existence of all the human family. The branch never can have an existence other than what it derives from the vine. The fact is, had it not been for Christ, there never would have been a human being besides Adam and Eve, and they would have been in hell long since. Such is the relation that the human family sustains to Christ.

Another consideration is, that the wood and constitution of the branch are exactly like that of the vine, in every respect. So we are of the same nature as Christ; He has taught us to believe so, and I am not ashamed to take it on His word. While we are in Christ we have the very nature of God. We speak this with all humility; but if God teaches it, we ought not to be afraid to take it upon His declaration. For the truth of this we have the Scripture warrant, and need no other. Thus the Bible talks of our being heirs of God, and joint-heirs with the Lord Jesus Christ, having a claim on all that God possesses. Is it possible that sinners will barter this high and holy possession for misery and degradation?

As the branch is in the vine, so are we, as believers in Christ, if we have not departed from Him. And even if we have, He has made arrangements for our return. Reference is made in the text to the condition of those who have thus departed from the living God, and who, by disobedience to Him, have prevented the light of heaven from being communicated to their souls, so that they cannot answer the design of their creation. Thus Christ says: "Every branch in me that beareth not fruit He taketh away." This is the real difficulty; and it is worthy of our most earnest consideration whether we may not be of the number of those who bear no fruit, and who are fitted only for burning. It is a well-known fact that any disease in the branch, anything which obstructs the passage of the sap, hinders the growth of the fruit. There may be leaves on it, and, to a certain extent, life in it, but there can be no fruit. The dresser of the vineyard takes note of all such branches, and if it is found that the disease is incurable, they are cut down and carried away to be burned. Now, when men sin, it breaks up the communication that may have existed between them and

Christ, and causes, as it were, the life from Christ to stop
before it gives them strength to bear fruit.

WHAT FRUIT DOES GOD EXPECT?

Now, perhaps it would be well to ask what fruit God
expects of His people in consequence of this relation
that exists between Him and them. The answer is
contained in the 5th chapter of Galatians: "The fruit
of the Spirit is love, joy, peace, long-suffering, gentleness, goodness, faith, meekness, temperance." God requires all these of every man. It is fully intended
that every man shall possess the love of which this
passage speaks—to love God with all the heart, and
soul, and strength, and mind, and our neighbor as
ourself.

God has made arrangements whereby every man may
be possessed of joy and peace. God never made men
to be miserable; He don't want any miserable people in
this world: He has made a place to put them in elsewhere. God is displeased with the sight of the miserable; it is a grief to Him; He has made arrangements
to have it otherwise; He wishes us to be joyful, to rejoice evermore. Our joy should be like the river which
flows summer and winter; not like the brook which
flows only in the season of rain, and becomes dry in the
season of drought.

The peace of God is not like the peace of the world:
"My peace I leave with you: not as the world giveth
give I unto you." God's peace cannot be broken up.
The world has a great time when everything goes smooth
with it—when it has plenty of money, the best of health,

and something to intoxicate. But the first adverse circumstance breaks up that peace. Such is the peace of the world. When we have it, it turns us crazy; and when we have it not, it makes us mad. It is quite different with the peace that Christ gives. It is continuous and abundant. We have as much of heaven, or may have, as we can bear. People think it a wonder that a man should clap his hands and shout, " Glory to God!" at such a meeting as this; but it is the joy of God that makes him shout. That kind of moping religion that has no joy connected with it, nothing but mourning and tears, is not the religion that God has made for us. The peace of the believer is the peace of Christ.

God also requires love of his disciples—not the love that loves only those who love us, but the love that loves our enemies and prays for those that despitefully use us. Such is perfect love that God requires us to possess. The fruit which God looks for is not anything that we do. All the graces mentioned in the passage cited as the fruits of the spirit are not acts, but dispositions—not things that we do, but spiritual qualities by which we are actuated. If a man is filled with love, there is no need to tell him to work: the wise plan will be to get out of his way, or he will run you down in the ardor with which he *does* work. You might as well try to keep the thunder still, or stop the mouth of Vesuvius, as to prevent such a man from working. A man was on one occasion travelling in the cars, and he seized the opportunity of exhorting the sinners who were travelling with him. As a matter of course, they became angry, and threatened to throw him out of the window, when

3*

one of the passengers said, "Never mind that man; I know him: he is only a pesky Methodist who has got religion, and can't keep still!"

As ministers, we ought to impress upon faltering believers the necessity of receiving the second blessing—entire sanctification of the soul, total delivery from the power and presence of sin. Without this it is absurd to ask any one to work for God.

Brother Abbott, when forty years of age, experienced religion, and the preacher meeting him immediately afterwards, said to him:

"Brother Abbott, the Lord has a greater blessing in store for you yet; He will sanctify your soul, as He has now removed your condemnation."

The reply was, "I will have it right away;" and going to his knees he never ceased praying until he had found it. It was entire sanctification that he sought and found, never dreaming of calling it "the higher life," or any other nickname of the kind. As soon as he had found it he sprang up from his knees and began in earnest; and his labors for the Lord continued for twenty years, and the devil never had a more troublesome enemy to deal with in all America. Such men will carve their way through every difficulty.

I feel disposed to call them "THE INVINCIBLES." You may throw them up anywhere, and they will always alight on their feet.

The washing of regeneration, and the renewing of the Holy Ghost, are as essential to the soul as the forgiveness of sins, and should be earnestly and perseveringly sought until God's grace shall make us perfectly free in Christ Jesus. And this is a favorable time and place to seek this great blessing. On the day of Pentecost, at the first meeting which was ever held for the special purpose of the promotion of holiness, the Spirit of the Lord was mightily present, and three thousand souls were converted. Let us pray and expect that a like result may attend this meeting for that purpose.

TESTIMONIES.

A Sister.—"The love of Christ constrains me to speak. 'My peace I give unto you;' that peace I have this morning. I have given all to Jesus, and he gives all to me."

A Brother.—"My cup runneth over."

A Sister from Baltimore.—"I rejoice in a present and very full salvation. I am full of gladness that I am one of the least of God's children. I *am* the Lord's, and Jesus is mine. I love Him, and He loves me. He is the chiefest among ten thousand, and the one altogether lovely. Hallelujah! May this spirit spread from heart to heart!"

A Sister.—"I should not be able to rise here but that I am trusting in the Lord God. I can do all things through Christ strengthening me. I have not the joyous experience which some possess, but I have perfect rest, and can say my life is hid with Christ in God. The Blessed Jesus dwells in my heart, and moment by moment I am able to cast all my burden upon Him. I have proved Jesus. He has often tested me, but has never failed me. He has ministered to me in trial as no earthly friend could minister. Jesus does all for me."

A Sister.—"I read recently a little paragraph about the Cross which impressed me. It was this: 'The

Cross consists of two pieces of wood, one transverse with the other. This symbolizes our will and that of our heavenly Father; when there is a want of harmony, when our will is transverse with God's, there is a cross.' Thank God that this morning my will is lost in His!"

A BROTHER.—" I tried a long time to find this pearl; but I was never satisfied till I gave up tobacco, the use of it, and even selling it in my store; I have offered all, and God now saves me fully. I *know* that my Redeemer liveth."

A MINISTER FROM NEW JERSEY.—" I feel that the blood of Jesus Christ is applied to the washing away of all sin, notwithstanding a consciousness of past weakness. One year only has passed since God revealed himself in Jesus as an all-satisfying portion. Since that time it has been with me one constant scene of revival."

A MINISTER.—" I feel it a privilege to be here. I am satisfied in Jesus. He is present in great power in my heart. The very firmament reveals Him to my soul."

A BROTHER.—" I can bring a good report of this way. It pleased God to call me from among gamblers, revilers, and blasphemers in the city of New York. At the age of nine years I broke away from the restraints of my mother, but God heard prayer and followed me by His Spirit till I yielded to Him, and by faith I heard Him speak my sins forgiven. Afterward, without even knowing that it was duty, I consecrated all, and while at work in my shop God opened the windows of heaven, and poured out upon me the fulness of His Spirit; and now I feel every day the life of God flowing through my soul. When converted I could not tell where to find one passage of Scripture, but in four days I was out in the sea of perfect love. Glory to God!"

AN AGED BROTHER.—"Under the weight of many years and unusual bodily weakness, I came to this ground, scarcely expecting to join in the utterances of praise to the Great I AM, but I find it impossible to refrain. Forty-eight years I have been in this way, but never felt so near to heaven as I do to-day."

A BROTHER.—"After a bitter experience, and terrible contest, and deepest conviction, I was enabled some years since to yield all to the Lord and He filled my soul with himself. A short time after this I was called to look upon my worldly goods as the flames were consuming them, but I could rejoice, and felt to thank God that I had that in my heart which the fire could not burn."

CHAPTER V.

SERMON BY REV. GEO. C. WELLS, OF TROY CONFERENCE.

Isa. vi, 5–8.—" *Then said I, Woe is me! for I am undone; because I am a man of unclean lips, and I dwell in the midst of a people of unclean lips: for mine eyes have seen the King, the Lord of hosts. Then flew one of the seraphim unto me, having a live coal in his hand, which he had taken with the tongs from off the altar: And he laid it upon my mouth, and said, Lo, this hath touched thy lips; and thine iniquity is taken away, and thy sin purged. Also I heard the voice of the Lord, saying, Whom shall I send, and who will go for us? Then said I, Here am I; send me.*"

THE text is an account of a very remarkable occurrence, intended to designate Isaiah to the prophetic office. The whole is representative of the majesty and holiness of the Divine Being, in whose presence seraphim covered their faces in token of conscious insignificance and unworthiness, and cried out in responsive plaudits, " Holy, holy, holy! Lord God of hosts!" A view of God produced in the mind of the prophet such a sense of his own defilement, that he took up the affecting confession : " Woe is me! for I am undone; because I am a man of unclean lips, and I dwell in the midst of a people of unclean lips : for mine eyes have seen the King, the Lord of hosts." This deep conviction of impurity was followed by the symbolic application of a live coal from the altar to his lips by one of the seraphim, who also said to him " Lo! this hath touched thy lips, and thine iniquity is taken away, and thy sin purged." Then he heard the voice of God asking for a messenger :

" Whom shall I send, who will go for us ? " and Isaiah answered, " Here am I ; send me." God had a message to be borne, and the prophet, refined by fire, was ready to bear it.

We do not propose to consider all the wonders in this vision, but to look at this single thought—that individual Christians and the Church have

NEED OF BEING REFINED BY FIRE,

To be a power in the world. The single qualification which the Church needs for the accomplishment of her mission is holiness. When the prophet had a clear view of God in his holiness, he could do nothing but lament his pollutions, and confess his sins. In this state of pollution he had no intimation that God had a message for him ; but when the seraph had applied the fire and assured him that he was pure, then he heard the voice of the Lord, asking, " Whom shall I send? " and then he answered ; " Here am I ; send me."

From these facts, as well as from the universally corroborative teachings of the Bible, we learn that while God has messages to be borne to all men which shall prove a savor of life unto life, or of death unto death, to those for whom they are intended, He calls the Church first to be saved herself, and saved in a high sense, that her goings forth to all the ends of the earth may be with authority. God does not send sinners laden with guilt, even though they may bear a profession, to preach the Gospel to sinners. As well set a blind man to teach painting, or a deaf man to teach music, or a dumb man to teach oratory.

Let us now take a slight glance at the magnitude of

the work to be done, in order that we may see the necessity of the power of the Holy Ghost to accomplish it.

The work is, in the first place, to convert the Christianity of the day, which substitutes mere numerical or other considerations for that which is spiritual and vital. The work is to preach the Gospel in all its truth and power, until all become illuminated with the light of love, and energized with the life of God; until the whole professing Christian Church shall become conformed to the will and image of Him who loved the Church, and gave himself for it that He might sanctify and cleanse it, and present it to himself a glorious Church, without spot or wrinkle, or any such thing.

The work is, secondly, to spread a living Christianity, until every nation and kindred and tongue shall fear God, and give glory to Him.

If the work were to convert men to nominal Christianity, nominal Christians might do it; if it were to convert men to formalism, formality might make parade of the exteriors of religion, and lead many to assume its outer garb. But since it is to make men new creatures in Christ Jesus, to diffuse experimental and practical Christianity, experimental and practical Christians alone can hope to succeed.

The difficulties to be overcome all show the necessity of that courage and strength which pertain to a holy Church. But she can easily contend with the difficulties that are without when she stands upon the high vantage-ground of inward purity.

The agencies in her own body which oppose the progress of the Church are scepticism, formalism, conservatism, and worldliness.

SCEPTICISM IN THE CHURCH.

This is lamentably prevalent, even in the hearts of many of the professed friends of the Saviour. It is manifest by their dull, drone-like movements in soul-saving, and their reliance upon human skill rather than divine power. It is to be feared that the great doctrines of Justification by Faith, and Regeneration by the power of the Holy Ghost, which the Bible represents as a sudden change from darkness to light, which makes the bondman free and the child of sin and suffering an heir of glory; and the doctrine of the witness of the Spirit, whereby God assures the believer, as strongly as he is assured of his being, that he is saved now; and the doctrine of holiness, of salvation from all sin, as attainable and retainable by all men in the present life, and of obedience to God, and of a present appropriating faith as the condition of the divine favor; it is to be feared that these old doctrines of the Bible are to a lamentable extent ignored by no small proportion of our Zion. This scepticism may not have found expression in our creeds or on our tongue, but it has taken up its abode in many hearts. Our religion possesses too much a negative and too little a positive character. We preach and talk too much of the philosophy of religion, rather than religion itself. We make parade of creed rather than press the truth upon the heart until paleness and trembling evidence that its power has been felt. We deliver moral essays to the people as bright and as clear, many of them, as an arctic night, and as cold too. We preach to the head rather than to the heart. We try to educate men into Christianity instead of urging them to faith in the Lord Jesus Christ. We lean too much on hope, not enough on God ; too much on rhetoric, not enough on the Holy Ghost. We want logic and rhetoric, but we want more of God. Our influence is paralyzed by an undue reliance upon externals—an educated ministry and costly church edifices to attract the fancy, and influence caste and numbers. We want an educated ministry, but let it graduate at the cross. We want learning, but also lips and hearts that have been refined by fire. Instead of the attractions of architecture, we want our church edifices to glow with the radiance of divinity, so that the people shall see the Lord in His holy temple. We want numerical strength, but at the same time we want more of Christ. Because the external is more relied upon than the internal, the Church has too often failed in her efforts, and turned her back upon her enemies. We think to advance it like any other organization, and then God shows us our madness.

FORMALISM

Is the next great difficulty to be overcome. This is the representative of death ; and formalists are the tubercles on the lungs of the Church, causing the consumption of her life. Their influence is one of torpor. They have no creative force nor energy. Their very strength is weakness ; all that it produces is a delusive dream : its glory is corpse-like. The danger does not consist in having a form, for this is directed by the great Head of the Church ; but the evil is the putting of the name for the thing, the sinking of religion into its mere appendages, the making of the form an end rather than a means. With the formalist, everything that is really spiritual is gross extravagance. Earnestness is enthusiasm, and everything that rises above the freezing-point is fanaticism. " Let your moderation be known unto all men," is the text that embodies all the theology of the formalist. He may be an enthusiast in business, and feel that the magnitude of his work justifies it ; but in everything pertaining to his religion, moderation is his watchword, and every emotion is schooled according to this.

Nearly allied to this, and proceeding from it, is

CONSERVATISM,

Which seeks to preserve that which is established. It appropriates the names of Christianity, truth, and charity, and extends the right hand of Christian fellowship to a moderate degree of error. It deprecates no religion at all, while too much religion is no less an evil in its eye. It would strengthen the weak and weaken the strong, apply fire to such as are cold, and ice to such as burn, and it claims to be the umpire in religious fervor, and judge whether a man has too much religion or too little.

The only true conservatism in religion is to be found in keeping within the Bible limits. Whoever has no religion, or less than the Bible warrants, needs to be exhorted to strive after it; whoever has more religion than the Bible allows,—which requires the utmost of every physical and moral power,—he is to be checked and brought down to the Bible standard. Dr. Cumming, the eloquent English divine, says: "Some people say that we ought to have more moderation. The apostle says moderation is good. In your preference of form, yes. In your love of the world, yes. Pray be moderate in these things; but how can you be moderate in

Christianity ? Did you ever hear of a man being mod erate in honesty ? Moderate honesty would be positive theft. Did you ever hear of a moderate truth ? A moderate truth would be a lie. If a thing is right, you are to do it with all your heart ; if it is wrong, you are not to do it at all. The moment a man becomes earnest in his attachment to the truth and in his worship of the living God, that moment men will declare that much religion has made him mad."

So far is moderation from being recommended, that Christ said distinctly, " Thou shalt love the Lord thy God with all thy heart, and with all thy soul, and with all thy strength, and with all thy mind." Not much moderation in that !

The next difficulty in the way of the Church's growth arises from

WORLDLINESS.

The lust of the flesh, the lust of the eye, and the pride of life hinder in many cases the growth of holiness, and eat up every green thing in thousands of redeemed souls. It is beyond all controversy that there is in the Church a love of money, which the apostle declares is the root of all evil. A man is known by what he lives for, and multitudes seem to live only to amass wealth. It is to be feared that this spirit of worldliness in the Church is drinking up the very life-blood of thousands. By the operation of this spirit is the angel of mercy hindered. The world was never in a better state for the reception of the Gospel. The heathen intellect is waking up, and everywhere, weary of their worship and disgusted with their idols, they are stretching forth their hands unto us for help. The men are in readiness to go; the money is in the hands of the Church,—all that she needs to evangelize the world. Why, then, is the angel of mercy hindered? All that we ask to accomplish the great ends for which the Church has been founded and preserved is, that the means squandered by professed Christians should be thrown into the treasury of the Lord.

WE ARE PROUD.

We are proud, and pride is one of the greatest hindrances to the spread of the Gospel. Its dreary emptiness is seen wherever the cross casts its shadow. Its upas breath is everywhere working death.

CONFORMITY TO THE WORLD.

There is proceeding from this a spirit of conformity to the world in appearance and conversation, a disposition to catch the passing gale that blows from the world. And when you defraud religion of its peculiarity, you defraud it of its life, and sink it to a mere name. You may just as well strip the sunbeam of its light as religion of its peculiarity. Every Christian is peculiar; God, the Bible, and religion made him so. Just in proportion as the Church becomes like the world, she ceases to be the Church of God. In her present position she is too much like a noble ship tossing about in a boisterous sea, driven by the angry winds, and making but little headway. She should be as a great ocean steamer, with her heart of burning fire, which, in spite of storm and tempest, impels her toward the peaceful haven.

I would not be understood to claim that there is deterioration in the Church. I believe there never was a time since the apostles when her heart beat more in unison with the heart of Christ than now. Her bounds are enlarging on every side, but without a corresponding increase of power; there may be activity at the extremities and a fearful torpor at the heart.

OBSTACLES FROM WITHOUT.

We come to speak of obstacles from without. Two-thirds of the whole family of man are yet to be rescued from darkness and brought to the cross. To encounter and overcome every difficulty, and to spread a pure faith throughout the world, is the work of the Church, for which nothing but the power of God can fit her. The Church is to be the depository of truth, and the grand design is to oppose truth against error, righteousness against unrighteousness, purity against corruption; to give to the world an example of the spirit of Christ until sin shall blush in shame.

But in the accomplishment of this work there are difficulties to be overcome. There is no victory without a struggle. The world, the flesh, and the devil are in leagued hostility to the cross of Christ. The demoniacal nature of unregenerate man has suffered no abatement since it hung the Saviour on the cross. Victory can never be achieved by the might of merely nominal Christians. What! Send forth a company of imbeciles in the form of professed Christians to take the world by storm? They are better fitted for a hospital. You might as well attempt to bombard a fortified city with snow-balls, or to storm it with an army of manikins, as to think of taking the world by the might and prowess of merely nominal Christians. The work needs living, breathing, faith-inspiring men, who count not their lives dear unto them, and who sing and shout with a conscious certainty of triumph.

I have referred to the magnitude of the work and the difficulties to be overcome, not to baffle the courage or abate the ardor of the feeblest disciple of Christ, but that the Church of God may gird herself in proportion to the greatness of her work, and the difficulties that stand in the way of its performance. In the face of difficulties like these we see that the Church, like Isaiah, must be refined with fire to accomplish her mission. Just in proportion to the holiness of the Church is her power. Men may reason about Christianity, may reason powerfully and truthfully, and so as to sweep away all opposing arguments, and yet these arguments may not affect the conscience and the heart. But there is a moral power in holiness that disarms argument. All the vigor of the soundest logic may be rejected, but there is a moral power in the personal experience of salvation that must produce conviction in spite of everything.

It was the spirit of holiness in John Knox that gave him such power with God and constrained Mary Queen of Scots to declare that she feared the prayers of John Knox more than all the armies in England.

SPONTANEOUS POWER IN HOLINESS.

You might as well attempt to check an earthquake as to prevent the going forth of the spirit of holiness from a soul washed with blood, or a church refined by fire.

What are force and opposition to a saved church, in which God dwells? If need be, He shall hew her enemies to pieces; if brought in a strait place, He shall make for her a way through the mighty sea. The

Church may burn in the fires of persecution, but, like the bush of Horeb, she shall not be consumed. Oppositions to a saved church are like the weights to a clock —they keep her going. Persecutions are only the winds which fill the sails and drive her onward to her destined haven.

Holiness is an expansive energy. It will diffuse and communicate, and whenever kindled in the heart the man will feel like Jeremiah when he says a burning fire is shut up in my bones; and when God calls for a messenger he will cry out, Here am I; send me.

Holiness excludes selfishness. Its possessor loses himself in his mission; so loses sight of self, that ease and honor, and position and riches, and everything of earth is as the small dust in the balance compared with the fulfilling of his mission, to serve God and to save souls. Holiness is a spirit of sacrifice. A holy church is one that gives up all to God—reputation, influence, position, life itself—and with a calm dignity, determined to know nothing save Jesus Christ, and him crucified, says—

> "Here, on this altar, Lord, I lay
> My life, my soul, my all."

And more and more is this spirit coming upon the Church. The fires are being kindled, our sons and our daughters are receiving a baptism of power, and having their lips touched with a live coal from off the altar. May God kindle it anew in hundreds of hearts at this meeting. This is all that the Church needs. With such a church as this, when God calls for messengers the response will come up from every part of our Zion: Here am I; send me.

And such a church there shall be, for the mouth of the Lord hath spoken it; and already, as we have said, the fires are kindled, and the Church is feeling that it is specially charged with the salvation of the world, and soon it shall have to come to this, that he that is least in Zion, and he that remaineth in Jerusalem, shall be called holy, and every one that is written among the living in Jerusalem.

But we are to bear in mind that this is an individual work. We are not saved by bundles, but singly and alone. Many have been endowed with this power. God is among us at this meeting; God is among his saints, giving strength, for they have received power since the Holy Ghost has come upon them. Shall not many others enter into this rest? Oh that God would make every soul to hunger and thirst after righteousness, and to cry loudly to God that they may be refined by fire!

We sung at the opening, we have sung it many times since, and I would that all would sing now from the very depths of the soul, " Refining fire, go through my heart!" I would that we might break out in this language to-day, not merely in the language of our lips, but of our hearts, hungering and thirsting after righteousness, turning away from everything else, and asking here that satisfying portion. I would that this might be the language of every one's heart on this stand, in the middle of this ground, and on the very outskirts of this congregation.

> "Refining fire, go through my heart,
>   Illuminate my soul;
>   Scatter thy light through every part,
>   And sanctify the whole."

CHAPTER VI.

BISHOP SIMPSON'S EXHORTATION

GIVEN AT THE CLOSE OF REV. MR. WELLS'S SERMON.

I HAVE no doubt there are many here who would be glad to have a view of that seraph of whom we have been hearing, who took a live coal from the altar and came and touched the lips of the prophet; and could you see that seraph now, methinks you would anxiously ask that your lips might be touched with the same burning coal.   For there is such an immense work to be accomplished, that you and I often feel to say, "Send us;" and the Spirit impresses upon us the need of special qualification for the great work.   But we cannot see the seraphim, and yet, though invisible, angels are here.

> " Angels now are hovering round us,
>   Unperceived they mix the throng ,
>   Wondering at the love that crowns us,
>   Glad to join the holy song."

And it is easy for the Master to bid them wave their wings over us, or to come and whisper peace to our souls.   But, thank God! we need not ministering angels to come and fold us in their arms, or to cover us with their wings, for Jesus sends the Holy Spirit, in accordance with the promise:—"But the Comforter, which is the Holy Ghost, whom the Father will send in my name, He shall teach you all things, and bring all things to your remembrance, whatsoever I have said unto you." The Comforter, sent from the throne, Jesus has commanded to come to your hearts; and this morning he wants to welcome you into the family and Church of God. Do you fancy you are seeking the fulness of the blessing of the Gospel of peace? Seek it not as though it were far away, not as though by loud cries you must bring the Almighty near; seek it not as though Christ were not willing to come to you. No, no: God has prepared for us a fulness of life, a fulness of joy! Christ stands just by the door of your heart. Listen to that fond, deep voice this morning, as he gently knocks, and says, "If any man will open the door I will come in unto him and sup with him, and he with me." He whispers to the heart just now—not a seraph, not an angel, but Jesus himself, by the holy Comforter, the sent of God,—and are you unsatisfied and waiting? All the power of God is round about you, all the mercy of God is flowing towards you, the Son of God wants to encompass you, and the Spirit of God to fill you with an ocean of boundless love.

It is not necessary now that we travel down into the valley to find the pool of Siloam, and wait for the coming of the angel to trouble the waters, and for some strong man to lift us and put us in. No: the fountain is all around us, and flows divinely clear. Here is the Son of God waiting at this very moment to wash all our sins away. Have you a single stain upon your heart? Come to the fountain. Have you trouble and sorrow? Come at once to the Saviour and receive joy and comfort; for, thank God, there is room in His heart for all. How many have stepped into that fountain already,

and found it a sovereign balm for every sorrow and defilement! Thank God, cleansing power is there still.
It is here now; we may have it just where we are—
just as we are: open the door and let the Saviour come in.

You say this is difficult. Yes, it is difficult to break
down all barriers; but it may be done. Just remove
the bolts, and open the door. The Lord that made you
wants to remake you, and the Spirit that breathed life
into Adam at the beginning, is waiting to breathe life
into your soul. You may be dead in trespasses and sins,
and yet God can take you, as He took the lifeless body
of Adam, and breathe into you as into him, and you
may become a living soul. God can bring the corpse
to life, and he can do a great deal more than that. The
bones may be scattered, the sinews may be removed
from them; they may be very dry, and lying at the
mouth of the caves of earth; and looking at these dry
and scattered bones, I may well ask, Can these dry bones
live? And yet God can breathe upon them and they
shall live. God sends us in His name to say "Dry bones,
live!" Thank God, the power is now as mighty as in the
days of old; and the dry bones shall live, and there shall
rise up an exceeding great army to praise the living God.

Some that were very near to death at the commencement of this meeting have felt a moving as in their
very bones already; and a great many who were sick,
and infirm, and weak, and poor, God has touched as
with the wires of the battery of divine power, and their
souls have been filled with the fulness of divine love.

And if there be one in the very outskirts of the congregation who to-day has a single desire to find Jesus, I
tell him he may come now and find this grace; for even

now God can encircle every sinner in this congregation in the arms of His love. The people of God are going up the mountain, higher and still higher; a clearer light is visible. It increases as they ascend, and every hour they are having brighter views of the land of Beulah. Its ways are glorious with the sunlight of the steps of the redeemed who have walked there. While God's children are getting all these visions of the Better Land, come you to this same Saviour, come to this same Jesus; and He that saved us and brought us to himself is willing to receive you also.

It may be that some one will ask, "If I do receive the power of the Spirit, shall I be kept when amid trials, difficulties, and temptations which obstruct life's path? How shall I endure when I go home and father and mother or other kindred may prove unkind? What will become of me when surrounded again with the associations of the world? Though happy here where all is song and praise, when my hands are given to business, and I come into contact with sinful men, shall I be kept in the peace and comfort of the believer?"

I answer, Not if you live as you used to live, not if you go in the way of sinners. But hear Peter when he says, "Blessed be the God and Father of our Lord Jesus Christ who according to his abundant mercy has begotten us again unto a lively hope . . . who are kept by the power of God, through faith, unto salvation, ready to be revealed in the last time." Here is the secret of it, kept, not by your husband, not by your parents, not by the Church, not by the ministers preach they ever so learnedly and so eloquently—NO, NO:—kept, not by angels, not by cherubim, not by seraphim—kept "*by*

the power of God ! " That's enough. The power that
made the world, that holds the universe in its course, can
keep us. That power is around us, beneath us, above
us, and, thank God ! in a certain sense we can say, that
power is within us. Is it in you this morning ?

"Kept by the power of God, through faith ! " The
power is able to keep you if you have the faith, and this
faith is the realized gift of God to all who truly seek. As
I look over these converts and those that have stepped up
into the higher life, and then at the resources and in-
strumentalities for their safe keeping, I feel as Elijah did
when encompassed by the Assyrian hosts. You know
Elijah's servant came running to his master, and, with
fear and consternation in his looks, told him that he was
surrounded by his enemies. And Elijah, looking up to
heaven, said, "Lord, I pray thee, open his eyes that he
may see." The young man was very wide awake in ordinary matters. He had very clearly perceived the dan-
gers ahead. And yet the prophet prays God to open his
eyes that he might see. And when his eyes were opened,—why, there was the prophet just as he was before,
and there were the Assyrians just as they were before.
But yet there was a change ; for when the young man
looked out, behold, the hills were covered with horsemen
and chariots of fire. God had opened heaven and sent
its legions down to earth. God had encircled his servant with the hosts of heaven to protect him. I tell you,
young converts and grown Christians, you will be kept
by the power of God if you have faith. Look out this
morning beyond this grove, beyond this platform, beyond these trees and yonder blazing sky, and what do
you see ? Chariots and horsemen of fire ! If God thinks

it necessary he can send them down and take you up to glory, as he did Enoch and Elijah. But that is not best for you. It is better to stay here, and it is just as easy going to heaven through the sick-bed and the grave, as by the chariots and horses of fire. The same Saviour and the same angels are around you there, and you can sing,

"Jesus can make a dying bed
   Feel soft as downy pillows are;
 While on His breast I lean my head,
   And breathe my life out sweetly there."

If I had the choice now whether I would go to heaven in the chariot of fire, or enter the grave first, I would prefer the grave, simply because I would go the way Jesus went. That is the way his people have been going in all ages. Patriarchs and kings, prophets and martyrs, have gone up by the same door through which Jesus entered. Our mothers and fathers have passed in —some of them very recently—by the same door. I know they are there. I have almost seen them translated as they went up to glory. And, blessed be God! we are going also. The children and friends of these glorified ones, we are on the way, and we shall be kept by the power of God, through faith, unto salvation. When you go to your homes, do not go with trembling and fear; only keep humble and look to Jesus all the time for help. Go home believing. Take Jesus with you, and He will bring His Father and the holy angels with Him. Go into no company where you cannot take Jesus with you; do nothing in which you cannot ask His assistance; say nothing that Jesus cannot approve, but give yourself wholly to the Lord.

At meetings like this, the soul forms many good resolutions; and I think, this morning, many of you have felt that you have a work to do. I do not know what the work is, but each has his work; and let me say to you, go in the strength of Israel's God, and do it resolutely, unflinchingly, perseveringly; and may God help and bless you, and finally take you home to glory.

TESTIMONIES.

A Venerable Minister.—"I feel I should say I am resting in Christ, and Jesus is my all in all. Forty years ago I left everything behind, to labor as a Methodist preacher, and I never had any other business at all than that which belonged to a Methodist preacher. I have noticed that 'holiness to the Lord' never drove people away from me. Whenever I had that on my banner, they gathered around me, rough and stern as I may have been naturally. When I left holiness the people left me, and I have noticed that true of other men. The intellectually weakest will find they have an attractive power when possessed of this grace. Learning would not gather them in, and then constrain them to cry for mercy; but when holiness to the Lord is the impulse of the preacher, they will gather about him, and never cease their importunings until they are saved. You need not be afraid of failing to go on aright when you get this perfect love, for, bless God! there is Almightiness in holiness. Do not hesitate, lest afterward you should be overcome; for it is the eternal rock, and 'the gates of hell shall not prevail against it.'"

A Sister.—"Many years ago I heard the Lord say in the Episcopal church, 'Thou shalt love the Lord thy God with all thy heart.' I resolved to obey, and for a long time tried to do so in my own strength, until the Lord in his kind providence made me acquainted with the people called Methodists, through whose teachings I apprehended Jesus as the Saviour, as I had never done before. The promise has been verified to me, ' He shall deliver thee in six troubles, yea in seven there shall no evil touch thee.' God has graciously given me every member of my family to go with me, and I find Him a perfect Saviour."

An old Sea Captain had witnessed the love of God on the ocean as well as on the land. " There have been some beautiful thoughts thrown out here, but I was much impressed when in Philadelphia, some time ago, meeting with a dearly beloved friend, who said, God had given him a New-year's gift in the class-room—the Scripture sentiment, ' In Christ's stead.' I took it as mine also, and resolved to go out and act as Christ did, and regard it as a privilege. Last Monday morning a poor fellow came from Blackwell's Island prison very much reduced in pocket, of course. ' My father,' said he, ' was licensed by John Wesley.' I thought, as best I can I'll carry out my purpose ' In Christ's stead.' I said, 'My friend, come and I'll give you your breakfast.' Afterward I said, ' Christ will accept you if you will accept him,' and I seemed to love him, body and soul. This is what grace does for me. It plants within us the great heart of Christ, and helps us to be simple in heart and life. I want to magnify the grace of God, that he has rescued and so wonderfully helped me. I did not know my letters when I was thirty years old. If we only follow Christ all will be well. Let us resolve to do so now."

A Minister.—"My soul has been exceedingly blessed here. Oh, what a steady, sweet, solid, heavenly peace has been pervading my soul from the very commencement of this meeting! It seems to me I never attended a camp-meeting where the tide of grace kept rising so constantly; where there was no jarring, and where every breath was fragrant with Christ. I praise the Lord for the increase of interest on this theme in our beloved Zion, and for the evidence that the precious doctrine of perfect love is getting a firm foothold in this country. Go where you will, and you find Presbyterians, Baptists, and others, walking in this light, and their ministers are more generally interested in it. Some important religious conventions have of late given special attention to the need of the Church of a higher life.

"I have been praying for such a divine influence to come down here, that through us it might be spread all over this land. Oh that God would unite his children to seek for holiness, so when they go hence, north, south, east, and west, they would exhibit the power and sweetness of every Christian grace. I love sinners, and to those of you who know me I need not say I have been laboring earnestly for their salvation for eighteen years past. In this meeting we may be fully anointed for the work of soul-saving, and those from Maryland and Maine, Rhode Island and Virginia, New York, Vermont, and the far West, South Carolina, Pennsylvania, New Jersey, and all these regions round about, gathered with one accord with these hosts of God's elect. We should be so baptized from on high, that henceforth we should be instrumental in gathering many souls into the fold of Christ. God grant it!"

CHAPTER VII.

SERMONS OF REV. B. M. ADAMS, OF NEW YORK EAST
CONFERENCE, AND REV R. V. LAWRENCE, OF NEW JER-
SEY CONFERENCE.

MR. ADAMS'S SERMON.

. *Acts* i. 8.—" *But ye shall receive power after that the Holy Ghost
is come upon you : and ye shall be witnesses unto me, both in Jerusalem, and in all Judea, and in Samaria, and unto the uttermost part of
the earth.*"

THESE words were spoken by Jesus just before He ascended to heaven. His disciples were not prepared fully
to go forth on the great mission set before them. They
were living near the geographical centre of the then
known world, with the various philosophies and govern-
ments of men against them, and these they were to meet.
But they were poor and unlearned men ; true, they had
been under the greatest of teachers for three years, but
yet they were comparatively unprepared for their great
work. They needed what was promised in this text, the
coming upon them of the Holy Ghost that should endue
them with power. Men are necessarily and naturally
worshippers of power, according to their conception and
appreciation of it, whether it be physical, moral, or intellectual power, whose manifestations more immediately appeal to their sympathy. The man that develops
an unusual degree of physical strength sways a moral
sceptre over a very large class of persons. Everybody
admires muscular ability. This is one reason why men

attend the race-course, and await with eager expectation the account of every prize-fight. Such is the worship or veneration that people have for mere power. Men, again, admire the powerful in nature; a magnificent cataract will attract visitors from a distance of thousands and thousands of miles; and they will sit looking at and admiring it until their feelings become warmed and their hearts seem to partake of the very spirit of the natural scenery which they contemplate. It is so, also, with intellectual power. An unusual degree of mental energy, intensified by thought and enriched by learning, causes the possessor of it to stand upon a platform of imperial elevation above his fellows. Many men possess a sort of commanding, magnetic influence which assures their pre-eminence and authority wherever they go.

There is another species of power that men know very little about. They will surely know more about it in the future; that is the spiritual power that is spoken of in the text. If you add to those natural endowments whose influence and authority are everywhere recognized, the spiritual power secured by the coming of the Holy Ghost, the man thus endowed has attained to a most commanding influence. We have a noble example of this union of the natural and the supernatural power in the person of the Apostle Paul. Physically he was not a large man, but he must have possessed an iron frame to endure the sufferings and bodily trials to which he was subjected. He had intellectual endowments in a superior and commanding degree, and then he was anointed with the power spoken of in the text, and it made him a monarch among men, a position which he holds to-day, and will probably hold throughout all eternity. Paul stands out before the minds of men to-day as one of the most imperial men whom God has ever given to the world. Now, the power spoken of in the text is spiritual, which, brought into contact with physical power, overcomes it; or brought into contact with the psychological force, overcomes that singly, or even combined with every other natural power; thus it stands out in single grandeur above all other exhibitions of power that the world has ever seen, and brings all in humble submission before the great God of the Universe. Such is the power spoken of in this text.

THE MAXIMUM OF POWER.

There are comparatively few men imperial in the realm of physical and intellectual power, or that possess in an eminent degree the magnetizing psychological force previously mentioned. But here is a power that is accessible to everybody, under the conditions and according to the measure of every man's capacity to have it. I do not believe that all men can be equally powerful spiritually, and accomplish the same results in working for God. There is a great deal more work expected of an engine of a thousand-horse power than one of a hundred-horse power; and yet it is the same power, steam, which drives both. There are small minds, and great minds, as there are engines of small and of great power. You take the small mind and fill it with this spiritual power spoken of in the text, and it will accomplish all that God designed it should; you may take the great mind and endow that with this spiritual power in addition to its own natural gifts, and it will be much more powerful in proportion to the natural ability which God has confer-

red upon it.   What is wanted is the spiritual power inspiring every man, woman, and child to the maximum
of effort.   They would then be capable of the greatest
measure of success in the work of God possible for them
in view of the primary conditions of their existence. And
the possession of this spiritual power is the normal condition of the soul,—placing it exactly where God meant
that it should be, in exact adjustment with his plans, so
that his influence and spirit may pour through it and
pervade it in every part.   It may influence some men a
thousand times more powerfully than others, and cause
them to produce results a thousand times more important.   Would that the great power of God were poured
through every man to the accomplishment of the divine
purposes.   " Ye shall receive power after that the Holy
Ghost is come upon you ; and ye shall be witnesses unto
me," so that your words shall be in power.   You know
it does not depend so much on the size of the machine
as on the strength of the power that drives it.   The bul-
let is powerless in my hands, but put it into the rifle
and it becomes an instrument of death.   This idea properly expresses that of the varying measure with which
different men are inspired with the spirit of God in the
proportion of their capability.   I believe that the baptism of the Holy Ghost is felt and admitted in all the
deepest philosophies of the human mind to be the normal adjustment that God designs for all.   I believe that
this baptism is supremely reasonable in the eyes of the
world, whether they admit it or not.   Wherever you see
a man brought into this condition, it is shown that there
is a power superior to every other power in the world.
What was the Roman government, with all its persecu-

tions and hostility to the Cross of Christ, but as the mere sprig of a tree which trembled and snapped in the hands of the God whom it despised? This is the power which will sooner or later take hold of this world and hang it up on high as a trophy of the power of God; and to every one upon these grounds He will give it if you will only put yourselves in a position to receive it.

CONDITIONS, CONSECRATION.

I will now speak of some things that are preliminary to the attainment of this power. In the first place, there must be an entire consecration of ourselves in our wholeness—our property, as a part of ourselves, and our influence, as the outgrowth of ourselves. There must be a wholeness, or rather a wholesaleness, in our consecration. We must have not merely a minute consecration, going down into the particulars of our being, but after all the particulars are examined carefully, we must be ready to say, "If there is anything more that I know not of, I will give it all to God; if there is any new force developed by the exercise of these forces of which I know, then I give this to God." Now it will be admitted by all, that when the Holy Ghost is received, it gives people a supremacy and a commanding influence and power, of which they have had no previous experience. Simon Magus was very well acquainted with this, and very ready to acknowledge that the apostles had a power that he did not possess, and he thought he could purchase it with money. You will find that some of the very topmost heights of spiritual attainment stand very close to that descending line, that, after all, may send one down to perdition; and we must be continually on the watch, for even our affections may betray us. This matter of consecration must be wholesale, must take in all the life, all the thought, all the mind; all that we can think of, all that we know, and all the consequences which for the present we are unable to see. I want to speak of this, because even we preachers make mistakes in regard to it. We wonder often that the Holy Ghost does not come under our preaching. We preach the truth, and are under a conviction that we are in earnest, and preach with fervency and power. Yet the result is not an abiding one. Allow me to say, brethren, that this power is a spiritual power, and leads men to decide at once; and if decision for good is not the result of our preaching, it is because we have not made that *entire* consecration of ourselves to God of which I have been speaking. This is where a great deal of our preaching fails. It is truthful, eloquent; but the Power which appeared at Pentecost is absent, and men are not led to decide for God. An eminent Doctor of Divinity in the Methodist Episcopal Church once said to me, " Brother, I do not understand it: I preach with all my might, and as well as I know how, and yet, after care and prayer, I do not succeed in leading souls to God." The reason of this failure is, that whilst radical and important truths are preached, the great fundamental truth, that which embraces and underlies all the others, is forgotten. No matter who or what you are, success in preaching will only be fully realized after entire consecration to God.

FAITH.

Entire consecration leads to faith. This is the second preliminary. I do not believe any one can thoroughly believe in God unless he has this entire consecration of which I speak. When you have made an entire consecration of yourself to God, you can believe. In fact, when you have this entire consecration, you have belief in God. When, eighteen years ago, I first came to believe in this great fundamental truth, my recognition of it sent me on a thousand leagues ahead in force and feeling. I then tried to make my consecration entire, and give up all to God, as far as I knew; and God helped me, and the Spirit bore testimony to my heart that my consecration was entire.

Make, then, this entire consecration, and the Holy Ghost will come upon you at this meeting, and fill you with a power that you never had before. The nature of its influence I cannot describe; but "Ye shall receive power after that the Holy Ghost is come upon you." And ye shall be witnesses to God, even though you may be unconscious of the fact.

I might say a great deal about the effect produced on different minds by the action of this communicated power, but I will only say that it makes everybody natural. It makes some people boisterous in their manifestations, and other people still. Some may have power that manifests itself in noise like the thunder, and some silent power like the lightning.

RESULTS.

I only wish now to notice some of the concomitant blessings attending the manifestation of the power of God.

And, in the first place, it takes away all fear. Fear is the result of weakness. You take a man of good physical strength, and he walks the streets with an air of confidence and pride, as if perfectly conscious of safety. So, when a man is filled with the Holy Ghost, he is not afraid of anything that may stand in his way and endeavor to obstruct his passage upward. Why should a man fear who is endowed with the fulness of the Holy Ghost? There never was a better example of this result of the power of the Holy Spirit than the Apostle Peter, at one moment without it, trembling in the presence of a servant-girl, and the next moment crowned with it, standing up before a hostile mob, and preaching the Gospel without the shadow of a fear.

Another blessing attending it is that it will make you lovely in life and character; but as the love-producing power of the Gospel has been brought so fully before you here, it is unnecessary for me to dwell upon it. It will make you capable of submitting to the smallest and most annoying inconveniences. The baptism of the Holy Ghost makes men sweet in private life, as it makes them fearless and undaunted in public.

There is one prolific source of fear in this world—I mean the almighty power of God ; for there are men so peculiar that they are afraid to do anything that will offend God, simply because God is so great. And then there are others that are entirely destitute of fear, owing to the tremendous consciousness of their own strength. Allow me to illustrate the first consideration.

Thirty or forty years ago, my father was in the habit of telling a story of a man who had been through the last war, who had a son thirteen years of age, and he had trained that boy to obey him carefully and perfectly in everything. On a certain Sunday afternoon he sent the boy on an errand to a distance, charging him to be back, without fail, at sundown. The evening proved to be tempestuous, and a river which separated the boy from his home was soon swollen to a rapid and fearful torrent. The father's heart yearned after his boy, wondering whether he would return; and at last he wandered to watch for him at the swollen river's bank. Toward sundown the boy appeared and urged his horse into the fearful current. The horse drifted, borne by the torrent, down the stream, and the father traced his steps to where he thought the animal would reach the shore. When within a short distance from the shore, the boy in his agony cried out:

"Father, save me!" And the answer was:

"Cling to your horse, my son, or I will flog you to death."

The boy had no other alternative, and soon the stern father was weeping like a child on the neck of his son. Despite the hard schooling to which his feelings had been subjected, nature proved conqueror at last, and every other feeling was lost in his rejoicing over the boy's deliverance. Some people fear God like that. Others, however, are so filled with the spirit of God that they have no tormenting fear. Perfect love casteth out fear; and this perfect love comes of perfect consecration and perfect faith. Consecrate yourself to God, and then believe, and it is yours; and you shall be so endued with the Holy Ghost, that obedience shall be not of fear, but of joy; not a task, but the play of your life.

"Ye shall be witnesses unto me" also, saith the Lord, to testify of this grace; to praise God for its bestowal.

And oh, when the longing soul finds this bliss, how does it break forth in utterances of thanksgiving and testimony of God's abounding mercy!

Dear brethren and sisters, are you coming to God to get this blessing here, to be fed from God now? Remember God is willing, and waiting in love to satisfy you now. One day my only boy was away from home,—and we make a good deal of the baby at our house, as all parents may do. We had been for some time expecting his return, but he did not come at once. I was up in my study when I heard the door below shut quite hard, as though some one had come in. My heart was in a flutter, when in a low voice I heard the boy call his mother, but she was not within hearing at the moment. Hearing his call, I said, "What is it, my son?" "Oh, I am so hungry!" said he; and then down-stairs I went, two steps at a time. I gave him suitable food, and while I did it, oh, how my heart went out toward him and yearned over him! and just then God said to me plainly, by His spirit, "If ye, then, being evil, know how to give good gifts to your children, how much more shall your heavenly Father give the Holy Spirit to them that ask him!" And the whole of my soul felt the logic of this appeal. Oh, yes! if I, a poor weak man, down here on earth, delight in supplying the need of my child, my Father in heaven, rich, and infinite, and omnipotent, is willing to give you, and wants to give you, this great blessing. I have not much in this world, but to buy a meal of victuals for my hungry child, if I could not do it otherwise, I would sell my tools, my books, and everything else; and so would you. I have heard mothers say, as they bent over their children, that they would willingly die for them, and I believe it. How much more intensely does God love us, and how much more willing is He to give us the Holy Ghost.

I had thought of saying something about keeping this blessing, but I leave that. Oh, let us get it! There is a terrible responsibility resting upon us to get this; and getting it and improving the grace we receive, God will help us to keep it until we go up to see the glories of heaven, and reign with Jesus forever.

MR. LAWRENCE'S SERMON.

Jeremiah viii. 22.—*"Is there no balm in Gilead; is there no physician there? why then is not the health of the daughter of my people recovered?"*

THE prophet bewails the condition of the Jewish people, his own people, who were in deep trouble and affliction. The very bones of their fathers had been dug from their graves and scattered with irreverent hand throughout the land. The glory had departed from the nation, and instead of being famous among the nations of the earth, they had now become a byword and a reproach. The prophet likens their misfortunes to the diseases which afflicted the people notwithstanding there was a remedy provided which was sure to effect a cure. They had fallen into sin and forsaken the Lord their God; and the earth became as iron; their prosperity passed away; God made their fields to cease to yield; famine so raged over the land that the very mothers of Israel were obliged to eat their own offspring. And yet all they had to do was merely to obey God, just to do what he bade them and their prosperity would return to them; and yet this they failed to do, refused to do, and, as a consequence, famine, and invasions, and sicknesses, and distresses, continued to afflict the people. It was a review of the condition of the people that extorted from the prophet the lamentable cry of the text, "Is there no balm in Gilead; is there no physician there?" You perceive that this passage of Scripture has a very easy application to our own condition and to the state of the Church of God at the present day.

In the first place, I propose to show that the Church is yet fearfully diseased; in the second place, that provision has been made for a perfect cure; and in the last place, to make a practical application of the text to our own souls.

DISEASE AND SYMPTOMS.

In the first place, the Church of the living God is yet fearfully diseased. Sin is the great evil of the human family. It entered at first with Adam, has descended all down the ages ever since, and now, confined to no particular clime or country, produces disorder of all kinds, moral and physical, and is a source of misery and death to the people. It is true it is in the first place a soul-disease; but then it is the cause of all the ills that flesh is heir to as well. A portion of the human race, and an ever-increasing proportion, the part included in the Church of God, profess to have been cured of this soul-malady, and there are individuals throughout the Church that have been entirely cured of it, entire holiness of heart having superseded this fearful state. There are others who are yet fearfully diseased, though by their actions they seem to say, "See how sound I am!" Inward diseases in general have their outward manifestations; and this is no exception to the general rule. It is more important that we should know how the case stands with this than with any other disease; and may God aid me to search hearts here just as they will be searched in the day of judgment, when every stain, however small, shall be made visible before all the universe.

ABSENCE OF JOY.

In the first place, the absence of the joy which God intends Christians to feel is a sign that the Church of God is not yet entirely rid of this terrible malady. God's people are to be a happy people, and I tell you that if this happiness that Christ gives to his followers is in the heart, it will manifest itself in the life and conduct,— in the beaming countenance, in the earnest shout of glory, or a serenity of face that never seems to know a cloud. It is true it may have tears to shed, tears of sympathy with the sorrows of one's household or of those around us, and yet in the heart there is a well full of the joys of salvation. A common surface-well will get dry, but artesian wells in dry times have plenty of water in them, and sometimes send it in sparkling jets far above the ground. The perfect Christian has an artesian well of joy in his heart. Many of God's people seem to have just about as many carking cares and weary anxieties as the people of the world. If you visit the homes of many Christians, of many who are indeed the people of God, you will find about as much care sitting on their brows as you will find anywhere else. It is because they are not yet entirely healed of that moral malady within.

ABSENCE OF LOVE.

But then, again, the absence of brotherly love in the Church is another sign that the Church is not yet entirely healed. Now God's people are to be a loving people; they are to love one another with a perfect love. You know Christ said, "Another commandment I give unto you, that ye love one another;" and John, the loving disciple, says, "Little children, love one another." This is one of the signs of true discipleship; and yet how little of this true Christian love do we find in the Church of Christ! You will see old hatreds and prejudices down in the hearts of many of God's people, and they seem likely to remain there for years. And even if they do not appear in words or deeds, they are seen too often in the contemptuous curl of the lip which stings like the fangs of the serpent. If every evil word spoken by one brother or sister against another were an arrow that went straight from the heart of the speaker to the heart of the person spoken of, the air would be darkened as in the midst of an Indian fight. And if some of God's people had their houses converted into forts—as indeed they might be, since they live in a state of war—there would be a surprising number of fortified castles in the Christian world. All this only too plainly shows how it is with the heart.

DRESS.

The general appearance of the Church in respect of attire is also proof that she is not yet entirely healed. I believe that religion covers the dress of God's people. It is true that it does not proscribe any particular color for the dress, or any particular cut for the coat, but it rules out all extravagance and all that is brought in merely for show and vanity. I think that is the Scripture rule, and when I see any one bedecked all over with those things which are merely for show, I argue that there is something the matter down in the heart. Pride in the heart will show itself in the outward appearance, in the style and dress, and when we see it we have a right to conclude that the heart is impure.

SPIRITUAL DYSPEPSIA.

There is another sign of this diseased state of the Church referred to by the apostle, when he says, "I have not fed you with meat but with milk, because hitherto you were not able to bear it." They had the spiritual dyspepsia, poor people, and could not digest the strong meat of the Gospel. The signs of the physical malady are well known, and the signs of the spiritual malady are equally known. Too many of our preachers feed their flocks merely on the milk of the Word, and it too often happens that the milk is so diluted with water as to have lost even the character of milk. It is only milk and water, and very weak at that.

WEAKNESS.

There is still another sign that I wish to notice, and that is the weakness of the Church in its contests with the world. Those that are warring against the Church of the living God seem to laugh at her. It is said that a year or so ago the Wesleyan Church in England had

decreased in membership. In order to bring back the
old power, a Doctor of Divinity proposed that the ministers should put on the gown again. Our old Methodism seems disposed to go with ritualism as well as the
Anglican Church in this country. We have departed
from the old land-marks. The same spiritual power
which our fathers possessed is all that we need to bring
back the old prosperity of the Church.

THE REMEDY.

I am to proceed, in the second place,·to show that
though the Church of the living God is not yet cured
of the old malady, there is sufficient remedy at hand.
Upon Calvary is found the balm of Gilead, and if the
Church is not cured, it is not God's fault. Every one
of you believes that God has made provision for the entire extirpation of the old disease. Is there no physician
there? Yes, there is a physician, Jesus Christ, who has
all the qualities of a good physician. Now there are
two things necessary to qualify a physician for his
work. The first is a pathological knowledge of the diseases to which the human body is subject, and the
second is, a knowledge of the remedies necessary to
effect a cure. Jesus Christ possesses all knowledge of
the diseases of the human soul, and surely we ought to
have confidence in Him. He dwelt here in the midst
of sin and wore our nature, and can sympathize with the
most terrible case that can come before Him. When
Jesus Christ practises among His people, it does not
matter whether they are rich or poor, high or low.
But another important question, " Has Jesus the remedy?" Blessed be God! He has the remedy in His

own blood. "The blood of Jesus Christ, His Son, cleanseth from all sin." It is an infallible remedy. It has been tried by white men and black, by poor men and rich. I tried it myself once, and found it an infallible balm. There was a soldier, a Christian, once, who was asked by the officer for the watchword at night, and he said, "The precious blood of Jesus." There was a comrade soldier who heard this strange watchword, and could not rest until he had bowed himself before the Lord.

There is another question. Has Jesus Christ had unfailing success? Yes: in every instance in which the patient has complied with the conditions of the cure, a cure has been effected. Just let us step back eighteen centuries, to the foot of that mountain from which Jesus has been preaching. There is one of those poor despised creatures who is afflicted with the leprosy. He is alone, for the people are afraid to go near him, and he makes his way toward the Saviour, and an old Pharisee, with a proud curl on his lip, wonders what Jesus can do with that chronic leper. So he comes to Jesus, and says, "If thou wilt, thou canst make me clean." And Jesus says, "I will: be thou clean." And the leper goes home to his father and mother, who had disowned him so long, healed of his disease.

And now others come to Jesus, for at evening they brought to Him all their sick, and all who were possessed of devils, and He healed them. They bring them all to the feet of Jesus—a good place that for the sick. The mother with her dumb daughter, and the possessed of the devil, and the blind, and the lame—all come up before the Saviour, and now I see them stand there, and oh, what a group! And they begin to cry to Jesus, and

Jesus, with the gentleness of an infant and with the majesty of God, stretches forth His hand, and cures all their diseases. And I do suppose that there were many happy homes around Jerusalem that night. Do you not remember the time when your father and mother came home converted, what a happy time you had? We will in imagination visit that little domicile just outside the walls of Jerusalem, and there stands an old woman weeping because of her son Benjamin who had been sick five years, and his brothers have taken him to Jesus; and his mother trembles lest he should die ere he returns. Oh, the depth of a mother's love! it is only surpassed by the love of God. But who is this coming along towards the house? It looks like Benjamin—but no, they *carried* him away. And yet it must be Benjamin, and so he comes home healed, and no more to be the victim of disease; and methinks there was joy and praising of God in that house that night. But, says one, these were only physical cures. Don't you know that he forgave sins also? We will go up to Calvary and find another instance to convince you of this. For they accused this blessed Jesus and hung Him upon the cross, and nature seemed to die with its great Creator. And another poor soul comes to Him there, a thief who had been nailed to the cross. He was a guilty sinner who saw beneath him a yawning hell. And what is to become of him? Is he to die there? Just then the blessed Holy Ghost led him to notice a man hanging by his side, and something within seemed to say, " It is the Saviour, it is Jesus," and the earth beneath grew sick and murmured, " Jesus." And looking up he saw written, " This is the King of the Jews;" and he said, " Lord, remember me;" and Jesus said, "This day thou shalt be with me in Paradise;" for

> " The dying thief rejoiced to see
>   That fountain in his day;
> And there may we, though vile as he,
>   Wash all our sins away."

My dying brother, look away to Calvary. Is there no balm in Gilead; is there no physician there? Yes, there is, and he is here to-day. You have come here to be sanctified, and you may be sanctified now on this very spot. The only reason why the Church is not entirely sanctified is, because she has not asked to be sanctified. I need not urge you to this. The blessed Holy Ghost is here now. This is a great camp-meeting, and I am looking for another that will assemble up there before the throne, and all will come—Coke and Wesley:—and Paul will rise up somewhere from old Rome—we shall all rise up, early in the morning, I suppose, and ascend up there and look at that great Physician. I am to be there. I am booked through. I have just got my baggage checked and my passage paid.

[At this point the enthusiasm was intense; shouts of " all the way through " and others resounding from every part of the platform. The preacher sat down evidently exhausted, whilst the large audience burst out simultaneously in the words of the hymn:

> " The dying thief rejoiced to see," &c.

Then the congregation was invited to come closer towards the stand, and under the fearful excitement to which the exercises had led, the most appalling shouts for mercy were heard, and the most earnest supplications uttered.]

CHAPTER VIII.

SERMON OF REV. JOHN PARKER, OF NEW YORK EAST CONFERENCE.

Ezekiel xxxvi. 25, 26, 27.—*" Then will I sprinkle clean water upon you, and ye shall be clean : from all your filthiness and from all your idols will I cleanse you. A new heart also will I give you, and a new spirit will I put within you : and I will take away the stony heart out of your flesh, and I will give you a heart of flesh. And I will put my Spirit within you, and cause you to walk in my statutes, and ye shall keep my judgments and do them."*

THIS is one of those portions of the Old Testament which indicate the mind of God toward his people in all ages. I do not believe it was intended merely as a promise to the children of Israel in view of the affliction and distress which their idolatry brought upon them. It promises personal sanctification, and appeals, therefore, to all the people here and everywhere. I know it, if for no other reason than this, that it exactly answers to my own experience before I came to the fountain of Christ's blood, and it most beautifully illustrates the experience I have had of the cleansing power of the Gospel, during the past twenty-five years.

Rather than dwell upon the thoughts suggested by the text in regular order as they arise, I will direct your minds to the general subject; and though there are a great many hearts here which do not need my instructions, there are others that do not enjoy that rest in full measure which God has promised to his people. To them I am anxious more particularly to speak. The preaching from this stand, so far as I have been present to hear, has been very precious indeed, but mainly directed to those who love the Lord Jesus Christ in sincerity and in truth. There are many persons present who would like that this should be the day of their deliverance; I want to talk to such this morning.

HOLINESS INSURES COMMUNION WITH GOD.

There is a promise in the text of a moral state which, enjoyed by us, brings us necessarily into most blessed communion with God; I say necessarily, for if we walk in the light as He is the light, then He and we have fellowship one with another—not merely Christian fellowship, but the fellowship of God in communion with His children. God loves himself because He cannot discover in himself any imperfection whatever. If He should find anything against which His holiness should protest, He could not love himself, nor us, nor demand of us a holy life. Loving himself, He loves us and all who, like Him, are holy. It arises as a necessity from this relation, that the man who walks in the light as God is in the light has fellowship with God. This moral state in which the people of God are placed in relation to Him is variously spoken of and described in the Word of God. It is spoken of, for instance, as " purity of heart," " perfect love which casteth out fear," " going on to perfection," and so on; and these expressions, I think, indicate that it is the intention of God that we should live in this state of grace, which is our normal condition.

MEANING OF THE TERMS.

What do we mean by perfect love? I think we mean that as love is the centre of all grace, so when it is present all the other graces of the spirit are perfected in the same degree in our hearts. The state of perfect love includes not only perfect love towards God, but perfect love towards man. It is not an exclusive love, in which we should love God and hold a relation of perfect indifference to everything else; or that we shall think only of divine things to the neglect of the affairs of this life. It is that supreme love that prefers God to everything else, and only loves other things in reference to Him. The other terms used to express this moral state are fully understood by you, such as "entire sanctification." This means that we are entirely consecrated to the service of God, and made holy by the blood of the Lord Jesus Christ, our dear Redeemer. The term "holiness" relates rather to the outward manifestation of the inward principle of sanctification. Holiness is what you do; sanctification what God does for you. God's holiness consists in perfect harmony between the relation that He sustains to created intelligence and his conduct; and ours in the harmony existing between our relation to God and man, and the conduct we manifest towards God. All this holiness comes out of the heart that has first been made clean by the blood of the Lamb.

RELATION OF SANCTIFICATION TO JUSTIFICATION.

And now, in reference to this blessed work of entire sanctification, what do you mean by it in relation to the work of grace that has been begun in many hearts here? I would not have you undervalue your justification. Ye were born, "not of blood, nor of the will of the flesh, nor of the will of man, but of God." Being justified, you are now God's children; and you are always to remember that such is the relation that you bear to God. There was a prince once travelling with his tutor. He took the opportunity, on a certain occasion, of asking the tutor what course of conduct he ought to pursue under certain circumstances. The answer—and it covered every circumstance that could possibly arise—was, "Always remember that you are a king's son." Always remember that you are the children of the living God.

There is an essential difference between the work of our justification and its concomitants, and that active sanctification of which we have been speaking. In our justified state, love, which is the essential element of all grades of religious life, is imperfect, being often mingled with selfish motives and earthly feelings; with fears and terrors which oppress the soul. It is true that we have no fear for the morrow, for we know that He who feedeth the ravens will not forget the children of His love; there is no fear of the judgment—how shall I stand in that great day? For He who bought me with His blood shall bear me through this fully absolved from blame. When the heart is sanctified fully, all selfish fear is taken away; the blessed word of Christ is experienced in its reality, "Come unto me all ye that labor and are heavy laden, and I will give you rest."

In the justified state it is quite common that the presence of a corrupt nature should be felt. Even amid

4*

the joys of adoption, how common is it to feel vexed and oppressed under the presence of evil thoughts and of evil tendencies, which too often manifest themselves, even at our own fireside!

If you were to fill a glass with water from a roiled stream and then allow it to stand until all the impurity had settled, you might lift the glass up into the sunlight and you would discover nothing but the transparent water; but shake it or disturb it, and again the sediment spreads all through the vessel. After a season of favorable circumstance and rest if we look at our hearts as the sun of righteousness may shine upon them, we may behold no impurity; but is there no sediment, which, if stirred by temptation or trial, would soon spread through our natures? Our tempers are very often excited; but in the state of entire sanctification these tempers are subdued and the old stony heart is taken away, —that unfeeling heart, which has been one of the deepest sources of anxiety, is renewed. Without this, how many things do you see that should be done, and yet there is no response in the heart, and they are too often left undone. Has not this been the very plague of your life? I will take it away, says God, and give you a heart of flesh, which shall be responsive to every voice of duty and of love.

Again, in our justified state we are dissatisfied with our religious experience; and this is true, not of those alone who have become backsliders, but it is truest of those who are most devoted and careful and honest in the sight of God, and it continues so until they have become the recipients of this blessing of perfect love. This is one great sorrow of the Church's heart.

Many preachers try to quiet the cravings of the people, which they may deem too keenly felt; but often while the hungry soul is begging for bread it receives only a stone. They are pleading for something which is clearly presented in the Word of God as attainable, for something which they know others have obtained, and hence their peace is broken and their spirits are sad. If they could only realize the blessed state spoken of in the text—the state of entire sanctification, having all their pollution taken away and their stony hearts made hearts of flesh—then there would be perfect love and peace in the soul.

There are also at times distress and fear concerning our future safety. Up to the point where we enter into the promised land of perfect love, there prevails in our minds a fear of the future. "What if at last I should fail! What if I should never reach the haven of rest at my Father's right hand! What if, notwithstanding all my religious desires, I should, after all, be a castaway! I have days of no joy, days when it seems as if God had forgotten me; and what if, at last, when the good are gathered around the throne of God and the Lamb, I should be cast out from the presence of God!" When I was yet a young man, having just been converted, with nothing to comfort me but the idea, just formed, of the fatherhood of God, though ambitious for learning and desirous of doing something in the service of my Master, I was the victim of that spirit of fear as to my future; this continued for six months, and then God revealed His perfect love to my heart.

If other proof is needed of the possibility of this state of perfect love, I would refer to the founder of our eccle-

siastical system.   Attempts have been made to misinter-
pret the meaning of Wesley in regard to this glorious
doctrine.   John Wesley says, in his sermon on Patience,
when describing a visit that he had made to the congregation of that good man, Thomas Walsh, that he did
not find a single person among them who did not experience entire sanctification as a second blessing distinct
from that of justification.   The Scripture testimony is
plain and decisive on this point.   Look, for instance, at
that passage from John: "Every branch in me that
beareth not fruit he taketh away; and every branch
that beareth fruit he purgeth it, that it may bring forth
more fruit."   Mark you, the branch is in Christ, or it
could bear no fruit.   It is in Christ and bearing fruit;
but it needs purging that it may bear more fruit; and
not until this purging process is accomplished does it
bring forth fruit to the honor and glory of God.

The branch must have support as well as purging.

Give a man God to lean against, and he will cast his
branches on the further side of heaven's walls, and angels will pluck the fruit.   There was a time when you
were tempted and the temptations were pleasant.   Being born of God, you cannot sin while the seed remaineth in you.   Tempted are you, then, and does the temptation oppress you?   It shows that there is a conflict
going on between the flesh and the spirit, and the spirit
will help you to triumph in the end.   Here is a barrel
of powder: I throw upon it a pitcher of water, and it
does no harm; I throw a lucifer match into it and there
is an explosion.   Sin is the gunpowder in your heart,
and the devil's match will explode it.

It then appears that perfect purity is attainable in this

life; but lest there should be any doubt about it, I will consider further. It is admitted that this must take place at some time; and there are only three agents in the accomplishment of this work of cleansing—the word, the spirit, and the blood. When is that cleansing accomplished? That excellent minister, Mr. Jay, says death will finish the work. What is death? Death is merely the absence of life, as darkness is the absence of light—is nothing. Can nothing do this greatest of somethings? But then, it is said, this is done just before death. But why five minutes or ten minutes before death? If God can do it five minutes before you die, can He not do it ten minutes, ten hours, or ten days before?—then why not *now?*

How long a preparation is necessary to get this state? This will depend upon three things. First, your previous spiritual condition. If you do not have it, the cause may be your secret sin, your living apart from God. Is not that the fact? You are living close up to the line of worldliness, and the law of the Church cannot follow you. And there are others who come and seek, and they obtain a blessing, and they call it entire sanctification, whereas it is only deliverance from backsliding. Secondly, by the degree of your consecration. In the language of brother Adams, you should stand outside of all you have and fence it round, and say, All is God's. Another point is the fulness of your belief that Jesus can do it just now. The devil takes you often and gives you a shake, and your Sunday clearness is all muddled. This is the reason of your unhappiness. There is a fountain where defilement can be washed away, and the soul be robed in the livery of heaven.

Approach these circles of pure white in the heavens, whither in imagination we go, and as we come down to earth, we ask, remembering what we left, "Who is fit for heaven?" This kind of reasoning, since I was a boy, has led me to say, "Though I go in rags, I will go up there." I had been crossing the ocean for thirty days, without friends, and with but little food—only God. And as I came in sight of that forest of masts in New York Bay, I heard a crash, and the anchor dropped, and the yellow flag was raised, and we were obliged to ride quarantine. So men have to hoist their yellow flag right in sight of the port of heaven, because there is disease on board. Oh! cleanse yourselves from secret sin; consecrate all that you are and all that you have to God; and with full faith in the power and willingness of Jesus to give it to you now, you need not unfurl the yellow flag, but with full sail enter the glorious port of heaven!

TESTIMONIES.

A Sister.—"All fear is gone. I never expected to see such a morning as this till the morning of the resurrection. With humility I speak it. This perfect love in my soul casteth out all fear. In a dream, a short time since, I thought I was drinking water in heaven from the fountain of life, and in it there was no sediment, but it was perfectly pure. So I drink this water now; and God has taken the sediment all out of my heart, as well as from the water he gives me to drink. That illustration of brother Parker's was blessed to me years ago, and I hope it may never be forgotten."

A Brother, from Trenton.—"I used to look sidewise

at brother Parker, several years ago, when he was stationed in our place, and preached, as he did, the doctrine of holiness. I thought then he was preaching a strange doctrine, though I was a steward in the church. But I have come to think differently about it; for afterward I saw the truth of this, and that it was the glorious privilege of believers; and by grace I entered upon its enjoyment, and found it something tangible; and now I like to talk about it; and for several years I have had a meeting in my house every week for the promotion of this work."

A MINISTER.—"What a wonderful change God has wrought in my feelings! The devil made use of brother Parker years ago, as a stumbling-block to me, because he taught this doctrine, and I was prejudiced against both it and him. God had to take me across the Atlantic to rid me of this prejudice, and then make me like a little child, so that I was ready to sit at the feet of any one, so I might learn of Jesus. Then, when I came to this, I was made to know this blessing for myself; and since that time I have rejoiced in it."

A BAPTIST MINISTER.—"I am increasingly happy. I have been made happy before, but I am happier to-day, for I have the joy of purity. The sun, by some strange influence, shining upon the waters, lifts them up above the earth, and as they ascend the sediment and impurities of earth are left behind, till at last these waters form the pure and beautiful clouds. Once the water of these clouds was contaminated with the sediment of earth, but now the sun has purged it, and it exists as the pure water of the heavens. So, though impurities cling to the soul, when the sun of righteousness shines upon it, and the mighty love of Jesus is shed abroad by the Holy Ghost, the impurities are taken away, and the pure water of life rises in the soul, a living well. Years ago I had the beginning of this perfection of love; but now God is all in all, and the sun, moon, and stars are under my feet, and I already catch ravishing views of the Ethereal Temple. I thank God for this sanctification camp-meeting. I shall remember it in eternity!"

CHAPTER IX.

SERMONS OF REV. J. A. WOOD, OF WYOMING CONFERENCE,
AND REV. J. R. DANIELS, OF NEWARK CONFERENCE.

MR. WOOD'S SERMON.

1 *Thess.* iv. 3.—"*For this is the will of God, even your sanctification.*"

Go where you will in this country, and you will find a great interest upon the subject of Christian holiness. It is the great interest in the Church and the land to-day, and God is advancing it in many ways. He has lifted His mighty arm and taken away the great curse of American Slavery, which but a little while since was the great question in the Churches; and now the idea that most occupies the mind of the Church is holiness. The great felt want of the Church everywhere is greater aggressive power, and indeed with all sincere Christians we find that those who are walking nearest to Christ do most earnestly desire this power; for it is a mistake to suppose that those who have come very near to Jesus have reached a place where they can go no further.

Wherever we present this subject, especially if we do it, as we always should, in the spirit of Christ, and with the power of the Holy Ghost, we find always an interest in it, for its want must always be felt by the sincere heart until it is realized.

In just so far as a man has within him a tendency to sin, does the devil have an ally in his heart. Bishop Janes has well said, that "when the devil comes to a man who is but partially sanctified, he finds some property, something that is his, there, and the man is disposed to sympathize with the temptation; but the heart that is fully sanctified is free from all inward inducement to sin." If a man love God *with all his heart*, necessarily he must have a pure heart; but loving God *supremely* does *not necessarily* involve full salvation. I have often heard brethren say, "I love God supremely." Most certainly you do, or you are an idolater; for a man must love God supremely, better than he loves any or all other beings or things, to be a Christian in even the lowest sense, but this is not necessarily a love which excludes all antagonistic feelings. I understand, however, that the term *holiness*, which has reference to moral purity of the heart in connection with entire devotion of the person and the life to God, does involve perfect love to God and man; so that Wesley's definition of this precious grace is the correct one. It is purity of motive, intention, and will, which conducts the whole heart to God.

REASONS FOR SEEKING.

I wish now to notice a few reasons or motives which I think should lead every one to seek this precious fulness, this entire sanctification, this gospel purity, and to seek it now.

One reason, and to me a very important one, is, that it will bring out in the believer's heart the most satisfactory evidence of his justification. Do you know, brethren, that vast numbers of those whose names are upon our Church records are not clear in the light of justifying grace? Do you know that there are multitudes who have not "the witness of the Spirit"? Alas! How many live in a state of constant doubt and anxiety as to their justification! I have marked this, and you have not failed to observe it. If the faithful pastor presses this question personally upon the members of his flock, as to the present witness of the Spirit to the fact of justification and adoption, he will find multitudes who will confess that they have it not. Now, I say that this grace will settle this question forever, so that you shall constantly know of your acceptance with God. Not that I would teach that there are degrees of justification, but at the same time the clearer light of personal purity will bring evidences to the believer's heart that will necessarily drive away his doubts. I have known many who were never fully clear in the light of justifying grace, till they had experienced the fulness there is in Jesus.

I would carefully guard against underrating the great work of regeneration, for I believe that if the standard of justification were held more prominently and clearly before the people, we should find less difficulty in bringing the Church up to the idea and experience of entire sanctification. Those who have, as Wesley suggests, been in the lazy beaten track, those are they who most disparage sanctification; but show me a man who is anxious to do all his duty and to fulfil all the good pleasure of God, and I will show you a man who is in sympathy with salvation to its fullest extent.

And how blessed is this experience, to be able to grasp

all this, to be where he knows constantly that he is a child of God; to have a clear assurance that God is indeed his Father; and to be able to cry out with perfect confidence " My Lord and my God!"—I am inclined to the opinion that I should preach this subject less, and have need to preach it less, if the Church of God were more generally in the clear light of justification. I believe that many have justification restored in seeking for purity, for the reason that they have before refused to seek for purity. God requires the Christian to have a pure heart; and if he measures his steps wilfully back into the wilderness, he must suffer loss, and he may have God's favor restored when he is seeking purity. But if a man is in doubt whether he is backslidden or not, let him first seek the evidence of God's favor, and then not rest till he is fully sanctified.

ANTIDOTE FOR BACKSLIDING.

Another reason for seeking this, and which is nearly related to what has gone before, is that it is the surest protection against backsliding. Though the possibility still remains, yet sacred and ecclesiastical history conspire with experience to declare that few who enter this grace, really and fully, ever apostatize. Peter was weak as a child, and cowed before his enemies till he received this baptism, but after that he lived a hero and died a martyr. And so was it with the "one hundred and twenty," and so has it been with thousands; this glorious grace has nerved them to withstand manfully the assaults of all foes, and having done all, to stand.

RELIANCE.

I remark again, that this grace will enable you to rely

upon the atonement of Christ with a steadiness and a completeness of confidence that nothing can disturb. How often have you occasion to lament the weakness of your faith in and love toward the Lord Jesus Christ? Let me say to you that at the point where your soul enters into this precious rest, you will find a confidence and trust that nothing can disturb. You will be enabled to rest upon the atonement of Jesus with such a consciousness of its preciousness and power as no influence can disturb or remove from your breast. Hence, the erroneous notion of some that Christian purity excludes the necessity of constant reliance on the atonement. It is the direct reverse of this. No man sees his need of the atonement more clearly than the man whose heart is thoroughly washed in the blood of Jesus Christ. No man feels the merit of Christ's atoning blood so constantly as that man whose heart is washed in the blood of Christ. Fletcher said, " To suppose that Christian purity excludes the need of the atonement is not less absurd than to suppose that the perfection of navigation excludes the need of the ocean as a great reservoir of water." Let your hearts be cleansed in the blood of Jesus and you will know the sweetness of living a life of faith on the Son of God. There is a vast difference between the faith that a man exercises while under the influence of sin and that which he exercises after grace has pressed out every unholy element from his heart.

And then Christian purity reveals Christ more fully to the heart. How often the believer looks away sorrowing and saddened with the thought that he experiences so little of the preciousness of Jesus! You read that He is the chief among ten thousand and the altogether lovely; that in Him dwelleth all the fulness of the Godhead bodily; that He is the brightness of the Father's glory and the express image of His person; that He is the rose of Sharon and the lily of the valley; and you chide yourself that you cannot feel it with the intensity you desire. My brothers, there is a standing point from which you can see the King in His beauty, and whence He burns into your very soul the conviction of His excellency. This perfect purity of heart brings Christ so near that you are constantly conscious of His presence and smile in your heart.

During the first ten years of my ministry I used to sit and weep in sorrow over the depressing consciousness of a Saviour at a distance; I felt, as every true minister must feel, the need of a present Christ; and nine years ago, before some fifty ministers of the Wyoming Conference, the blessed Jesus let his grace come in a stream from heaven upon me, that so filled my soul that for three hours I was conscious of nothing but that Jesus had me and that the heaven of heavens was streaming through my full soul. Since that day I have realized a new experience of the presence of Christ, and everything in the light of my justification has been wonderfully intensified, and I have experienced and do constantly experience the meaning of perfect love in a pure heart.

GROWTH IN GRACE.

Another reason why you should seek this precious grace is that it will wondrously minister to your growth in grace. You wish to be a faithful Christian, to climb the hill of Zion, to reach the highest summit of Christian experience. Get Christian purity, and you will realize the most steady and rapid growth in grace possible this side of glory.

But, you ask, "When a man's heart is cleansed is not this the climax?" There never was a more pernicious error than that which teaches that there must be ten, twenty, or thirty years intervening between partial and entire sanctification, and that when this is reached there is an end of growth. What God wants is to have your heart cleansed *now*, and then to have you realize a rapid growth in grace through the entire period of your probation. Holiness is moral and spiritual health, and just fits a man to grow most rapidly. Come to Christ at once and obtain this purity of heart, and your growth in grace and knowledge will be unsurpassed, nay, unequalled in all your previous experience.

But, says one, "I do not know about this leaping into the experience of ten years in a single hour or moment." No more do I. Do not, I beseech you, confound Christian purity with Christian maturity, for they are distinct, though related. We do not teach that a man may become a mature Christian in a moment; but we do teach that he may become a pure Christian at once, in an instant. And that will give him a chance to become mature; for the great reason why we have so few mature Christians, is, I apprehend, that there are no more pure Christians in the Church. Come, then, now, to Jesus, and experience what is the privilege of every believer, —have your heart cleansed from all sin.

MR. DANIELS' SERMON.

2 *Cor.* xiii. 11.—" *Be perfect.*"

W HEN the apostle wrote this letter to the Church at Corinth its holiness had been interrupted by false teachers, and great corruption and confusion had follow-ed as a consequence.   After urging them most faithfully to the work of correcting the errors of the Church, he gives utterance to the words, "And this also we wish, even your perfection," and exhorts them in the language of the text, "Be perfect."   In presenting this doctrine of Christian perfection in a sermon, I have always felt a large degree of solicitude; not that I have any doubts in regard to it as a doctrine fitted for the people, and as a matter of individual experience with believers, but in view of its vast practical importance, in connection with the fact that there are so many different views upon the subject.   But I thank God that during the time that has elapsed since this ground, and these trees, and this stand, and this bower of prayer, and these tents have been con-secrated to God, there has seemed to be but one senti-ment here, and all admit the glorious privilege which the believer in Christ possesses of being made perfect in love.   Looking to God for illumination such as He only can impart, coming here with the earnest prayer that His word may be brought home with power to every heart this morning, we feel confident assurance in direct-ing your minds yet further to this great privilege of the believer.   We call this blessing Christian perfection, and distinguish it, as did the fathers, from the absolute perfection of God, the perfection of angels, and Adamic perfection, for neither of which do we contend.

And that for which we do contend refers not at all directly to the development of our mental capacities, and hardly at all to the excellence of our external actions; but rather to a sense or consciousness that the graces of the Holy Ghost are produced upon our hearts and perfected within us. The various expressions which we feel at liberty to use as synonymous terms in speaking of this subject—such as entire sanctification, perfect love, perfection, holiness—all refer to the same state of grace.

Now that we have these preliminary explanations fixed in our mind, let us proceed at once to meditate upon the experience of this grace, and to consider some of the blessings attending it.

REPENTANCE.

First in the experience of the perfection at which we aim, there is a consciousness on our part of perfect repentance. The repentance exhibited in the day of our conversion is such as implies a sorrow for the sins we have committed. It leads us to confess our sins to God; we have forsaken them with the determination to indulge in them no more ; and there is in this godly sorrow a perfect hatred for the sins that we have previously committed. This prepares us for the exercise of that faith which is the only condition laid down in the Gospel for our salvation. He that is perfect in his repentance continues thus to regard sin to the end of his life. What, says one, shall we be repenting after being justified freely by the grace of God, adopted into His family, and made of the number of His children ? Yes. Shall we be repent-

ing in sorrow for the sins of our past lives after that God
has perfected our sanctification and applied His love to
our hearts by the agency of the Holy Ghost? Yes. If
we have once committed sin—even though now forgiven,
if our repentance is perfect we shall always sorrow that
we ever offended God. There was a time in my own
experience when I was not justified—when I was led to
see the necessity of turning again to God and repenting
anew; and there was a time when, somehow or other, I
seemed to have pleasure in referring to the sins of which
I had been guilty; and I have sometimes thought that
I could detect this feeling in others. This idea of perfect
repentance is well illustrated in the story of the little
boy whose father trained him up strictly in the line of
duty. The father told him that when at any time he
had committed any evil deed he must drive a nail into
a certain tree; and then when he had done any action
that he believed to be good, he was to draw out a nail.
The boy did as he was commanded, and soon the tree
seemed to be filled with nails. Presently, however, as
the boy's good disposition came to triumph more completely over his evil propensities, one nail, and then another and another, was extracted; and the boy, conscious of doing good, would return day after day to remove a nail, or nails, as the case might warrant. After
a while all the nails were gone, and he made a statement
of the fact to his father. The father smiled on him with
approval; but the little fellow, when his father was com-
mending his well-doing, burst into tears. The father
was surprised, and asked the reason of this strange emotion. "Father," said the repentant boy, "I am glad to
have you smile, but the marks of the nails are in the tree

yet, and I remember that I have offended you and incurred your displeasure." It is so with the believer. Though the heart seems to be beating in perfect sympathy with the heart of the great Master, and seems to be responsive to every Christian duty and every noble feeling, yet he remembers his sins, and grieves over the fact that he has ever offended his heavenly Father.

PERFECT FAITH.

Perfect faith is included in this perfection. This involves the casting away of self-confidence, and a full appropriation of the blood of Jesus. How slow we seem to be in learning this; and how slowly some have seemed to learn it who have been experiencing the blessing of God at this encampment! A number with whom we have talked on this subject, who have been seeking earnestly for the blessing of purity, have told us, "I have consecrated all that I am and all that I have to God; I believe it to be my privilege to have this blessing; I believe that God will sanctify me, that I shall enter Christ's perfect purity, and the perfection of love; I believe that God will give me, in the name of Jesus, all that I ask of Him, and I am determined to wrestle on, to strive on, until God grants my request." Just as though the mighty saving depended upon their wrestling and struggling with God, and that God would reward that, instead of taking hold, as is our privilege, of the promises of God, and by naked faith claiming, without this earnest physical struggle and mental effort, our promised inheritance, and saying in full confidence, He *does* save me. Such a faith as this would be a power in the hands of God's ministers. What a power would it be to the minister coming from the closet to the pulpit, after having cast away all confidence in self, and being filled with the Holy Ghost; how sweetly and how powerfully would God apply the word to the hearts of the hearers! May it be so in a wonderful degree this morning.

And then, with this experience how would the Church advance the interests of the Master's Kingdom; how would God use the Church as a whole, as he now does the individual members who have obtained this glorious light!

PERFECT HUMILITY.

Again, there must be perfect humility as a result of this state of perfect purity.

Some appear to think that the doctrine of Christian perfection is opposed to humility. The contrary is just the fact. If Christian purity is opposed to perfect humility, or humility in any degree, why, I ask, are not the earlier stages of grace in a proportionate degree, opposed to the same? When a sinner is first brought to a sense of God's favor, he is humbled before God; and while walking in the light of justifying grace, and conscious of a continual advancement in the divine life, the believer sinks deeper and deeper in humility before God. Then if God proposes to carry on the work of his saving power while in a state of justification, shall he not in much larger degree when He perfects His work of cleansing in the heart, cause the mind of the believer to sink to profounder depths of humility? I have no sympathy with any other perfection than that which keeps one low down before God.

PERFECT SELF-DENIAL AND HOPE.

Then perfect self-denial is included in this experience. The soul chooses that which will tend to the glory of God, rather than to its own gratification. It has been said of the wife of Howard, the celebrated English philanthropist, that on a certain occasion when her husband—who had come into the possession of unexpected means—contemplated a trip to London, she would not undertake the journey without careful inquiry whether the money could be expended in a way that would contribute more to the glory of God and the good of His creatures. The matter received a careful consideration, and though the trip would have been very pleasant, both to her and her husband, it was finally postponed, in order that the expenditure of money which it would entail might be devoted to the support and comfort of a poor neighbor. Do we not too often refer in such matters rather to our own pleasure and convenience than to the glory of God? This state of perfect love is a state of perfect self-denial, leading the Christian to consider the glory of God and the good of others, to the exclusion of merely personal pleasures.

Again, the believer is made perfect in hope, and, coupled with all the blessings of salvation, he has a confident expectation of heavenly glory. Perfect hope is entirely the result of the perfection of the other graces of the spirit of God in the heart. They are the most sure of heavenly bliss who are the most trustful, the most believing, the most humble, and who exercise the greatest amount of self-denial. What a sublime expression of this feeling is seen in the words of the

apostle, which it is the glorious privilege of every believer
to adopt: "And all things work together for good to
them that love God, to them who are the called according to His purpose." It is this precious perfect hope
that enables him to say in times of trial and suffering and
doubt, "These light afflictions, which are but for a moment, work out for me a far more exceeding and eternal
weight of glory."

PERFECT LOVE.

There is also included in this perfect state a perfect
love to all mankind. The objects for which the Saviour died become the object of our affections. This
will be exhibited not only in the attentions that we
show to friends, but it will include also the utmost kind-
nesses towards an enemy, and enable us, in strict conformity with the requirements of God's word, to render
good for evil, to bless them that curse us, to pray for
them that despitefully use us and persecute us.

And then, how this will qualify us for advancing the
interests of Christ's kingdom, each in his particular
sphere of labor! Satan never seems to succeed, never
does succeed better than when he infuses into the heart
of the Christian a spirit of retaliation against real or
fancied wrongs. Blessed be God! this grace of love can
be perfected in us, is perfected in us, and becomes the
sweetest pleasure of the believer's life.

But this perfection is not shown merely in our personal intercourse with men; so great, so enlarged, so
comprehensive is it in the heart of the believer, that
there is a complete consecration of time, of talent, of

money, of everything at the demand of God for the good of the world and the saving of humanity. Such is an indication of what is included in this perfect love, and love is the foundation of every other grace.

We must love God with all the heart, with all the soul, and with all the strength, and with all the mind. This must be the guiding motive in every word spoken, in every thought entertained, and in every deed accomplished. With this there comes a sense of the absence of all disposition towards man-fearing or man-pleasing, unless it be the disposition to please all men to their edification; to become all things to all men if by any means we might save some; and the mind is positively impelled by love to the fearless performance of every duty that God may lay upon us.

Oh that we might realize by faith this blessing now, and feel all the impelling conquering power of love!

> " Sink down, ye separating hills,
>   Let sin and death remove;
> 'Tis love that drives my chariot wheels,
>   And death must yield to love."

EXPERIENCE.

A few words now of my own experience, and I close.

A few years ago it pleased God, by the instrumentality of a Baptist sister, in the house where I was then boarding, to lead me to a prayer-meeting in Camden. For three years previously I had not been within a church, but had spent many hours in gambling and drinking saloons. Ten days afterward I attended another prayer-meeting, and here in the second religious meeting which I had attended for three years I went to the altar as a penitent seeker, and God mercifully spoke peace to my soul. Never since that time have I had any doubts of my salvation, nor have I once since that day wilfully offended against the law of God, nor have I had any desire to do so. That God soundly converted me I have no doubt, and with my conversion he implanted in me an earnest desire for the salvation of my fellow-men which soon led me into the work of the ministry. During the first year of my ministry I remember with what pleasure I was permitted to preach the Gospel to the very associates with whom my days of sin were spent,—the firemen of Camden,—and with what power the fruits of the Spirit were produced under that preaching. At Perth-Amboy I first began to feel the need of this perfect love, this entire sanctification. Before going there I had learned in conversation with a brother that there were many "Palmerites" in the vicinity, and I was cautioned to be careful not to offend against their peculiar doctrines upon this subject. I went there, and during all the time of my residence there these "Palmerites" did not cease to pray for the entire sanctification of their pastor. They gave me no rest. I prayed for sinners, and preached to sinners, but the "Palmerites" persisted in praying for me. I was not disposed to believe in this doctrine of entire sanctification, and only came to receive it under the preaching of a Congregational minister, the Rev. Henry Belden, sometime afterward. But when I took the Word of God for its possibility, and applied the promises by faith to my own soul, then God revealed himself to my heart with a fulness of glory of which I had before no conception. I stand in the light of that blessing to-day, and expect ever thus to stand; and oh that all you may taste its joys, and taste them now!

5*

CHAPTER X.

TESTIMONIES.

THE spirit of testimony was so graciously bestowed at Vineland that God's children realized, in an extraordinary degree, that they "overcame by the blood of the Lamb, and the word of their testimony." To many the work of God was confirmed as they witnessed to what had been wrought in their hearts. We furnish our readers with some of these experiences, given from overflowing hearts.

A MINISTER who had charge of this special service said:—"This is an adjourned meeting for testimony, so you must resume on the theme of the first part, which was PERFECT LOVE."

WE MAY BE ENTIRELY SANCTIFIED SOON AFTER CONVERSION.

A BROTHER.—"I was converted to God in the city of London, when the whole family, parents and thirteen children, were out of Christ. But God in infinite compassion sanctified my soul in three days after I was converted; and then the first requirement God made upon me was to testify of this before my father. I promised I would, and I went to his house, and fulfilled my covenant promise to God. My father said, 'You are crazy; you used to be a good and pleasant boy, but you have got so much religion that it is changing you, and you must either leave the Methodist Church or leave my house.' I said, 'By the grace of God I will never leave the Methodist Church.' 'Then leave my house,' said he; and I did. God made use of that circumstance, and it proved the beginning of conversions in the family; and now father and five of the children are in heaven, and I am joyfully following on to meet them there."

A BOND OF UNION.

A BROTHER.—" When I came here I doubted the propriety of this meeting, as it was a little out of the order and working of our camp-meetings generally, and I said this to my minister; but this feeling has all been swept from me, and I now feel that in the specialty of this meeting we have the great bond of union of the Methodist Church." [A Voice—" Yes, and of every other church !"]

Many witnesses could not be heard, on account of the large concourse of people and the distance of some of the speakers from the stand; yet there was great and even profound interest all over the meeting.

CAN THIS BLESSING BE RETAINED?

A BROTHER.—" Though seventy-four years of age, I enjoy the liberty in Christ which I had when twenty-one years old, and much more; for during twenty-four years I have experienced perfect love."

A BROTHER.—" Fifty years ago I received a token from the Scotch Presbyterian church, by which I could be received to the communion. For forty years I have been preaching the Gospel, and now I have the same blessing which I had then. Timid friends advised me not to preach, lest I should not live worthy of so high a calling; but I committed myself unto God, as the keeper of the soul, both able and willing to take care of us, and He has kept me from sin, unto salvation, and I expect He will continually keep me."

A BROTHER.—"I am eighty-one years old, and I bless God for full salvation."

CONSTANT CLEANSING.

A BROTHER.—"I was in the parlor of a brother's house when I entered into perfect love, some years ago, and ever since I have been questioning whether I am a Methodist or a Baptist, but I believe on the whole I am a Baptist. I believe in immersion, and I have it every day, for every day I plunge anew into the fountain." [Great sensation, followed by several persons speaking at once, in different parts of the congregation.]

A SISTER.—" I am 'filled with the Spirit' of glory and of God, and am going up." [Many of the people and the ministers were weeping and shouting, and some of the ministers said, they never saw anything like such great demonstrations in their lives.]

SAVED FROM SELF.

A SISTER.—" Between four and five years ago God, for Christ's sake, sanctified my soul, and I believe that I died to sin, but not entirely to self; for I think it requires more grace to die to self than to die to sin. I have been in the habit of working in meetings, but I could not here, and God showed me that it was self that was in the way, and the Lord Jesus took me down in the valley of humiliation, and there graciously removed these fond considerations of self, and helped me, as never before, to say, 'Thy will be done;' and now I say, I will speak in this meeting, or keep silence, as Thou wouldest have me. In this path I find the crucifixion, so I can say, 'I am crucified with Christ.' It has resulted in much clearer light, and I have passed into a much broader and deeper experience. It is a losing of self in Christ. 'It is no longer I that live, but Christ liveth in me.'"

DUTY AND BENEFIT OF PROFESSING THIS BLESSING.

A SISTER.—"Glory be to God for this grace which I have enjoyed for many years, and which, for all this time I have been in the habit of professing in the Methodist Church! Then the Spirit desired me to speak of it in other churches, and I have done so, and have been most gloriously baptized there; and if God will dwell in such a heart as mine, he will surely dwell in any heart."

REV. BRO. L.—"I was brought up a Presbyterian, but heard Methodist preaching frequently in my youth. Eight or nine years ago I entered upon the blessing of holiness. I have had some dark seasons, and some lapses, when I could not say the blood of Jesus Christ cleanseth from all sin, but for the most of the time the light has been very clear and my experience satisfactory. I have been trying to preach on the subject both since and before I received the blessing, and one of the strongest sermons I have on the subject was prepared before I entered upon this experience, and I have found occasion for but little alteration in it. I have held special meetings for the promotion of this blessing in my different charges, with varying success, but have afterward heard of good results not witnessed at the time. I have found it very advantageous to me, and to the churches where I have been stationed, but I desire more of its fulness, that I may preach it more definitely and powerfully."

FILLED.

A SISTER.—"I could not get an opportunity to speak yesterday, but feel I must now witness for Christ. I had clearly realized the necessity of my being sprinkled with clean water, and I prayed earnestly and consecrated myself fully, and He did cleanse me from all my sins, and now I am filled with love, and could bathe His feet with my tears."

A SISTER.—"Previous to this meeting I had never been satisfied with my experience, and I came here hungering and thirsting after righteousness; and, blessed be God! I have been filled, and now realize, as never before, that I am cleansed from all unrighteousness. Now I desire to have my life witness to this blessing."

A BROTHER.—"God has saved me in a glorious degree, for which I would like to praise Him with more powers than I now possess. I came here hungering for a deeper knowledge of Jesus, and am conscious of some remains of self. Oh, pray for me."

> "Oh, to grace how great a debtor
> Daily I'm constrained to be!
> Let thy goodness, like a fetter,
> Bind my wandering heart to thee,"

was sung very earnestly.

A BROTHER.—"I am now the Lord's, unreservedly, and so sweetly rest in him."

A BROTHER.—"I can say of the stream of this salvation,

> "'It runs divinely clear,
> A fountain deep and full.'"

A Brother.—"I came here to catch some of this hallowed fire, and I have not come in vain; and now I mean to carry it back to the Black River country, and spread it along the banks of the St. Lawrence."

A Sister.—"Bless the Lord for the grace of God I now feel! I can keep my seat no longer. When God baptized me with this grace I felt I had something to do. This, indeed, is a revival of primitive Christianity."

HOW A MINISTER FOUND THE BLESSING.

A Minister.—"I found this blessing of a clean heart nineteen years ago next month. When I was received into Conference I was sent to follow a very popular man, and it pleased God to put me in great straits. I was greatly afflicted with the fear of man, and sometimes, before the congregation, I would lose my place and way. Once, I remember, that having my eyes closed in prayer, I imagined myself turned around, and that embarrassed me much when I opened my eyes and arose from my knees. I was considerably confused in my experience, and while in this state I took up and began to read Wesley's Plain Account of Christian Perfection. When I had read it about half-way through the Spirit of God said to me, as though it was the voice of a man, 'This is what you want.' I put the book away and kneeled down and said, 'O Lord, if this is what I need I will never rest until I find it, and by the help of grace I will never sleep again till I have it.' I thought I had a great work on hand, and so I brought in wood and water enough to last several days, and other things in proportion, and then said to my wife, 'I am going down to the barn, and will never come back till I get this blessing.' As I was going I felt that if I owned the whole world I would give it if I had not said this to my wife, for we can sometimes lie to God easier than to man. Reaching the barn, I got into my carriage and kneeled down, and it was a sober time with me indeed. There I stayed and wrestled with God, and some time toward morning the Lord came into my soul. Hallelujah! He satisfied me that the blessing was mine, and it has been a cardinal idea ever since, that if any man will plant himself here, and say, 'Lord, I will stay right here till I get this grace,' God will give it speedily. I arose and went to the house, and I found that my wife had been up, too, praying for me, and I said to her, 'I have received it;' and then it seemed to me as though the bottom of heaven's reservoir had come out, and floods of glory deluged my soul. The Lord told me to go nine miles and tell a dear friend about it, and I went, and God convicted him for it, and he sought and found it, and not many months after died and went to glory. I stand fast in this grace to-day, and mean ever thus to stand."

BENEFITS OF THE BLESSING.

A BROTHER.—" I have been reading on the doctrine of Christian perfection, and I am firm believer. Attending a church where the invitation was given for those who sought for this blessing, to go forward, I embraced the opportunity, and I never had such comfort and religious enjoyment as since then. Pastoral visits are now a pleasure, whereas they were before an irksome duty; at the family altar, too, I have most delightful seasons, and souls even there have asked for prayers. I do not find sanctification altogether what I thought it would be, as I supposed it would be fair-sailing all the time, and that temptations, if they came at all, would have no effect upon my mind. When I realized my mistake I was somewhat disappointed, and asked if I could have been mistaken. Upon reflection I thought I had not, and so I would give glory to God. When a temptation came I thought it was from without, and I would go immediately to God, and say, 'Lord, haven't I given myself to Thee? Yea, I have: and now save me, and let me do Thy whole will,' and such a joy and peace would come as I cannot express. I do not hold up the standard as I should, and I ask your prayers."

A MINISTER.—"I feel that this experience has benefited me in every respect. I used to feel great trouble about my preparation for the pulpit, but this is all gone. It is very pleasant now to prepare for the pulpit, and when I have made the best preparation possible, and then go to the pulpit, I feel that I am in the hands of the Lord to be used in any way as he may direct. I have thrown the responsibility in this respect upon the Lord, and he has taken it, so that doing what I can I can leave the issue with God. Whatever God would have me say in the pulpit, I am ready to say, and if the Good Spirit suggests something in the pulpit of which I had not before thought, I am ready to say that, and if the Lord should be pleased to let me break down, I am satisfied with that. I find myself now always ready for the work of God. I am not compelled to go to the prayer-meeting or class-meeting to find Jesus, for though I highly prize these and all the means of grace, I now meet Jesus upon every corner, and all along the lines of duty,—in the services of the sanctuary, visiting the sick, at the family altar, in my closet and study, and everywhere.   I have enjoyed and am enjoying this camp-meeting very much, and feel that my soul is full. Everything here and all about here seems to be love. God's smiles are my light and my joy, and I can sing,—

> " 'Not a cloud doth arise to darken my skies,
>   Or hide for a moment my Lord from my eyes.' "

CHAPTER XI.

1 *Thess.* iv. 3.—" *This is the will of God, even your sanctification.*"

THE doctrine which specially interests us here has, by some, been entitled the pearl of doctrines, the great central idea of our holy Christianity, the fount of present personal experience. It is doubtless for this reason that it has been the object of fierce assault, both in the Church and in the world, more or less, ever since Wesley's days.

This great doctrine has been strangely perverted by some, and by others greatly abused. The doctrine of justification by faith has scarcely been less opposed in the Romish Church than has this doctrine in the Protestant Church. Some of this opposition may have been occasioned by an incorrect and unjust apprehension of this great doctrine itself, but the great cause of it is, I apprehend, the natural hostility of the human heart to it until the soul is drawn toward it by the Holy Spirit.

I do not propose at this time, nor intend at any time, to preach this doctrine dogmatically. I wish to place myself, with these friends who even now are giving me their attention, in an attitude of waiting for divine enlightenment. I do not wish to, nor will I, place myself in a controversial attitude, nor allow myself to be placed there, for this controversial spirit has been a great hindrance in the past.

I ask you, however, to listen for a while, and to give me a special interest in your prayers, while we consider some things which relate to the character and possibility of the experience of the believer in these things. And remember, my friends out there in the congregation, that you are as much interested in this as I am, or as the apostle himself was. If it implies duty, that duty is just as binding upon you as upon me; and if it involves privilege, that privilege is just as desirable for you as for any other.

Before we proceed to formularies of doctrine, you will allow me to premise with one or two thoughts. To unfold this doctrine of entire sanctification to one who has no experience of the grace, is exceedingly difficult, if not, indeed, impossible. The Bible does not attempt it, but after setting forth the privilege itself, teaches that this and all kindred truth must be spiritually discerned. "If any man will do His will he shall know of the doctrine." We come at this and all similar doctrines more through the experiences of the heart than the reasonings of the intellect. Do you doubt this? Then attempt to answer an objector to the doctrine of regeneration, and you shall find that he will comprehend your reasoning in much the same proportion as his heart experiences that of which you speak. We are vastly more concerned, now and always, with the experience itself than with the particular terms by which to express that experience. Entire sanctification, holiness, purity, Christian perfection, full redemption, full assurance of faith,—all these terms are employed to designate this grace, nor may we except to any of them, since all are divinely given; and we venture to infer from this great variety of terms in the sacred record that we in turn may exercise some license in our choice of words. One may like one term better than another, while the experience may be, and must be, according to the gospel standard, materially the same. We must each follow the leadings of the blessed Holy Ghost in giving expression to our experience as in all other things.

STATE THE DOCTRINE.

Let us now proceed to state the doctrine as we understand it.

If we should define entire sanctification as an entire consecration of one's self to God, with the present acceptance of Jesus as our perfect Saviour, some of you might think this to be rather its condition than the thing itself; and yet the condition is so related to the experience, that it is with difficulty that we distinguish between the two.

CONSECRATION.

Let our first inquiry, then, be with regard to entire consecration. This, of course, must include self, time, property, and, in short, all possible things of us, or connected with us. But, just at this point, some one may inquire, " What is the difference between the consecration necessary at conversion, and that which we are called upon to make in seeking this richer grace?"

In our view, the difference will appear in four particulars :

In the first place, when we come to God for pardon, we are dead,—"dead in trespasses and sins;" but when we approach God for this richer grace, we have powers that have already been regenerated, and hence are living. Hence said the apostle, "I beseech you, brethren, by the mercies of God, that ye present your bodies a *living* sacrifice."

The second difference is this: When we come to God for pardon, we seem to generalize and mass our offer of ourself, saying very sincerely and reverently,—

> "Here, Lord, I give myself away,—
> 'Tis all that I can do."

But when we would entirely sanctify ourselves to God, our consecration under the new and greater light becomes more careful, and intelligent, and specific, and if it is entire, it is not only myself, but these hands, these feet, these senses, my judgment, my will, my memory, affections, desires, imagination, principles, practices, hours, energies, influence, reputation, the world, friends, worldly substance, home, *my all*. At last we seem to say,—

> "More shouldst Thou have if I had more."

I give thee all I know, and all I do not know. Some have been careful to write out their consecration. This was the case with President Edwards.

The third difference is, that when we thus come, yielding ourselves up intelligently and specifically, there is likely to arise in the mind some peculiarly trying test. It may be a very little thing, but it is none the less formidable or trying. Taking an apple in Paradise would

seem to have been a very little thing; but what stupen-
dous results followed. The test to you, my brother,
may be some little thing connected with your habits,
associations, or adornments, but it is important. I
know not what it may be with others, but it will be ex-
plicit. It may involve some doubtful employment or
indulgence, which was not discovered before, or it would
have prevented your justification. It may be your hesitation or delay, and because of this your experience has
been feeble and sickly. Before you can have this testimony there must be the most thorough submission, and
this covers all things.

The fourth difference is, that the *object* of the two
dedications is different. When you came to God at first
you were filled with grief and condemnation, and you
came to sue for pardon. Pressed down to the gates of
perdition, you exclaimed, " Oh, wretched man that I am!
who shall deliver me from the body of this death ?"
You wanted then to be raised to the condition of childhood. But in seeking purity you are already a child, and
you want now an increased ability to do and suffer all
the will of your heavenly Father.

So much for the first part of the formulary of entire
consecration. It will be entire if we make it to cover
that test which God brings before the mind.

ACCEPTANCE OF JESUS.

But we represent entire sanctification, also, as the acceptance this moment of Jesus as a full and perfect Saviour. This, of course, suggests an exercise of faith,
" not of works, lest any man should boast." If sanctification were consecration, then, it being our work, we could

boast; but it being through the blood of Jesus Christ our Saviour, it is not our work, but God's. Consecration brings us upon believing ground. When we take away all the obstructions, when we yield ourselves without reservation or hesitation in the entirety of our being, and have the witness of the Spirit to that consecration, then we come where God can and will fulfil our desire. Mark this point. When we hunger and thirst after righteousness, feeling that we cannot live without it, and dedicate ourselves to do, or dare, or die for Christ, and at that point rest our faith on the Lord Jesus Christ, then the gift comes. We must rest our faith upon Jesus. There is none other upon whom to rest it. I know not how long you may rest there before the blessing consciously comes; it may be a moment or more, but the blessed Holy Ghost will come to you so that you shall see, and feel, and know, and enjoy its verity and preciousness as never before, and you will be constrained to say,—

> " 'Tis done ! Thou dost this moment save,
> With full salvation bless."

Observe, that this cleansing is not for the future, not for a day or an hour, but for the present moment, and always for the present moment. One moment is given and the blood cleanseth; another, and the blood cleanseth; and thus are we constantly dependent upon this blood, and are constantly cleansed. As we live by breathing, so the Christian lives by believing. Our breath is the bond that unites soul and body, and faith is the bond that unites our soul to Christ.

EXPERIENCE.

What, now, is the experience consequent upon this blessing?

I answer, It is twofold.

In the first place, it is purity. The Psalmist says, "Wash me, and I shall be whiter than snow." Oh, let us think of this for a moment. *Whiter* than snow, not white *as* snow. Oh, what purity this involves! Jesus speaks to the heart in answer to its prayer, and says, "I will: be thou clean."

The second consequence of this grace is a more regular and continuous growth in grace and in the knowledge of our Lord Jesus Christ. Before this we were now rejoicing, and now lamenting; now upon the mountain, and anon in the deep valley; and after weeks and months, sitting down to review our experience, we have been unable to say definitely that we have made any considerable progress. But when we receive Jesus as our perfect Saviour, then we grow steadily and constantly. We may not always have sunshine and flowers upon our way, but this grace will enable us to go on in the darkness as well as in the light, over thorns as well as through flowers. Remembering that the nights and the thorns are intended to help us along, we say Amen to them. We have found the rock, and we stand upon it.

You may ask us whether we teach or believe that the sanctified never sin. I answer, that the sanctified do not wilfully sin, but they may through the wiles of the adversary be led through mistake into that which is sin; but if this is the case, when that soul sees it, you will find it at once hying away to the fountain to be cleansed.

It may be asked again, Do not these views degrade the blessing of justification? I answer, No. When Jesus does the work of justification He does it perfectly; and this is a great work, one we can hardly exalt too high. When sin is forgiven, all sin is forgiven; but at the same time this is not entire sanctification, and no intelligent theologian claims this. If you insist that God could do a perfect work at first, and therefore should do it, we answer, that would do very well as an *à priori* argument, but not as an *à posteriori* argument. And besides this, the work is a perfect one in itself, but this other work is something which lies beyond it.

Look in nature. Is there not first the blade, then the ear, and then the full corn? But the blade is as perfect in itself as is the full corn in itself. " Oh, yes," you say, " that is just what we believe, that we are to grow to this." But it is an egregious error to suppose that because you are sanctified your growth is ended. Indeed, growth is only steadily realized in the sanctified experience. I believe there is growth in the justified state, but it is spasmodic; but in the entirely sanctified state it is steady, and I can conceive of no time here or hereafter when we shall cease to grow if we abide in Christ.

Another will ask if we believe that the justified are ever lost. We answer with emphasis, almost with indignation, No! But who are the justified? They are those who, having been forgiven, obey the commands of God. And how many commands there are about entire sanctification! and these must be obeyed. No, my brother; you cannot treat this grace lightly without losing your justification. Our Father will bear with you, for He is long-suffering; but if you continue to wonder and doubt too long, it may be to your everlasting overthrow.

NEED OF THE CHURCH.

Is not this experience of entire sanctification the great need of the Church, and is it not the great want in individual experience?

I like to look at this practically. I pass through a congregation, go to their class-meetings, and hear their experiences, and I conclude they are children of God and desirous of doing His will. God blesses them in their religious services, but they say, " Our experience is not what it should be." There is a conscious lack. They want closer communion with God, and ability to go forward in work for God, and they want the testimony within. They want heart purity before God. They want rest in God, for there is a difference between peace and rest. Some say they have peace, but not rest. Their experience is not full and satisfying. What is it now they want but what we call, in Methodist parlance, entire sanctification? And this is to be had by the Holy Ghost. Oh, that He may shine, this hour, upon many minds!

The text declares this is the will of God, and we all agree that nothing is comparable to the will of God. We think of this as the efflux of the Divine Glory. It was that will that brought you to Christ in the first instance, and will you not allow it now to lead you to this bright fulness? Oh, why do you not avail yourself of your privileges, and thus come to Jesus? You wonder that sinners do not come to Christ; but is it not a greater wonder that you who have tasted the good word of life, when the Spirit invites you to those richer joys should hesitate just as your unconverted neighbor hesitates? Perhaps you say you do not understand it. Just so says your unconverted neighbor. He does not know, and you do not seem to remember, that it is spiritually discerned.

But "some who profess this grace bring dishonor upon it." Yes; but this is just what your unconverted friend says of professors of religion. So you see, when we press you close you answer just as the unconverted do. My brother, I hold you fast to this truth, "This is the will of God, even your sanctification." I lay it on your conscience, be you minister or layman, be you male or female, be you near or afar off; I say to you, with authority given of the Holy Ghost, "This is the will of God." If you go away without this, I believe you will travel into darkness. Pass this around, and let every one say, "This is the will of God, even *my* sanctification."

POWER OF THE CHURCH.

And this will be the power of the Church. During the centenary year we heard much about the numbers of the Church. But it is not numbers, nor fine churches, nor ecclesiastical polity, nor theological schools, nor ritual that constitutes power. These are all well in their place; but purity, after all, is true power. This has ever been so, and ever must be. / In 1760, as Wesley recorded in his journal, a very extraordinary revival commenced in Yorkshire, then extended to London, and

finally crossed to Ireland, and was the beginning of the
societies at Dublin and Limerick.   This progressed till
the societies of Ireland seemed wrapped in revival influence.   Wesley explicitly says, that wherever the work
of holiness spread, the work of God generally revived.
Dr. Stevens, in his admirable History of Methodism, insists
that this doctrine of Christian perfection was the great
potential idea of Wesleyanism; and what was true then
is true now.   This power which comes through purity
and by self-consecration is a mighty one ; for, giving up
ourselves, we receive the Divine fulness, and we are
strong because filled with the Almighty Spirit; the
body and the soul are filled with almightiness.   Oh,
what a sublime idea is just here !   And this power is not
confined to us who experience this, but it is felt upon
the outside world.   Why is it that the erecting in this
wilderness of a standard having upon it, " Holiness to
the Lord," has attracted such multitudes ?   Why is it
that so many unconverted are listening with such attention ?   Because of the presentation of this always attractive theme, and this because it involves the exaltation of Christ.   And why does it exalt Christ ?   Because
it declares He is a great, present, precious, complete
Saviour, and He has said, " And I, if I be lifted up, will
draw all men unto me,"—and that is true in more ways
than one.   Will you not then let Christ draw you now
to himself ?   Will you continue to cling to the world, or
will you give it up and let Jesus take you into the land
of Beulah, where the birds sing and the air is all joy ?   All
may have this grace, not to die by alone, but when responsibilities are upon us and temptations around us.   To live
is more than to die ; for to live is to toil, but to die is to go

home. If you would fill your death-chamber with quiet, let Jesus fill your heart with himself, and then fill your own life with obedience. Life is a journey upon the edge of a precipice, and a step may launch us over,—are we ready? We may have Christ in us, the life of our life, and the soul of our soul, making our hearts stout, and our hands strong, and our life joyous and useful.

Some may accuse us of one-idealism, but surely we cannot urge a more glorious specialty than that which brings us together here, for there is an intimate connection between the sanctification of the Church and the conversion of the world. You all remember that immediately following the dedication service here, before a sermon had been preached or an invitation given, there were persons who sought and found Jesus as their pardoning Saviour. We have the strongest convictions upon this subject. I look around to-day and recognize different faces, some from Delaware, some from New York, and others from Philadelphia, all friends cherished and beloved, to whom I would gladly give worldly good, if I could, and if it would be a blessing; and yet I would rather give every one this sanctifying power than the material universe.

I have been wondering whether we shall sit down together in the heavenly kingdom. Oh, my precious friend, shall it be so? Shall we all shine and shout while we make the heavenly arches ring, ascribing to God glory, dominion, and blessing, and power forever? Remember that without holiness no man shall see the Lord.

I love this way. Under a sermon by Bishop Hamline, at about this hour of the day, I made the consecration. I had been very thoughtful for some time; but I said,

"Now I will, I do, give these hands, these feet, this body, my soul, to Jesus; my heart to be His home, and my life to spend in His service." I laid myself upon the altar, and I said, "The altar sanctifieth the gift;" and then peace, full, perfect peace, came unto my soul. I had had peace before, but never anything like this. I almost feared to go to sleep that night, but I slept and woke, and Jesus was with me. I went then to my friends Bishop and Mrs. Hamline, and told them of this, and in the telling of it I was conscious of a blessing. Mrs. Hamline said, "Let us have a season of prayer;" and while one after another prayed, the witness of this came into my heart with all the clearness of noonday. Do you wonder that with this experience I stand here to-day and advocate this glorious truth? O young men, be holy! This is the grace you need. Sunday-school teachers, and class leaders, Presbyterians, Baptists, Congregationalists, Lutherans, Episcopalians, Friends, let us all be holy, and then shall the Church be "fair as the moon, clear as the sun, and terrible as an army with banners."

CHAPTER XII.

SERMONS OF REV. B. POMEROY, OF TROY CONFERENCE, AND REV. B. W. GORHAM.

MR. POMEROY'S SERMON.

I HAVE come down to Vineland to say Amen to the religion of Jesus, and to declare opposition to the worldly, powerless, Christless systems of the present day, which are coming in upon us like a flood. Though conscious of my inability to preach in such a place as this, I thought, nevertheless, that if I should refuse I had better go home and hide myself out of sight. I hardly know what I am going to say to you, my friends. The ministers of the Troy Conference usually let me talk as I please, and put up with anything I may say, and I want to feel just as much at ease in this place. I have no particular ambition to preach a systematic sermon. I am anxious to speak only the truth to you as the Spirit may give me utterance. I am not very particular in my choice of a text, but I think this will answer my purpose as well as any other:—"*Now unto him that is able to do exceeding abundantly above all that we ask or think, according to the power that work-eth in us, unto him be glory in the church by Christ Jesus throughout all ages, world without end. Amen.*" (Eph. iii. 20, 21.)

To be happy when everything is happy around us is

nothing marvellous. The world understands this. But
to be happy when there is nothing that is possibly calculated to make us happy, is beyond our comprehension;
and to be happy when everything about us is calculated
to make us miserable, is one of God's marvels. Paul
and Silas were happy when no human being could say
why they were happy. They had been put in the inner
prison for their devotion to their Lord; and yet so great
was the noise they made in praising God, such was the
outward expression of their inward joy, that they were
requested to leave the prison. They praised the Lord
at midnight, singing, perhaps,—

> " Come on, my prisoners in distress,
>   My comrades through this wilderness."

A strange place to be happy in, and yet they were
happy, and were at last led out in triumph. And the
Spirit which enabled Paul and Silas to be happy in
prison is with us.

TOPICS.

There are three thoughts or topics in the text: first,
what God is to the Church; second, what the Church is
to God; third, the relation which God bears to the
Church, and the Church to God, is world without end.
Amen. Now, though I think I could live and die
speaking and preaching about the last of these topics,
the first will be sufficient for the present—what God is
to the Church.

Without stopping to say what He is not, I come directly to this strong assertion: He is salvation to the
Church; and I mean more than you think I do. I do

not mean to say that salvation is one work amongst others—that it is a mere accident; but I do wish to say that salvation is the great, the grand leading idea of the Infinite—that it is the grandest idea that ever loomed in the fog of eternity, and there is no other work really in God's hands. If He does anything else, it is with reference to salvation. And this is a work of necessity which has been brought upon God through the rebellion of men and angels. I wish to say that this is the great work of the Infinite, of the Three—one God. Do not then, in your faith, be pestered with the idea that in asking God to save you, you are asking Him to go out of His course of action. When you come into God's order of saving, you intercept the great moral currents that are drifting Godward everywhere. It is just as God has contrived it. He has not only contrived His word and His works, but His worlds, for salvation. We are not to think that this is a little place down here, that may almost get lost sometimes, and forgotten in view of the immensities around us. This grove, at the present time, is the most public place in the whole universe of God. Heaven is around you here. Hither do angels come to learn the mysterious lesson of God's grace. All the Creator's worlds and works are subsidiary to the one idea, the salvation of the human race.

It is said there were two full moons in one month a little time ago, and astronomers say the like had never been known since the world was made. What is to be inferred from that? Why, that shows that the first series of revolutions has but just ended. Think of that, mortal, and hold thy breath! Six thousand years in bringing through the first figure in the dance of worlds!

Suppose the angels were to go out from their thrones and, stopping at some distant star, ask what all these worlds and system of worlds were for, and the answer should be, " To see how pretty they would look," would they not be ashamed? But suppose they were told that all these were to serve the race of man, that man was the favorite of God, and that all these contrivances were so set that all come with their swelling flood of good to man, that all is laden with blessings for him, they would break forth into pæans of praise. Everything in the heavens and in the earth subserves the purposes of God towards man. Not this little world merely, but God has put demon and devil into the harness and bids them work for the good of man. God has subordinated everything to the one grand idea of the salvation of man, so that we can bundle all up together and exclaim in the words of the apostle, " All things work together for good to them that love God." Not death, nor devils, nor anything else, can counteract this great decree. God is equal to the work of saving us, and He has come forth to this work, not only with all His vast retinue of worlds, but with His providence and grace. Man began favorably. He started originally with a fair prospect; he was a natural Christian, and walked with God as neighbor with neighbor. But the devil persuaded man to sin, and then and there heaven's favor departed, and every light in the Paradise went out for him, and angels turned their back upon ruin too dark for eyesight; and man became a failure, a perfect failure. Did God abandon His original idea? Did He give up the case as hopeless? No, my friends. He went into a wonderful compact by which He

changed the very throne of heaven to meet the exigencies
of the case. I do not say that the nature of God was
changed, but that He changed the manner of communicating himself to man. And He made this new order
of things; made these new names for the Godhead.
For Jesus Christ is a recent name; it has only been
known a little while, and it is a name that suits the
sinner best. It indicates His vast work. He is made
Jesus Christ to suit the emergencies of the case.

Sanctifier is a modern name; and it is ordained to
express the new work of the Holy Ghost, the third person in the Trinity, which is necessary to be carried on
in consequence of the fall of man. If we could read
the chart of God's original design, we should find no
single intimation that He designed the loss of a single
human soul; but we might read as the title-page of
His chart, "Who will have all men to be saved." And
He does it and decrees it, and has adjusted himself and
His worlds to it. And to every man walking under
these heavens to-day, I want to say that if you are lost
you will be lost against the decree of God, against the
will of God, and the Word of God, and the worlds of
God, and the providence of God. You have got a hard
passage to find your way through all these.

You are resisting influences that make devils tremble
in hell, and that would almost waft devils heavenward.
Oh, get out of this place before the upper and nether mill-
stones come together and grind you to powder. God
has decreed your salvation.

The Infinite was taken by surprise by a second rebellion, so to speak, and space was all taken up with
the original plan. God had no place and no space for

a lost human soul. The original plan had absorbed the universe, and God was obliged to say, " Depart from me, ye that work iniquity, into everlasting fire, prepared for the devil and his angels." That's all the place there was for man. There was no idea of having a lost sinner in the universe, no arrangements made for a lost soul. But when God comes to his natural work, His divine work, how easy and how Godlike it is : " Come, ye blessed of my Father, inherit the kingdom prepared for you before the foundation of the world." You will have no objections to the angels being there. Before the foundation of the world, coming out away back to the very beginning of things, away beyond the morning when the Lord laid the foundations of the earth, and put down the corner-stone of the universe, a mansion was prepared for the glorified from the foundation of the world. He is able to do exceeding abundantly above all that we can ask or think. He is able to do it here. The Lord Jesus proposes to save man just where he went to ruin. An old Methodist once told me that to have a camp-meeting in his time they were obliged to go away six miles out into the woods, to be beyond the influence of the men of the world. " But," said he, " we stood our ground." " Great standing," I answered, "to go six miles out of the world, and then talk about standing your ground !" Now, God stood His ground, and He is going to stand His ground right here, and this is one of the great secrets of the triumphs of the Cross. He will save a soul just where the evil was done. Now, we did not tell the Southerners to get away to Canada, and set some trap to get them out of their homes; but we went down to their fortifications and breastworks, after they had fixed them up to their hearts' content, and took the line on the point that they had made for themselves, and conquered their devilishness there; and that means something. Now, the Lord proposes to save man just here, and not to kidnap him and hurry him off, with the devil at his heels, to the moon, and save him there. God will save man here, and pass him round, and hold him up for devils to froth and foam at to their hearts' content. That's a specimen of what Christ will do. He will save a soul here, and dress him in white garments, and bear him up through all the fogs of hell, and he will come out without spot or wrinkle, or any such thing.

God does not merely straighten out the branches: He gets to the root of the matter. There was a man once who said he had cured his son of the crime of theft, and on being asked how he had done it, he said he had tied his hands behind him! God does not merely make a man moral. The devil don't care for morality, he is not afraid of that. Now, Jesus Christ proposes to begin not with the limbs or the trunk. He goes down into the snarl and snag of the roots, and takes the cause out there. The physician will tell you sometimes that he can't cure the disease, but he can make you die easy. I tell you we have a Physician who is equal to the disease of humanity, who will completely heal the wound, and cover up the scars, so that there shall be neither spot nor wrinkle, nor any such thing. My father had eight different ways of punishing me, and, though he found occasion to administer them all, I continued disobedient and rebellious, until God changed my heart. I went home on one occasion, and my father said to me, "Benjamin, you have given your parents more trouble than all the rest of the children." I felt bad, you may be sure, especially when I thought for a moment of the eight different kinds of punishment. "But," said he, "I have one thing more to say, you have been a greater comfort to your parents than all the rest of the children." That's Benjamin the unregenerate, and Benjamin after Jesus Christ has made him a new creature. And don't you think I should be true to Jesus Christ—must be true to Him? I was brought up a Presbyterian, and hated the Methodists with a perfect hatred; hated them so much that I took delight in pestering the little children. But God converted me without any revival at all. The first prayer-meeting I ever attended, I held and conducted myself. I remember when, at the close of the meeting, I went out into the open night to finish my prayer. I looked up into the sky, and lifting up my hands, said, "Glory to God!" My brother, who saw and heard me, took hold of my hand, and said, "Benjamin, it's wicked to look up to the sky and say, Glory to God." For the height of perfection in Massachusetts at that time was solemnity, and my brother thought it was not solemn enough to look up to the sky and shout "Glory to God." I heeded him not, my heart was too full, so I moved further off, and looked up to the stars again, and said, "Glory to God," again, and I have not got over it yet. I was the first person that joined the Methodist Church in that place, and I joined it because I found in its communion what I could not find anywhere else.

Now, I do bless the Lord Jesus Christ for saving me as he has; and I want to continue talking on this theme,

God's way of saving His people. When God cures a man He don't begin at the tip of a man's fingers, He don't tie his hands behind his back to keep him from stealing. Hands never stole: it is the heart that steals. God begins at the fountain-head; God makes the heart right, and then He lets us go, and we go clean, and all that a saved soul has got to do is to keep in the faith.

CONCLUSION.

Mr. Pomeroy concluded with an exhortation to the congregation to see that they be saved into uncommon things. The mystery of religion is beyond expression, beyond all thought. But let us seek its fulness, and then its contemplation will be eternal. He began on a very small capital, but it had been increasing ever since. There is no such thing as the soul's coming to a standstill. New developments of the love of God in Jesus will be growing upon us throughout all eternity.

MR. GORHAM'S SERMON.

Acts ii. 47.—"*And the Lord added to the Church daily such as should be saved.*"

THE better rendering of this is, The Lord added to the Church daily such as were saved. The Acts of the Apostles is a remarkable book. It is the first book of Christian history. It is fact illustrating theory; it tells us how the Gospel prospered when its forces were first brought to bear upon human society. The things that God makes require no second thought to make them perfect. God made man's body, and no new bone or nerve or muscle or tissue has been found necessary in the lapse of thousands of years. God made the universe, and the great machine went at the first and went correctly. God made the Gospel, and from the day when the judgment of God laid Ananias at the feet of Peter, to the day when its chief apostle, lying in a heathen dungeon, said in the face of martyrdom, "I am ready to be offered "—all declares that the Gospel is the power of God unto salvation to every one that believeth. This text tells us, within the compass of an aphorism, how the Church fought and conquered at the first; how when she stood without prestige, when her members and friends were few, and enemies many and mighty, when the infant Church found herself confronted with Jewish and heathen superstitions all armed with the instruments of martyrdom; how then she conquered, conquered steadily, conquered rapidly, conquered always. My object now is a very simple one indeed. I wish, first, to call your attention, in this short passage, to one fact in it, and secondly, to go back of this fact and seek after some of the foundations of it.

THE FACT ANNOUNCED.

The simple fact is, that there was an increase in the Church, that there were members added to it. This is a vital fact, for it is the sign of life in a church. The Church never conquers when she sleeps, but she always conquers when she is true to her Lord, when she is in a state of spiritual health and activity. I do not speak of accretions to the ecclesiastical body, but I mean additions to the Church of God, additions of men and women who are spiritually alive. This is the sign of the life of the Church. The absence of it indicates her torpor, her death. The presence of it is her endorsement before angels and the world. This is the very condition of her life, the fact upon which hangs the perpetuity of her existence, and she must live by this if she live at all. She lives by conflict and victory, and, like the army of Hannibal in the heart of Italy, she must conquer, or she must die. If there were to be no converts during the next fifty years, then at the end of these fifty years Christianity would be extinct on this continent, for the Church perpetuates herself from age to age by conquering. Every soldier of the cross is a captive taken from the ranks of the enemy, brought into the ranks of Jesus, and trained and inspired and moved by the Holy Ghost.

But this accession of which the text speaks was an addition to the Church in Jerusalem, where the great Head of the Church, not more than ninety days before, had been put shamefully to death, on the occasion of a public festival. In this very city now, a great revival has come, and hundreds of men and women are enlisting under the banner that bears the name of the Crucified. In this very city the Lord has given a great outpouring of the Spirit's power, converting three thousand souls in a single day. And now the thunder-storm has settled down into a steady rain, a regular equinoctial. God Almighty grant that nothing may occur to thwart this order of God here. May God grant us a steady rain of blessing; not in New Jersey merely, but in every other State, whether represented here or not.

This was a steady and a rapid increase; the Lord added *daily* to the Church of such as were saved. Men were so ready to join the Church that they could not wait till the next Sabbath, or the next sacrament. They pressed around the altar, and even when they knew that possible martyrdom lay in the path of every one of them, these men and women hastened every day claiming to be registered as disciples of the Crucified.

Then this was the work of the Lord. The *Lord* added to the Church daily such as were saved. There was no other church with whom the apostles could raise a disturbance and induce a number of their members to side with them. There was no proselytism. The whole thing was of God: The Lord added to the Church daily such as, being saved, were likely to get to glory, people that you might look upon, and say, " They will go through with it, at all events." Their eyes were opened, and they were ready to say, " Though it cost me my position in society—and it certainly will—I give up all for this Jesus." And that is to some people about as much as they can afford to give up for Christ, to give up caste, to stand disgraced, to go down from one of the upper-ten to some lower position in society. These men knew that it would cost them that. They could stand by and see their goods despoiled. They fully expected all this. And they knew that in all probability they should be obliged to go to the stake as the result of it; and yet the people said, each for himself, " I will be a Christian." Of such people you may safely predict that they will be saved. You see people sometimes, and you shake your head, and say, " I don't know about that ; I am afraid it won't hold out." But there are others of whom you never have many fears, and these were all of this character.

THE CAUSE.

This fact, that there were so many additions of saved men to the Church, when viewed with all the surrounding circumstances, is a remarkable one, and one for which we may well ask the cause.

Jesus, as he was about to ascend to heaven, said to His disciples, "Tarry ye in Jerusalem until ye be endued with power from on high." He had endeavored to interpret to them the Kingdom, but they did not understand His sayings until after He had arisen. So He said to them, "Tarry ye in Jerusalem." "Ye shall receive the Holy Ghost not many days hence." "The spirit of truth shall come and lead you into all truth." That was a very remarkable measure of truth which Christ used here,—"*All* truth." God gives not His truth nor grace to us by measure, only as the measure is infinite, and all may come and be filled.

Was it true, then, that the men who had consorted with Jesus for three years were not quite ready yet to preach the Gospel? They had sat at His feet, had travelled with Him, had listened to His conversation 'and understood something of His heart and feelings; and is it true that three years of such schooling as that was not quite enough to prepare these men to preach the Gospel, especially when their only business was to witness what they had seen of Christ's life, of His travels, of His miracles; what they knew of His crucifixion, and especially of His resurrection? And besides this, Jesus had said to them, "Go ye into all the world, and preach the Gospel to every creature." Was it true, then, that they were not yet prepared for this work?

Yes, this was true; and so they were bidden to tarry in Jerusalem till they should be endued with power from on high. Now, if these men, who had thus walked and talked with Jesus for three years, were not ready for their work till they had tarried for the baptism, who is, or can be, prepared for the great work of the ministry till the holy anointing comes upon him? Nay, who is ready to be a laborer for Christ, aside from the ministry—and all the members of the Church are to be laborers—without a similar baptism of the Holy Ghost? I do not see that human learning in any measure is able to qualify any one to bring sinners to Christ. As far as the mere statement or utterance of the word was concerned, these men were prepared without this baptism; and I do not see that in this respect we can be better prepared than were they. What modern repeater of the mere facts of Christ's life has any advantage over such a man as Peter? He could say, 'I know all about this man Christ. I remember, when at my house, He spoke to my mother-in-law, who had been some time sick of the fever, and she arose instantly. I remember that, a short time afterwards, as He was preaching under the verandah in the court of my dwelling, four men came and lifted off the tiling, and let down a sick man in his bed—I think I see him now, so pale and ghastly, he scarce could speak; but I remember the imperial look of Jesus, as the sick man was let down before Him by four cords, and I remember how Jesus, with a single word, bade the man be well, and he arose, took up that whereon he had been lying, and went away grateful and astonished. I was there when He fed the five thousand with five loaves, and I

saw Him when He came walking upon the liquid bosom
of the deep. I was with Him when He wept beside the
grave of Lazarus, and heard His voice ring through the
chambers of the sepulchre, and presently Lazarus
stood before us, a well man, who had been dead for
days. I saw Him on the cross on that day of terror.
I remember how, at nine o'clock, or thereabout, I
heard the terrible hammer that drove the spikes into
His hands and feet. I remember the rumble and shock
of that fearful earthquake, and how the stony darkness came over us at noonday; and how, in the terror
of the moment, even His murderers were constrained
to cry out "This is the Son of God!" John and I
ran on the morning of the first day of the week to
His sepulchre, but He was not there. I was present
when Thomas, who had refused to believe till then, put
his hands on the prints of the nails, and cried out "My
Lord and my God!"

Where, now, I ask, is the modern Apollos who can
argue and reason about the facts of Christ's history with
greater effect than Peter, who had seen it all? If Peter
needed the Holy Ghost, am I sufficient without it? If
Peter, who lived in the year of grace 1, and from that
up till 30 or 50, was unfitted for this work without the
baptism of the Holy Ghost, am I, who live in the year
of grace 1867, or any one of the brethren on this platform, equal to the work without the same baptism of the
Holy Ghost? God knows we are not. Is the truth
mighty? Yes; but it is the truth accompanied and
driven by the Holy Ghost that is powerful to the pulling
down of the strongholds of Satan; and the man who
has the Holy Ghost, and whose reliance is upon the

Holy Ghost, and not on his own word, or eloquence, or address, that man carries with him the certainty of victory, and that man alone. The cannon-ball or the minie-ball is perfectly harmless but for the powder and fire behind it. The Holy Ghost, and nothing else, can make the truth of God to triumph.

IN EARNEST.

These men were in earnest, thoroughly in earnest. They had had their own ideas of who should be greatest, and all those selfish questionings, in times past; but all that is forgotten now, and they are on their knees with one heart and one mind. Christians, when upon their knees, are very strong people. All animosity and selfishness were laid aside, and they were of one spirit.

Now, when the day of Pentecost had come, this people had a very remarkable meeting. One morning, they were all with one accord in one place. That's very remarkable, they were all there—a hundred and twenty members in the Church at Jerusalem, and there were just a hundred and twenty of them at this meeting. And it was not a meeting to hear John Summerfield, or Bishop Simpson, or any other great man; but it was a prayer-meeting. They began it at seven o'clock in the morning, and when Peter began to speak it was about nine o'clock. Commend me to such a Church as that. I would go to such a meeting if I knew where it was to be held, if I had to cross the continent. All at meeting, and all with one accord! And while they prayed, there came from heaven a sound as of a mighty rushing wind, and it filled all the place; and there appeared unto them cloven tongues, like as of fire, and they were all filled

with the Holy Ghost, and began to speak with other
tongues as the spirit gave them utterance. And mark
the spiritual revelations and renovations that took place.
See Peter, the self-sufficient apostle, who a little time
ago was ready to do battle in his own strength, and yet
shrinking in the presence of a servant-maid : see him
now as he rises to address that congregation under circumstances of peculiar difficulty and delicacy. Before
him are the murderers of his Lord, and yet, under the
influence of the power from above, he speaks with such
resistless energy that these very murderers cry out under his searching and awful word. Peter was a new
Peter; he had risen to a new altitude, and had found
a new latitude, and had received a spiritual force and
energy of which he never knew anything till that day.
It was so with the others. Their rivalries and conten-
tions were all gone, and, under the influence of this
new power, they were henceforth to be, till the era of
their martyrdom, simple as children, but bold and daring as lions. With the spirit of martyrdom in their
souls they went everywhere preaching and publishing
the words of the grace of Jesus.

And the congregation felt its influence too. A congregation is always ready to follow its leader, whether
to the heights of spiritual enjoyment or into the depths
of formalism. All great reformations and all great
defections have come by the ministry. The Church
has followed her leaders, and they will be held responsible before the great white throne.

The Church at Pentecost received the baptism of the
Holy Ghost, and these men showed by their after-con-
duct how complete was their consecration, and how

thorough was the cleansing work wrought in them; for "they that gladly received his word . . . . continued steadfastly in the apostles' doctrine and fellowship, and in breaking of bread, and of prayers; and fear came upon every soul."

FEAR.

With this baptism the Church became an object of a kind of majestic fear. There is no way for the Church to maintain the respect of the world, but to bear that perfect impress of the Lord which carries with it such a fear. When the world finds there is nothing in the Church that is dangerous to its sensuality, when they can go up to these great churches and find that they are only wooden guns, their fear and their respect are lost together. If the Church would hold the respect of the world, and hold it in awe before her, she must herself hold hard by the throne of God. When a government loses its power it also loses the respect of its subjects. This is strikingly illustrated in the case of Mexico. So, in a family where there is no parental government, no power of control, the children do not respect the parents.

The world desires to see in Christians unmistakable indications of power, and unless these indications are seen, they cannot respect us. Men know they are wrong. The whole great sinful world knows it is wrong, and they respect most that Church and minister who will put the fire of truth upon their hearts, and then they will come like flocking doves to their windows.

Oh, what mighty power clothes a divinely baptized

Church! May God send it upon us now. Here we are to-day, and in addition to our numbers, we possess magnificent church edifices, colleges, academies, presses, tract societies, and mission societies, and have Christian legislation on our side. Besides all this, we have great postal routes. Why, Paul had to send Phebe to Rome, a distance of seven hundred miles by sea, and not much less if she went the whole journey afoot,—for there were not even stage-coaches in those days. Paul had to send Titus to Ephesus and Colosse to carry an epistle there. You can send an epistle there now for fifty cents or less. Last Sunday I preached in Pittsburgh, a distance of nearly four hundred miles from here, and expect to preach there on the coming Sabbath. The work that I can thus do in a week, Paul could not have accomplished in a month. How, then, stands the count? If eleven ministers, with five hundred church members, could accomplish so much in fifty years, and without these facilities, what ought eighty-five thousand ministers, with ten millions of Christians, to do in fifty years with these facilities? When the Church shall be clothed upon with the power of God we shall soon be in the neighborhood of the millennium. Did each member of the Church accomplish the salvation of only one man in each year, in one year the church members would be doubled, in two years we should stand four to one, in three years eight to one, in four years sixteen to one, in five years thirty-two to one, and in six years sixty-four to one; while in less than seven years the millennium glory would be here. [Shouts of Glory! Glory!]

God knows this is what we want. The world is

waiting for it, angels are waiting for it, the old martyrs that dared to die for Christ are waiting before the throne to see the Church come up and take hold of this work. God help us to do it!

The preacher, after the conclusion of the sermon, desired that all those in the congregation who would just then, and with all their hearts, give themselves to God, should immediately come forward and kneel at the seats in front of the stand. Some two or three hundred at once responded, and they came from all parts of the congregation. He then asked all the ministers who would humble themselves before God and seek for a great Pentecostal baptism, to retire from the stand and kneel with the other seekers. To this they every one, to the number of fifty or more, immediately responded, Brother Gorham himself going with the rest. How impressive was this scene, as ministers and people bowed together, first in silent prayer and consecration, and then in groanings, and subdued but earnest and intermingling prayer, and this often broken in upon by shouts of praise. Many will never forget that scene, nor how the Spirit took them into hitherto unknown depths of humility; nor how they realized the sweet baptism of the Holy Ghost coming upon them, enabling them to realize, as they sang,—

> " 'Tis the very same power
>   They had at Pentecost;
>   'Tis the power, the power,
>   That Jesus promised should come down."

CHAPTER XIII.

CONCLUDING—BISHOP SIMPSON AND FAMILY— CONVERSIONS
—PREACHING—OTHER SERVICES—FAREWELLS

FROM the hour that the first glad song of praise
broke the stillness of the Vineland woods, or the first
prayer of that tented grove ascended to our Father's
throne, sprinkled with the merit of Christ's blood, it
was known on earth that this camp-meeting, for a
specialty—the expediency of which was so generally
doubted, and the holding of which was so considerably
opposed—would be a heavenly success. Yea, many
praying ones had received answer from God assuring
them of His presence ere they left their homes. The
proportions of the meeting were great, and the spirit
wonderful, so that the reader who was not present can
hardly realize how the great deep of the human soul
was moved upon by the breath of the Lord. This
ever-present and all-powerful Spirit resulted in excellent order, deep humility, holy trust, heavenly fervor,
godly zeal, brotherly love, childlike simplicity, and a
divine unction that sweetened and sanctified all things.
There was nothing assumed, nothing extraneous, nothing officious, and nothing deleterious. The Com
mittee of Direction seemed to be divinely directed.

BISHOP SIMPSON AND FAMILY

were present through the meeting. This highly esteemed servant of Christ and the Church came to the camp with considerable physical prostration, resulting from recent illness, but mingled very freely in the various exercises at the stand and in the tents. Offering the opening prayer at one of the preaching services, " he seemed to catch the heavenly fire, and, rising in the might of earnest faith, he continued pleading until showers of blessings fell on all the people, whose hearts seemed to burn within them as they waited and worshipped before Jehovah." Elsewhere we have given the Bishop's exhortation, which was accompanied with an heavenly unction to the hearts of the multitude. We give the following from the pen of one who was a witness to the scene described: " The Bishop spent the Sabbath at Cape Island, officiating at the re-opening services of a beautiful Methodist church. Returning to camp on Monday morning, some one spoke a hurried word in his ear, and immediately he repaired to Kensington tent, where, looking in over the throng who stood around, he saw his own son, in the midst of a group of dear friends, bowing in broken-hearted penitence and prayer. Tears came fast rolling down his face, and the way being opened, he proceeded to the spot and knelt down by the side of Charles, a noble-appearing man, to point him to the Lamb of God. As the Bishop led in prayer, his own spirit all bathed in sympathy, we thought we had never witnessed a more deeply impressive and affecting scene. Subsequently we saw this son, the subject, doubtless, of ' ten thousand prayers,' stand up and confess the Lord Jesus, as

did his precious mother and wife, all of whom are fervent in spirit, and with renewed consecration seem to
say and sing—

> " 'Nearer, my God, to thee,
> Nearer to thee!' "

It is permitted us to add, that after months rolled
away, and this noble and manly son lay sick, and was
swiftly approaching the river of death, over which he
soon passed, he said, "Mother, I shall bless God to
all eternity for the Vineland camp-meeting."

CONVERSION OF SINNERS.

It was thought by some who had not sufficiently
reflected upon the very close relations of a holy church
to the awakening and conversion of sinners, that there
would be few or none of such cases at this meeting.
But this feature of the work began the first night, and
continued to the last.   There were not a few of these
that were marked.   We give some illustrations of this.
A Christian woman, with her unconverted husband, of
about middle life, was present.   After one of the preaching services, a meeting for prayer and consecration was
commenced before the stand, and a great company of
those seeking entire sanctification were there.   This
woman arose and said she wanted this blessing, but
her husband, who was near her, wanted her to get in
their wagon and go with him to their somewhat distant home.   One of the ministers asked him aloud if
he would not allow his wife to remain just ten minutes
to seek this grace.   To this he consented, and she
immediately entered the group of praying ones, and
kneeled with them, he remaining just outside the circle,

standing, and with his hat on. Before the expiration of the ten minutes she arose, and with a bright light playing upon her countenance, bore testimony that the blood of Jesus Christ had cleansed her from all sin. As she was proceeding to join her husband, the minister who had obtained consent for the tarrying asked the husband if he would not prolong his stay just fifteen minutes by the watch, to allow the people of God to pray for his conversion. Quite promptly, but with seeming indifference, he consented. All now centred their prayer for this man, he remaining on his feet and with his hat on. The minister took his watch in his hand, and announced the moments as they flew. One and another went to him, and entreated him to uncover his head and kneel down, but for some time without avail. By and by, as prayer took hold on God with great energy, the hat was taken off, then another struggle, and he sat down, then more importunate prayer, and he kneeled, and soon was crying earnestly to God for his salvation. The minister announced "twelve minutes gone," and the people seemed hushed into the stillness of faith, and in a moment the man arose and said, "I feel I have been a great sinner, but I feel God is forgiving me; and now I must leave, but please all pray for me, that at home with my wife I may serve God, and at last meet you in heaven." As they left, the children of the Lord were praising God that so great a work could be wrought so soon:

The following is from the pen of a Friend, an intelligent Christian gentleman, and an influential member of a firm that employs several hundred men.

"While walking around the circle one day I met one

of my workmen. He was a man of about fifty years
of age, generally kind and indulgent to his family in the
use of the unusually large wages that he earned by his
trade, but often profane in his language, and subject to
fits of violent passion. In one of these he had, a few
weeks before, driven his family from the house, and
beaten his youngest son till his Christian wife, in fear
for the boy's life, had to interpose, and resolutely say
that he must strike her before he should again assault
the boy. He was a peculiarly interesting, open-hearted
man, but had so long withstood the claims of Christ in
the midst of a religious community, that there seemed
little hope of his conversion.

"Addressing him, I said, 'John, I have been watching for your soul for two years, and now I want you to
become a Christian TO-DAY!'

"We sat down, and I again told him, as I had several
times done a year before, the story of the cross, solemnly
pressing the gospel of salvation home upon his heart.
He listened respectfully, saying but little; but when
we were about to part, and I asked him if he would not
kneel while I asked God's blessing upon him, he replied
with characteristic frankness,—

"'Well, I am much obliged by your kind interest in
me, but, to be honest with you, I am really not now
interested. I have sometimes felt these things deeply
at meetings, but I have no interest in the subject now;
I feel nothing.'

"He, however, consented to kneel, and a brother
joining us, we bowed before God. The prayer ascended,
that as Jesus, in the days of His flesh, had looked upon
the faith of those who broke through all obstacles to

place their beloved sick before Him, and had said, 'Son, thy sins be forgiven thee!' so now He would look upon the poor sin-sick soul whom we brought to His feet, and in mercy make him whole. It was a bold request, but God was present in remarkable power.

"Almost immediately the man broke down, weeping and pleading for mercy. His wife, who, seeing my conversation with her husband, had followed us into the tent as we turned aside for prayer, now stood behind us. Very soon after, our prayer was answered in his conversion, and she received, as he rose from his knees, her now Christian husband with a joy better conceived of than described. As he left, he exclaimed, 'I am a new creature in Christ Jesus!'

"I suppose that *hardly ten minutes* had elapsed between the time of his expression of entire want of interest and feeling, and his confession of Christ as his Saviour.

"I learned afterwards that besides his wife's prayers during probably thirty years for his conversion, some of his fellow-workmen had selected him as apparently the most unlikely to become a Christian, among several hundred who worked together. I also found that the wife of a fellow-workman, a mother in Israel, had been awakened in her tent about twelve o'clock the night before, and had found herself so praying in the spirit for this man, that she could not go to sleep again.

"When he came among some of his Christian fellow-workmen, and told what God had so marvellously done for his soul, their joy was unbounded. More than anything that I have ever seen, its expression made me un-

7*

derstand how David must have felt when he danced
before the ark. They embraced one another, and
wept and laughed for joy as they welcomed the poor
sinner so suddenly snatched from the snares of the
fowler.

"This man has for about two years, under my own
often almost hourly observation of faithful walk,
'adorned the doctrine of God our Saviour in all things,'
so far as human observation can discern, and demonstrated, were such demonstration needed, that the whole
glorious chain of events—the wife's long-continued
prayers, the selection of this man by his comrades for
special prayer, the midnight intercessions of the aged
saint, the word of testimony, the power of God in the
camp, and the laying of him at the feet of Jesus to be
healed,—all these events were but the links in the chain
of God's marvellous purposes of grace to the profane
sinner. "Lord, increase our faith in the present power
and immediate results of thy testimony to holiness."

There was a vigorous effort made to keep the account of
the numbers of those who were converted, but the work
went on so rapidly and in so many tents, as well as
before the stand, that it was found impossible to keep
such a count. On every hand the evidence seemed to
abound that the number was large, and eternity only
can reveal how many.

THE PREACHING,

As attested by the effects on the congregation, was
excellent. Many a hearer will never forget some parts
of the various sermons which our space has compelled

us to omit. Rev. J. S. Inskip, Rev. Mr. Johnson, Presbyterian; Revs. A. M. Barnitz, A. C. Rose, W. G. Browning, W. T. D. Clemm, P. E. in Baltimore Conference; L. C. Matlack, and Rev. Bros. Stratton, French, Dunn, and McLean were of this number. It was often observed that, no matter who was the preacher for the hour, there was increase of the divine power at each successive service. Often after the close of the sermon, or the exhortation following it, there was such a manifest power of the Spirit falling on the great congregation, that it seemed futile to think of inviting the great numbers who were desiring to come to take places in front of the stand. The whole enclosure of the tents would, therefore, be regarded as an altar, and the congregation invited to esteem it so, and to kneel before the Lord and give themselves to Him. The compliance was astonishingly general, and there was the greatest solemnity resting upon those who did not go so far.

OTHER SERVICES.

The Love-Feasts, of which there were two, and the Ministers' Experience-Meeting of an hour and a half each day, were, if possible, of still more thrilling interest than the meetings generally held in the tents. The extended "Bower of Prayer" was generally filled at the season of service there, and it was not unusual to see two or three hundred persons seeking the blessing of Perfect Love there. The meetings in this place were frequently led by those successful servants of Jesus, Dr. and Mrs. Palmer.

The hour of secret prayer at noontide was both a no-

ticeable and profitable feature of the camp. As the
hour arrived every tent was closed, the walking about
the ground was almost discontinued, and the hum of
conversation was quieted, while God's children came
face to face with Him in secret prayer. That, like in
some great manufactory in those unseen places, there
was power generated, who can doubt?

The Sacramental Service was held on Thursday
night, to which the evening was devoted exclusively.
Before entering on these services thanks were unanimously tendered to Rev. A. E. Ballard, Presiding Elder
of the District; to R. J. Andrews, Preacher in charge
of Vineland M. E. Church; and to C. K. Landis, Esq.,
proprietor of the town of Vineland.

Prayer was offered by Rev. Bro. Lawrence of the
Newark Conference. Revs. Geo. Hughes, of Newark
Conference, J. A. Wood, of the Wyoming, and A. Hunt,
of the New York Conferences, addressed the congregation, improving the occasion to give such counsel or
comfort as they deemed most for the glory of God.
The emblems of the broken body and shed blood of
our Lord Jesus Christ were distributed to nearly a
thousand persons. This solemn scene, at night, and in
the woods, with the glare of the camp-fires falling on
these commemorating disciples, made it a time of unusual interest; but the Spirit itself intensified that interest, as that first supper of Jesus and His disciples was
remembered, and was followed swiftly by the thought
that these now partaking of the consecrated emblems
would never all again receive them together until they
shall be received in our Father's house on high. These
thoughts commingling with the sacredness of their vows

to set themselves apart for God, and the recollections of
the happy hours spent together in the tented grove,
made it an occasion that will remain fresh in the recollection when most other things shall have faded
from memory. After this service the people formed in
line and marched around the enclosure, singing as they
went, and after reaching a designated place, shook hands
with ministers and each other, giving their "God bless
you," or "Farewell," or "Be faithful;" and thus ended
the first National Camp-Meeting for the promotion of
Christian Holiness.

Manheim.

CHAPTER XIV.

OPENING.

THE SECOND NATIONAL CAMP MEETING was held at Manheim, Pennsylvania, commencing on the Fourteenth of July, 1868, and closing on the Twenty-fourth. A beautiful section of country and a majestic forest, excellent water and well-prepared grounds, necessary concomitants of Camp meeting, were all here. There was no experiment involved now, in calling upon the people from all over the land to come to this Jerusalem, to *Worship the Lord in the beauty of Holiness*, for all fear of failure had been dispelled by the baptism of the Holy Ghost sent down upon the people at the Vineland Camp. They came together praying, but in joyful anticipation of Pentecostal results. From the hour the grounds were formally consecrated, the meeting went on with increasing fervency and power, so that it has been said by competent authority, that probably there were as many sinners converted as at any camp meeting ever held on the continent. Hundreds of others received the witness of God's Spirit that the blood of Jesus Christ cleanseth from all sin.

SERMON OF MR. WELLS.

1 John i. 7.—" *If we walk in the light, as He is in the light, we have fellowship one with another, and the blood of Jesus Christ His Son cleanseth us from all sin."*

THE doctrine of this text is this :—The Christian's progress from pardon to purity—a true Christian walk, resulting in an experience of entire holiness ; or, the walking in a justified state leading to the efficacious blood of Jesus, in which the believer, by an act of faith, experiences an entire cleansing from sin.

Let us inquire—In what sense God is in the light, and how this light pertains to all believers ; what is implied in walking ; and what in walking in the light, and having fellowship with God ; and how such a walk leads to the blood of Jesus, and the entire cleansing of the nature.

The metaphors light and darkness, in the Scriptures, represent the opposite extremes of knowledge and ignorance, truth and error, purity and corruption, happiness and misery. Everything that is gloomy and wicked and terrible is represented by darkness, as " the children of darkness," " the works of darkness ; " and outer darkness is the final abode of the wicked.

LIGHT.

Everything cheerful and pure and blessed is represented by light. The Gospel is a light, the Holy Spirit is a light, the path of the just is light, believers walk in the light.

Light is a strong and beautiful metaphor to represent intelligence, purity, and happiness, and in this sense it is applied to the Creator as well as the creature. His nature is light; He is the Father of lights; He is clothed in light, and dwelleth in light. St. John says, "This then is the message that we have received of Him and deliver unto you, that God is light, and in Him is no darkness at all."

Light is a fit emblem of intelligence, because it is a medium of discernment and communication, and without it there could be no intercourse or knowledge. This world itself would have become a mere ball of ice, swinging in silent darkness, and devoid of every living thing, but for the word of its Creator, "Let there be light."

Light is also an emblem of purity. There is nothing in nature so pure and undefilable. It can neither be stained nor stagnant, and though it shines upon the most poisonous miasma, it is ever a bright and spotless splendor representing the perfect purity of God.

Light is an emblem of happiness. "Truly the light is sweet, and a pleasant thing it is for the eyes to behold the sun." Light fitly represents the perpetual and infinite blessedness of the Divine Being, and himself as the source of all good and happiness. Thus God is light, yea, "the Father of lights." He is the source and fulness of light, like the sun shedding his rays upon surrounding worlds without being diminished in splendor; and, unlike the sun, God is an uncreated light, self-existent, immutable, eternal, and enlightens the universe of mind and matter with the bright splendor of His own being.

The Scripture assertions, therefore, that "God is

light," is "clothed in light," and "dwells in light," represent to us the divine effulgence of His infinite perfections, and particularly the combination and diffusion of His knowledge, holiness, and happiness, all which originate in Him, and flow forth from Him, flooding the world with divine illumination.

The Scriptures so invest Him with light, and He is so revealed in light as to inspire the doxologies of earth and heaven; and tongues angelic and human join in the lofty utterance, "Glory to God in the highest!" as if there was no other suitable language above or beneath when the divine effulgence shines forth. Every other word seems beggared and utterly inadequate to the utterance of astonished thought and ravished emotion, when God is revealed, but the word glory. This word is heaven-born, and belongs to the dialect of seraphim. Angels brought it to earth, and rolled it over the plains of Judea. Earth caught it up, and sent it back again to heaven, expressive of devout praise for the shining of divinity upon the darkness of humanity.

When the incarnate God appeared in Bethlehem the wise men of the East saw only the glimmer of a solitary and mysterious star; but a multitude of the heavenly host, of keener vision than they, saw in the manger the bright and morning star of the world, and the air of Bethlehem trembled with their announcement of the glorious sunrising of redeemed humanity, and angelic praise for its dawn, "Glory to God in the highest, on earth peace, good will to men." And when Simeon took the child in his arms, he saw His glory, and with the inspiration of prophecy exclaimed:—"A light to lighten the Gentiles, and the glory of thy people Israel."

When He was transfigured, the bright rays of His divinity darted through His humanity, and shone out in such brilliant coruscations that His countenance shone as the sun in his strength; and in such light and glory He was revealed to John in Patmos.

But all our views and conceptions of Him who dwelleth in light to which no man can approach, and the splendor of whose being dazzles and obscures as well as reveals, are necessarily very imperfect; but enough of this glory is manifest to demonstrate the truth of His word, " God is light, and in him is no darkness at all."

My next remark is, that light pertains to the nature and walk of Christian believers as it does to God. Not the full blaze of the light of God, but the light of a man and a Christian—a light that God has kindled within him, and that makes a halo of brightness around him—not unoriginated and eternal light, but light communicated from the fulness of the Divine Being, " For God who commanded the light to shine out of darkness hath shined into our hearts, to give the light of the knowledge of the glory of God in the face of Jesus Christ."

In Malachi it is said, " Unto you that fear my name shall the Son of Righteousness arise with healing in his wings." It is always night with a sinner. He belongs to the kingdom of darkness, and he is held by the power of darkness. The kingdom of God is a kingdom of light. The day of salvation is a day of glorious sunshining, and with its dawn comes the call of God, "Arise, shine, for thy light is come, and the glory of God is risen upon thee."

The children of God are the children of light; to

them " the Lord God is a sun " as well as " a shield."
Christ is the Sun of Righteousness: the truths of the
gospel and the Holy Ghost are the rays of this divine
sun, darting into the mind benighted by sin, penetrating
the heart mantled in moral midnight, burning away the
murky mists and fogs that rise from the low grounds of
depravity, and making the mind and heart all luminous
with the light of God.

Oh! the blessed call. Oh! the astonishing deliverance, when God calls men out of darkness into his marvellous light. It is not in the midnight that Christians
grope their uncertain way to heaven. No! no! Nor
yet in the dim starlight, or under the glimmer of the
moon, nor in the twilight, but in the bright sunlight of
the day of God's presence and favor.

Christ is the Sun of Righteouness. Most significant
expression. He is the light of righteousness, and upon
them that fear the Lord He arises and shines with healing in His wings. His light opens their dull eyes from
the troubled sleep of sin to see the morning of salvation
spreading upon the mountains, and the dark shades of
the night of sin hastening away. The Sun of Righteousness so outshines the natural sun that it is said to the believer, " The sun shall be no more thy light by day,
neither for brightness shall the moon give light unto
thee, but the Lord shall be unto thee an everlasting
light, and thy God thy glory."

Believers are begotten of the light, born of the light,
and hence are called children of the light, as God is the
" Father of lights." Said the apostle :—" But ye are all
the children of light, and the children of the day ; we
are not of the night, nor of darkness. For ye were

sometime darkness, but now are ye light in the Lord. Walk as children of the light." Christ said to His disciples, " Ye are the light of the world." " If thine eye be single, thy whole body shall be full of light." " Light is sown for the righteous, and joy for the upright in heart." " Unto the upright there ariseth light in darkness." " The path of the just is as the shining light, that shineth more and more unto the perfect day."

Such is the light of a saint of God; all luminous within, and all luminous without. The Sun of Righteousness to him suffers no eclipse, but shines uninterruptedly, and makes it light all about him, and all the way through to glory. The lamps of eternity are hung out on either side of the narrow way, so that you cannot keep that path and walk in darkness. He that walks in the path of the just never gets lost, never is overtaken with night, but he can see each step, for the light shines all the time. Midnight is on either side, and if he steps out darkness is upon him, but never while he is in the path of the just.

I pass to inquire next,

WHAT IS IMPLIED IN WALKING?

Walking is a voluntary and uniform forward movement on the feet by consecutive steps. It is an activity that implies and requires life. Dead men never walk. As applied to the Christian it signifies that he has spiritual life and activity. A Christian cannot be sepulchred and buried amid the silence of the dead. You will find him among the living, and amid the stirring and tremendous events of life, and by the activity and energy of his spiritual life making events and shaping events that will be heard from in eternity. He is on a pilgrimage from the City of Destruction to Mount Zion, the city of the living God, and he is *walking* it.

Again: The Christian walk signifies uprightness. The natural walking posture is an erect one. This is the Christian's posture—not one of cowardly, servile crouching and creeping—not one of stooping, and bending, and bowing to adjust himself to human views, and practices, and policies, and Satanic suggestions. The Christian's position is upright. He stands up for the truth, and stands up for Jesus, even when it costs him something.

But walking is not simply standing up; it is motion. The Christian moves in the way of duty, and toward heaven. This walking is not only motion, but it is voluntary motion. He moves of choice. He is not walked by another—*he walks*. He is not dependent on outward influences nor inward impulses, nor irresistible agency, but he moves himself. The motive power is within him, and like a man walking so he goes forward by his own effort in the path of duty.

Walking is also a uniform and regular motion, step by step, and but one step at a time. It is not simply promiscuous exercise—not leaping, and bounding, and dancing, but regularly and consecutively setting one foot forward of the other, and thus advancing.

Such is the Christian's walk—a regular and uniform movement forward, step by step, advancing to the city of God. Every duty is a step toward the kingdom.

Walking is a *forward movement.* One can hardly be said to walk who takes one step forward and then one backward, or who steps to the right or left. This is simple exercise, not walking. So the Christian's walk is a forward movement. Each step is in advance of the last. He progresses from one point to another by walking. Every act of obedience and of faith brings the Christian nearer to God, and holiness, and heaven.

WALKING, AND LIGHT.

I would next ask your attention to the combination of the two figures in the text—walking, and light.

As to the mere fact of walking, sinners walk, but they walk in darkness; they stumble, and know not at what they stumble, because the darkness hath blinded their eyes, and they plunge headlong into darkness that is utter and eternal. The difference between a saint and a sinner is that one walks in light and the other in darkness. They are both on a journey to eternity; but they travel different roads, and to a different destiny. The one is all night and darkness, the other all day and light

But what is the light in which the believer walks, and what is walking in it?

We reply in the general Scripture language, "Whatsoever doth make manifest is light." Whatsoever opens the understanding to discern clearly the way of life, and whatsoever makes the path of duty and the way to heaven a plain path, and an attractive and blessed way, is light.

But to be more specific, walking in the light is:

1st. Walking obediently. Said the Apostle, "I have no greater joy than to know that my children walk in the truth." And the Psalmist said, "The entrance of thy word giveth light. For the commandment is a lamp, and the law is a light." The commandment is

light, because in this God teaches us what we must do
to be saved. In the light of every command we may
distinctly read the handwriting of God, " This way to
glory," " This do and thou shalt live." Every truth of
God's word is a ray of light from the eternal throne.
To follow it is to follow the sunbeam that leads up to
the glorious Sun of Righteousness, and in a path so
plain that " the wayfaring men, though fools, shall not
err therein."

2d. The believer has also the light of God's countenance. " Blessed are the people that know the joyful
sound ; they shall walk, O Lord, in the light of thy countenance." God's countenance is dark with the frown of
anger to the ungodly, but when a penitent believes in
Christ, His anger is turned away, the cloud of frown is
lifted, and God's countenance is light with approval.

3d. The believer walks also in the light of the Holy
Ghost. On the day of Pentecost, when he was fully
given, his visible symbol was fire, " cloven tongues, like
as of fire, sat upon each of them," indicative of the wondrous illumination of the Spirit, and the wonderful utterances of truth and experience under that illumination.
And if the tongue of fire sits not now upon the head of
the disciples, yet the living flame of the Holy Ghost
burns brightly in their hearts.

It is the province of the Spirit, as an illuminator, to
take the things of God and show them unto us. It declares to us our adoption, our sonship with Christ, and
our heirship to all the treasures of eternity. " The Spirit
itself beareth witness with our spirit that we are the
children of God." Thus light from the three Persons of
the Godhead, as well as from the inspired Word, shines

upon the believer. No wonder that with the first breaking in of such light upon the soul that has long lain in darkness he should be enraptured and overwhelmed. Oh! there is true significance in the oft-repeated utterances of the newly converted soul, that he has been brought into the light, that the room was light, that everything around him seemed to glow with a heavenly light, that the sun in the heavens shone with an increased brilliancy, that the faces of the saints beamed with light, that he seemed to be in a new world where everything was praising God. The light is in his own soul, for God has poured down light from heaven upon him. He has become a child of light. He belongs now to the kingdom of light, and no wonder that amid the gleaming of truth in his soul, and the shining of the Holy Ghost, and the smiling of God's countenance, and the rising of the Sun of Righteousness, everything should look luminous with glory. There was no such shining as this in the kingdom of darkness.

Now let him walk in the light, and it will never abate but will steadily increase. There is no growing dim, and flickering, and going out of the light to him who walks in the narrow way. Yet the faintest light is at this end of the path, and the strongest at the other end, as we near heaven. " The path of the just is as a shining light, that shineth more and more unto the perfect day." If from the hour of conversion any man has experienced an abatement of his first light, it is not that the narrow way has become beclouded and dark, but he has stepped out of it. There are but two roads for us to travel to eternity—one narrow and the other broad, one light and the other dark ; and God will never light up the broad way for our accommodation, nor will He ever let the light go out in the narrow way.

LOWEST STATE.

I pass now to remark, that to walk in the light as He is in the light is the lowest possible state of grace in which we can walk and be the children of God. We must do this to be accepted of Him in any sense. We must do it to retain the favor of God. We must do it before the attainment of entire holiness. We must do it in the process of its attainment. The very first question to propound to a seeker of holiness is, "Are you now walking in the light as God is in the light?" If not, you must first be converted or reclaimed before you can be a successful seeker of holiness.

Now, in proof that walking in the light as God is in the light pertains to the lowest grade of Christian experience as well as the highest, I refer you to Christ and His apostles. Christ said, "I am come a light into the world, that whosoever believeth in me should not abide in darkness." Not whosoever is sanctified, but whosoever believeth. "He that followeth me shall not walk in darkness, but shall have the light of life;" "Ye are the light of the world," is nowhere limited to those who are entirely holy, but is addressed to all the disciples. St. John says, "If we say that we have fellowship with Him, and walk in darkness, we lie, and do not the truth." But fellowship with God is based upon adoption, and pertains to all Christians. Fellowship is a family life, and signifies the friendship, intercourse, and communion between God the Father and all His children. The weakest believer has fellowship with God, the merest

8

babe in Christ—as with a family on earth where between parent and child look answers to look and smile to smile —has communion with God. " If we walk in the light, as He is in the light, we have fellowship one with another;" that is, the soul and God, as the text means, have communion with one another. There is a blessed friendship and intercourse between them. He communes with God and God communes with him, and then "the blood of Jesus Christ His Son cleanseth from all sin."

But walking in the light, as He is in the light, no more implies the entire purity of the nature than walking in the light of the natural sun by day implies the perfect health of the body. And just as a man with a measure of strength may walk out in the light of the sun, but with secret disease lurking about the heart; so a man may walk in the light of God, but with moral disease yet lurking at the seat of life, and insidiously working there, and that must be kept constantly under the control of the Great Physician, or it will increase and spread, and over-match all human skill and power, and end in eternal death.

Or, using another Scripture figure, the newly-converted soul, receiving the good seed, may, in the genial light of the sun, send up a golden harvest of righteousness, and peace, and joy in the Holy Ghost; but with the living roots of depravity, called by the Holy Ghost " roots of bitterness," secretly ramified all through that soil, and that God must deaden and hold in check, or they will spring up and trouble him, and defile many. Said the Apostle to his own brethren, confessedly believers in Christ, who were walking in the light, " Looking diligently lest any root of bitterness springing up trouble you, and thereby many be defiled." Said the Saviour, "Every branch in me that beareth fruit, He purgeth it that it may bring forth more fruit." And yet the branch is in Christ; and "If any man be in Christ, he is a new creature," and he "beareth fruit." He is, therefore, a true Christian, a fruitful Christian, and yet God purgeth him.

There is, then, in every such branch, in every such Christian, something to be purged from, something beyond the reach of human power, something of moral evil and defilement that limits our fruitfulness, and is so commingled with our very life, and so tenacious of its place in our spiritual being, that it will not die out of itself, and no human power can expel it. Its removal is the work of God. It requires the skill and power of the Infinite to separate it and take it away. "He purgeth it," not that it may die and go to heaven, but that it may live and be more fruitful. This shows that sin yet remains, even in those who walk in the light.

Do we inquire why, when God brings a man into the light of conversion, He does not effect a complete renovation of his nature, and make him, at a word, pure as a seraph? or, in other words, "Has not God power to make a man holy in a single act? What necessity, then, for dividing this work?"

We reply that Infinite Power is guided and applied by infinite wisdom. His power might have created the world as it did Adam—in full maturity. His power might also have made him a perfect linguist, a perfect mathematician, perfect in mind as well as in body; but His wisdom ordained the attainment of knowledge and strength by another process.

His power might have prohibited the entrance of sin into this world. He might have held Satan bound in chains, so that his hellish breath should never have blasted earth, and so that there never should have been a polluted human heart, and thus have precluded the necessity of atonement, and made man a saint without a Saviour, and a seraph without blood. But infinite wisdom restrained His power, and suffered the fall, and then instituted and executed redemption, and man is saved through the blood of Jesus. Why, it does not become an earth-born worm to inquire when God has not revealed.

God has power to make a believing penitent in an instant as pure as an angel; but His wisdom has ordained, first, to forgive him, and shed abroad in him His love, and adopt him, and pour light upon him, and then lead him in the light to the fountain of atoning blood, to be washed from all sin.

While we are assured in the Scriptures that the babe in Christ is yet carnal, that the fruitful branch in Christ must be purged, that the believer who walks in the light as He is in the light must be cleansed from sin, that the beloveds who cling to the promises must be cleansed from the filthiness of the flesh and spirit;— while all this teaches us that sin remains in the heart of a believer though it does not reign there, that its pollution continues though its power is broken, and while Christian experience is found exactly to accord with this divine teaching; yet we are nowhere taught that sin in the heart of a believer is destroyed or washed away, but by the blood of Jesus applied by faith and in an instant.

LIGHT NOT CLEANSING.

Though we are to walk in the light, yet the text does not teach us, nor does any other Scripture, that light has any cleansing properties for a corrupted soul. It is nowhere intimated that the soul's defilement can be bleached out by the gradual process of the shining light. Light is nowhere invested with power to purify the heart. The province of light is to shine—to shine away our darkness, to make our loathsome depravity visible; but when we have seen it, and our souls sicken at the sight and groan for deliverance, God takes us then to another element; another agency is provided for our cleansing, even the blood of Jesus. The light shows us our need; in the blood we find our remedy. The light discovers to us our defilement; the blood takes it away. The light leads us to the fountain; in the blood of the fountain we wash and are clean.

The Christian walks, and walks in the light, but he does not walk himself pure; he does not walk into purity, but he walks to the fountain, and the blood cleanses him. There is no Christian effort or exercise that can purge a soul from sin. There is nowhere the slightest intimation that one step can wash away one stain; that the gradual advance of a Christian by consecutive steps of obedience is attended by a gradual cleansing of the heart, tinge after tinge departing, till every stain is gone. It is not said, if we walk in the light as He is in the light, the light shall make us pure, or by walking we walk away from our sins. No, no! There is no such merit as this in walking; but "the blood of Jesus Christ His Son cleanseth us." In the light we walk to the cross, and there we are cleansed by blood.

The Christian must "grow in grace and in the knowledge of God," and by every step of walking in the light he does grow ; but there is no measure of the knowledge of God, or of the love of God, that can crowd out inborn depravity. It can no more be removed by growth than the growth of a tree can destroy the worm at its root, or the growth of a child destroy hereditary disease, or the growth of the wheat cast out the pernicious roots in the soil.

Neither will these roots of bitterness ever die out or rot out of themselves, as the roots in the earth. Depravity is a most desperate thing, and wonderfully tenacious of life. You cannot shine it out, you cannot bleach it out, you cannot walk it out, you cannot grow it out; it survives all your theories, it outlives all your efforts ; it is a living and deadly thing, and it clings with the grip of hell and the tenacity of Satan to your soul. It has conquered humanity and bids defiance to Deity, yea, to everything in heaven, earth, or hell, but the blood of Jesus. But here is a Divine Energy that conquers it. It yields quickly, yea, instantly, to the blood, the efficacious blood of Jesus. "The blood of Jesus Christ His Son cleanseth from all sin."

The certain and infallible result of walking in the light is, that it will lead speedily to the fountain of Jesus' blood. Not walking for a period and then ceasing to walk, not for a season in the light and then groping in darkness, but a steady walk in the light reaches soon the blood.

The light, if followed, will soon flash conviction for holiness upon him who follows it, deep and pungent as when first awakened. Not conviction of guilt, for he who walks in the light has no guilt. Not a sense of condemnation—" There is, therefore, now no condemnation to them which are in Christ Jesus"—but a conviction of indwelling sin. That light will shine into the depths of his heart, and show him the great deep of depravity that he has never been able to fathom before. It will flash all through that charnel-house of incipient and abortive sins, and discover to him such a mass of unholy passions, stunned and deadened by the grace of God,—of suppressed desires, of smothered feelings, of principles of enmity and rebellion only held in check by grace, all making such a body of death, yet hidden within him,—that he will loathe himself, and long for the power of God to remove these relics of moral death, and for the blood of Christ to wash out their foul stains. This, when a believer thus sees himself, is conviction for holiness—when the Spirit takes him down into this workshop of iniquity, where unholy thoughts originate, where lust is conceived, where pride has its seat, where love of the world lays its schemes, where malice plots its mischief, and where sin has its home and plants its engines of destruction. If he walks in the light, that light will bring him down into this sink of iniquity, where he will see

> " Such dark and grainèd spots
> As will not leave their tinct."

Such a discovery of inbred sin yet dwelling in his heart, though not suffered to break out in his life, cannot but be a painful conviction.

Let him follow now that ray of light, and while it

shows him the plague of his nature, and enables him to make a full discovery of his foes, and his weakness, and his want, it will lead him also to groan for inward purity. A sense of want will so press upon him as to cause him to exclaim—

> " My restless soul cries out oppressed,
>   Impatient to be freed;
> Nor can I, Lord, nor will I rest
>   Till I am saved indeed."

Yea, such intense desire for purity will take hold of him that his heart and flesh will cry out for the living God, and his language will be—

> " My heart-strings groan with deep complaint,
>   My flesh lies panting, Lord, for Thee;
> And every bone and every joint
>   Stretches for perfect purity."

Let him follow that ray of light and it will lead him next to an unreserved consecration to God. Not the consecration of anything new, for he is already the Lord's when in the light; but he renews the offering of himself with reference to a new state of grace, a holy heart, and a holy life. He sets himself apart now to be a subject of the all-cleansing blood of Jesus. He offers himself to God now in view of a distinct experience, a distinct confession of Christ, and distinct labor for the promotion of holiness.

He has come now to the fountain opened for sin and uncleanness; he stands upon its brink; the light has led him there, and he waits the cleansing. Waits? He need not wait one moment. "Behold, now is the ac-

cepted time, now is the day of salvation." Faith alone
brings him in contact with the cleansing blood. One
resolute, venturesome, desperate act of faith, and the
great salvation is obtained; a belief not merely that
God will do it, nor a cold intellectual belief that God
has done it, and calmly wait the witness, but the bold,
positive utterance of the soul, " HE DOETH IT;" and then
and there he will feel the warm, gushing blood of Jesus
applied, and flowing all through his polluted soul, leaving not a spot nor a stain, and the blessed word is verified in an instant, " Though your sins be as scarlet, they
shall be as white as snow; though they be red like crimson, they shall be as wool." There is no pollution so deep
but the blood flows to it; there is no depravity so dark
but the blood washes it away. Is depravity sin? Is
enmity sin? Is pride sin? The blood cleanseth from
all sin; and in this fountain the believer is made in an
instant so completely pure, that the eye of Omniscience
even discerns not one stain. It cleanseth from all sin.

INFERENCES.

With a few inferences we close. We learn from it,

1st. That to be a Christian in the lowest sense is a
very exalted state. There are very many who have so
fearfully let down the standard of true piety, that they
take conviction for conversion, and conversion for holiness; who fancy that holiness is deliverance from *sinning;* that to be holy is to be saved from open transgression, and that a believer may live in sin and yet have
favor with God.

In distinction from this, we learn from this subject
that it is a wonderful thing to be a Christian at all;

that the lowest grade of a Christian is saved from guilt, saved from pollution, saved from sinning, and walks in the light as God is in the light.

2d. We learn from this subject the great reason why so many are indifferent to Christian holiness, why so many are opposed to it, and why so few enter into it. They do not walk in the light, steadily justified before God.

It is impossible for one to be a true Christian, and walk very long in the light, and read in that light the Divine command, "Be ye holy, for I, the Lord your God, am holy," and read of the wonderful provisions of the Atonement, and the precious promises of God's Word to cleanse him from all sin, and remain indifferent to this great work of grace. Indifference to holiness is evidence that a man is under the power of darkness. Opposition to holiness originates from the same cause. It is strange indeed, that Christian holiness should have any enemies or opposers; but it is no more strange than true. And these are found in the Church as well as out of it —in the pulpit as well as in the pew. They were to be found in Wesley's day, they are to be found now—men who not merely question and warn, but who hate and revile. The reason is they are not walking in the light, for the light leads every man towards holiness; and when you hear professors talking of Christian holiness just as sinners talk, and when they are feeling just as they feel, and thinking just as they think, there can be no doubt about their position,—they are the real enemies of holiness.

And this enmity arises from the rejection of light. Oh! how many have been convicted for holiness; but the flashing light has been to them a painful glare, revealing to them duties that they were unwilling to perform, crosses that they were unwilling to bear, sacrifices that they were unwilling to make, a narrow way in which they were unwilling to walk; and they have closed their eyes against the light, and God has withdrawn it from them, and they dwell " at ease in Zion."

It is but a short way from pardon to purity to him who walks in the light,—no farther, proportionately, than from Egypt to Canaan. The reason the Israelites wandered so long, and their carcasses fell in the wilderness, and they never entered the land of promise, was that they walked disobediently; and the great reason so many wander for years without entering this Canaan of rest, and fall by the hand of death without it, is that they do not walk in the light.

A few months, yea, weeks or days, yea, a shorter time than this, will bring to the fountain him who walks in the light; and the washing which was commenced and in part accomplished at conversion will be completed, yea, completed in an instant, for it is not by works, but by faith. And hence now, " If we walk in the light, as He is in the light, we have fellowship one with another, and the blood of Jesus Christ His Son cleanseth us from all sin."

CHAPTER XV.

MR. MUNGER'S SERMON.

" *Sanctify them.*"—JOHN xvii. 17.

IN considering this subject it is important that every
step should touch the Rock of Ages ; therefore we reverently inquire for the real meaning of this petition. Our
thoughts may be indicated by two words—*what* and
when—what did Jesus mean when He prayed " Holy
Father, sanctify them," and when was this sanctification
to occur ?

Christ prayed first for His personal disciples ; afterwards for all who should believe in Him through their
word.

The meaning of this petition is indicated in part by
the preceding petition, " Holy Father, keep them."
This implies a definite religious experience already attained, in which they were to be preserved, and to which
the sanctification prayed for was to be supplemented.
What was that experience already attained by the disciples ?

1. They were disciples, and as such had faith in

Jesus as the Saviour of men. The first utterance which attracted them to Jesus was "Behold the Lamb of God which taketh away the sins of the world!" The genuineness of their faith and love they had proven by the actual abandonment of all for Christ's sake, thus accepting the severest test of discipleship ever proposed by the Saviour. Christ not only accepted them as disciples, but called and ordained them to the ministry and apostleship of His incoming kingdom. They exhibited a most ardent attachment to Him. "Let us go that we may die with Him," said the most timid and doubtful Thomas. And at the last supper they all declared that they were ready to go with Him to prison and to death.

On the other hand, Christ acknowledged the sincerity of their love and the genuineness of their devotion, in terms which can never be applied to unregenerate men. He called them His "little children," His "friends;" and as such gave them the sacramental bread and wine, with the promise that He would drink it new with them in the heavenly kingdom. Hear Him again: I go to prepare a place for you. Because I live ye shall live. My peace I give unto you. I am the vine, ye are the branches. Abide in me, continue in my love. To His Father He said of them, Thine they were, and they have kept Thy word; and, Thine are mine, and I am glorified in them. I have kept them in Thy name, and none of them is lost save the son of perdition.

Had they remained unregenerate to that hour, they all were the sons of perdition. But the Saviour puts that matter beyond question by the terms and symbols employed to set forth the relations existing between

Himself and them.   No one can for a moment suppose that Christ could contradict His life, works, and teaching by applying these terms to unregenerate men, for " except a man be born again he cannot see the kingdom of God."

When Jesus prayed " Holy Father, keep them," He distinctly recognized this antecedent experience ; and the burden of His desire was that they might be preserved in that faith, consecration, and love.   The next petition, " Father, sanctify them," must supplement this. It was not a prayer for what was a work already done, but for something to be done.   This shows that the sanctification here prayed for was not the initial sanctification of discipleship, nor their official consecration to the apostleship and ministry, for this had already been received.   What then was it but the completion of their heart-cleansing, and their endowment with those spiritual gifts which Christ had just promised should attend the approaching baptism of the Holy Ghost ?   But if they were already true children of God and heirs of the kingdom, what need of another work, sometimes called a second blessing ?

Their life answers this question most satisfactorily. We trace their history to within ten days of Pentecost, and find elements of weakness and disaster sufficient to overthrow the entire Christian movement.   We find in them the very same evils which afflict and enslave so many of God's dear children to-day, and which if allowed to remain will produce the most fearful disasters to the individual and to the Church.   Their history evinces a strange admixture of faith and doubt, of seeing and not seeing, of learning and forgetting, of courage and cowardice, of strength and weakness, of firm purpose but unsteady practice, of self-renunciation and self-seeking, of charity and bigotry, of humility and pride, of meekness and ambition, of brotherly love and family jars, of sweet concord and painful disputes, of sincere desires to serve Christ and a wish to be honored of men. Peter was strong-headed but weak-hearted, sincere and ardent, zealous even to rashness, but unsteady, and at times cowardly. James and John, by reason of their impetuous tempers, were called " sons of thunder " or commotion. Disciples with such natures involved a special need; and hence, perhaps, Christ kept them near Him, and in the inner circle of His life granted them extraordinary privileges. His work needed their peculiarities of original temperament, and they needed His special grace in order not to break down in the work given them. That brave heart which dared to draw the sword single-handed upon the multitude was a necessity ; but it needed to be disciplined to wait for orders from on high, and then obey them. It needed the *dash* which threw Peter into the sea, but it needed also a steadfast faith which would not yield. An aged slave testified that when God sanctified her soul He gave her a holding-on faith. With this she walked in triumph the angry sea of slave life forty years, and entered the haven with shouts of victory. Now when Jesus prayed for the sanctification of His disciples, is it not evident that the burden of His heart respecting them was just this, that all these elements of weakness inherent in their original constitution, or acquired by habit, should be removed, and what they lacked should be supplied, and every power and peculiarity should be wholly purified and consecrated, and employed under the Divine supervision in the Master's work ? It meant evidently that they should be cured thoroughly of the leprosy of inbred sin ; that Peter should be cured of his cowardice, and be made steady as well as strong; that James and John should be cleansed of their bigotry, so they would not forbid a disciple casting out devils " because he followed not with us." The sanctifying power would take from them that vindictiveness which would call fire from heaven upon the Samaritans because they would not receive the Lord, would cure them of that ambition which sought office in the kingdom, and of that evil desire which disputed who should be greatest. The prayer answered would deliver Philip from his lingering thirst for sensible manifestations. It would wonderfully change the cautious, doubtful, despondent Thomas, whose fear to venture settled into a wilful unbelief, saying, " Except I see I will not believe ;" and enable him to enjoy the blessedness of those who, having not seen, believe, and believing, rejoice with joy unspeakable and full of glory.

But the sanctification for which the Saviour prayed in behalf of His disciples was not only a deliverance from moral evil, but also an endowment with spiritual gifts. It was not only a release from bonds, but the possession of heavenly powers and privileges. The all-comprehensive gift was the entrance of the Father, Son, and Holy Ghost into the purified heart, to abide there, as in God's holy temple. This Trinity, said Jesus, should come into them and abide with them at " that day," and thus they should be "*filled* with all the fulness of God." This distinguishes the Pentecostal sanctification from every antecedent phase of their religious life. The completeness of the cleansing, and of the Divine occupancy and control, form the crowning glory of this grace. When God should be enthroned in the heart and reign supreme, He would dispense spiritual gifts according to His pleasure; and that pleasure was indicated to the disciples by the Saviour in His last discourse before His death, as recorded in the 14th, 15th, and 16th chapters of John. "Ye shall receive power," said Jesus, "after that the Holy Ghost is come upon you." Power, complete and abiding, expresses the fulness of these gifts. The various elements of this power are unfolded by the Saviour in those chapters. They comprise a fulness of light and knowledge by the teaching of the Word and Spirit; a fulness of peace and joy, by the indwelling God; a fulness of fruitage by the Holy Ghost in answer to prayer and labor. "At that day ye shall *know* that I am in the Father, and *ye in me and I in you.*" The Divinity of Christianity as well as our personal relations to it, but especially the amazing grace of an indwelling God, are so attested to the sanctified heart, that they are beyond question or doubt. • Therefore said Jesus, "At that day ye shall *know.*" And this was to be abiding: "My father will love him, and we will come unto him, and make our abode with him;" "And He shall give you another Comforter, that He may abide with you forever."

II. When, according to the design of the Saviour, was this sanctification to be received?

This question is determined by the object sought. The *time* of the work is plainly shown from the *object* or design of the work. The main current of thought in the whole prayer seems to be about this: "Holy Father, keep them; Holy Father, sanctify them; that they all may be one in us, that the world may know that Thou hast sent me and hast loved them, and that they also may be with me where I am, that they may behold my glory." In this series of petitions, reaching from earth to heaven, one thing depends upon another, and the sanctification here prayed for is the pivot of all. We may express the connection and relations of the thoughts thus: Keep them, that they may be sanctified. Sanctify them, that they may be kept. Sanctify them, that they may be perfect in us, that they may be with me in the vineyard work and in the harvest-home. Sanctify them, that they may be preserved, united in one, and ultimately glorified. Keep them, by cleansing them from those tendencies which incline to apostacy and sin. Keep them, by investing them with power from on high, that they may be more than conquerors. But in order to this keeping of them, must be their sanctification. Therefore, as the keeping is here, so must the sanctification be here. Sanctify them that they may be one. But as this unity of the Spirit in the bond of love is designed for earth, so is the sanctification which is the only way to do it. Sanctify them, that they may be with me and behold my glory. Holiness here, and heaven hereafter, is the law of God's changeless economy. But Jesus designed more than this: He came to save the lost, and this work in the Church was to bear directly upon that object of His mission. Hence the prayer runs thus: Sanctify them, believers, that the world may know that Thou hast sent me and hast loved them." Speaking of the baptism of the Holy Ghost, Jesus said to His disciples, "At that day *ye* shall know that I am in my Father, and ye in me, and I in you." The sanctification of the Spirit would satisfy them of the Divinity of Christianity, and of their own participation in its richest blessings. And the same sanctification enjoyed by His Church was to convince the world that both Christ and His Church are divinely loved and commissioned. Sanctify them, "that the world may know that Thou hast sent me and hast loved them." But when and where is the world to be thus convinced? Not after death, not in death, but while it is called "to-day." The world is to be converted, instrumentally, by a sanctified Church: "Create in me a clean heart, and uphold me by thy free Spirit; then will I teach transgressors thy ways, and sinners shall be converted unto Thee;" "Sanctify them," said Jesus, "that the world may believe." But the world must believe before death; therefore the Church, which is to convince the world, must stand up before it in this life, sanctified wholly, and preserved blameless by the power of an indwelling God. Nothing is plainer than that Christ contemplates this sanctification for His Church while on the field of battle; for a Church thus sanctified, and that only, can conquer the world. "Blessed be the Lord God of Israel, for He hath visited and redeemed His people, and hath raised up an horn of salvation for us . . . . to perform the mercy promised, and to remember His holy covenant; that He would grant unto us that we, being delivered out of the hand of our enemies, might serve Him without fear in holiness and righteousness before Him, *all the days of our life.*"

MR. LAWRENCE'S SERMON.

2 Peter i. 1.—" *Precious faith.*"

THE text, like its Divine Author, introduces itself; and hence, without waste of time about the threshold, I may proceed to the subject itself—" Precious Faith." Consider:

I. The nature of faith.

II. Its preciousness.

I. The nature of faith. Much has been written and spoken concerning the nature of faith, but nothing more to the purpose than those words of St. Paul,—" Faith is the substance of things hoped for, the evidence of things not seen ;" which sentiment might be run into another mould: " Faith is conviction that the Bible is the Word of God, and confidence in the fulfilment of the promises therein contained, as soon as ripe for fulfilment, or as soon as conditions are complied with."

1. Faith is conviction that the Bible is the Word of God.

Men have some of the best reasons conceivable for believing this proposition. Among these are three common-sense presumptions, and two facts.

First, it is presumable God would not leave man without a revelation of His will for his guidance. Two things are undeniably true. 1st. Man is ignorant. He does not know much until instructed by a superior intelligence.

Second, God is illimitably wise. This needs no proof. He who made all things knows all things.

Now can you, on the supposition that God is wise

and good, bring yourself to believe that when man needed knowledge about the vital questions of life, and God had it for him, that He would withhold it? Man's powers and faculties, if managed aright, will make him and all around him happy; but if managed amiss, will make himself and all around him miserable. Can you believe that God would leave man in ignorance of the manner in which he should manage his own powers? that He would set up an engine and start it, and give the engineer no knowledge of it, or control over it? Common sense says God would make a revelation of His will to man.

The second presumption is, that God has made such a revelation. Many thousands of years have passed since man sprang forth from the creative hand of God, and as soon as he lived he needed the divine law to restrain and guide him. Hence God's statute of laws and book of instructions must have been compiled, issued, and distributed long ere this, and we aver it is now in the world.

The third presumption is, God's book must have something about it that distinguishes it from all other publications. The very idea of a revelation implies this; for if there is nothing about it that marks it as a book from God, it might as well not have been issued at all. If you receive a letter from father or mother, you discern its authorship by the handwriting, by the terms used, by the signature. If Charles Dickens should issue a new work, but withhold from it his name, the literary world would at once detect its authorship, for there is but one Dickens. And does not God possess individuality and originality of thought and expression? Some hypercritics have been considerably troubled that the Bible was not written in their style, and perhaps it is a pity! If God has written a book it is in His own style, of which there can be no counterfeit. The Book of Divine laws is in the world, and so unique and peculiar that it cannot be counterfeited, mistaken, or hidden.

2. Consider now the two facts.

First, there is no book, if you lay the Bible aside, that comes up to what common sense would say a Divine revelation should be. You cannot claim that the Koran, Book of Mormon, or any of the musty Indian manuscripts come up to this standard. So, putting the Bible aside, the world is without a word from God to this day.

The second fact is, that the Bible is just what we might antecedently suppose a Divine revelation to such a creature as man would be.

It gives us the information we need concerning God, Satan, ourselves; the means of recovery from the fall, the nature of holiness, sin, heaven, and hell.

No item of information that man needs is in this book denied. Such considerations as these carry us along to the conclusion that the Bible is the word of God. And this is the first layer in the masonry of the temple of faith.

2. The second branch of faith is, confidence that the promises in the Bible will be fulfilled upon compliance with the conditions. We believe to the saving of the soul when we ascertain just what God's promises are, and then take just what they offer.

God says, "Do thus and so, and I will forgive and

bless you;" and now it is for us, according to our best ability, helped by the Holy Ghost, to do just what He tells us, and then to *believe* that God does His part whether we *see* that it is done or not.

We may just here mention some preparatives to faith. 1st. Knowledge of the promises. 2d. Mental and actual renunciation and forsaking of sin. You cannot believe God saves you while you are holding on to any known or suspected form of sin. You may try to work yourself up to the believing point, but it is all of no use until you renounce sin. 3d. Consecration of your all to God.

Now you are ready to take God at his word. You are a sinner—you feel it. Your sins burden you. In your repentance and agony you cry out, " Who shall deliver me from the body of this death ? " You look into the Book of God, and find these words of Jesus : " Come unto me, all ye that labor and are heavy laden, and I will give you rest." Immediately you cry out, "Here, Lord, I come. I am the burdened, laboring soul invited by Thee. To Thee I come; no other help I know. I believe Thou dost impart the promised rest." And though no change for the moment is felt, yet the soul rests in full confidence that the work is being done, and perhaps the very next moment has cause to say, " Thanks be unto God, who giveth us the victory through our Lord Jesus Christ." But should the witness be some time delayed, the soul still rests on God, in a manner that seems to say,—

> " Wrestling, I will not let Thee go,
> Till I Thy name, Thy nature know."

Or are you seeking entire purity of heart ? Conviction of inbred sin has been felt ; the soul is hungering and thirsting after righteousness; the consecration has been made; all is cast down at the Saviour's feet, and now the soul wrestles and agonizes for the blessing. What more can be done? The word of God is opened, and here stands out the promise: "What things soever ye desire when ye pray, believe that ye receive them, and· ye shall have them." "Precious declaration!" you cry; "I desire a clean heart."

> "Nothing less do I desire
> Than Thy pure love within my breast;
> This, only this, do I require,
> And freely give up all the rest!"

"Now, Lord, I have done all that is required of me, according to my best understanding; and though I have not as yet the witness of the Spirit, yet I believe Thou doest the work: I now receive purity. On the strength of Thy word I believe it."

"But," asks one, "would you have me believe that I receive when I have no sensible evidence thereof?" Yes, having prepared your soul by help Divine as just shown, God would now have you honor Him by just such a faith as this.

In temporal matters men often believe that they receive without any sensible evidence—believe on the strength of a promise. There is a man along the street that I wish to see. I ask, "Sir, can I see you at your office directly?" He answers, "Yes, as soon as I go down to the wharf and get some goods. I have hired this porter and his cart for that purpose."—"Are the goods at the wharf now?"—"Oh no; they are on the steamboat coming up the river; I sent for them by a trusty expressman who has never deceived me, and I *am receiving* them. Hark! do you not hear the bell? They are at the wharf now." And down he goes and returns with his goods. " Believe that ye *receive* them, and ye shall have them." This is not unreasonable; for Jesus, our daysman and intercessor, has gone to the throne of the Father with His blood, to purchase pardon and purity for you and me, and can you not believe that you *do* receive?

> " The Father hears Him pray;
>   His dear anointed one,
>   He cannot turn away,
>   The presence of His Son."

Look up in faith, and say:

> "'Tis done; Thou dost this moment save—
>   With full salvation bless,
>   Redemption through Thy blood I have,
>   And spotless love and peace."

Faith never doubts the word of God. When she is conscious that the conditions have been complied with, she says, " It is done; He is faithful who hath promised."

We have many remarkable instances of this kind of faith recorded in the word of God—instances in which God has been trusted against feeling, against human reason and philosophy so-called, and yet He was always found true to His word.

See Abraham sitting in the door of his tent! God tells him to take his son to a mountain in the land of Moriah, and there give him for a burnt-offering. Without conferring with flesh and blood, he prepares for the journey and the awful service; and on the morning of the third day I see him on the top of the mountain, with the altar built, fire kindled, Isaac bound, and the knife raised to strike the blow. "What now, Abraham, thou wilt not slay thy son, and thus make the promise of God of none effect? Has not God said, 'In Isaac shall thy seed be called?'"—"Yes, I know that is the promise, but now God has commanded me to offer Isaac for a burnt-offering, and I will do it, for God will raise him from the dead."—"But didst thou ever see one rise from the dead that had been cut in pieces and burnt to ashes?"—"No; but the same God who made the *promise* has given the commandment, and the command shall not make war on the promise, and God will raise Isaac for the promise' sake." How the Patriarch's faith carries him above the dust raised by feeble human reason! Abraham knew that God's promises would march right forward to fulfilment. Believe that ye receive, and ye shall have.

Behold that woman down there by the river Nile! It is Jochebed, the wife of Amram. She has the infant Moses in her arms. "Woman, what art thou doing here? Knowest thou not that the crocodile and other river monsters prowl here for their prey? It is no place for thee and helpless little Moses: get thee back to Amram's tent, and save the life of thy precious boy." As the tears fall from her eyes, she answers: "There is no safety for Moses at home, for Pharaoh's officers were there yesterday to kill him. And now I have prepared this bulrush boat, into which I shall place the child and launch him out, and let God take care of him."—"Why, you don't see God anywhere hereabout, do you? but see, yonder is a crocodile ready to devour your child."—"No, I don't see God, but He is here, and will take care of my child, for I have His promise." She executes her purpose, and the waves gently rock the sleeping child, until Pharaoh's daughter comes and takes the boy to the king's palace, that God's will may be fulfilled.

There is an old man in the streets of Jerusalem: "Well, Simeon, a few days more and you will finish your course."—"I shall not see death until I have seen the Lord's Christ."—"Simeon, is there any more sign of His coming now than when the fathers fell asleep? What reason have you to suppose that the Messiah will come during the few days yet allotted you?"—"The Holy Ghost has told me so, and I shall yet see Him."

Unbelief says, "The old man is surely demented." But soon Simeon goes up into the temple and sees Mary with the infant Jesus, "to do for Him after the manner of the law;" and Simeon immediately recognizes Him. "Mary, I would hold your babe a moment," and taking Him in his arms, and looking down into the depths of those eyes divine, his soul filled with the joy of assurance, he exclaims, "Now, Lord, lettest thou thy servant depart in peace, for mine eyes have seen thy salvation." God's word never fails. Trust Him for full salvation now, and you will prove His promise true, and He will save you from the last foul taint of sin.

> "Oh for a faith that will not shrink,
>   Though pressed by every foe;
> That will not tremble on the brink
>   Of any earthly woe."

II. Let us consider the *preciousness of faith*. And yet its preciousness has been appearing all along in the preceding reflections. "And what shall I more say," only to sum up what has already been expressed?

1. It is precious as the means by which spiritual life is conveyed to the soul. I was dead in trespasses and in sins. The Great Physician was a great way off, methought. Faith brought Him nigh, and kept Him in my soul until I was fully restored; and now "I live, yet not I, but Christ liveth in me, and the life I now live in the flesh, I live by the faith of the Son of God, who loved me, and gave himself for me."

2. Faith is the medium by which the soul is kept in communication with the fountain of life. "The just shall live by faith," and they live well at that.

3. Precious, because it takes the soul to the all-cleansing fountain, and keeps it there. I want to keep this blessing of perfect love, and take it home with me. I have upon my heart the honey-dew of salvation, and I would carry it with me where'er I go. Faith has engaged to insure me against the loss of this blessing.

4. Precious as the " shield " against the "fiery darts of the wicked one." The musketeers of hell are out shooting souls. Faith in God will defend you, quenching every fiery dart.

5. Faith is precious because she gives us a glimpse of Home once in a while, to cheer us by the way. Heavenly home ! Fall not those words sweetly on the ear ? It is " just over there." Sometimes it seems afar off. Clouds and fogs intervene. Doubt, an infernal magician, conjures up dark mountains between us and that cherished spot. But faith draws aside the veil of clouds and fogs, makes the mountains skip away like lambs, and shows us the goodly land with peace and plenty blessed.

6. Precious faith also takes away the sting of death.

Apart from the faith of the Son of God, we are never quite free from the fear of death. You may be tired of life. Disappointment may have murdered all your earthly hopes. Disease may have destroyed all the remains of health. Your home may have lost all its loved inmates. The wish to live may have died out of the soul. And yet you shrink back from death. What is beyond? Whither will the dark-winged messenger lead us? Will not the ills before be worse than those from which you are escaping?

Faith solves these questions, and opens to you the gates of paradise. A soldier was dying on the battle-field, far away from home and friends. An attendant asked, "Are you ready to die?"—" Yes."—" To what church do you belong?"—" To the Church of Christ." —" Of what persuasion are you?"—" Persuasion! persuasion!" exclaimed the dying man; " I am persuaded that neither life, nor death, nor angels, nor principalities, nor powers, nor things present, nor things to come, nor height, nor depth, nor any other creature, shall be able to separate me from the love of God which is in Christ Jesus our Lord;" and he was gone. Faith conducted him to yon crossing on the river of Death. Faith is precious—precious all the way along from the altar of conversion to the hour of final dissolution.

" Have faith in God." Faith brings forgiveness, holiness, happiness, and heaven.

During the delivery of the above sermon, those anxious to consecrate themselves fully to God were first asked to rise; then, at a suitable time, those believing their consecration received or accepted, were asked to

do so ; and afterward those believing that God sanctified the gift, were also asked to stand on their feet.
Hundreds arose every time, the Spirit of God was wonderfully poured out, and at one time it seemed that the
congregation would get beyond the preacher's control.

CHAPTER XVI.

SERMON OF REV. A. E. BALLARD, OF NEW JERSEY CONFERENCE.

Heb. xii. 14.—" *Follow peace with all men, and holiness, without which no man shall see the Lord.*"

THE theme of Holiness is one of the most important as well as beautiful of Holy Writ. It is the grand object of all Christianity, and the central doctrine of *all* its states. It is the gospel's splendor-flaming city set upon a hill—beautiful for situation, and the joy of the whole earth. A sight of its bread of life excites delightful hunger in the soul ; a glance at its living waters produces joyous thirst; a vision of its paradise compels a longing for the fragrance of its roses ; the flashes of its glory stimulate a desire for steady noontide currents ; and whenever presented to the sincere Christian soul, it *appears* both one of the most important and beautiful doctrines of the word of God.

I understand the terms " holiness," " perfect love," and " wholly sanctified," to mean one and the same thing, and to refer to a state of Christian character attainable by any child of God, at any period of its Christian career. I understand " perfection," in its general application, to mean that maturity of spiritual existence, when the soul has grown through all the phases of its life to "the measure of the stature of a man in Christ Jesus." With this distinction kept in view it is possible that some of the confusion otherwise enveloping this subject will pass away.

Except in incidental sentences the Scriptures never argue this subject. They discuss repentance and justification in elaborate and exhaustive forms, but never holiness. They assume it as a fact whose self-evidence precludes dispute. No argument could make plainer the fact that we exist, and no argument could make plainer the doctrine of holiness. Strike that from its position in the gospel scheme, and there is nothing left to argue; for one who would ignore it must ignore not only particular passages, but the sum of all the Scriptures.

Probably one reason why it has been so seldom specialized as a pulpit subject is because it is really the foundation of *every* pulpit subject. Yet it is a happiness to know that this delightful experience is now being pressed upon the churches as a north star among the brilliancies of the Atonement, and a sun among the circling orbs of Faith and Hope, by whose power and glory the people may be lighted, not only into a higher and more beautiful Christian life, but also a more vigorous and powerful Christian aggressiveness.

Our Methodism has always so accepted it. Upon the necessity of spreading holiness over these lands, its organization was founded. To that point its literature has always converged. Its ministers have ever rolled such a gospel in words of holy flame from burning hearts and lips. Many of her members, in all ages,

have been its living witnesses, and to-day larger numbers than ever are pressing into its enjoyments and tes-
tifying to its truth.

I do not think it a doctrine difficult either of comprehension or experience. It is not a matter appreciable
only by the highest intellects of the Church, and to be
enjoyed only by her more intelligent members; but
something so entirely devoid of mystery, that the wayfaring man, though a fool, may understand. All that
is actually needed is the plain Bible, illuminated by the
spirit of truth, which God will give for the asking—
and illustrated by the experience of those who have
been able to tell the world of its enjoyment. With
these, or even without this last, any one may both see
and feel that the doctrine is of God.

I do not intend to employ these pages in nice distinctions. Whether holiness is simply justification, whether
it is an extension of justification, or something entirely
distinct from justification, are questions which I shall not
take your time to argue. If you are living in its enjoyment, these questions are easily settled for yourself; and
if you are *not* so living, you are as yet scarcely competent
to their decision. Like the new birth, it needs the revealings of experience for the full illumination of these
delicate distinctions. The general outline is appreciable
by intellect alone, but the inner knowledge depends upon
spiritual revealment. We must be *inside* the house in
order to *exact* interior description, and otherwise no
amount of outward calculation can furnish the picture.

I merely assume that the Apostles urge upon the
Church a state of religion transcending that enjoyed by
many of her members in that day. I assume, also, that

the experience of the Church in all the ages since has corresponded with that state of facts, and that the circumstances are the same to-day as at any former period of ecclesiastical history. And then, ignoring all side issues, ask the one earnest, pleading question, Are *you* holy?

If you are *not*, are you struggling for its attainment? If you are, are you laboring for its extension in your soul, or are you giving the most of your attention to the mint and anise and cumin, while you neglect the weightier matters of the law of holiness.

Holiness is being RIGHT. Right in inward feeling and right in outward life. A life that fulfils Christ's law in its externals, and a heart that fulfils it in the emotions. It is a will that is unquestionably controlled by that same law, and which controls in turn every power of the inward nature, so that body, soul, and spirit are in perfect harmony with the one grand law of God.

In an attempt to make it plain, I think it important that our views be neither too high nor too low, but *level* with the Scriptures, and so it is defined as a HUMAN HOLINESS. The developments of holiness, as they array the Eternal Father, would not fit me. Its glory shimmering from angelic robes is too brilliant to suit me. The difference in our natures would make their degree of holiness unholiness to me, and with all reverence I say I do not want it—nor do you. What God expects is something which assimilates itself with all the needs of a *human* nature, and nothing more; something which will permeate that nature like an atmosphere, filling it with health and blessing; that accepts the new birth as an introduction into spiritual life, and gives itself to that new life as strong and vigorous health; that enables him to look with holy rapture upon the islands of the sky and exclaim, " The heavens declare the glory of God;" that fills his vision with the sunlight filtering through the forest branches, or sparkling, gem-like, on the ocean, or flushing the mountain-tops with gold, or flooding the evening horizon with beauty, or tinting the soft green of the verdure, or brightening the flower diamonds of the plains, or kissing the pellucid waters of the brooklets, and impels him to feel that the earth is full of the glory of the Lord; that inspires his adoration in the study of celestial science, as he beholds how He hangeth the earth upon nothing; that comports with all the sweet relationships of domestic life, and lends a deeper tenderness to parentage, a more sacred beauty to filial affection, a closer affiliation to brother and sisterhood, and an intenser affection to the bonds of married life; that elevates all the *refreshments* of his nature, teaching him how to slumber in the security of love, to eat and drink with a sense of the Divine presence bathing him in blessing, and enabling him, in whatsoever he does, to do it to the glory of God; a holiness which demands the whole of our human nature for its exercise, and releases us from every demand which would transcend that nature.

It is not only a holiness compatible with human nature, but with FALLEN human nature. God's infinite pity bends down to what is our exact condition NOW, and circumscribes His law to that condition. The spiritual orbit circled by unfallen Adam is too high for me, for I am fallen below it. The pure glory which now adorns the brows of the just made perfect would not reflect rightly from mine, for their sphere is still

beyond that of Adam in his innocence.   In the onward
progress of being we may reach these, but *now* they
would, if fitted upon *us*, present the anomaly of a being
living above his order, and thus break the harmony of
the creation.   But such holiness as can fit a nature
which, though fallen, may be pure, I *do* want, and it is
made my privilege.   Holiness, thus adapted, conse-
crates even my mistakes, by showing the holy rectitude
of the intention.   It brings the divine smile even when
the flesh has failed in its godly labor, knowing that He
sees the spirit willing even if the flesh is weak.   It does
not allow us to forfeit our sense of the divine approba-
tion when a mistaken deed has wrought injury to the
cause of Christ, because it feels that *He* knows the
meaning was to bless that cause.   It shows him that
God is well pleased when he is in the severest trial or
sorest temptation, because the will has no thought of
yielding to its enemy.   The atonement takes all these
broken stones in his spiritual temple of character, and
cements them with the blood of Christ till Divinity de-
tects no flaw.   The ignorance and weakness which fill
his life with their mistakes are passed through the loom
of that atonement till all their strands are woven into
the robes of universal holiness.

It is also a PROBATIONARY holiness.   There is no pin-
nacle upon its loftiest temple from which we cannot
fall.   Adam stood upon its heights, and yet he fell.   Angels stood still higher, and yet were cast down.   Judas
was numbered among the Apostles, yet Satan entered
into him.   So long as we are in the flesh it is possible
to descend.   There is not the same extent of danger,
however, to one who is holy, as to others; but still there

is danger. His watch-towers must be occupied; he must wash in the crimson springs which bubble up in his pathway, in order to be safe and clean, yet his position is far in advance of others. For those others, one unsubdued passion may open the gate of the soul to its assailants, or one lukewarm feeling infect the rest with cowardice; but for him, with the nature *all* subdued to God, viewing with deepest hatred its past rebellion, struggling with vehement longing to revenge itself upon its adversary, and filled with love for the rightful ruler of the spirit, the fortress of the soul is far less likely to fall than if it were not holy.

It is a PROGRESSIVE holiness. As there is no height from which we cannot fall, so there is none from which we cannot rise. The principle of holiness is an ascending angel, and our simple motto is to "follow her." When, as a babe in Christ, the cleansing process is received, that angel stands upon the straight and narrow way and bids us follow her. As a youth in Jesus he is beckoned onward. In the maturity of Christian manhood he is still to follow holiness. In the ripened mellowness of Christian age he is to acknowledge no other leader. In all the perplexities of providential dispensations when he cannot see his way, he is still to follow holiness. When his way crosses the valley and shadow of death he need fear no evil, but only follow her. When he takes up his line of travel from the Jordan shores to the eternal throne, he is still to keep her in his view; and when he chooses his pathway across the broad eternity, he simply follows her as the only one in which he can eternally rise in the sight and enjoyment of the Lord.

It is a COMPLETE holiness,—one that does not admit

of the smallest departure from the will of God concerning us. That will is narrowed down to the circle of our actual circumstances, but it must be completely met. It might be called a small but perfect image of Christ in the soul. There must be no resting-place for the serpents of anger within the heart. They must be driven out of it and crushed; not only crushed, but killed; not only killed, but their poisonous bodies hurled from the soul and the stain of their venom washed away with atoning blood. Not only this, but every egg must be crushed which might afterwards be warmed into a viper life. There must be no idol left of pride. Its every shrine must be broken and the cross heave the rubbish away. The lurid lamp of malice must both be extinguished and destroyed, and its fragments swept from the soul. In place of these and kindred evils, the graces of the Spirit must form the face of Christ within us. Peace must dwell there—perfect peace—not freedom from trouble of mind or the overflows of sorrow, but a peace with God, which no opposing motion can disturb. I once lost two darling children, and when standing by their coffins the whole human nature quivered with agony, and wished to lie down with them in the grave where they were being placed. But below the surface of those heaving waters there was the completest peace. *He* went down beneath that surface sorrow, and where *He* was all was calm. Above, the waves were rolling, but in the centre of the soul the calm was undisturbed. Another of these features is a full and confiding SUBMISSION to the will of God, whether that will be expressed in Providence or the Bible. The soul asks no questions as to whether a thing is pleasant, but only whether it is the will of God. Its performance may cause deepest anguish, but like the martyr in the flame, the very anguish praises God, and would not have it otherwise. His will is married to the will of God, and they twain are one. As the Christian lady, when asked, " if God gave her a choice, whether she would prefer to live," replied, " she would not make a choice, but would refer the matter back to Him," so does the holy soul decline all responsibilities of its own, and confides alone in the wisdom of the Father. Still another feature is LOWLY-MINDEDNESS, esteeming others better than ourselves. The charity that hopeth all things covers the defects of others with the broadness of its mantle, while their excellences glow in the light which it reflects. When the soul takes its own privileges into the account and contrasts them with the opportunities of others, it is so penetrated with its own unworthiness that it esteems itself " less than the least of all saints." Any spirit that attempts its own exaltation by saying, " I am holier than thou," is a mistaken one, for holiness demands exactly the opposite experience.

Yet another feature is PERFECT MEEKNESS in the soul. When it is reviled pity takes the place of a desire to revile again. The harshest words of reprehension are accepted as necessary parts of God's loving discipline, and, therefore, borne without resentment towards these whips the Father uses. It is so penetrated with Christ's meek spirit that whatever *He* did, the very attraction of the act impels it to do also. There is such inward harmony between his soul and Christ that the deeds of Jesus are repeated in his dispositions, and find their images daguerreotyped upon them.

The *expression* by which these features may be more

fully known to be those of Jesus, is Love—that viewless bond of perfectness. The radiance of those features is in the glow love borrows from the Father's face when they are upturned toward Him. With God's splendor upon them it is impossible to look at their fellow-men with any other spirit. Men may be evil or unthankful, but the glow cannot be dimmed; for its glory is from God and flows as steadily as the pulses of its life. Many waters will not quench it, icy coldness will not chill it; for love is God's own light, and evil has no power against it.

The magnitude of these images of Jesus differs in different individuals, and at different times in the same individual, according to their development in spiritual life. The plates from which they were God-printed show them larger or smaller, according to the growth in grace. They are in all cases a higher life, but higher in proportion to the spirituality previously enjoyed. In the babe in Christ, or the older Christian who may have recently experienced holiness, the features may be infantile, but they will broaden with advancing growth; and while a higher life is found in the health of soul that forms the state of holiness, a higher life will also be found in the advancement of that holiness itself.

Every man can be conscious whether he meets this character and possesses this image. If you find that these things are in you and abound you are holy, whether you know it for this blessing or not. If these features are not there you are *not* holy, no matter what you may have previously estimated your condition to be.

It is said, sometimes, that "holiness can be no after-work to the spiritual birth, else that birth would be imperfect." This is true as far as it applies, but it does not apply as far as the objection assumes. God's work in the new birth is simply to give LIFE. This He does and does perfectly. But almost all the forms of life with which we are acquainted demand a further work after their birth in order to a perfect health, and so does this one. This further work accomplishes its purification, and this we call Holiness. Some will not seek it because it appears so difficult a matter. Difficulties there are, it is true, but none so great as are involved in living a single day without it; for in the one case it is simply using the medicine which restores to health and afterward is manna to the taste, and in the other it is a struggle for the maintenance of the life under the vitiating power of disease.

Others refuse it because they fear it will dishonor Christ. Once holy, say they, and will I not be saved by holiness instead of Christ? But this is a mistaken view. Christ is the soul's physician, and receives more glory for healing the soul than simply keeping it alive without removing the disease—more glory for constantly applying that healing power and keeping it in strongest vigor, than for simply giving the palliatives of disease that merely keep it from death.

Some refuse because they think they will throw contempt upon the glorious work which God has done for them in regeneration. But there is no such contempt in this. A Christian life, even without Christian health, is nowhere undervalued. A ship half rigged is immensely better than no ship at all, for it is far easier to complete the rigging than to build the ship from the foundation. But there is no contempt thrown upon what is done to say that she needs the rigging in order to safely navigate the waters, and that she cannot live among the breakers or enter the harbor without it.

Its attainment is preceded by a spiritual repentance for the past. A glance along that past will bring up before you neglects of duty—not through ignorance, not through mistake, but through determination to neglect. It will show you deeds that were wrong—not through ignorance, not through mistake, but whose righteousness was doubted at the time of their performance. It will show you your guilt in neglecting to remove the evil of your nature long ago, which was the will of God concerning you; and from all these a fresh repentance will come to your soul, which is the first step toward the experience of holiness.

The second step is a spiritual sorrow over the remains of corruption in your nature. You cannot feel that corruption as a crime chargeable to you, but you can feel it a sorrowful fact that it is there. Sorrow, as you feel it over your crippled child, whose misfortune you did not cause, and yet sorrow because he *is* a crippled child; sorrow deep enough to make you long for its complete extirpation from the nature.

A third step is a belief in the possibility of its attainment. Besides the fact that holiness is the entire basis of Christ's religion, the Scriptures clearly prove it in other forms. God commands it, and it is insulting to Him to suppose its execution an impossibility. He promises to do it, and it is a deeper insult still to doubt the performance of a promise. He tells us to pray for it, and it would be cruel trifling to bid us pray in vain. He presents numerous examples of it, and it is putting ourselves above Him to dispute His judgment of these men. Besides this, large numbers of people who have lived without reproach have asserted its experience, and it is a blackening of their characters to deny it. Large numbers profess it still, and while we take their word for every other phase of their experience, it is not consistent to refuse it here. If you can believe the Gospel at all, you can believe it in the possibility of attaining holiness.

A succeeding step is a belief in the possibility of its attainment NOW.

Crucifixion is not a mode of death requiring years for its accomplishment, and crucifixion is the Gospel mode for sin's destruction. The use of the atonement spear will make an instant matter of it. God acknowledges but one principle in the duties He demands of us or the privileges He accords unto us, and that principle is now. Upon all the Gospel principles, if the work is accomplishable at all, it is accomplishable now. Before the perusal of these pages is finished, I assert, in the light of the eternal judgment, that you may, if you will, do all that is requisite to the attainment of a holy heart.

Next in order comes a consecration of the nature correspondent with its present capacity and knowledge. In the consecration we made preceding the justification of our souls before God, this was done, but performed only up to the knowledge and capacity existing then. When the knowledge of impurity first dawned upon us, if a fresh consecration correspondent with that added knowledge and capacity had been made, the inward holiness would at once have been accomplished, probably without any sensible knowledge of special change beyond an elevation in religion. But if it has not been done; if your nature, with its present knowledge of its defects, and capacity for the reception of God, has not been laid on Christ's altar just as it is, the experience of holiness is an impossibility until you yield this point.

It needs next a belief that God accepts that entire consecration *now*. It ought not to be any more difficult to believe this at this time than it was at the beginning of your experience. God's naked word was enough then, and it ought to be sufficient now. Over and over, in varied forms, He says He *does* accept it; and we ought not to doubt anything that is a plain expression of the Almighty word.

Then we take our last step,—a belief in Christ, who is our sanctification, commensurate with the consecration that we have made. Consecration, and a belief that God accepts it, while it implies faith in Jesus, is yet not that active personal appropriation which makes the blessing ours. When we *first* believed, He was accepted simply as the sufferer upon the cross. Now we are able to go higher, and while we do not leave the cross, we also clasp the throne. We blend both the suffering and the glory in our acceptance of the intercession plea of Jesus for our personal holiness *now*. Then *wait*, and it will come. It will flow over your justification with a perfect peace. All the grime upon your soul will disappear. All that you cannot do for yourself Christ will do for you. Your joy will be filled with purity. You will be inspired anew for your Christian labor; you will have greater boldness in your Christian profession; your light will burn and shine till men will glorify God. May God incite you, without a moment's delay, to enter upon its possession!

CHAPTER XVII.

SERMON OF REV. J. W. JACKSON, OF PHILADELPHIA CONFERENCE.

John xiv. 22.—" *Lord, how is it that Thou wilt manifest Thyself unto us, and not unto the world?* "

SUBJECT: THE BELIEVER'S VISION OF GOD.

IT was the eve of Christ's departure from the disciple band. His great public ministry had ended; and, in the quiet circle of His chosen, Jesus was solemnizing the most significant of all the Jewish festivals, in its typical character, as a symbol of His own sacrificial death—the great object now hastening of His manifestation in the flesh, in the firm conviction of the nearness of which He had come to the feast at Jerusalem. The traitor, in the beginning still present among the twelve, had gone out from the circle which he had long since deserted in spirit. The Saviour, seizing the moral uses of the passover in their deepest significance, had consecrated them to holy transactions of a higher kind, which were to be repeated in the Church of the Lord until the day of His second coming.

And now the conversation that had mingled its current of living, loving words with the other duties of the hour rose in its sublime import, until, revealing Christ's whole heart of love, it revealed Him to them in the whole fulness of His divine nature.

Of all Jesus Christ's recorded conversations, this, the last, is the most memorable, most wonderful. Memorable and wonderful for the occasion, when Jesus knew that His hour was come that he should depart out of the world unto the Father, going by the way of the cross, for the world's redemption. He was about to leave them. It was this one thought that smote the hearts of those who had forsaken all to follow Him. To go away, and whither and why, they but dimly if at all comprehended, although He had beforetime showed them how He must go into Jerusalem, and suffer many things of the elders, and chief priests, and scribes, and be raised again the third day ; they only knew that to be with Christ, to have the joy of His personal presence, to listen, to look upon Him—that, to them, was heaven, life ! To be separated from Him was death ! Poor human hearts, throbbing with the sympathy and love of personal companionship, how the threatened going of their Lord, whither they could not follow now, troubled them ! So sweet and loving, so confidential and truthful, had been their intercourse with Him, could anything lighten the dreadful darkness of the world's solitude without Him ? In part the design of this last discourse is to satisfy the questionings of such human grief—to teach the doctrine of the spiritual presence of Christ as its consolation, and as the comfort, not merely of the disciple band, but of all those who shall believe on Him through their word ; to teach the necessity of His bodily absence to such spiritual presence—that He who, in such loving companionship, had gone with them would still be guide, comforter, companion to them, and to all who are made partakers of like precious faith.

I go away! A little while and ye shall not see me, and again a little while and ye shall see me, for the Holy Spirit shall testify of me. I go away *from* you, but *for* you. My going shall not leave you comfortless, for I will come to you. Going—I go to prepare a place for you. Coming—it is that I may receive you unto myself. You shall not be left to grope in the night darkness of utter loneliness; I will be your companion; I will show you the way; for all your troubles faith in me is the antidote. Be not troubled; let not this departure sadden you. Yet a little while and the world seeth me no more, but ye see me; because I live ye shall live also. Love me, and ye shall be loved of my Father. Love me, and I will love you, and will manifest myself unto you.

In the midst of such communications concerning the profound spiritual relationship which exists between a believing and loving soul and a living and loving Lord, the question of our text occurs: "Lord, how is it that Thou wilt manifest Thyself unto us, and not unto the world?"

It is as if Judas (not the traitor) had said, "How is it that we shall see Thee and others see Thee not? What mean these strange, mysterious sayings of Thine, about being seen no more by the world and yet being seen by us? Our hearts are saddened at being separated from Thee; it is a consolation to know that such separation is not final, and without compensation; but how canst Thou return to us, and how may we abide with Thee?

What means this wonderful secret companionship to him who loves Thee and keeps Thy words, incomprehensible to him who loveth Thee not?"

We know, my brethren, by blessed experience, that Jesus promised a real, personal, but spiritual relationship to himself, such as fills the measure of the soul's need—a manifestation of himself such as only the divinely illuminated soul can understand. Not a manifestation of God to the bodily senses; that were impossible, for God is a spirit. Not such manifestation of God, of His eternal power and Godhead being understood by the things that are made, as leaves idolatry and atheism without excuse, and demonstrates the undevout student of nature to be mad; for men may thus know God, and glorify Him not as God, but become vain in their imagination, and darkened in their foolish hearts. No, not such a revelation of God as glows in the stars or blossoms in the trees—not an intellectual revelation to philosophic faculty, to perceptive reason, but a manifestation to the inner consciousness of the loving purified heart, a consciousness of the divine presence in the heart, through holy affections, moral sensibilities purified. "Blessed are the pure in heart, for they shall see God." It is the condition of the affections which makes it possible to see God, to recognize God "manifested unto us and not unto the world." For "with the heart man believeth unto righteousness."

"We speak the wisdom of God in a mystery, even the hidden wisdom which God ordained before the world unto our glory." "As it is written, Eye hath not seen nor ear heard, neither have entered into the heart of men, the things which God hath prepared for

them that love Him. But God hath revealed them unto
us by His Spirit, for the Spirit searcheth all things, yea,
the deep things of God." "Now we have received, not
the spirit of the world, but the Spirit which is of God;
that we might know the things which are freely given
to us of God." "The natural man receiveth not the
things of the Spirit of God; for they are foolishness unto
him; neither can he know them, *because they are spiritually discerned.*" "*But we have the mind of Christ.*"

Oh wonderful mystery! Oh glorious experience! A
heart experience, not susceptible of exact statement, yet
really, definitely true; an experience for which no argument can be framed convincing to him who has it not, yet
mounting to the dignity and certainty of divine assurance
to him who, passing from death unto life, has received

> " The unknown power,
> And felt His blood applied."

To the world, to those who deny a spiritual religion,
such a doctrine seems the illusion of a dream. "How
can these things be?"

We would not, my brethren, lower your conception
of the sublimity of this manifestation of God and
Christ to the believing soul, in referring to those analo-
gies and illustrations which it has in other departments
of human experience, differing, it is true, in being the
highest of which the soul is capable, and in the preparation necessary to the soul, as a condition precedent to
its attainment. We frequently say, "I cannot express
myself." Now, in ordinary knowledge—in the knowledge that is attained unto by study, and that is capable
of intellectual statement, such expressions are but the

flimsy expedients by which ignorance seeks to appear wise. What a man knows he can express; and the extent, definiteness, and clearness of his knowledge may be measured by the definiteness and clearness of his expression. What he knows well he can express well, for he thinks in words. Words are the motion of his thoughts. But in the department of feeling, of emotive experiences, language only expresses the fragments of his thought, the shallow places in the heart; there are deep places where the plummet of words may not sound out to others the unknown depths of which we are painfully or joyfully conscious, where, by the very vagueness of our language, we most nearly approximate the communication of the otherwise incommunicable. The fear and trembling which came upon you, which made all your bones to shake, defies all your power of expression adequately to communicate to another; that exquisite emotion of joy that swept all the chords of heart harmony is but feebly echoed by the lips. Even your intellectual and æsthetic enjoyments cannot be communicated to any one indiscriminately; your auditor must have the same or similar culture, or your words are to him but sounding brass and tinkling cymbal; you speak in unknown tongues if your words describe excursions into unknown regions of intellectual effort.

On such a day of brightness and beauty as this, amid the thousand odors of summer that charm the air with fragrance, a new and strange sweetness is borne to the sense of smell; you direct a companion's attention to it; should he fail to recognize it, there is no argument for it by which you may convince him of its existence; you

can but affirm it. To one destitute of the sense of
smell you cannot communicate by words the sensation
which is knowledge; the blind you cannot teach to distinguish colors; to the deaf you cannot convey the
sweet and subtle joys of sound; they are destitute of
the conditions of such experiences. How much greater
the impossibility of a communication of the secret of the
Lord, which is with them that fear Him, to those who
fear Him not.

But do we not often long for such a manifestation of
Christ as the disciples had in the visible, bodily presence
of Jesus—the Word made flesh and dwelling among
them? Have we not felt that an intimation of His
presence by the ordinary channels through which
knowledge comes to us would make it easier to live
ever after by the faith which is the evidence of an unseen God? The very seclusion, silence, unresponsive-
ness of God, has been to us a pain. We pray, and no
audible voice answers. We ask, and no form gathers
shape upon the horizon. Have we not thought: Oh, if
I might but see Him, as Peter and James and John saw
Him upon the Mount of Transfiguration; if I might
but look for one passing moment upon that loving face,
as Mary or Martha or their brother Lazarus looked!
Could I but thus *see* Him, how would faith grow to
giant strength as it fed upon the sweet memory of His
loving look! This was the error of the unbelieving heart,
that Christ exposes and corrects in this and in many
other passages of His teachings. It implies that God
has no other than bodily manifestations for our bodily
senses, such as the natural world affords, which is not
God, only a sign and effect of His presence. God has

no body. He is a Spirit. What is there, then, about
Him to present to your senses? Did He assume form,
to satisfy the cravings of eye and ear, that form would
not be God, only the mask or disguise of God. By the
natural sense we should not find God, as the world by
wisdom knew not God. Were such a sensuous manifestation of God possible to each and every longing soul,
would it satisfy? It did not satisfy the world nor the
disciples when God came in Christ's person. He came,
and began both to do and teach. Never man spake as
this man spake. He taught as one having authority, and
not as the scribes. The wonderful works which He did
were self-revelations, as truly as His words declaring
Him to be the Son of God, with power. What was the
effect? " The Pharisees also, with the Sadducees, came,
and, *tempting*, desired Him that He would show them a
sign from heaven." And even in that hour, when the
divine in Jesus shone out most resplendently, glorifying
the Son of man, and when God was glorified in Him,
they discerned only the natural, and took that for the
divine, in so far as they considered Him divine. Philip,
" so long time with Him," now in the very Holy of
Holies of His moral manifestations, while shrouded by
His human form, but uttered the longings of the unsatisfied heart of all, as he said, " Lord, show us the
Father and it sufficeth us."

Would it not be so again? This is not the soul's rest
in God, the adulteration of the spiritual kingdom to
the low conditions of our natural life, but the lifting up
of the mind, its purification up to the range of the
spiritual kingdom. God's manifestations are to the
quickened, regenerate, sanctified soul—manifestations

precious, clear, abiding, to the loving, obedient spirit. Faith, working by love, purifies the heart; and the pure see Him whom, having not seen as John saw Him, we love; in whom believing, we rejoice with joy unspeakable and full of glory. Oh, yes! to the soul, clean through the Word which He has spoken, there is a sense of the Divine presence more real than a sense of the presence of any human being. Christ is more really present than if I could touch Him, or hear His loving human voice.

There are hundreds here to-night to whom Christ has thus come; to whom there is given the sweet, clear, satisfying consciousness that He is near them, that He dwells in them and they in Him. Nearer to Him than trees are to their roots; nearer to Him than streams are to their fountains; nearer than body and soul and breath and blood in their intimate conjunction is Christ with every loving, obedient heart to whom He manifests himself.

This is the mysterious teaching of our text. How it comes I do not know. "The wind bloweth where it listeth, and ye hear the sound thereof, but cannot tell whence it cometh or whither it goeth." How God touches our heart I do not know, but by the divine inward trembling, the sacred awe of such hallowed communion. I know in these celestial hours that there is such a presence of my Christ God, not to the body, but to the spirit, cherishing, inspiring, enlightening, forming a companionship more intimate, sweet, enduring, than that of any earthly relationship, sweeter than that of friend with friend, of father and son, of mother and child.

Do you, my unconverted friend, regard this in your

spiritual ignorance as the ravings of a wild, distempered enthusiasm? It is but the effort to interpret that spiritual consciousness of the divine presence, when God comes to the soul, not through the eye and ear gate, but by that inward way, plain to those who know it, inexplicable to those who know it not ; when He comes fulfilling His gracious promise, that He will manifest himself to His people and not to the world. That you cannot understand it is true, because it is spiritually discerned ; that I cannot communicate it is true, because it passes the limits of human expression by the very elements of infinity and eternity which inhere in a Christ-inhabited and purified heart.

Ever since language has been written, poets have endeavored to describe the wealth of human hearts as they blossom out in the sweet ecstasies of human love. Have they done it ? On what page of human literature is written that song which tells fully of that love which inspires the heart of a friend to lay down his life for a friend ? Where is the mother's love told in language that does not mock, by its paucity and meagreness, the living mother's undying love ? If the rapture of that hour when one human heart touches another must remain unsung, how shall I speak of that unspeakable joy when God's heart touches ours, and the love of God is shed abroad in our hearts by the Holy Ghost which is given unto us !

> " Angels, assist our mighty joys,
>   Strike all your harps of gold ;
>   But when you raise your highest notes
>   His love can ne'er be told."

Philosophy or poetry cannot describe the ineffable joy

of a soul in the rapture of this love. The secret of God, known and felt, is real forever after.

The practical question to us is the condition on which this soul-vision, this manifestation of God to spiritual consciousness, depends. A spiritual intuition demands such moral dispositions as shall render you susceptible. The eyes clouded with worldliness and sin see not God. The ear recognizes not His voice amid earth's Babel jargon, crying lo here, and lo there! with its many-voiced allurements from God to plunge the soul in worldly cares. To see and to know God we must enter into His kingdom, be transformed by the renewal of the mind. A supernatural kingdom has its supernatural law, demanding a supernatural birth, a supernatural life. The manifestation of Christ to us by the Holy Ghost can only be received by those who, by a simple, pure, childlike, unreserved consecration of themselves to God, in loving obedience and keeping of His word, say, "Speak, Lord, for thy servant heareth." Then will Heaven open, God will manifest Himself to your soul, and you shall abide with Him. The intensity and fervor of such communing increases with its repetition. The more we know of God, the more we long to know. As the appetite grows by that it feeds upon, so the soul communing with God increases in the intensity and fervor of its desire for such communion. The soul's knowledge of God is in proportion to the purity and fervor of its aspirations, the strength and vigor of its faith. To them that believe He is precious. "If a man love me he will keep my words, and my Father will love him, and we will come unto him, and make our abode with him." A manifestation of God's presence is felt, unknown to other men ; a peace enjoyed, pecu ar to the child of God.

How great are the incentives to holiness! It is the secret of all spiritual enjoyment, the key to all spiritual knowledge.

Bodily enjoyment depends upon physical vigor, upon the harmony of every part of the bodily system with the laws which govern our physical being. The eye and ear put forth only their best exertions and bring back only their best results as they are brought under the discipline of continuous training. The skilful hand is the educated and continually practised hand. The scholar will tell you that the intellect submits to the same law, and that the pleasure and success of study depend upon its continuity ; that the suspension of mental culture, for any great length of time, is not merely the loss of time, but conflicts with the favorable and happy use of mental power. More imperatively does the spiritual mind demand continuous and uninterrupted dwelling in exalted companionship with the holiest, loftiest, sublimest objects of thought. The growth of the sacred principle within must be most sacredly guarded. The earliest symptoms of declining vigor in spiritual affection must be carefully watched against ; the feeblest tendency toward the low and sensual must be checked. The power of the soul must be kept in constant use, to be able to comprehend the divine manifestation.

I turn to those who, in the darkness of the natural unbelieving heart, are without the vision of God ; whose sin shuts, bars, bolts the door at which a loving Saviour now stands knocking, crying, " If any man hear my voice, and open the door, I will come in to him, and will sup with him, and he with me." Do you, listening to this feeble effort to realize in contemplation the heights and depths of spiritual enjoyment which flows from communion with Christ, from a sense of His spiritual presence by the believing heart, turn away from spiritual religion as if it were but a poetic fiction, and ridicule its fervent utterances by these saints of God as if they were but fanatic ravings, grounding your hope of the future upon the morality of your life? I do not mock at your morality. I do not depreciate its value. I hope that you are all that you claim to be in your outward life. But I know—I have only to look abroad upon the world to see it—that a morality left to the guidance of the unregulated impulses of a carnal, unregenerate heart, is feeble, fluctuating, contradictory. I point you to a morality superior to yours in the kind of duties to which it gives prominence, and the light in which it presents them, but whose great superiority is in its motive power—the love of the Lord Jesus, the love to Him that flows out in submission to His will, who, having done all for us, claims us for His own. "Ye must be born again." "Without holiness no man shall see the Lord."

By the beauty of holiness; by the joyous rapture of holiness; by the freedom from sin, which has its fruit unto holiness and the end everlasting life, I beseech you come to God. "Him that cometh unto me I will in no wise cast out." *Amen.*

10*

CHAPTER XVIII.

1. *Thess. i.* 5.—" *For our Gospel came not unto you in word only, but also in power, and in the Holy Ghost, and in much assurance.*"

WE understand the term Gospel to mean glad tidings, or a revelation of the grace of God to fallen men; and this includes the whole scheme of salvation, as revealed by Christ. The term is used, however, in the text in the sense of instruction also; and hence the Apostle says, " Our Gospel came not unto you in word only, but also in power, and in the Holy Ghost, and in much assurance." St. Paul would not have us understand by the term " our Gospel," that he was the author of it, but the dispenser only. Not our Gospel by original revelation, but by ministerial dispensation. The Apostle announces first to the Thessalonians that the Gospel came unto them not in word only; that is, it was not simply by preaching or reasoning. We do not understand by this that he ignored reason, but he simply states that it was not by this only. He desired that the truth should not only play around the understanding, but go deeper, and reach the heart.

IN WORD.

It is right that the Gospel should come to us first in word. Before I can hope to bring an infidel to seek

God, I must convince him of the being, excellence, and claims of God. Before a sinner can be induced to seek salvation in Christ, he must be convinced of his own sin and danger, and of the ability and willingness of Christ as a Saviour. That the Gospel does come in word, and is designed to come in word, is beautifully presented by divine authority in the inspired Scriptures, in the calling and appointment of the ministers of God from the various walks of life. Moses was called to his high communion whilst in charge of the flocks of Jethro. Gideon, the great champion of his age, was called to be the instrument in overthrowing the gigantic power of Midian, while threshing wheat with his father's bullocks at the wine-press of Ophrah. Matthew was summoned to attend his great Master while collecting the harbor dues at the port of Capernaum. Peter, John, and Andrew, while busied with their nets and boats, were called to become fishers of men.

There can be no doubt that in the calling and appointment of these men the great Head of the Church designed adaption. There were the Son of Thunder and the Son of Consolation, and there is the same beautiful diversity to this hour in the Church of Christ: " And he gave some apostles, and some prophets, and some evangelists, and some pastors and teachers, for the perfecting of the saints, for the work of the ministry, for the edifying of the body of Christ, till we all come in the unity of the faith and the knowledge of the Son of God unto the measure of the stature of the fulness of Christ." As in a forest there is diversity among the trees, as every garden has diversity of flowers, and shrub, as each field has its varied crop, as each face has its peculiar features, with countless varieties of expression, and each body its varied organs; so we trace the same singular yet beautiful diversity in the intellectual charácter of God's servants. Luther and Knox, who have been called the Elijahs of their times, had their vocation in preparing the way for the Zwingles and Melancthons—the gentler messengers of peace. He has men whose province it is to carry the assaults into the enemies' works, and also those distinguished for organization and ingenious in device. He has others whose vocation is neither pulpit nor platform, synod nor council, ecclesiastical debate nor stern polemics, but the quiet duties of the study and closet; men who are thinking while others are acting, doing in their own way a secret work, without voice or ostentation; who could not stand the shouts and clamor of Carmel (we thank God there are Elijahs who can), but who love to carry their influence amid the homes of Israel, and amid the schools of the prophets. Now we should thank God for this unity in diversity, and diversity in unity. The division of labor, so needful in social life, is illustrated with equal force and beauty in the diversity of gifts and operations in the Church—each in his own way and sphere laboring for one common end. In the building of the temple of old, the rough mountaineers of Lebanon were as much needed to hew down the cedar trees, as Hiram of Tyre's cunning workmen to prepare and cast the mouldings of brass, and carve the delicate interlacings of gold. We should never depreciate one spiritual workman's avocation at the expense of another's; every hammer, and axe, and tool of iron is required to shape the varied parts, but all are working for one end—the bringing forth of the topstone, with shoutings of "Grace, grace unto it!"

IN POWER.

But, says the Apostle, "Not in word only, but also *in power*." "That is," says Clarke, "with such manifestations to your eyes and to your hearts, as induced you to acknowledge that this Gospel is the power of God unto salvation." The word power in the text is used by the Apostle in the sense of influence, and its influence is felt in its nicely adjusted claims in man's sentient nature. And in this we see its adaption to meet the felt necessities of the human soul. We are never out of the range of its promises and hopes; youth cleanses its way by taking heed to it, as to the word of God; age stays its feeble steps upon the staff of its promises; in it is found a word for the widow and the orphan, "A father of the fatherless and a judge of the widows is God in His holy habitation." If you are in trouble, God is a present help. If you are sick, you have written for your encouragement, "Is any afflicted? let him pray," "for the Lord is nigh unto them that call upon Him." And when dying we hear the Saviour's voice speaking those words, heard of old among the tombs of Bethany, "I am the resurrection and the life."

The Gospel in its power is like the great law of gravitation. Making no noise, its voice is not heard; yet governing, controlling, keeping the minutest atom in its place, and the most magnificent orb within the limits of its orbit. Its influence is not like electricity—confined and sparkling ; but, like the electric power that runs through all nature, giving beauty to the tints of flowers, and making, under God, the harmony of all created things. It is not speaking religion, but living religion ; this, my brethren, is the noblest creed, the richest eloquence, and the mightiest power. One of the grand distinctions of the Gospel, as separate from other schemes of human elevation, and by which we see its superior adaption to man's moral exigency, is love ; to this noblest of all principles the Gospel makes its highest appeals. Its foundation, the Atonement, was laid in love; the principle on which it is propagated is love; the conquest it is to achieve is the extinction of hate ; the cement by which it will unite the ransomed universe is love. And when this power shall be realized, the sorrowing world may dry up her tears, and complaint shall give place to praise ; and the Church, permeated with the sanctifying power of grace, will then thrust out her commissioned sons, glowing in the Redeemer's matchless love, to preach this Gospel with power. Imagine the effect if love, this mighty power inherent in our Gospel, were in full operation to-day.   Why, this world would soon be transformed into a paradise ; the moral desert would be changed into a fruitful field, and Eden would appear again in all its beauty and glory.

IN THE HOLY GHOST.

Again, the Apostle says, " Our Gospel came not unto you in word only, but also in power, *and in the Holy Ghost.*" Man's nature is so corrupt that it requires the application of an extraneous agency to renovate it.   The ancient Greeks and Romans had not these enlightened views of the nature and effect of moral transgression that we have; but the very worst had a lingering conviction that some great moral blight had passed upon the human soul, and they felt themselves the victims of sin; they recognized its dominion as the secret of their ills, and every school in ancient Greece had its prescription for its removal, every philosopher some great system which, if accepted, he thought would be to the world a complete relief. There was a sense among all the heathen, that moral transgression was in some way the root of all evil, and that unless the evil in man's heart could be eradicated, human sufferings could never be removed. They did not know that Christ should come a Redeemer from sin; but this was what they blindly desired, and He is exactly what meets that desire, for "in Him we have remission through His blood, even the forgiveness of our sins;" and it shows the profound philosophy of this blessed Gospel, that Christ came into the world not merely to ameliorate man's outward state, but to expel from his heart the cause of his misery, and by the removal of the source of the evil, to ameliorate gradually, and ultimately to remove altogether, the evils that oppress him. The evils that affect society are not like driftwood lying upon the surface, which you may sweep away with a strong arm; but they are like the gnarled roots of ancient oaks, that have struck deep into the heart, and intertwined with the very feelings, affections, appetites, and passions of the soul. So much so that none but He who made man can be the physician who can cure him; and, blessed be God, just when our need was sorest, God sent forth His Son, born of a woman, made under the law, that we might no more

be the slaves of sin, but receive the adoption of sons.
Thus we have in Christ Jesus, as the Redeemer from
sin, a response to the inmost, the deepest desire of fallen
humanity. But we want something to bring this truth
home to our hearts, to stereotype it there, and to make
us know so as to realize it. Like the wax and the seal,
it wants some power to bring the two together and
make the impression. The gold may be prepared for
the die, and the die may be perfected for its work, but
they must be brought together. And not only so; you
may lay the one upon the other, and press them with all
the weight of your human arm, and produce no visible
effect; but place them both in the right machine, and
apply its power, and with one stroke the coin comes
forth, bearing the image and superscription which fix
its current value. This may give you some idea of the
fact that power is needed to stamp the human soul with
the likeness of the glorified Saviour.

But we must have something more than human agency
to make the truth of the Gospel a living thing in the
soul. Thank God, we have this agency in the Holy
Spirit, for we are His workmanship. Created in Christ
Jesus, even when we were dead in sin, He hath quickened us together with Christ, and raised us up together,
and made us sit together in heavenly places in Christ
Jesus. And the measure of the mighty power by which
the new man is created is according to that which He
wrought in Christ, when He raised Him from the dead.
Thus it is the Spirit that quickeneth. As Christ incarnate was a supernatural embodiment, or manifestation
localized in space, so the Holy Spirit is a supernatural
indwelling force, by which Christ is perpetuated in the

world, universalized in all localities, and brought nigh to every being in every place.

Christ and the Spirit are complemental forces, and both together constitute a complete whole. Without the Spirit the efficient working of the model set before us in the divine beauty of Christ and His death would find us dulled in understanding, blurred in perception, and held fast in the penal bondage of our sins; approving the good before us only faintly, desiring it coldly, reaching after it, if at all, impotently. Only by the Spirit of God can we be freed from the shackles that bind the soul to sin.

The eagle chained to his perch lifts his eye heavenward and longs for liberty, and often, stretching his wings, essays to rise; but the chain, which he can neither break nor cast off, holds him down, and he may not rise aloft and soar in his native air till some power greater than his own shall set him free; nor is there freedom for us till the Holy Spirit sets us free. But when Jesus says to the Spirit, Loose him, and let him go; let him fly; let him spurn the earth, and on the wings of faith and prayer soar away upward to the gates of glory; then we rise. Oh! we praise God that our Gospel has come to us, not in word only, but also in power and in the Holy Ghost, to enlighten our minds, to attest our adoption, to cleanse from moral impurity, to promote our sanctification, and to seal upon our hearts the first-fruit of the glory yet to be revealed.

MUCH ASSURANCE.

But more than this. The Apostle in the text says our Gospel came *in much assurance.* Wesley says, "literally, with full assurance." We understand that the Gospel came unto the Thessalonians with an evident conviction of its truth; that the Holy Spirit left no doubt upon their minds as to the general truth of the doctrine, or the safety of their state while trusting it. And our Gospel, my brethren, comes in the same manner to-day, with much assurance, adapted to man's moral exigency and to the felt necessities of the human soul, to the satisfaction of every sincere inquirer after the truth as it is in Jesus, assuring the conscience of its part in the Redeemer's blood. We have abundant assurance of its truth; and this is what we want. Before I go into battle I want to know that my sword is forged of trusty steel; before I go to sea I want to know that my anchor is wrought out of the toughest iron; before I set out on my journey I want to know that this is sterling money. So in religion I want to know if my hopes rest on sand or solid stone; I want to know that the wealth of the Spirit is mine. You know that he who has his wealth in the banker's safe walks light-hearted through the gloom of night, though thieves be all around. Even so the man who has the assurance in his heart that he has treasure in heaven; he is prepared for the worst that can befall him. And when misfortunes come to take away his wealth, or disease to take away his health, or calumny to take away his reputation, or death to take away his life, he sings,

"Let sickness blast or death devour,
   Heaven will recompense my pains;
 Perish the grass and fade the flower,
   Yet firm the word of God remains."

And this is the testimony that the Gospel brings.

The believer says, I went to Jesus weary and heavy laden, with a sense of sin and presentiment of judgment, and He has lifted away the load from my soul, and enabled me to rise as on eagles' wings, to run and not be weary, to walk and not faint; He has bound up my broken heart, and poured balm into my wounded spirit, and made His consolations to be richest and closest where my sorrows were deepest. It is not conjecture, but irresistible conclusion; not fancy, but transfiguring fact. I have the assurance in my heart that His blood is mine to cleanse me from all sin, His righteousness is mine to cover me as with an, imperishable and spotless robe, His power is mine to protect me, His intercessions are mine to sustain me, His promises to comfort me, His grace to enrich me, and His glory to receive me when the toils of life are over. Webster says assurance means firmness of mind, undoubting steadiness, intrepidity. Brave men meet danger with assurance. I recollect reading that when Marshal Massena was marching at the head of a body of Napoleon's victorious troops through a gorge in the Alps, a vast avalanche of snow descended from the heights above and swept into the valley below some hundreds of his soldiers. And on the very verge of the snow that was swept into the ravine beneath was a drummer boy, who, undisturbed amid the peril, continued beating the march he had commenced before the avalanche fell, until every soldier had passed through the gorge; this was his own funeral march, for he then sank down to die. It is said that one of Napoleon's greatest marshals never felt himself perfectly calm and self-possessed till the dead lay in thousands around him, and the tide

of battle seemed rolling against him.   This shows how
human nature in circumstances of great trial may feel
great calmness, and do its duty with unflinching nerve;
but if ambition and discipline can do this, the religion
of Jesus can do more.   It made Daniel calm in the
prospect of certain death.   It made Polycarp regard the
flames only as a chariot that should waft him to glory.
It made the apostles feel that bonds, imprisonments, and
death were no calamities, but blessings, because they
took them from scenes of suffering, and conveyed them
to realms of glory.

"Thou wilt keep him in perfect peace whose mind is
stayed on Thee."   And such is the assurance enjoyed by
the child of God, that he says, Though the mountains
were cast into the midst of the sea, and though the
earth should shake with the swelling thereof, yet my
Father hath made with me an everlasting covenant of
security.   Therefore I rejoice, and am exceeding glad.
Did you ever notice the remarkable expressions in the
Scriptures, where a Christian is described as one with
Christ ?   Why, every time I read them, I seem to get
nearer the cross, and my soul receives a new impulse
heavenward.   Wonderful language !   You never say a
servant is in his master, or a pupil is in his teacher.   Such
language would be intolerable.   And yet the whole New
Testament is full of similar expressions : " There is no
condemnation to them that are in Christ ; " " I knew a
man in Christ ; " " That I may be found in Christ Jesus,
not having my own righteousness."   Then why does Paul,
the accomplished scholar ; why does Luke, the classic
evangelist, use so strange an expression as "in Christ " ?
The answer is, that the relationship of a Christian to

Christ is totally unlike the relationship of a servant to his master or a pupil to his teacher. And therefore a new form of expression is needed to embody and unfold it. The believer is in Christ, as a branch is in the vine from which it grows. He is in Christ by a union as close and as real as the living limb is in the living body of the living man. So that if I am in Christ, His sympathies are mine, His life is mine. An apostle said, as if just to unfold and express this very idea, "I live;" but correcting himself, "yet not I, but Christ liveth in me; and the life that I now live, I live by the faith of the Son of God, who loved me, and gave himself for me." Oh blessed assurance, to have our life hid with Christ in God,—you in Christ, and Christ in you, the hope of glory. Not an ancient recollection, not a glorious name, not a word of eloquence and beauty, but your very life! Therefore I am safe, and can confidently say, "Nothing shall separate me from the love of God." Every wave of trouble lifts me higher on the Rock of Ages, wafts me nearer to the heavenly shore.

Look up, then, ye children of my Father. Your salvation is not only nearer than when you believed, but it may be nearer than you suppose. Even now the cry may be sounding in heaven, "Room for another saint, a crown for another head," and the next turn of the road may bring you in front of the gates of glory. And what next? Why, angelic welcomes, and a house not made with hands, eternal in the heavens.

> "No sickness there;
> No weary wasting of the frame away;
> No fearful shrinking from the midnight air;
> No dread of summer's bright and fervid ray."

Care has no place in that realm of ceaseless praise
and song.

> " Its tossing billows break and melt in foam,
> Far from the mansions of the spirit's home.
> No withered flower
> Or blasted bud celestial gardens know ;
> No scorching blast or fierce descending shower
> Scatters destruction like a ruthless foe.
> No hidden grief,
> No wild and cheerless vision of despair,
> No vain petition for a swift relief,
> No tearful eye, no broken hearts are there."

CHAPTER XIX.

SERMON OF REV. H. MILLER, OF PITTSBURG CONFERENCE.

Eph. iv. 24.—*" True Holiness."*

THE Bible proposes no philosophical solution of the philosophical question, " Whence came moral evil ? " But how shall moral evil be removed ? and how shall man, the subject of its blight, be restored to purity, happiness, and heaven ? are questions to which divine revelation gives no uncertain reply.

Holiness is the grand essential element of Christianity, the all-comprehending requirement of the Gospel; and its pursuit should therefore engross the thought and engage the energies of every man ; and hence the conditions of its attainment and the means and methods of its culture are subjects of infinite interest and importance.

Will you accompany us thoughtfully and prayerfully in a series of statements on the doctrine of holiness ?

1.— HOLINESS IS MORAL LIGHT.

" The eyes of your understanding being enlightened, that ye may know what is the hope of His calling, and what the riches of the glory of His inheritance in the saints, and what is the exceeding greatness of His power to us-ward who believe, according to the working of His mighty power." The soul has eyes as well as the body ; or, to speak without a figure, man is the subject of a perceptive faculty. This, in his natural state, is closed by sin, and the soul is shrouded in moral gloom, so that there is no spiritual perception of spiritual objects.   The testimony of St. Paul on this subject is exceedingly emphatic : " The natural man receiveth not the things of the Spirit of God, for they are foolishness unto him, neither can he know them, because they are spiritually discerned." " He shall lead you into all truth," said Jesus of the Holy Spirit. When his quickening and enlightning power rests on the understanding, a great tendency is excited to inquire after the truth, to cause us to pursue it daily, and that truth exerts, more and more, its own sanctifying influence on the soul, revealing to an adoring mind a world of beauty, a God of grandeur, and an eternity of terror and glory.

> " He comes from thickest films of vice,
> To clear the mental ray ;
> And on the eyes oppressed with night,
> To pour celestial day."

2.—HOLINESS IS MORAL, OR SPIRITUAL LIFE.

The Word, incarnate and glorified, is the source of spiritual life. The Holy Spirit, under the redemptive economy,—the regenerating, life-giving Spirit,—is the purchase of the Saviour's death, and the gift of His love.

" Ye shall be baptized with the Holy Ghost not many days hence," said the risen Redeemer to His inquiring disciples, just before He ascended to " the excellent glory," amid adoring myriads of attendant angels, and " the spirits of just men made perfect."

After the baptism came, on the day of Pentecost,

Peter stood up in the midst of the excited multitude and said, " This Jesus hath God raised up, whereof we are witnesses; therefore being by the right hand of God exalted, and having received of the Father the promise of the Holy Ghost, He hath shed forth this which ye now see and hear."

The giving of life is one of the most surprising instances of Divine power, and is convincingly manifest in that change which renders a man what we call religious. He is invested with what we may justly style a supernatural character.

Lately he regarded only earthly things, but now he can no more rest in them than an angel can ; and, like an angel, his only bliss is in beholding and adoring God.

What is the cause? Paul supplies an answer: "And you hath he quickened, who were dead in trespasses and sins."

Are you dead with Christ, by virtue of spiritual crucifixion, and alive from the dead by the power of the resurrection, so that sin hath no longer dominion over you? "Have ye received the Holy Ghost since ye believed?" Oh, for the prayer—

> " Jesus, my life, Thyself apply ;
> Thy Holy Spirit breathe."

Oh, let us have done with our formalism, our ritualistic worship, cold, comfortless, dead. " God is a Spirit ; and they that worship Him must worship him in spirit and in truth." Oh, for the wrestling of prayer, the glowing of love, the soaring of hope in all our religious assemblies. Some professors of religion are mere spiritual effigies instead of living, burning witnesses for Jesus.

Life, deep, glowing spiritual life, is the great want of the Church—men and women pardoned, sanctified, hungering and thirsting after righteousness, crying with devotional ardor, "I am crucified with Christ, nevertheless I live; yet not I, but Christ liveth in me; and the life which I now live in the flesh, I live by the faith of the Son of God, who loved me, and gave himself for me." This is the beginning of that life which shall be consummated in heaven. "He that believeth on the Son, *hath* everlasting life."

3.—HOLINESS IS MORAL FREEDOM.

Religious liberty involves the right of adopting and enjoying opinions on religious subjects, and of worshipping God according to the dictates of conscience.

But the liberty of which we speak is freedom from the dominion of appetite, passion, lust, and to live in obedience to the dictates of the higher faculties, the teachings of inspired truth, the promptings of the Holy Spirit. There is a slavery of mind, of spirit, that is cruel, tyrannical, and degrading, and compared with which, the severest form of bodily servitude is perfect freedom. But there is also a liberty for the soul that is joyous, ennobling, and exultant. "Ye shall know the truth, and the truth shall make you free." "Whosoever committeth sin is the servant of sin. If the Son, therefore, shall make you free, ye shall be free indeed." It shall not be a simulated freedom, but real, genuine.

If the religion of Christ could not deliver from the tyranny of sin, it would do little for man. However

long the habits of sin may have remained, and have in-
terwoven themselves with our interests, yet must they
give way before the all-powerful Holy Spirit. "Where
the Spirit of the Lord is, there is liberty." A man cannot do the good which his enlightened will prefers, till
God works in him not only the will but the power.
Hear Paul: "For the good that I would I do not; but
the evil which I would not, that I do. I find then a law
that, when I would do good, evil is present with me;
for I delight in the law of God, after the inward man;
but I see another law in my members, warring against
the law of my mind, bringing me into captivity to the
law of sin which is in my members. O, wretched man
that I am! who shall deliver me?" Is not that about
as far as a great many get in religious experience? "in
captivity to the law of sin," crying, "Who shall deliver
me?" There is a better way, good brother. Listen
again to Paul: "I thank God, through Jesus Christ our
Lord, for the law of the Spirit of life in Christ Jesus
hath made me free from the law of sin and death."

"Glorious liberty of the sons of God," free from pride,
passion, appetite, lust, all that pollutes and degrades an
immortal creature. "A man, to be a man, must rule
the empire of himself—in it must be supreme."

We boast, as a nation, of our political freedom, our
civil liberties, and rejoice in the emancipation of three
millions of human beings, long held under a dark and
degrading bondage; but are there not a greater number to-day with fair skin, intelligent, educated, refined,
wealthy, in positions of trust and power, many of
whom are the victims of a more degraded vassalage,
the slaves of appetite and passion?

Is it not affecting to think of the numbers who bear
the holy name of Christian, who bow at the altars of the
Church, receive her sacraments, swell her songs, contribute to her support, pray for her triumph, who are,
nevertheless, the slaves of lust and perverted appetites?
Are we free? Do we govern, or are we governed?
Does the brute run off with the man? There is freedom for thee, blessed freedom, " through the blood of
the Lamb."

What signify shackles on the limbs, if the soul be
free? Paul and Silas were thrust into the inner prison
at Philippi, and their feet made fast in the stocks, but
their dungeon was bright with the glory of God, and
they could sing exultingly—

> " Redeemed from sin, and free indeed,
>   We taste our glorious liberty."

4.—HOLINESS IS MORAL BEAUTY.

" Let the beauty of the Lord our God be upon us."
" Worship the Lord in the beauty of holiness." " The
beauty of the Lord " consists in those excellencies and
perfections which constitute His character, and the display of those perfections in the redemptive economy.

" The beauty of holiness " in man is the possession
and reflection of the Divine image. We are made
" partakers of the Divine nature," " of his holiness."

It was complained of Homer that he made his gods
live like men ; but it is the distinguishing glory of
Christianity that it enables men to live like God—

> " Into a saint exalts a worm,
>   A worm exalts to God."

We have seen persons of fine proportion, symmetrical

features, fair complexion, and expressive eye, whose spirit and behavior made them exceedingly repulsive.

On the other hand, we have known persons not especially attractive, whose sweet temper, genial spirit, and obliging manners have excited our admiration and won our hearts.

> "So beauty, armed with virtue, bows the soul
> With a commanding, but a sweet control."

How unlovely is even the religion of some persons—repelling instead of attracting by their austerity and moroseness of temper. "Sour godliness is the devil's religion," is an expression attributed to Mr. Wesley. Who would wish such a religion as that? Rather let us seek the piety of which it is said—

> "Mild, sweet, serene, and gentle is her mood,
> Nor grave to sternness, nor with lightness free;
> Against example resolutely good,
> Fervent in zeal, and warm in charity."

God designs that Zion shall be the "perfection of beauty." "Let your light so shine before men that they may see your good works, and glorify your Father which is in heaven." "So shine"—with such a divine effulgence—"shine before men, that they may see your good works, and glorify your Father."

We owe it to the Church, to the Master whom we serve, whose honor we are solemnly pledged to maintain, and to the interests of perishing humanity around us, to render our religion more attractive to the world, not by lowering but by elevating its standard. Nothing but inward sanctity can give beauty and persuasive power to the Christian life.

5.—HOLINESS IS MORAL PURITY.

Christ expounded and enforced the purity and spirituality of the Divine law as Jewish rabbis had never
done, or His disciples ever heard—uncovering the
human heart, touching the secret springs of action, and
insisting on purity of thought, feeling, intention, affection.

Anger is murder, and lust adultery, according to the
showing of the "Teacher sent from God." Moral purity
is the great demand of Christianity; the interpretation
of its doctrines; the significance of its provisions; the
teaching of its symbols—water, blood, fire—and the
burden of its promises.

If there is one thing more than another which distinguishes the prophecies of the Old Testament in their
relation to the New, it is the fact that the Gospel
should be characterized by its demand of, and provision
for, holiness. "And a highway shall be there, and a
way, and it shall be called *The way of holiness.*"
"Then"—when the Messiah should open the "fountain in the house of David for sin and uncleanness"
—when the dispensation of the Spirit should come—
"Then will I sprinkle clean water upon you, and ye
shall be clean; from all your filthiness, and from all
your idols will I cleanse you; a new heart also will I
give you, and a new spirit will I put within you; and I
will take away the stony heart out of your flesh, and I
will give you a heart of flesh; and I will put my Spirit
within you, and cause you to walk in my statutes, and
ye shall keep my judgments, and do them."

With reference to these and similar prophetic utterances, the Apostle says: "Having therefore these promises, dearly beloved, let us cleanse ourselves from *all* filthiness of the flesh and spirit, perfecting holiness in the fear of God."

There is a question that presents itself just at this point which demands an answer. What is *sin?* With reference to man's voluntary action it is "the transgression of the law," but evidently the teachings of the Bible authorize us to say that it is more—that it includes not only voluntary evil actions, but a corrupt and depraved nature.

Sin exists in man in two forms; he is the subject of guilt and of depraved principles. "Original sin is the corruption of the nature of every man that naturally is engendered of the offspring of Adam, whereby man is very far gone from original righteousness, and of his own nature inclined to evil, and that continually." Suppose we drop the word "original," and say that sin corrupts the nature of every man. Every act of voluntary transgression is corrupting. It is of the very nature and inevitable tendency of sin to deprave. Yes, sin is an infernal virus which infuses its poison through the whole intellectual and moral being. How otherwise can we interpret the language of the Bible. "The whole head"—that is, the intellect—"is sick, and the whole heart"—that is, the moral nature—"is faint; from the sole of the foot even unto the head there is no soundness, but wounds, and bruises, and putrefying sores; they have not been closed, neither bound up, neither mollified with ointment." What an affecting and humiliating description of human nature, drawn by the pencil of inspiration!

"Is there no balm in Gilead; is there no physician there?" Yes, blessed be God,

> "There is a great Physician near;
>   Look up, O fainting soul, and live;
> See, in His heavenly smiles appear
>   Such help as nature cannot give.
> See in the Saviour's dying blood
>   Life, health, and bliss abundant flow;
> And in that sacrificial flood
>   A balm for *all* thy grief and woe."

From sin—its guilt, power, love, pollution; its in-working and its outward manifestation—you may be cleansed, cleansed *now*. Oh, come to the "fountain." "Wilt thou be made whole?" Careless, Christless one, wilt thou come to Jesus for pardon and cleansing? Wilt thou fall at His feet and cry, "Heal my soul, O Lord, for I have sinned against Thee"?

Or wilt thou stay away from this Saviour who died for thee, and who invites thee so compassionately to His arms; and, refusing to believe upon Him, wilt thou go into the presence of the Judge Eternal with the burden of unlamented and unexpiated guilt resting on thy conscience, and the stains of depravity spreading themselves over and sinking into the soul?

Professed disciple of Jesus, are you pure? Do you enjoy, or are you even seeking, with earnest, heavenly longings, this "uttermost" salvation? Hear the voice of mercy: "If we confess our sins, He is faithful and just to forgive us our sins, and to cleanse us from all un-righteousness." Hallelujah!

> "Cover'd is my unrighteousness,
>   Nor spot of guilt remains on me;
> While Jesus' blood, through earth and skies,
>   Mercy, free, boundless mercy, cries."

6.—HOLINESS IS MORAL PERFECTION.

We are aware that the terms purity and perfection are generally regarded as identical in meaning, and that they are mostly used interchangeably in the discussion of the doctrine of Holiness; but they are not so employed—not generally, at least—in the teachings of Christ and the Apostles.

We need scarcely say that the philological import of the words is not precisely the same. Yet St. John employs the term " perfect love " as identical with purity of heart—" Herein is our love made perfect."

Mr. Wesley allowed that purity of heart is sometimes attained in regeneration, but that such is not generally the experience of the saved. So that the work of holiness may be more or less complete in what we call a regenerate state.

Purity of heart—in the sense of " perfect love," according to St. John—" freedom from unholy tempers and from the carnal mind," is the precious blood-bought privilege of every child of God, and may be attained at any moment, when the faith upon which it is conditioned is exercised, whether it be in the instant of justification or at any subsequent period. The general tenor of inspired teaching, corroborated by actual experience, is, that holiness in its incipient stages is imperfect, progressing from the point of beginning to its completion. This seems to be the order of the Divine procedure. The plan of redemption was gradually unfolded through a period of forty centuries, until the Incarnation. And the familiar parables of our Lord are to be understood as referring not only to the diffusion of His kingdom

11*

through the earth, but also to the development of the empire of grace in the individual soul. "The kingdom of heaven is like unto leaven, which a woman took and hid in three measures of meal, till the whole was leavened." "First the blade, then the ear, then the full corn in the ear." Now these parables, while they denote imperfection and growth, do not necessarily imply impurity.

Take these passages from the Sermon on the Mount: "Blessed are the *pure in heart*, for they shall see God;" "Blessed are they which do hunger and thirst after righteousness,"—which may be the experience of the "pure in heart"—"for they shall be"—not cleansed, not purified, but—"filled."

And the prayer of the Apostle Paul for the Thessalonians: "And the very God of peace sanctify you wholly; and I pray God your whole spirit and soul and body be preserved blameless unto the coming of our Lord Jesus Christ." Such a "blameless" state does not preclude further growth. The exhortation still retains its appropriateness, "Grow in grace."

We are persuaded that Christians are not sufficiently concerned about this, or they would exhibit a greater beauty, symmetry, and force of character. A man with one arm, or with one as large again as the other, is not a perfect man—there is not proportion.

In morals a man may be generous, but captious; affable, but proud. So in religion: one man may prize humility, another patience, a third charity, &c., but the perfect character exhibits all the Christian graces, and seeks their improvement.

Take two of the passages from Philippians, and see

the difference between perfection of character and perfection of development. "Not as though I had already
attained, either were already perfect." Here is perfection of development—unattainable on earth.

"Let us, therefore, as many as be perfect, be thus
minded." Here is perfection of character, attained by
Paul and some others, but not by all—"as many as be
perfect," &c. We hope you will read the whole chapter.

It is a life, an attainment above the ordinary level
of Christian experience. Have we this perfection of
character, and are we reaching up toward higher and
sublimer experiences of spiritual excellence and Divine
fellowship? The grace that makes a man a Christian,
implants within the soul the desire, the purpose to be a
perfect Christian; and the standard of perfection is
approached in proportion to the rapidity of the assimi-
lating process which conforms us to the Divine holiness.
"Be ye holy, for I am holy," is the authoritative command of Jehovah, reiterated in different forms and with
varied phraseology in the Old Testament and the New.
Such a "commandment is exceeding broad," but it is
upon us, nevertheless, founded in eternal reason; and
with the promise of infinite aid, we are to make the
sublime attempt to meet its demands.

We are to be holy because God is holy, and as He is
holy—that is, we are to aim at the holiness of God, infinitely above our reach, it is true, but the more favorable in consequence to moral development and spiritual
growth—the very altitude of the standard furnishing
opportunity for unlimited progression. The incarnate
life is the pattern to which our conformity is enjoined.
"Let this mind be in you which was also in Christ

Jesus." The contemplation of the Divine holiness, as revealed in the character and life of Christ, is an exercise commended by its philosophy, as well as by its scriptural authority, as essential to eminent attainments in piety. The law is universal, that the voluntary association of two intelligences will necessarily lead to an assimilation of character—the stronger moulding the weaker to its higher nature.

Men take their mental cast, their style, from the authors they read, and it is equally certain that the moral nature, for good or evil, is affected in the same way. Hence the advantage and the superiority of Christianity to all other systems of religious worship, in placing before the mind for study and contemplation the infinitely holy and glorious Being which it reveals. A young artist places before him a painting of superior workmanship, and endeavors to produce a copy. The first effort is very imperfect ; it may be, bearing little resemblance to the original ; the second is better, and every successive effort approaches nearer the piece he would imitate, until, studying all the while closely and intently the minutest features and shades of the original, he presents an exact copy.

It is thus St. Paul states the law of spiritual assimilation in the transforming power of communion with God, in the passage : " But we all with open face beholding as in a glass the glory of the Lord, are changed into the same image from glory to glory, even as by the Spirit of the Lord."

" A soul in commerce with the skies " will be drawn thitherward. " I feel the pulling," said a Christian lady in an experience meeting. The homely utterance contains a profound philosophy.

"Enoch walked with God three hundred years," growing more and more spiritual, and in his moral nature going up, up, up, till the last ligament that bound him to earth was severed, and he passed to the fruition of God and the fulness of heaven.

> "The change the soul would scarcely know,
> Made perfect first in love."

"Let us therefore, as many as be perfect, be thus minded, and if in anything we be otherwise minded, God shall reveal even this unto you," "that ye may prove," in experience, attainment, blessedness, "what is that good and acceptable and perfect will of God."

"Follow peace with all men, and holiness, without which no man shall see the Lord." Think of this, ye who slumber within the pale of the Christian Church without moral purity. O remember that it is enacted in the conclave of heaven, enrolled in the eternal decrees of the courts above, and written in lines of living light in God's last and perfected revelation to our race, that none but "the pure in heart shall see God." Inspiration from heaven, come upon us; impulse divine, move us in the right direction!

What a glorious system is Christianity! May we believe all it reveals, obey all it prescribes, enjoy all it promises, until the measure of that enjoyment shall enlarge itself into the boundless blessedness of heaven.

> "In all our way through life the Gospel sheds
> Its kind and healing beams o'er all our woes;
> And when our days are done, it lights the path
> That leads us on to brighter, happier scenes;
> And it will live and shine when all beside
> Has perished in the wreck of earthly things."

CHAPTER XX.

BISHOP SIMPSON'S SERMON.

[We take the following sketch of this masterly sermon from the *Methodist Home Journal*, being unable to obtain elsewhere so good an abstract, and a full report being beyond our reach, as we had no reporter at Manheim.—EDS. PENUEL.]

The Bishop announced as his text:

Romans viii. 14.—" *For as many as are led by the Spirit of God, they are the sons of God.*"

WE would gladly give the entire sermon of the Bishop, if the great demand laid upon our columns by the long report of the many services of the week would permit. We present the general line of argument, although no ordinary report can give any idea of the mighty power of the eloquence that swayed the immense congregation gathered before him.

He said: There are presented in this text two facts. 1st. That men not only may be, but are, led by the Holy Spirit of God. 2d. Such as are led by the Spirit of God are the sons of God.

Around these two facts there spring up a great many questions which reach as high as heaven, and are important as Eternity, and touching both God and human nature. God may not expect that we can perfectly answer these questions, because we cannot comprehend the whole of infinity. There are many minds that doubt the possibility of the statements just made as facts, and suggest that such ideas approach the nature of enthusiasm. They fancy there is nothing that can be clearly understood concerning the Spirit of God.

They think that man lowers self when he submits his mind to be led by any other—say he ought to stand up in his own majesty—guide his own way—have self-reliance, that he may thus rise by his own powers to all that God designs him to be.

Now we can assert that to be led by the Spirit is a fact—yet we do not presume to answer the question how, and to what extent, man may be consciously led by the Holy Spirit of God.

We regard the fact as most reasonable, although many skeptical minds deny entirely, or doubt the possibility of such transaction, because the Holy Spirit is unseen. We regard it as most reasonable, because all through this human life God has subjected man to leadership. In childhood to a father's training—a mother's care—placed under professors to be taught in science, law, arts, &c.

Man must be regarded as existing not only for this world, but, having two natures, he is fitted to live in two worlds. The body is of the earth, and has connections with everything earthly. I am related to all I see about me—earth, air, sea—to the animal and vegetable crea-

tions—and I know there is in me more than body. I
know there is thought, and feeling, and that which
governs and controls body that is not physical.

I have love, and I feel that there must be an attraction of soul to soul. Is there not much about me to
teach it—am I in harmony, in fellowship with tree,
mountain, sea, and can I not hold soul-fellowship? If
there is no such intercourse, then there is a strange dis-
cordance in my nature. God has made the soul susceptible of impressions from soul. What is this wonderful thing of talking about my soul going out to your
soul, through the medium of air?—wave acts upon
wave, and the air is in action, and a thought expressed
in my word reaches your ear, and the same thought
thrills your mind—distance makes no difference if the
medium is right. Thus my mother guided me by the
simple influence of words upon my soul—her sweet
thoughts guided me—just so her spirit overwhelmed
and controlled mine—I felt her voice, her hand, her
soul, on mine. Now I ask, if the spirit of a mother
can thus influence me, why may not the Spirit of the
great God? "He that formed the ear, can He not
hear?"

Reference was made to the philosophy of Coleridge,
and the fallacy of the argument thoroughly exposed.

I can rely upon God more than upon my senses.
God's Word is the limitation. There is fanaticism, but
this limitation will keep it from us. We may not go
beyond God's Word; just so far as my experience goes
on God's Word, I am on safe ground. Bad spirits may
come to me with suggestions, and I may be deceived
if I rely upon my own impressions; but where God

speaks in his Word, and I find an experience corresponding with that Word, I am safe. Some of the leadings of the Holy Spirit will be discovered to result in increased love for the Word of God. By the study of God's Word we are instructed, and God will never teach you by prayer what you may learn from His Word. Some would supplement the Word by prayer. We must cling to the Word and the Testimony, and never go beyond the revelation. Let none add thereto—there is no new revelation—the Word of God is the only sufficient rule of faith and practice.

Again, it leads by way of prayer, "Because ye are sons God hath sent forth," &c. When the Spirit of God is in the heart, it teaches us how to pray—no man can say, "Our Father," but by the Holy Ghost. No man can truly say that Jesus is Lord, without the Holy Ghost, and this gives him feeling through and through.

Out of the depths we cry unto God. He leads us down into the valley of humility, that we may be exalted —what groaning it inspires—instance Jacob wrestling, &c. There is a depth of experience that comes out of these soul-struggles, through intense groanings. There never has been a man of power in the world but has been led through intense groanings to preparation for victory. Luther, before the Diet of Worms, and Wesley, in his deep spirit-longings, demonstrate this truth. These are followed by seasons of great joy, peace, and victory. True, the workings of the Holy Spirit are very different with different individuals—some are extravagant in expression; others very peaceful and quiet, but moved by the same Spirit—I have gone to houses of mourning and witnessed the great difference in expressions of grief; some with great outcry gave expression to feeling, while others had a grief too big for tears.

Some of the most rapturous death-beds I have ever seen, have been those of the most quiet Christians; they have been so manifestly with God, that I have wanted to send messages by them to friends in heaven. I am not very demonstrative, and am more deeply moved in quiet and retirement than in great gatherings.

Reference was made to God's manifestation of Himself to Moses, and to the belief that He finally died of glory. Attention was directed to the fact that the endearing title of this text is not found under former dispensations.

Believers are not called sons of God in the Gospels, but they are spoken of as children after the day of Pentecost, and the Epistles are full of the expression. In these they are frequently called "sons of God." Again, there is a likeness to God in His children, for we are formed in His image. We are sons here, but what we shall be afterward, who can declare? In one of the lowest senses, this likeness consists in knowledge. We are to be like God. In nature we discover family likeness both by the physical and spiritual. Take two children of the same parents, who may be raised in different families, whose mother was a tender and intelligent Christian, and great thoughts will impress and move both. I have noticed that families, however poor, if truly religious, have always become intelligent families. I have looked over the great men of the age and have traced this fact in their history. (He referred to the men who were boys in his childhood and who had risen to distinction.) Christianity will lead to greatness of thought, feeling, and influence. I used to wonder why men had these great questions under consideration—Christianity will lead to all the great questions of the world. It is marked by boundless benevolence everywhere and to all persons.

A beautiful illustration of the magnetic storm was introduced that thrilled the entire audience.

He closed with a reference to the future glory of the Christian: " Beloved, now are we the sons of God, but it doth not yet appear what we shall be; but we know that when Christ shall appear we shall be like Him, for we shall see Him as He is."

A TEA-TABLE BLESSING.

A WONDERFUL scene was witnessed in one of the boarding tents on Monday evening at tea-time. Some two or three hundred were sitting at table, in the act of commencing their repast. A group of five or six, two or three of whom had just entered into the blessing of perfect love, and one had just been converted, were sitting together. Their hearts were full and eyes were streaming. One of them broke out and praised the Lord. Another followed, and another. The fire ran up and down the tables. At this juncture a young lady from Philadelphia, the daughter of a preacher, began to preach—yes, preach. Her soul, lips, eyes, face, all on fire. The people arose from the table, weeping and shouting, and after lingering around a season, went off with hearts thrilling; the most of them leaving their meals all but untouched. Another such tea-table scene was never, perhaps, witnessed.

PENTECOSTAL POWER AND GLORY.

ON Monday evening after sermon, the power of God descended in a most wonderful degree upon the whole congregation. All were called upon to kneel in silent prayer before God. A vast congregation was present, and nearly all knelt, or bowed the head. The writer, being much fatigued, left the stand in the midst of the scene, and went up along the left-hand outside aisle. Such a sight he had never seen before. Silence reigned. Thousands were in the attitude of prayer. An awful presence seemed to rest upon the multitude. You could hear heavy breathing, as if they were crying. There were suppressed sobs, and praises too. Deep-drawn sighs, as if burdened hearts were breaking. A minister found a sinner alone, no one paying any attention to him, crying for mercy. God had found him.

There were those who insisted that at one time they heard a sound, a strange sound, as of a rushing, mighty wind, and yet as if somewhat subdued and held in check over that prayerful congregation. The writer went to his tent, far back from the circle, but God was everywhere; the people were still, as we may suppose they were that night when the Death-Angel was going about slaying the first-born of Egypt.

It was an awful season. Souls were wrestling with God. God, from the archives of memory, was unrolling to many the long, long list of their sins. Unfaithful church members were looking, with a shudder, over the dreadful past. The people were face to face with God.

PUTTING IN THE SICKLE.

On Wednesday evening the ministers present were sent out into the congregation to bring sinners to Christ. In a short time the slain of the Lord covered the ground. All around, in every direction, you saw groups engaged in prayer. From fifty to a hundred penitents were in the altar in front of the stands. Far up towards the head of the ground ministers could be seen pointing kneeling penitents to Christ. Without doubt, scores were that night converted to God. The harvesters had been preparing for days, and that night they put in the sickle. Such scenes are rare—have been far too rare in the past. May we be so true to our God in the future, that they may be often reproduced.

MISSING A SERMON BUT CONVERTING SOULS.

The Prayer Meetings held at Manheim were almost without number. At the stand, in the great tents, in scores of smaller ones, in family tents, during the interval of preaching, the tide of prayer was ever rolling on. A Philadelphia lady had a desire to hear a certain minister preach. Just as she was going out to hear him, a penitent soul was brought to her tent door, and she stopped to pray with her. Another, and still another came, and by the time the sermon was over, the three were converted to God. She missed the sermon, but converted three souls from the error of their ways.

MR. McDONALD'S CLOSING ADDRESS.

DEAR BRETHREN AND SISTERS :—We are about clos
ing these memorable services, and shall soon be at our
homes.   Home will not be Manheim.   A few words of
counsel may not be out of place.   There are many
things that a sanctified soul should *avoid*, as well as *do*.
The road to heaven, though a most delightful way, is
not a path of flowers ; it is sometimes rough and thorny,
and we need not only to be shod with the preparation
of the Gospel of peace, but to be informed of some pit-
falls and dangerous points.

FIRST.— *You should avoid all unnecessary controversy.*

There are many in your vicinity who not only oppose
holiness, but they will seek to draw you into controversy on the subject.   They like controversy much
better than personal experience.   They will manage to
hold still while you relate God's wonderful dealings
with you, and then seek to continue the controversy.
Do not fail to remember that the man who is ready for
controversy is not ready for full salvation.   Holiness
is not the end he seeks.   He has no love for it, and
only seeks to confuse and confound you.   Such controversy is generally attended with a warmth of spirit
which has a tendency to cool the ardor of our love, and
leave us weaker than when the combat began.   Better
put into the hands of such a one some good book on
the particular point in dispute.   When Paul was to be
tried for his life, his only defence was the relation of his
experience, and how Jesus met him in the way.   We
cannot do better than follow his example.

SECOND.—*Avoid indolence or inactivity.*

God did not sanctify you to release you from labor. There are no retired Christians. There are no gilded saloons for gentlemen and lady passengers here. The command of the Master is, "Go work in the vineyard." A holy Christian is never idle, never uselessly employed. Our mission is the grandest of human missions, and to fulfil it we must be clothed with the pure robes of personal holiness; upon our forehead must shine this jewel of heavenly brilliancy. We must supplicate as Abraham did for the doomed city; as Moses, in behalf of his rebellious charge; as Jacob, until he had power with God and man; like Daniel, with supplication, fasting, and ashes. Be like Alleine, "insatiably greedy of the conversion of souls." Let your desire for the conversion of souls occupy your thoughts, sleeping and waking. Do something for God. Do not be idle. God has no place for idlers.

THIRD.—*Avoid a censorious spirit.*

You will have much to try your faith. You may be called "fanatics," and "second-blessing seekers," and that too by members of the Church.

Your minister may regard you as a troublesome member, and suggest that you had better not say so much about holiness. We know one such minister, who declared that the greatest nuisance in his Church was an old disciple of Jesus, and lover of holiness, who had stood like a pillar of brass for more than forty years, a pure-hearted defender of this blessed grace, and who was regarded by the great mass of the Church as an apostle of goodness. You may find it difficult at such times not to make some reply. But remember that many eyes are upon you, watching your every word. Do not utter one harsh or unkind word against your minister. Do not report that he needs conversion, or that he does not feed you. Better tell all this to the Great Shepherd. If He can bear with them, you ought not to complain. Pray, as Sammy Hick used to pray for his minister, "Lord, touch fire to him."

Do not scold the Church because they do not come up to your standard, but let them see that you love them, and are anxious to have them become "partakers of like precious faith." There are many who are confused, and do not see this subject clearly. Some have been misled by others, and for certain reasons have more or less prejudice against the doctrine. Your lives, if uniform, humble, and active, will do much to disarm them of prejudice and bring them to the fountain.

FOURTH.—*Do not take your particular experience as the standard for others.*

It is seldom that any two persons reach the same point in Christian experience by the same process in all particulars. One enters into the *most holy place*, rapturously exclaiming,

> "O for a thousand tongues to sing
> My great Redeemer's praise,"

while another reaches the same point, but with feelings best expressed by—

> "A speechless awe that dares not move,
> And all the silent heaven of love."

One shouts lustily; another feels deeply, but says nothing. Do not think that everybody must do as you do. We differ in our education, and in natural temperament; and our religious experience is shaded more or less by these. We cannot help it. One may "meditate on these things" until the heart is lifted to heaven in sweetest musings. Another may "sit and sing himself away" to a bliss that fills the whole heart. Another may "cry out and shout" at the revealings of the Divine presence. My musing brother must not complain of my singing or shouting brother, and they in their turn must not complain of his musings. While there are different manifestations, it must be remembered that all is by the same Spirit.

In regard to the matter of dress, of which much is said, do not be too confident that you only are right. Our education has much to do in modifying our faith in these matters. Do not conclude that the Spirit is grieved by everybody who does not accord with you. A safe rule for all to follow in such matters is this: Let your adorning be such as not to attract attention or remark from any one. Be neither so old-fashioned as to be regarded as a fossil of a past generation, nor yet so much in style as to impress most minds that you think more of your external adornings than you do of a "meek and quiet spirit." Be sure that your adorning is internal, not external.

FIFTH.—*Avoid all unnecessary extravagance.*

Persons of an ardent temperament frequently do many things not in keeping with the rules of etiquette. This may be expected. But be careful when you come to "visions and revelations." Do not conclude that God has made a confidant of you to bear special messages from Him to His Church. It is only when some honest but misguided souls lose their way that mischief is done. God has been scandalized by some who profess this *higher life*, by claiming the power to impart the Holy Ghost, and heal the sick, and do many other things much more objectionable. Keep clear of all such associations, unless you would have your good evil spoken of. Avoid all extravagance of voice, and gesture, and everything except humble trust and loving obedience.

SIXTH.—*Do not imagine that you must be a religious pugilist.*

If called upon to rebuke sin, do it in such a manner as to convince the gainsayer that you are a loving follower of Jesus. But do not fight everybody. You will do quite as much by prayer as in any other way. Most of you are called as witnesses for the truth, and not as defenders of the faith. Do your appropriate work.

SEVENTH.—*Be very careful in your confessions and professions of holiness.*

It is better to *confess* Christ than *profess* holiness. It is our duty to do both. If Jesus has saved us, there is no reason why He should not have the honor of it. But let all understand that you are not so anxious to publish this to the world as you are to glorify God and honor the blood of Jesus. While you must do it to retain the blessing, be careful that it be done with humility.

FINALLY.—*In the discharge of your religious duties do not be governed by feeling, but by faith.*

Do not be spasmodic in your religious duties, but let principle govern you. Do not take it for granted that when your feelings are gone you have no faith. Sometimes we are left as barren of feelings as a desert of flowers. God will test us and prove us, that it may be seen that we prize Him more than His gifts. Carry this God-given blessing with you wherever you go; and may Heaven and earth witness to the genuineness of the work here wrought; and may eternity reveal the fruit of this mighty change!

RESULTS OF THE MANHEIM MEETING.

These can only be measured in Eternity. Hundreds of souls, filled with the Holy Ghost and baptized with fire, going out into the world to bear their pure and burning testimony all over the land, there cannot but follow results for good innumerable and incalculable. Here upon this sacred and in this retired spot, many ministers of our holy religion, and many members of the Church of Christ from far and near, found themselves able to make their sacrifice complete, and as they did so they received of the Divine Spirit the witness of their entire sanctification and the anointing of power which made their hearts courageous to dare, and their tongues and hands mighty to do for Jesus, and hence, as the necessary sequence, the work ceased not, but rather widened and mounted higher when the meeting was closed and the laborers had returned to their homes.

From all parts of the land has come the news of victory for Zion. As an illustration of this, Rev. R. A. Arthur, of West Virginia, writes as follows:

"The Camp-meeting at Moundsville, W. Va., held last August, was a wonderful success. More than one hundred were wholly sanctified. The influence of the meeting has been felt far and wide, so that in this region not less than five hundred have felt the all-cleansing blood of Jesus upon their hearts within the last year."

But what connection has the work of holiness here with the National Camp-meeting ? I answer :

1st. Rev. F. Ball, accompanying me to that meeting, received the sanctifying power of the Spirit, and bringing the fire home to his own charge in Wheeling, greatly promoted the work of holiness.

2. Ten Thousand brethren at the National Camp-meeting solemnly pledged themselves with uplifted hands to pray for the success of the Moundsville meeting ; and their prayers were heard and answered.

3. Rev. J. S. Inskip and wife, Dr. and Mrs. Palmer, Rev. John Thompson, and Rev. B. Pomeroy and wife, were, as it were, a delegation from the National Camp-meeting to the Moundsville meeting, and their eminent services greatly promoted the work of holiness. The Lord wonderfully blessed their labors.

4. Having been greatly strengthened and encouraged at Manheim, I have been enabled more perfectly and successfully to aid in carrying on the glorious work of holiness. The past year was the most successful year of my life. More than one hundred and fifty were wholly sanctified within the bounds of my charge.

I have deemed it due to the National Camp-meeting, and for the encouragement of the brethren connected therewith, to make the foregoing statements.

Awaiting with joy the glorious morning when the harvest shall be shouted home and the sheaves be numbered, let us praise our Lord and adore the Holy Ghost for such pentecostal seasons as Manheim. May God multiply them ; and let all the people say " Amen ! "

Round Lake.

CHAPTER XXI.

ROUND LAKE Camp-ground, a name which for many
years to come will be fragrant in the memory of thousands of the lovers of holiness, is a beautiful grove, situated some twenty miles from the city of Troy, in the
State of New York, on the railroad leading from Troy
to Saratoga Springs. The grounds consist of about
forty acres, finely situated upon an eminence, whose
crest overlooks the lovely sheet of water from which
the place takes its name, and are, indeed, "beautiful
for situation."

The space within the circle, as well as much of the
ground upon which the tents and cottages are built, has
been finely graded, and a substantial stand, capable of
accommodating some two hundred preachers with seats,
has been erected, in the cupola of which hangs a bell
which calls the worshippers to their devotions. In
front of this stand are seats for several thousands, and
all is finely shaded by forest trees, which spread the

greenness of their arching branches overhead—all constituting a grand and pillared temple, through whose arches and recesses the waves of worship swell like the song of seraphim.

Outside the circle are circular avenues running around the ground, which are cut at intervals and at right angles by streets radiating from the centre. Many of the avenues bear names historic in the annals of Methodism, as Wesley avenue, Fletcher avenue, Asbury avenue, etc., leaving upon the mind the impression that the spirits of the fathers may be hovering near to mingle in the ardent devotions of their sons and daughters.

*Pure water from springs upon the neighboring hills is brought to the ground by underground conductors, and, besides furnishing an abundant supply for use at various points, rises in a beautiful and constantly streaming fountain at the lower side of the grounds, just by the bookstore, and near the main entrance to the circle, imparting an air of coolness and beauty, and at the same time calling to mind the better and purer fountain which has been " opened for sin and for uncleanness."

ASSEMBLING.

Here, on the 6th day of July, 1869, commenced the third National Camp-meeting ever held in America, or in the world. Quite a number had reached the grounds during the week preceding; and on Sunday, the 4th, very interesting services were held; but not till Monday, the 5th, did the stream of life fairly begin to flow this way. Thence onward through the ten days of the meeting did the mighty tide of humanity flow and ebb, some single trains bringing thousands. A detail of men

from the Capital Police was constantly upon the ground
to preserve order; and so perfect were the arrangements,
and so manifestly was the Lord's hand present throughout the entire meeting, that very few arrests were made,
and not the slightest disturbance occurred to mar the
peace and order that reigned everywhere.

The lowest estimates put the number of people in
attendance on the Sabbath at twenty thousand; and
but for the fact that—by an express stipulation with the
Railroad Company, which every lover of God's Sabbath
must approve—no trains were run to the ground on
Sunday, there would have been many more. On that
day Bishop Simpson preached to the thronging multitudes in the morning; and three distinct services were
organized and simultaneously in progress in the afternoon.

The meeting continued from the 6th to the 16th of
July, with increasing manifestations of the Divine presence and power. The preaching and other religious
services were under the control of the National Camp-
meeting Committee.

The object of the following chapters is to give some
of the sermons, exhortations, testimonies, and experiences which so thrilled our hearts, when listening to
them, with the earnest prayer, that to thousands who
were not at this great feast, but who may read these
pages, they may be made a blessing in leading them
into the glorious light of the "full assurance of faith,"
and the experience of present and entire salvation from
sin.

THE FIRST SERVICE.

On Tuesday afternoon, July 6, the first public service of the meeting was held at the stand.

The service was introduced by singing the 536th Hymn, commencing—

> "Jesus, thine all-victorious love,
> Shed in my heart abroad;
> Then shall my feet no longer rove,
> Rooted and fixed in God."

The singing was followed by prayer and the reading of the Apostle's account of the wondrous baptism of the Holy Ghost on the day of Pentecost, when cloven tongues like as of fire sat upon each of the waiting disciples, and they were all filled with the Spirit.

MR. INSKIP'S SERMON.

At the close of these opening services, REV. J. S. INSKIP, of Baltimore, and President of the National Camp-meeting Committee, rose to speak. He said:

In consenting to address myself to the most responsible task I ever undertook in my life, I assure you that I am very much embarrassed. It is not that I am unaccustomed to speaking at camp meetings; it is not because of lack of confidence in these my ministerial brethren, nor in these people of God who hear me, that I feel thus; but I am embarrassed with the idea that this is the first service of this National Camp-meeting for the promotion of Christian holiness, and that it is necessarily to have something of a decisive influence upon all that is to come. O, that the Holy Spirit may make us mighty for God to-day, that this opening service may promote his glory!

I have had not a little difficulty in fixing upon the best line of thought to be presented at this time, but I propose, humbly looking to Almighty God for help, to ask you to contemplate with me the words of the Apostle to the Church in Thessalonica, as found in the 5th *Chapter and first clause of the 23d verse of the First Epistle: "And the very God of peace sanctify you wholly."*

I have no need at this time to say anything as to the fitness of holding a Camp-meeting for the special work of the promotion of holiness. God settled that question last year at Manheim, and we pass now directly to the examination of our text.

THREE INQUIRIES.

We may with profit inquire:—

1st. What is it to be sanctified wholly?

2d. How this state may be attained?

3d. The benefits that accrue from it?

I do not propose to give this theme a dogmatic discussion, and yet there are one or two points which it is proper and important all should understand with regard to the nature of this work, for we think that many have been in some measure mistaken in their interpretation of our views and doctrines upon this subject. We wish, therefore, at the outset, to state in a plain way what we understand it is to be wholly sanctified. The phrases and terms perfect love, purity, perfection, entire sanctification, and holiness, we shall employ as synonyms in this discussion. And now let us proceed to the subject.

SOMETHING ABOVE JUSTIFICATION.

1st. To be sanctified wholly is to attain to something beyond and above, and different from that which we experienced at the time we were converted to God. If I should not succeed in defining definitely the difference between the sanctification experienced in regeneration, and that which is entire in the subsequent life, I shall only have fallen into the difficulty of attempting to give a philosophical analysis of a practical theme.

We are often asked, "Is this difference one of kind, or of degree only?" We do not choose, nor think it necessary, to dwell upon this question, for the end we have in view is a practical one. When the sinner cries out to God, when under conviction for sin and under the condemnation of sin, his cry is for deliverence from that condemnation, and this he receives, together with a new heart and adoption into the divine family; and to the regenerate there is no condemnation, and yet every such one who follows the Spirit soon begins to press the cry of the Psalmist, "Create in me a clean heart, O God, and renew a right spirit within me." There is not a Christian man upon this ground but is deeply anxious that his soul may be made entirely clean; for if a Christian is not interested in this he must be a backslidden Christian. But there is in every believing heart this desire to be pure.

I do not say that when the soul is first saved it is not brought into a new life, for we all believe it is; but after thus experiencing to some extent the sanctifying grace of God, every Christian feels at times uprisings within his soul which clearly indicate that he is not *entirely* sanctified, and it is this that leads us to cry out with the Psalmist, "Create in me a clean heart, O God!"

CONSCIOUS DIFFERENCE.

2d. Let us observe, that while you may not be able philosophically to define the difference between these two states of the soul, yet of this difference every mind that experiences the two is personally conscious, and as I have before said, this question comes before us to-day as a practical one.

You know, my brother, or my sister, how there linger within the heart pride and passion, kept under control, it is true, but yet not destroyed. They live there yet. But we may have these things all destroyed and cast out, so that the nature within us may be radically revolutionized, and the bias of our hearts be all in the right direction. And oh, when a man has reached this state, how great is the advantage he has gained, and how much more easily does he triumph over his foes, for they are all without now, and none within. And this attainment is within the reach of every Christian, and is so taught by all our Methodist theology, and, better than all, by the Bible. I will not call attention particularly now to the teaching of our catechism, our discipline, our hymns, and our fathers upon this subject. I will only say that our whole ritual, and all our theological course as ministers, and our whole book of discipline combine with the word of God in holding up something above and beyond regeneration, as the possibility and duty of every believer. This is what the Apostle prays for in the text: "The very God of peace sanctify you *wholly.*"

THIS IS THE WORK OF THE HOLY GHOST.

3d. We must not forget that this is a work to be done by the Holy Ghost. I wish especially to press this thought upon all present. It is not wrought by human power, nor can it be, but it is by the power of the Holy Ghost, by which we come to a state of entire purity. In this state the soul loves God with all its strength; faith is not mixed with doubt; love is never mingled with hate; humility is not discounted by pride; patience is never paralyzed by petulance. In short, the whole nature is brought into perfect harmony with the Divine will; and all this mighty work is to be wrought in us by the power of the Holy Ghost.

There have been two extreme views upon this subject, both of which have led many astray. The first is the gradual theory, which teaches that we are to grow into this blessing, and which it seems to me ignores the fact of which we have just spoken, that this is a work to be done, if done at all, by Divine power.

The second view seems to make this agency to be a certain intellectual exercise, by which we are able to say that, having done certain things, we are therefore wholly sanctified. I pray that no such ideas as these may be promulgated here. We are here to teach that we are to be sanctified by the power of ALMIGHTY GOD.

It is sometimes said that justification is an act, or change in the mind of God toward us; while sanctification is a work wrought in us whereby we are changed. But this does not change the truth of what we have just said, for what God does in us is as much His work as what He does for us.

HOW MAY WE SECURE IT?

This, then, is God's work; but if you or I would have this power exercised in us and for us, we must put ourselves into the right relation to God. The sinner will not be pardoned unless he repents and believes in the Lord Jesus Christ, nor will the believer be entirely sanctified unless in humble penitence he believes in Jesus—trusts him for this work.

No uninspired man ever taught more correctly and clearly with regard to sin and repentance in believers than did John Wesley, and we shall do well to remember those teachings. He declares clearly what the Scriptures also teach, that if the Christian would be fully saved, he must come into that position where he will see and abhor the remains of sin that are still in him. And you, my brother, have reason to thus abhor yourself when you come to see the pride, and self-will, and love of the world, and movings of anger that you find still within. It will not serve the purpose to turn back to your religious life when it commenced, and try to satisfy yourself with this. No, no! How is it with you *now*, to-day? And when you have found out this, then repent, for the good old doctrine of repentance is to be received and practised by believers as well as by sinners, though not in the same sense.

But this is not enough. When you have had a look within and abhorred yourself, and repented sincerely before God, then go a step further. First look *at* yourself, not *to* yourself, and then give up all, and thoroughly con-

secrate yourself to the service of God.   There is much
that the Christian must give up if he would be entirely
the Lord's.   You cannot be as frivolous as are many professed Christians, nor as gay in dress as they are, for you
must speak, and act, and dress to please Jesus, if you
would be entirely his.   You must be willing to be marked
and known by your appearance, but more by your spirit,
as entirely Christ's.   And do not entertain the idea that
on this question you can be here to-day and yonder to-
morrow.   You must be steadily and constantly Christ's.
Between you and worldliness there must be a great gulf
fixed that can never be passed.   This matter of entire
consecration means much.   God help us to be thus consecrated.   We cannot do this without divine help, but
that help will be with us at every step, if we trust it.
If, then, you want full salvation, make a full consecration, and make it now.   This you may do; this it is
your duty to do, and to do now, cost what it may.

It takes some courage to do this; more, it may be,
than most of us have; more, perhaps, than I should
have possessed, had not God put me into a very close
corner, where I could not retreat without being incon-
sistent with myself.   I was in my pulpit preaching to
my people, and urging upon them the necessity of con-
secrating all to God.   I knew that a man's perceptions
of religious truth never get much beyond his experience, and that his experience is bounded by his consecration, and so I was urging this upon my people, and
urging them to do it now, when God said to me, so that
I could not misunderstand it, "*Do this yourself!*" and I
did it.   I made the consecration, and I knew I made it,
and I would rather have died that hour in my place in

the pulpit than not to have done it. I had no time to confer with flesh and blood, but I said at once, " Here goes for God and full salvation," and I was not long then in taking hold upon Christ, and I still cling to Him, and all hell cannot break the grasp.

When I made this consecration I knew full well what I had done, and I knew my people understood it, and there I stood in the pulpit, looking earnestly for a spot where to put my foot down next, but all was dark, and I could not see; but I said, " Here goes ; in the name of God, I will not go back," and I put my foot down in the darkness, and Oh, hallelujah ! there was a rock under it.

Oh, brother, come out, *come out*, COME OUT on the Lord's side ! Put your flag up to-day, and leave it there, and put no halliards to it with which to pull it down ! .And I tell you, my brother, if you do this to-day, the power of God will take hold of you, and you will be saved.

Not by your reason and logic, saying I have done this or that, and therefore I am saved. That will not do. What we want is the fire of God that will burn up sin, and the pure flame of love that will burn on forever and forever.

We teach the people, then, not that they are sanctified because they believe they are sanctified. It is not faith in what we are, or what we have been, or what we have done, or what has been done for us, but faith in the Almighty Christ that brings us where we cry out with joy !—

> " Tis done, the great transaction's done,
> I am my Lord's, and He is mine."

This is done in answer to faith in Jesus, and this faith

should be reached at the moment of full consecration. Consecrate, and then believe. But believe what? That you are sanctified? No! But believe that the blood of Christ cleanseth from all sin. "Well, I believe this," says one. But do you believe that it cleanses *you?* "Why," you answer, "I cannot just say that." No, and you never will till you get a willingness to go through a humiliating process, which I pray God you may go through to-day. Many, and especially ministers, want to understand the philosophy of the work before they enter upon its seeking; but if you wait till you understand that, you will never take any step toward it at all. There are many things we cannot understand. I do not know how I was converted. I could not understand it, and yet I know the fact.

Pride also keeps many away. We want the blessing, but are too proud to seek it in God's way, and cry unto Him from the valley of humiliation. Some of you will quite likely be required to come to this altar to seek this blessing. God forbid that you should be too proud to do so.

WHEN?

But when may you have this blessing?

I answer, just when you dare believe that the blood cleanseth. And when shall this be? Why, *now*, if your consecration is complete: if you have digged this impassable gulf between your soul and sin. See that you do it to-day.

But "what must I believe?" "How can I do this?" Why, how can you breathe? I cannot tell you how I can breathe, nor can any other, and yet the process goes on constantly. So, just what is meant by believing I do not know as I can tell you, or how I did it I cannot explain; *but I know I did it, and that I do it.* What is believing do you ask? It is leaning on Jesus. A brother says, "Lean *hard* on Jesus!" Yes, lean *hard* on Jesus, so that you will feel that he is your sure support, your all in all.

THE RESULTS

of this will be that Jesus will put his hand under you, and his arm around you, and his mind into you. He puts his mind into you so that you have no mind of your own. Men sometimes say of another, "That man has no mind of his own; but he must do always just as his friend says." So let it be said of us, "They can do nothing only as Jesus bids them." "They have no mind but his."

In this state you will do right, because it is a luxury to do as God would have you to do, and you will find so much of the Divine in you as to lift you up, and hold you above the power of temptation. You will be tempted still; but let the whole of your nature be made pure, and though the enemy may come and howl around you, you will feel just as easy and secure when he roars as when he is quiet. Before I received this eternal tranquillity there were frequent and terrible storms; but now all is calm and peaceful as were the Galilean waves, when He had said, "Peace, be still!"

Troubles and trials still will come, but Christ is mightier than all. You will be thrust into the furnace still, it may be, but you are better off there with one like the Son of Man with you, than out of the furnace without Him.

If we would have the world converted to God we

must get the Church wholly saved. I know it is said that "these holiness people say nothing about the conversion of sinners," and yet sinners somehow get converted among them. There were more sinners converted at Manheim last year than at any other meeting I ever attended.

And now, what have we come here for? Is it to see these fine grounds, or this beautiful lake? No! No! I trust not; we have higher ends and holier aims. All the beautiful lakes of this beautiful world are worthless when compared with the lake of salvation.

We came to wash in this fountain; to lead souls to it; to get good and to do good, as a brother here on the stand says. Oh, let us begin to day and now. Seek earnestly, all you who are not now conscious of full salvation, that this glorious work may now be wrought in you; that, wholly sanctified yourselves, you may lead others to this great blessing.

AFTER THE SERMON

Those in the congregation who wished the blessing of a clean heart, and who had come to the meeting resolved to seek it, and who were ready in self-renunciation to seek it then and there, were invited to rise to their feet, and immediately upon all parts of the ground numbers arose, and while united prayer was offered to God, some entered into the rest of faith. Thus at the very commencement of the meeting was God's power present, giving assurance to believers that, through all the services to come, the fire of the Holy Ghost should burn mightily, as subsequent events demonstrated that it did, consuming sin and setting many hearts on fire with love and zeal.

CHAPTER XXII.

SERMONS OF REV. W. B. OSBORN, OF NEW JERSEY CONFER-
ENCE, AND REV. W. L. GRAY, OF PHILADELPHIA CON-
FERENCE; EXHORTATION OF REV. B. POMEROY, OF TROY
CONFERENCE; AND TESTIMONIES.

MR. OSBORN'S SERMON.

2 *Cor.* ii. 11.—" *Lest Satan should get an advantage of us ; for we
are not ignorant of his devices.*"

SATAN hates holiness and uses all his power to prevent
people from becoming holy. It is my purpose at this
time to call attention to a few of the devices of which
he makes use to accomplish this purpose. One of these
is

INDIFFERNCE.

Satan knows very well that as long as a person is not
interested in the subject of holiness there is no danger of his becoming holy, and hence he uses his utmost power to keep men indifferent. He tries to keep
them•away from all places where the subject is urged,
and he would have been pleased if you had not come
to this meeting, and he has tried to keep others away
from this place, and may have succeeded in many cases.

PREJUDICE.

Another of his devices is to prejudice the minds of

Christians against those who profess holiness and urge it upon others; and he will, if possible, in order to prevent others from seeking it, lead those who enjoy it into sin. And this is one among the many reasons why we should be careful to stand fast always. If he does not succeed in leading them into sin, then he will misrepresent the motives and words of those who profess this grace; and sometimes he finds good people even who will help him in this work. Have you never heard such say Brother A. or Sister B. has done this or that, and he or she professes holiness? Thus Satan prejudices the mind against it. Oh, do not let the devil cheat you thus! Examine this subject, and do not take our word for it, but look into God's Word and see what he says. If you will do this you will not be left long in doubt.

NOTHING IN IT.

If Satan cannot keep a soul indifferent upon this subject, he will then try to convince him that there is nothing in it, or that it cannot be experienced till death.

But it is a reality, and may be experienced now. In the First Book of the Bible we read of a man who walked with God. This is holiness, and when you and I can daily walk with God, there will no longer be any doubt about our holiness.

We read also of Job: and God said of him that he was a perfect man, and Satan, liar as he is, did not attempt to deny it. And that this might be tested God permitted Satan to buffet him; but I rejoice that, though the devil had a long chain in this instance, God saw well to it that the end was made fast, and that in the faithfulness of Job we have a demonstration that a man can cleave fully to God in the midst of the deepest afflictions of this life.

In the New Testament we have the repetition of the command, "Thou shalt love the Lord thy God with all thy heart;" and the Apostle prays for his brethren, "The very God of peace sanctify you wholly." So, too, there are the clearest of declarations of the necessity of holiness, as "without holiness no man shall see the Lord." And there are commands to seek and love it, as "Be ye therefore perfect;" "Be ye holy," and many others. And yet some say it is not in the Bible. Get the film taken away from your eyes and you will see that the Bible is full of holiness, and it is on the outside of it even—*Holy* Bible.

WITNESSES.

Then if this doctrine is not true, what is to be done with the many witnesses to it, and their testimonies, such as Wesley, Fletcher, Lady Huntington, Carvosso, Hester Ann Rogers, Summerfield, Fisk, and hosts of others? Thousands can testify to this; and to say it is unreal is to fly in the face of a multitude of witnesses who cannot be impeached.

NOT FOR YOU.

But Satan may suggest that, though possible for others—for the minister, perhaps—it is not for you. "Ministers ought to be holy," you may say; "but I am satisfied my temperament or circumstances are such that I cannot be." This is a device of the devil; for God declares that all may be holy and glorify Him, no matter what their circumstances or temperament may be. I am glad we are not all alike, for diversity is beauty, and God needs us all in our individuality; but I rejoice also that He can make us all holy, and wherever we are, living in the next house to Satan or in the same house with him, we may live all for God.

NOT NOW.

But then Satan says : " Though this may be for you some time, it is not for you now ; you must grow into it if you ever reach it." Growth in grace is a good thing ; but the devil often employs this phrase to keep us away from God. We are to grow in grace, and not into grace. We did not grow into justification, nor can we grow into sanctification. We may not know the exact time we were justified and renewed, but it was a work done for us ; so must our entire sanctification be a work done for us and in us; and God says it may be done now, and in an instant. A friend of mine attended a camp-meeting, and hearing much upon the subject of holiness, concluded that was what he wanted, and so he went to seeking it, but he sought as though it were a great way off. But soon the Spirit applied the question to him, "Will you consecrate all now ?" "Yes, O yes," said he, "I do it now, and look for salvation now ; " and down came the blessing, and he began to shout aloud. Put a "now" into your prayers for this, for it is a now salvation.

CANNOT KEEP IT.

Again, Satan will suggest that if you get it you cannot keep it. True, some have lost it, and such are to be pitied above all others. But there is no need of this. Follow the directions of the Bible, and the blessing will keep you, and keep you well, instead of your keeping it.

COSTS TOO MUCH.

Satan may also suggest that it will cost too much. Well, it does cost something. You will have to give up many things—in short, you must give all to God, and abandon everything which is at variance with purity. It costs all this, but it does not cost too much. Is any price too large to pay for a blessing that will keep you happy all the day, and all your days, and takes away the fear of man and the fear of death? Oh! praise the Lord for the perfect freedom this grace brings with it. A good Baptist sister once said that this blessing of holiness was nothing but dying grace. Yes, it is dying grace; but it is the best kind of living grace also, and no price is too great to pay for it.

FAITHFUL AND USEFUL.

Then this will make us faithful and useful. In one of the battles of the late war, a portion of our troops, under General Steadman, were retreating, when he rode up to the standard-bearer, and seizing the flag, cried out, "Retreat, boys, if you will; but this old flag shall not go back with you." They rallied, and were victorious. So with this blood-stained banner waving over us, and with God on our side, we shall conquer every foe. Oh, let us all seek this blessing. We want power in us that shall keep us at work for God, so that men need not be compelled to ask whether we are members of the Church. Do not let Satan overcome you, but seek this grace now and here, and God shall surely bestow it upon you.

SERMON OF MR. GRAY.

Matt. v. 8.—"*Blessed are the pure in heart, for they shall see God.*"

I AM sure, my brethren, if you knew how little I feel, and how incapable of meeting the great responsibilities that rest upon me now, you would not fail to pray for me.   These words must have fallen upon the hearts of those who heard them.   They prided themselves that they were better than other people, because they were chosen of the Lord—His peculiar spouse, the spouse of His covenanted mercy. Our Lord looked into the depths of the *heart* and saw its depravity; and that He might save them, admonished them of the necessity of having it made pure. Indeed, every careful reader of the Word must have been impressed with the great stress that is laid on the condition of the heart:—" For out of the heart proceed evil thoughts, murders, adulteries, fornications, thefts, false witness, blasphemies."

Men are just what their hearts are; no better, no worse.   They may appear to men to be right, and yet within everything may be wrong, nay, nothing but rottenness.   Men may be better than their sentiments, better than their creeds, better than their associations, but never better than their hearts. The heart is the foundation, and therefore is associated with everything in the superstructure, and it is the heart that gives character to the superstructure of the life; but first or last it should be our constant thought that God looks at the condition of the heart.   Every careful reader of the Word of God must have been impressed with the repeated and forcible statements of the deep depravity of the human heart. Reason and philosophy may suggest doubts as to these statements of the low moral condition of man, but no man that reads God's Word can fail to know that it is there considered as only and continually desperately wicked. In a state of nature there is nothing good in it. It is not in a defaced or deformed merely, but in a ruined and disorganized condition. The heart is wicked, not by the force of accident, or association, or example, or habit, or by inherent constitutional tendency, but is essentially defective; not by the infusion of elements, tendencies, and propensities that in themselves are absolutely wrong, but there is the coming up and welling out of depravity and wicked tendencies, because of inherent depravity. This soul ruin has come not because it was implanted by God, or because of our original constitution, or in consequence of birth or example, but because of the absence of the controlling influence of God's grace. Purity of heart is the absence of this erratic and depraved condition of all that antagonizes the nature and law of God. It involves a change of our relations, condition, and tendencies. Our relations are changed when we are absolved from punishment by Jesus Christ. Our condition is changed when we are put under the forces set in operation by Jesus Christ and the concurrence of our wills. Our tendencies are changed when we spontaneously do that which is good rather than evil. Purity of heart makes these tendencies in accord with the Divine nature and the Divine law, so that all the volitions and aspirations find their beginning and end in God. When a man's faith is in no way mixed with unbelief, heart purity so overrides and sinks self that the individual says, I live, yet not I, but Christ

liveth in me, and the life I now live I live by the faith
of the Son of God; and so far as the government of God
is concerned, he is in constant subordination or submission, when the whole machinery of the mind and soul is
in perfect harmony with what is written in God's Word.

Is this the condition of every one before God? Is our
faith unmixed with unbelief? Is there no unholy passion? Is God our supreme delight, and do we accept
with sweet Christian resignation and joy the trials He
sends, if so we can say,—

> " Give joy or grief, give ease or pain—
> Take life or friends away;
> But let me find them all again
> In that eternal day."

Heart purity is a privilege of every child of God. There
is a great difference between having the heart right in the
sight of God, and the Christian enjoying all his privileges in the Gospel. To the latter it is perfectly natural
to believe, and all the tendencies of his soul are towards
God, and all God's fulness is poured into his soul. This
is a state to which God's children in every period and
age of the Church, by the grace of God, have entered upon; and he must have read the history of the Church to
little purpose if he has not discovered this stream of
salvation. It was developed more particularly in connection with the Reformation. A vein runs through its
theology and biography, presenting this purity as the
privilege of the children of God. God's word admon-
ishes us of the importance of this blessing. But this
privilege is not reserved for a part of the Church, but
all may be pure in heart. God has no special adminis-

trations for one more than another. Those favored in Bible record were examples for us, and they could not be examples unless it was possible to be as they were. Those great characters were built up by faith.

HEART PURITY IS THE BASIS OF CHRISTIAN MATURITY.

There can be no maturity of character without heart purity. It is the great foundation stone, and it is laid by faith in the blood of atonement, and that at the present moment. It should be distinctly understood that every blessing God promises us in His holy word is instantaneously conferred, yea, every blessing. All these are to be received by faith; and the great difficulty is to tell the people what faith is. Why it is hearing God speak—in His word—it is seeing God. "Look unto me all ye ends of the earth and be ye saved." In view of these scriptural illustrations, we say the condition is the easiest God himself could invent. We have the power of sight, but this does not involve necessarily that we see, for the Bible says, " They have eyes, but see not." The only appropriate object of our gaze is Jesus Christ, hence we are called upon to look unto Jesus. The very moment an individual sees Jesus, sees Him as the mighty Saviour, sees Him in all His divine and God-like proportions, and so looks that every other object is excluded, that moment he is saved, and hence we say the blessing is received instantaneously. Then we can read the Bible and see beauties in it never perceived before, and we shall discover our privileges greater than we had known, for God takes his people up into the Mount of Vision still; and if a man would see God, let him be purified. The carnal mind cannot discern the things of the Spirit, but

God can take these things and show them unto us.   I thought I had never read the Bible previous to my sanctification four years ago, so new and clear was its truths after that important event.   I had preached twenty-five years before that, and had welcomed into the Church hundreds, and perhaps thousands ; and yet the Bible became like a new book.   Aye, purity is the very best medium to see God.   Spiritual religion cannot be rationally apprehended, and the tongue cannot describe it, but God can reveal it to the consciousness ; and if you would know the deep things of God, get your heart purified.

To have the heart made pure signifies special favor. It comes into God's special presence, and there is nearness to Him that never existed before.   There are many who live outside of the veil of the temple, and that is a great privilege.   I lived there many years and enjoyed it, but what is it compared to going into the holy of holies ?   Then there comes an uninterrupted union.   Then I do not go down from the Mount where God has taken me, and the vision continues, and the communion is uninterrupted, and yet I have my trials and temptations.

PURITY OF HEART IS THE TRUE SOURCE OF SPIRITUAL STRENGTH.

God's giants were all pure in every age.   What is the cause of all the weakness in the Church of which we all know and experience ?   If a man knows God is with him, if God is always before him, he cannot be a coward.   I do not know anything of power only as God puts it upon me for the moment.   I must hold on to

God, and so, as a brother said, "Every step he took he thought his foot would find no resting-place, but he found it came down upon the Rock of Ages." This is the strength which God supplies to those whose hearts are purified by His grace. I do not know that those professing sanctification always do more in the Church than others. I have nothing to say in vindication of them. Their works and their master must do that, and the kingdom of God cometh not with observation. They are a very quiet people, and the most quiet people in the world are those who have most of God. They do not seem to be the explosive part of the army of God. Though I would not set them above others, I know they are doing a great deal of good in my section of the country. They have power and are wonderfully active, inventive, and enterprising for God. I pity the man that waits in the market-place for some man to hire him. I am a Methodist of the third generation, and when a boy my mother took me to Church, and I heard a preacher tell about his experience of sanctification. Years passed away, and having been long a minister, I thought seriously of seeking and obtaining this blessing. Then the devil said, "You have labored hard to gain the ministerial position which you occupy, and there will be very little of you left in a short time if you take this path. Your brethren will give you the go by." Soon I concluded, sink or swim, live or die, I will be all the Lord's, and I have found the devil a liar on this subject. I never had the co-operation and sympathy of my brethren in the ministry to the degree I have it to-day, thank God. (Voices, " Bless the Lord.")

THE WAY TO SUPREME HAPPINESS IS THE WAY OF HOLINESS.

When a man sees God he is not careful to see anything else. (Glory.) When the soul sees God then it is satisfied. Yes, brother, sister, you want to be happy. I have been rejoicing for four years, day and night, both in the sunshine and storm. And storms there have been, some of the severest I have ever met. I have buried dear ones, and have had to part with some very precious friends, that I might do my duty, but never enjoyed so much of what might be called happiness as when my will is lost in God's will. When is a man happy? When his joys overbalance his sorrows, and that has been the way with me since I entered upon this blessing of purity of heart.

The truth is marching on. I thank God I had a mother that represented it in her life and experience, and my greatest regret is, that when I became a minister I did not fully follow her example; but when God purified my soul I could see the example of my mother as I had never seen it before, and though she has been dead many years, she yet speaketh. Will you have this purity of heart now? The Bible constantly says, "Now, now." Brother, get your heart purified and filled with God, and you will be mighty to the accomplishment of the Divine will.

MR. POMEROY'S EXHORTATION.

I am in a strait, friends, and I hardly know what to do. I feel considerably stirred. The brother has been talking about *purity*, and I want to say a word about *power*, for they run along together wonderfully. In a certain city I attended a meeting for the promotion of holiness, and a great many came forward seeking for power. They believed they were sanctified, but they had not power. When the Word of the Lord comes it makes a man ten times himself, and whoever is under the power of the Holy Ghost is a definite kind of power. He is not moving about by moonlight, not knowing what he seeks. If he is in need he knows it. Whoever is under the inspiration of the Holy Ghost is not only quick and powerful, but sharp. With this two-edged sword, he cuts and cleaves and anatomizes to the astonishment of all men, for it is a discerner of the thoughts and intents of the heart. I used to think if I had power it would make something of me ; but we want the power not to talk loud. I do not mean this round-swell, high-foam, white-capped kind, but that which makes me stay down, below, to sit and grow tall while you sit there. I mean the kind that keeps us in the valley, and to be very quiet there, for we have eternity to prove what we are, and we can afford to wait. *What is power ?* It is not superadded quality. It is not something tacked on to holiness that may be cast off. When you have holiness you will have power. Those who have this, are the men and women who are worth nothing, and yet ask no favors of any one this side the stars. They are holy on God's account, and if they break down it is at his expense, and they can afford to go on in this way.

The Christian's power is in his faith. What is strong faith? It is not in its quantity. It does not necessarily act out on a broad scope. It is unmixed faith, whether little or much. If it is like a grain of mustard seed it is strong faith, if it is unmixed. If we mix a little sight with faith we injure faith, and the admixture of anything with it is against the character of God. If persons cannot believe, you cannot help them by urging up their faith. The most effectual assistance is to smash in all their broken reeds, to break in upon their hopes, until they feel themselves ready to perish. Put a man down until he consents to lie on God's door-sill a spiritual foundling, too weak to cry, and then that man will believe as you bring him to Christ. It requires more exertion to disbelieve in ourselves than to believe in God. We are strong in the Kingdom and in God through what relates us to God. Fourteen cars went up on the train that passed here this morning, and the last car went as strong, seemingly, as the first. It had no power in itself, but the power was in the coupling. The power of faith is in the coupling. Just in proportion as your coupling to Christ stands, you are almighty, however weak in yourselves; and until this is severed Satan can do nothing with the Christian. No matter how ignorant he may be, devices of men or devils, nor the rage of hell, can move him as long as he buckles on to God. Now I feel a little better, but as though there was a volcano in me yet. I feel glad that old-fashioned Methodism can get up the biggest meeting on the continent. This means a revival of old-fashioned gospel power, and God is going to take care of this thing. Here is my hope of the world. Said a man who was up here, "They have Presbyterians, Baptists, Episcopalians, and Methodists, but they all love each other." Christ is wonderfully pleased to make all his little ones work together for the universal sway of His kingdom. We don't want books, and schools, and colleges, as much as the Holy Ghost. I would not have talked a few years ago as I am often constrained to do now—no, not to have saved the cause; but now I must speak when I see God's great programme laid out before me.

[Brother Pomeroy walked up and down the stand rejoicing in God, as the people sung with great power,—

"The cross of Christ I'll cherish," &c.]

TESTIMONIES.

A SISTER.—"Three years ago God forgave my sins and made me His child. One year ago at Manheim He not only broke the power of cancelled sin, but He cast it all out, and through the year He has kept me by grace. I am glad to be here, and I am happy in God while the stream of salvation flows constantly through my soul."

A SISTER:

"Just as I am, thy love unknown
  Hath broken every barrier down;
  Now to be thine, yea thine alone,
  O, Lamb of God, I come!"

This is my experience now, and I praise the Lord that He keeps me thus His own."

A Brother: "Thank God for a salvation that removes all doubt and fear. There is not a doubt in my mind to-night, and God the Holy Ghost casts out all fear."

Rev. Bro. C.:—"This is the kind of firing that brings the enemy down, and does execution for God. This is the kind of fighting that, according to John the Revelator, overcame the devil, for he says, 'They overcame him by the blood of the Lamb and by the word of their testimony;' that is, they got religion and then told of it, and the devil ran away, as he always will when God's people begin to use this kind of artillery, for the blood of the Lamb and the word of the testimony of the saints kills him. The Lord give us more of it!"

A Brother Minister:—"When but a youth I asked a class-leader in England what was the best qualification for a Methodist minister, and his reply was, 'A holy heart.' I began at once to seek it, and continued to do so earnestly, till one night while at prayer there came upon my soul something as sweet as heaven, and with it came the witness, clear, direct, and plain, that my soul was fully renewed after the image of Jesus. I rejoice in the same salvation to-day."

A Sister:—"I am glad that Jesus makes me simple enough to believe just what He says, and to believe it because He says it. I do believe in Him, and I am saved."

A Sister:—"I am beloved by the Father, redeemed by the Son, our Saviour, and sanctified by the Holy Ghost."

Rev. John Allen—"This is the one hundred and

ninety-ninth Camp-meeting I have attended in my life, and it is the best one of all. God is filling my soul constantly with His presence and glory, and I can say—

> " ' 'Tis done, the great transaction's done,
>   I am my Lord's, and He is mine.' "

A BROTHER.—" If there ever was a man who ought to be thankful to God for His mercy, I am that man. I am an old rum-seller, saved by grace; and if God can save a rum-seller, surely He can save any one. I rejoice that He saved me from that wretched business, and that He saves me from all my sins."

A SISTER.—" I live in a land where the sun shines all the day and all the year. O, blessed sunlight ! "

AN AGED BROTHER FROM KENTUCKY.—" Years ago, in Saint Mark's Place, in the city of New York, I learned what I never knew by experience before, that Jesus Christ hath power to save from sin. I have travelled seven hundred miles to attend this feast of tabernacles, and I rejoice that I am here. For thirty-seven years I have been fighting in the front ranks of Immanuel's army, and now I am looking for a discharge very soon. The sun is risen upon your old servant, and his soul is full of light and salvation."

A SISTER.—" The sea of the Saviour's love is all around me, and I feel as though I were floating upon an ocean of love that has neither bottom nor shore."

A BROTHER.—" I have been wondering all day whether heaven could be better than this. Jesus is so near me that heaven seems all around and within me."

CHAPTER XXIII.

SERMON OF REV. J. T. PECK, D.D., OF TROY CONFERENCE,
AND TESTIMONIES.

DR. PECK'S SERMON.

Heb. xii. 14.—*"Follow peace with all men, and holiness, without which no man shall see the Lord."*

WHENCE are the criticisms which stern Christians are disposed to bring upon themselves? The demonstrations of heart experience of which they speak, are but a small part of what passes in the Christian heart. The intellect has secrets which it refuses to reveal to the lips, and which it does not undertake to publish. The really humble, tender, thoughtful expressions of unworthiness, inward depravity, and deep-seated ruin which we hear, are never equal to the reality, and are only a few outward manifestations of a great perpetual system of heart scrutiny, which goes on inside honest Christian people. I have an idea that the searching criticisms we practise upon ourselves are based upon actual depravity, and are illustrated to us by the light kindly vouchsafed by the Holy Ghost. That this is the reason why we are searching ourselves, that God gives us the light of the Holy Spirit, the promptings of Divine influence to induce that search, I have no doubt; and in proportion as we are

honest, we are willing and thorough in that self examination. The heart yearnings which we have after the
power which will relieve us from our felt depravity, are
from God,—He himself pervades and moves hearts that
men may long to be saved from what they feel to be inward depravity. I raise the question, in connection with
these searching criticisms and heart yearnings, *What answer is given to them from God in the Holy Bible?*

THE SPIRIT CONVINCES.

There is a logical probability that the things which,
under the searching of God's Spirit, we condemn in ourselves, are to be resisted, overpowered, and exterminated
by the power of the Holy Spirit. That logical probability my brethren will see in the fact which I have assumed, but not proven—that the Holy Spirit points out
in the man the depraved state of the soul. Conviction
is a part of the great plan of Redemption, and is implied in it; and if it were not God's plan to condemn
and remove these depraved states, and supply their
place with what was right and holy, then the judicial
dispensation would supersede Redemption, and then
only punishment would follow, and that would be connected with despair, and not with hope.

The answer we should expect to prayers that God
himself inspires, such as David uttered, when in self-
scrutiny he lifted up his heart, hardly daring to lift up
his eyes, and prayed, " Create in me a clean heart, O
God, and renew a right spirit within me;" such as are
manifested in those who say, " As the hart panteth
after the water-brooks, so panteth my soul after Thee,
O God "—are to be found in some provision or ar-

rangement of God, which, I am sure, we may reasonably expect to see clearly delineated in the Gospel. As an illustration of the certainty that there is a remedial response from God to these yearnings of ours, I would introduce the saying of Jesus: "Blessed are they that hunger and thirst after righteousness, for they shall be filled."

EXHAUSTIVE TERMS.

Consider one fact, *Inspiration uses exhaustive terms* to describe the supply of these wants; and they are selected, it would seem, to express this supply in the strongest manner possible; and it seems to me that in this effort Inspiration labored under the burden of inexpressible thought. Hence the change of expression, and the adoption of one kind and another, in order to reach and convince the human understanding of truths which are too large for language.

The exhaustive character of this language is to be considered. Take a few specimens from the Scriptures of the Divine method of struggling to bring out this idea: "Be ye therefore perfect." This was uttered as the completeness of an idea, and it could not be increased in strength, and requires elimination, if it be applied to the work of piety in general. It seems as if God had selected a word, to try, if possible, to get out the idea that the yearnings after Christian perfection were provided for. I need not tell you that we are only pleased with what is perfect in itself. That is one reason why we are not pleased with ourselves; since, if we accept not the Gospel provision, we inevitably fall below a proper standard. We have also the word "sanctify," which radically means to make whole, and was so employed at first; but in the subsequent use of the word an inferior sense was attached to it, and it was graded downward, and, therefore, could not exactly embody the idea embraced in the prayer of the Apostle— "Sanctify you wholly," the emphasis being on the word "wholly," as much as to say, The ordinary use of the word sanctify has become less than the truth, and, therefore, requires an exhaustive epithet, and hence the word "wholly" is added. If you take the word "faith," you find that in its ordinary acceptations it is not strong enough to employ in regard to these intense heart-yearnings; and hence, in such a connection, it is "most holy faith," a kind of faith which reaches to the clearest and broadest privileges. Take the term "love"—it is a very precious word, and one of the very best in our language; but when you come to use it for God's preparations and our heart-yearnings, it is not strong enough, and the word "perfect" must be put in before it, and you have "perfect love." It was a short Gospel word to render adequately the great sum of the law— "Thou shalt love the Lord thy God with all thy heart, and with all thy soul, and with all thy mind, and with all thy strength." In this commandment there seems to be a strong effort of inspiration to get everything in, and to make the inventory perfect. It was arranged that the heart, or, properly speaking, the affectional part of our nature, should be all devoted, and then the mind should be subservient to it, to give it force and intelligent meaning. And then with the "might" and "strength," including everything in the physical manhood, and the manhood of the affections; in other words, all was to be given up to the exercise of love, that should be perfect love—so perfect that the law itself in the Gospel dispensation is filled up with it. If there be a caviller here, I presume he is satisfied that the language setting forth Christian privilege is as strong as inspiration could make it; that it employs as high, comprehensive, and intense words as possible, or as inspiration could choose out of language.

SCOPE OF THE TERMS.

Now, secondly, consider the scope of the terms used in answer to our heart-yearnings. I will mention three things:—

First. The scope is against all sin. The condemnation of sin in the Bible reaches to every form and degree of it. The great legal system manifested in Zion, and revealed in the Jewish sacrifices, is to be read in the Apostolic teachings, for the law system never departs from the Gospel system; its forms change, but the law is present everywhere. No man can put his finger on a law that condemns outward sin, but allows it in the heart. The law is everywhere searching; it goes down into the thoughts and intents of the heart. It is "sharper than any two-edged sword." There is no form of sin that is covered or tolerated by the law, and for the good reason that God's legal government is a unit, and His sovereignty is a unit. God never intended sin should enter the universe. He made angels and men without it. It is an infringement of His plan, and a disturbing element.

Second. In looking at the scope of these Scriptures

we shall find that every provision of the Gospel scheme points to heart purity or holiness. God has sent His Son into the world to save His people from their sins, otherwise His coming would be nothing ; and you understand it to mean nothing less than the realization of the relief of God's children from heart-yearnings, or rather the satisfaction of those yearnings. The great doctrine of Justification by Faith is illustrative, and we ask, " Why must we be pardoned ? " Evidently because our sins are in the way of holiness ; pardon is the preliminary to holiness. The whole Gospel of the Bible is for the purpose of making men holy, and its every provision points to nothing else, as the many guide-boards for miles around point to the city. You take out the very vitality of the Gospel when you take out holiness. I can see nothing left if you take out " The blood of Jesus Christ cleanseth from all sin ;" and the man who would take it out compels us to resist. If the covenant of the Bible means anything it means that provision has been made for our holiness, and therefore we hold to the doctrine of the Wesleys, that the Gospel is completely adapted to satisfy the heart-yearnings of the Christian for purity. There can never be anything in its stead. If an angel should come down from heaven and tell us, " After you are regenerated and made living Christians, even though you find in your hearts the remains of depravity, you should be satisfied, for there is nothing beyond it, no arrangement to make your recovery from sin entire," we are authorized by Scripture to reject it ; and if an apostle should rise from the dead and preach to us that " there is no blood that can cleanse from all sin," that apostle is to be rejected, for

" though we, or an angel from heaven, preach any other gospel unto you than that which we have preached unto you, let him be accursed." What is a gospel that leaves us in depravity ? No angel will ever teach it. There would be such a curse connected with lowering the standard of Christian excellence and privilege, that there would be no possibility of giving toleration to such a message, no matter where it came from. Our position, that the scope of the Gospel does respond to our entire wants, is the old position, the sound position, the revealed position, and not exceptional, as some would have you believe. The limiting of the accomplishments of God's purposes through death, or purgatory, is the exception, the invasion. Beyond a question, Christian history shows that a poor, simple-hearted brother who prays, " Create in me a clean heart," is perfectly orthodox. The man who says, " The blood of Jesus Christ his Son cleanseth us from all sin," putting in the word " *all*," is perfectly sound in the old theology. There has never been any other orthodoxy, and any contrary teaching is less than the Gospel ; and, therefore, in undertaking to show you the provision for the satisfaction of our heart-yearnings, I am easy in my argument. I am not struggling with casuistry, but am in the very easiest track which a novice could desire to follow. Ay, and the way for a scholar or an apostle to follow is right from the conscious impurity, to the blood that " cleanseth from all sin." The strength of this argument is in its truth, and in the Holy Spirit's mighty power to satisfy your longings for purity, and therefore I pass on. (Many voices: " Glory ! " " Glory ! " and " Amen ! ")

Notice now the

SYMBOLISM OF HOLINESS.

I have selected three symbols.

First.—*The Blood Symbol.*

In the old dispensation they took the blood of bulls and goats and sprinkled the Book of the Law and all the people, saying, "This is the blood of the testament which God hath enjoined unto you. Moreover He sprinkled with blood both the tabernacle, and all the vessels of the ministry. And almost all things are by the law purged with blood, and without shedding of blood is no remission."

Now that startling word "blood" would be the last one man would select for a symbol of peace or purity. There are no two things more unlike each other than blood and love, or blood and salvation, I mean antithetically considered. Yet the symbol is selected by Inspiration, for here it is: "Almost all things are by the law purged with blood." Blood stains upon the holy garments of Aaron; blood stains upon the altar of sacrifice, and blood is thrown out with hyssop branch upon the people. You connect blood with unholy strife, and with the death penalty. We can see its application in connection with man's demerit and destruction, but why is it connected with his salvation? By it we are conducted to one thing and one only, The Lamb of God that taketh away the sin of the world. This sacrifice points to something to come. The sacrificial lamb was a part of the great idea of being made holy through Christ. "For if the blood of bulls and of goats, and the ashes of an heifer sprinkling the unclean, sanctifieth to the purifying of the flesh, how much more shall the blood of Christ . . . purge

your conscience from dead works to serve the living
God?" In this blood is more than the chemist could
descry. If it had been examined through the micro-
scope, there would nothing extraordinary have been discovered; but examined by faith, and it is seen to be full
of God, "for in Him dwelleth all the fulness of the
Godhead bodily." Paul meant to say there was a divine
element rolling through all the blood of Jesus Christ.
How does it happen that that blood, so small in quantity,
has reached all through the generations of men, and all
around the globe, and is for all nations, kindred, and
tongues, and for you and me? Why, it was because the
symbol had in it the thing signified—expiation and divine
satisfaction—and the blood of Jesus is to tell us how
broad is the atonement. It is just as broad as the
Divine Sovereignty—it is Divine Sovereignty in redemption. It goes through every ramification of every soul of
all the race. The blood symbol helps us to interpret
the Scriptures in their meaning, and reach, and power.
Blood stains, it does not purify anything; but, in the sym-
bolism of the Gospel, it is the most thoroughly purifying
influence in the universe known to either God or man, and
I don't know how any creature could utter a more momentous truth than is heard in the song of the redeemed,
"Unto Him that loved us, and washed us from our
sins in His own blood, and hath made us kings and
priests unto God and His Father, to Him be glory and
dominion forever and ever." Now I know I am right.
The argument, you know, might seem to be a little
lower down than it ought to be, but the conclusion certainly is not. The declaration comes from the other
shore. While blood would render whatever it touches

impure, it is the only thing that takes away the stains of sin. You go up till you get to the drapery of Heaven, and it is white, and made white in the blood of the Lamb. This underlies all the efficiency of the work of grace; there is blood everywhere. In a convention of Unitarians the question was asked, Why do we fail where the Methodists are so successful? One answer was given from out of the honest convictions of a member's heart. We want a religion of blood, and an atonement of blood; we are lacking the power of blood.

Second.—*Let us look at the Water Symbol.*

If God by any means can make us to know what an immensely great system the Gospel is, and then to avail ourselves of its provisions, he will try another way. See how washing was employed. There was washing of pots and kettles, and the washing of garments. When any man did a wrong, he was to wash his hands, and remain unclean till evening. Washing is appointed and spoken of in the Scriptures, to show us the necessity of spiritual washing. "Then," for instance, "will I sprinkle clean water upon you, and ye shall be clean." In the use of the water symbol you reach baptism, and the word translated wash, is baptize, and means the symbolic use of water as of cleansing efficacy, that it may teach that our souls may be washed and made clean. It is said, "I will sprinkle clean water upon you," and then, "I will pour out my Spirit upon you." Here is the double baptism of water and the Holy Ghost, and that is indicative of the thorough and practical power which God will employ to make us clean in his sight. I showed you the blood as a symbol, now I introduce the water baptism as pointing to the power of the Holy Ghost in renovating the soul from all sin. Men were very vile, and it was to be kept in remembrance that the Church, composed of those who were once like all other sinners, had been made clean, and here is the testimony: "And such were some of you; but ye are washed, but ye are sanctified, but ye are justified in the name of the Lord Jesus, and by the Spirit of our God."

Third.—*I pass to speak of the Fire Symbol.*

A most expressive and powerful help to interpret the language of Divine revelation. You remember when Jehovah Christ commenced redemption in the Abrahamic family, there was a burning bush, and a voice spoke out of the fire, and revealed the fact that the Jehovah Christ was there, and was teaching His people that they were to be saved as by fire. When the children of Israel came out of Egypt the fire symbol was chosen, and it guided them, and when it veiled itself in the cloud it was fire still, and when the shade was given, it was there but was concealed. Elijah went to heaven in a chariot of fire, and symbolized that everything that could not rise up in flame would not enter heaven; pointing to the fact that the great judgment day will witness the burning up of the world.

Isaiah had a vision of the Lord sitting upon a throne high and lifted up, and his train filled the temple, and the cherubim stood above him, and they began to cry, Holy, holy, holy is the Lord God of hosts. The prophet saw in the light of that holiness that he was impure, and he cried out, "Woe is me! for I am undone; because I am a man of unclean lips, and I dwell in the midst of a people of unclean lips: for mine eyes have seen the King, the Lord of hosts!" What was the man to do? Why one cherub flew away having a live coal in his hand, which he had taken with the tongs from off the altar; and he laid it upon his mouth and said, "Lo, this hath touched thy lips; and thine iniquity is taken away, and thy sin purged." Immediately the power of cleansing by fire was realized. The great problem of prophetic mission was settled by fire. There was no missionary power in him, until God had taken fire from the altar, and with it touched his lips, and then he said: "Here am I, send me." The power of the fire symbol explains the plan of salvation. Zachariah heard from the Lord that in all the land two parts of the people should be cut off and die, but "I will bring the third part through the fire, and will refine them as silver is refined, and will try them as gold is tried." And what shall happen when they are refined? "They shall call on my name, and I will hear them; I will say, It is my people, and they shall say, The Lord is my God." The fire tried them and burned out all the dross from their souls, and then they went on their way rejoicing. The Covenant was connected with a burning fire. To those who were able to go through the fire, to them shall it be said, "I am your God, and ye are my people." The burning fire, the Old Testament fire, the old Jerusalem fire, shall help them.

Do you know this is New Testament doctrine?

"Every man's work shall be made manifest: for the day shall declare it, because it shall be revealed by fire, and the fire shall try every man's work of what sort it is. If any man's work abide which he hath built thereupon, he shall receive a reward."

You remember John said: "I indeed baptize you with water unto repentance;" which is the symbol of the weakest power, "but he that cometh after me is mightier than I, . . . he shall baptize you with the Holy Ghost, and with fire," which shall come down as the result of the atonement. When the fire came down at Pentecost, it came and sat upon them like cloven tongues. Everything that cannot stand the fire shall be burned up.

CONCLUSION.

As I close, I want you to realize two or three things that I hold to be of great practical importance in these relations. There is an utter inadequacy of moral growth in all humanly developed systems. The Divine requirement to " grow in grace, and in the knowledge of our Lord and Saviour Jesus Christ," is always applicable and practical, but it is not exhaustive at all, for there is no end of the possibility of growth. Not one of the symbols that have seemingly struggled to get the great idea of purification out, applies to growth. But the saving of the soul has an end, which the cutting off of everything contrary to God's will, and faith that he accepts us, brings in. There is no standard of development or limits to growth. Go through all the system and there is not a word that, rightly applied, will show any such limit. Again, there is a difference between clearing away the weeds, and the growth of the plant; between the growth of a sickly child, and a well one. All our dear friends who think they supersede the necessity of being purified speedily, by the idea of growth, fall outside of the entire terminology of the Divine system. There is not a word of truth in it, and it is a serious mistake to trust to growing into the state of purity. God has exhausted the Bible symbols to get before us this idea that is exactly opposite to that of the process of growth, viz., that sin can be really taken out, and this is the reason why we are urging you to have it done to-day. In this we glory, that whatever hinders our growth can be taken away now, by faith in Jesus. Let us bring our souls into the holy work. Oh, I should like to exhort if I had the time. (Voices— "Time enough," "Go on.") These young ministers are to cope with the devil in all his power. They are to grapple with Ritualism, Unitarianism, and Rationalism, and they must be well prepared for a vigorous contest, and they are to get the power for storming the battery, from heaven. They must go through the fire to have the dross burned up. They must be washed, to be clean. When I think about the young minister, as he may be clothed with power to shake the kingdom of Satan, and to bring down the throne of Dagon ; when I think of the very important work he is going out to do, it seems to me he should almost desire that neither sun, moon, nor star should arise until he had been filled with the power and might of the Spirit. It seems to me he should go as the herald of the new Dispensation, to hasten the time when it should be announced that the kingdoms of this world have become the kingdoms of our Christ. Oh! whatever else you neglect, do not neglect the blood; do not lack the baptism of fire. Oh! the world is to be overwhelmed with the glory of God, and grace is to cover the world as the waters cover the sea. God bless you and help you to realize the purifying grace.

TESTIMONIES.

A Minister.—"I feel inspired with hope by this Camp-Meeting. I see the rays of the Divine glory spreading all abroad from this place, and I believe they will shine far and near, and do something toward hastening the day when the world shall be filled with this light. Brethren in the ministry, we must preach this precious doctrine at home. I know it is sometimes difficult, but God will help us and bless us amid the worst difficulties. It used to be the case with me, that wherever I began, whether at pardon, or repentance, or prayer, or the judgment, or anything else, I would always drift toward, and end in the river of Perfect Love. But some of my brethren found a little fault, and I began to lower the standard. One day soon after, I went home with one of my class-leaders, who was a holy man. He soon began to walk the floor, and wring his hands, and pray and groan; soon I began to feel his groans going all through me. I asked him what was the matter, and he said, 'Oh, brother R., will you not be offended if I tell you? I know I am a poor unworthy child of God, and ought to sit at the feet of my minister, and will do so. But it seems to me you do not preach as you used to, and you do not talk in the class-meetings as you used to, and I fear you and I need more of the holy baptism.' He did this so humbly and lovingly, that I could not help loving him all the better for it, and I saw that I had fallen into a snare of the devil, and going down upon our knees together, there God delivered me and brought me again into a large place. I made then and there an irrevocable deed of myself to God, and then went to the Holy Spirit, and He put the stamp of His approval and authority upon it, and I felt that the great transaction was done; and in that grace I stand to-day. I have never dared since to lower, for an instant, this glorious standard."

A CONGREGATIONALIST BROTHER.—"This gospel of holiness is precious to my soul. This is not a Methodist doctrine, but it is a Bible doctrine, and one in which all the Churches of the Lord Jesus have an interest, and the truth of which every believer may experience. This morning I look up to my Saviour and am assured that He loves my soul."

A BROTHER.—"One thing that comforts and pleases me greatly here, is that everybody seems to want to help somebody, and everybody who speaks to me almost, does help me. I was helped last night, when one brother said, if God could afford to take him, he surely could afford to be taken. Brother Inskip helped me the other night, when he asked a brother who said he wanted power, if there might not be something selfish in the desire. I think I am arriving to such an annihilation of self, that this joy which is all around me, is getting into me. Brother Reddy helped me yesterday, when he said we must die to sin and self; and Oh, I felt as though I wanted to die thus, and be buried deep down, and be nailed into my coffin, so that I should never rise and break the sod. But I want to live too, to live with Christ, and have him live in me."

A MINISTER.—"This is what I found more than thirty years ago; and it has gone right on ever since. I have thought sometimes that it had almost died out of the Church, but then it would break out on the other side, and I would have to run to keep up with it. It would seem sometimes that a dam had been thrown across the stream, stopping the waters, but very soon they would break away and form new channels, and now it seems that it has become a mighty river in which we can all float our ships. A few years ago there were not forty souls in the Troy Conference who could say they were entirely sanctified, but now see where it is! It has gone outside the Methodist Church now and found its way into the Congregationalist and Baptist and other Churches. Yes, the Baptists have got it, and their river is flowing right along with ours. Oh, bless the Lord!"

A MINISTER.—"My soul is full. This Camp-Meeting is one of the kingdom slopes, where the children come to sun themselves. I see the morning star that will usher in the grandest day that was ever seen outside of heaven, and I expect to see that time shortly. I am glad I was not born before I was, and I am glad God has spun me out to reach this day ; and I see how God is going to bear me over every terrestrial summit without brushing. We need not go to heaven to find heaven. God will bring it right down here to us, and fill the world with it. I have a big programme before me, for I begin to see how God is going to spread His work by the instrumentality of a holy Church. And now, men of God, don't let up a hair in this work. Keep too upright to be bought, and too shrewd to be sold, and I will stake Methodism on the issue of Holiness to the Lord."

CHAPTER XXIV.

SERMON BY REV. A. COOKMAN, OF WILMINGTON CONFERENCE
—ADDRESS TO CLASS-LEADERS, BY REV. W. M^CDONALD,
OF NEW ENGLAND CONFERENCE.

MR. COOKMAN'S SERMON.

Ephesians, 5 chap., v. 18.—" *Be filled with the Spirit.*"

It cannot be necessary at this time, or in this presence, that we insist on the personality and divinity of the Holy Ghost. We shall take it for granted, that you all unhesitatingly subscribe to that fundamental article of our faith; that " The Holy Ghost, proceeding from the Father and the Son, is of one substance, majesty, and glory with the Father and the Son, very and eternal God." Living as we do under the better and more glorious dispensation of the Spirit, we should feel we are under more special obligation to this third person in the adorable Trinity, because He seems to come nearer to us, than do the other persons of the Trinity ; for while we think of the Father upon the throne of His majesty, while we think of Jesus Christ as the Advocate of our cause before the throne, you will observe that the Holy Ghost consents to come to us in our indigence and wretchedness, and to come to abide in us, that He might awaken, regenerate, and adopt us ; to bear witness, sanctify, strengthen, comfort, and help our infirmities.

THE HOLY GHOST IS A REVEALER.

He comes also to reveal in us the Father and the Son ; for as Christ was the revelation of the Father, so the blessed Holy Ghost proposes to reveal in us the Father and the Son, so that He might say, He that recognizes my presence and perfection, realizes the presence of the Father and the Son, ay, of the Divine Trinity in Unity. Is not this the explanation of very many passages of Scripture with which we have been familiar, as " Christ in you the hope of glory ?" Again Jesus said, " If a man love me, he will keep my words : and my Father will love him, and we will come unto him, and make our abode with him." And again : " I in them, and Thou in Me." Wonderful truth, that we may mysteriously, gloriously, and consciously be one in Christ ! May we not join in the ascriptions already heard in the upper glory, rendered to the Father, Son, and Holy Ghost ?

When the Holy Ghost comes into the heart it is not to speak of himself, but to talk of the things of Christ, and show them unto us. When one man's spirit impresses another, our attention is called to the person who communicates the truth, but the Holy Ghost comes to make the presence and power of Christ individually present to our consciousness. Will not this explain two things ? The first is the prominence given to Christ in all evangelical preaching. The Apostle said, " God forbid that I should glory, save in the cross of our Lord Jesus Christ." Now his soul was a type of all faithful souls filled with the Spirit. He was disposed to subordinate his own personality, and hold up· Christ constantly as *all* in all. Again, this will explain the almost exclusive reference of Christians, in the work of the Lord, to Jesus Christ. They seem almost to forget about the Spirit. To exalt Christ, precious friends, is the joy of my life. He is Alpha and Omega. We do not know, and never shall know all that Christ has done for us in redemption; and yet I submit whether it would not be well to love the Holy Ghost, to praise the Holy Ghost, and to be filled with the Spirit. I can understand, how subsequent to our sanctification, in response to our faith in Jesus, the Holy Spirit may come in an extraordinary degree, and we be filled with the Spirit.

I. It is now for us to inquire about

The Possibility of being Filled with the Spirit.

Hear Jesus: " They shall be filled." The Apostle prayed for the Thessalonians : " The very God of peace sanctify you wholly," and that He would preserve them " blameless unto the coming of our Lord Jesus Christ;" and then adds : " Faithful is He that calleth you, who also will do it." Peter, Stephen, and Barnabas were filled with the Holy Ghost, and the Apostle, directed by inspiration, charges upon us every one to be filled with the Spirit.

What are some of the benefits ?

I shall speak of three classes.

I.—BENEFITS KNOWN TO OUR PERSONAL CONSCIOUSNESS OF BEING FILLED WITH THE HOLY GHOST ?

When filled with the Spirit we shall be hallowed by its presence.

The awfulness of the presence of the Spirit to one who was filled, would certainly result in a subdued and hallowed state of soul, a sort of "silent awe that dares not move," and we should feel like stepping softly, and moving guardedly. With such it would seem highly proper to say, Our Father, . . . hallowed be thy name, or with the angels to join in saying, "Holy! Holy! Lord God Almighty!"

The soul filled with the Spirit would be

Filled with the Spirit of Love.

Love is one of the most beautiful fruits of the Spirit, for it is of the nature of the Spirit itself. The Spirit came to reveal the Father, and Jesus the expression of His love, and then what should hinder that love should fill the entire orb of our life; then we would love God, and His works, and all His creatures, and His Word. In the language of the Psalmist, "O how love I thy law;" and His people—"His people shall be my people;" and sinners—

> "O that the world might taste and see
>   The riches of His grace;
> The arms of love that compass me
>   Would all mankind embrace."

I have observed that those passages in our sermons relating to personal experience are usually accompanied with unctous power. Some years since, at the Penn's Grove Camp-Meeting, after the Holy Ghost had been given as a sanctifier, I found myself drawn out for more of God. I could scarcely define my feelings, but there was a going out after God. When surrounded one day with a few Christians, struggling up to enjoy God as never before, this suggestion came: "You have been trying to get up; are you willing to sink down?" "Yes," I answered, "any way; if I may find Him thus, let me sink in the depths." Then I began to feel I was going down, and with this there came a realization of love, as I had never known before, and it filled my body, soul, and my entire being. O how I loved His children, and His Word. I asked, "What does this mean?" "God is Love." This was the consciousness of love that filled my whole spirit.

It will develop in our personal consciousness a

Feeling of Rest.

When all our powers are harmonized, each with each, and all with God, what should prevent our having rest? The storms which before swept through our consciousness have all subsided. Jesus has said, "Peace," and there is a great calm. The spiritual antagonisms have been driven back, or rather have been converted into willing servants of God. There is a difference between peace and rest. Our country has peace but not rest, though God grant she may. O surely the soul that finds itself enclosed within infinity, will realize this experience of rest. O how rich and satisfying it is to be filled with the Spirit. So we have as benefits, a hallowed feeling, a spirit of love, and sense of rest.

II. WHAT ARE SOME OF THE EFFECTS UPON PERSONAL CHARACTER, OF BEING FILLED WITH THE HOLY GHOST.

You will observe that religion aims at character. It has respect for individual welfare, national development, and the world's good, but then these are not the primal aim. Our religion has respect principally to character. By character I mean that inward condition, or generic force that belongs to every human being. Character, in its higher form, is not due to any circumstances of the world. It requires more than this—the vitalizing, indwelling of the Holy Spirit. The Christian is the highest style of man. O, if we are concerned about our character—and who is not—then we must be filled with the Spirit.

What are the effects upon the character.

The Spirit will not develop anything little or vile.

An individual filled with the Spirit will be likely to develop like the Divine character, entirely separate from everything that is low or vile. Holiness is God's special attraction, and he is represented as being glorious in holiness. Archbishop Tillotson says of God's Holiness that it is not so much a particular as a general attribute, that spreads itself over the whole being. Take away holiness from His wisdom, and wisdom would be annihilated, and that would leave cunning. Take away holiness from justice, and you would have cruelty. Take away holiness, and you would have false piety; and take it away from truth, and that would leave falsehood. Holiness is His superlative excellence. This is His throne, for "He sits upon the throne of His holiness." Let us be filled with the Spirit, and then see how we will be separated from sin. Our wisdom, filled with holiness, will be very different from subtlety; our power will have no form of oppression; our sovereignty will be free from tyranny; justice, marked with holiness, will be our mercy, and it will not degenerate into

cruelty. You can trace out this thought in its ramifi-
cations. You will be elevated into the likeness of God,
and pass hither and thither a holy being, and in the religious character there is nothing mean.

To be filled with the Spirit.

You will develop a gentle character.

The gentle dove; the gentle dew; the still small
sweet voice, are images of Scripture illustrative of this
effect. I do not remember at this moment that wrath or
vengeance is ever predicated of the Spirit. He is infinitely gentle, and hence may be grieved, and I hope
you may all understand that there is nothing so easily
grieved as the Holy Ghost. When filled with the
Spirit, have you not found you were gentle in your
course, and words, and thoughts?

It will develop a wise character.

How can it be otherwise? If the third Person in the
Trinity comes to abide in our heart, fulfilling His own
promise in teaching us all things, revealing Christ in
our consciousness as our Wisdom, (and to me that means
more than the Church now conceives) we shall make
wonderful progress in wisdom. Not that a holy person
will not blunder; but God will help you to perceive
His truth. His character, modelled after the Divine
pattern, will be impelled by the Divine impulse. When
Jesus sent out His ambassadors, He said, "Be wise as
serpents and harmless as doves." That, I think, means
the blending of purity and prudence. The Holy Ghost
does not come to teach any new doctrine, or to testify of
Himself, but of Christ. The very best minds are likely
to be tempted in the direction of presumption; and I say,
let us be careful for the sake of holiness. (Amen.)

To be filled with the Spirit will involve a character that is holy, gentle, and wise.

III.—THE EFFECTS OF BEING FILLED WITH THE SPIRIT UPON THE PERSONAL LIFE.

FIRST.—*It will supply the secret spring and motive power of an earnest, faithful Christian life.*

The blessed Holy Ghost will come to write the law of God in your heart, and you will come to love the will of God. The Spirit will reveal the law, and then apprehending it, you will go joyfully forward in its execution. The Spirit will help us, so that, as Jesus was, we shall be willing to go and preach, pray, weep, and die—yea, die a hundred times for souls if we could lift them nearer to God.

It will give the ability to go steadily and successfully forward.

Here I enunciate the greatest glory of our Christianity. I know there are a good many who deem the great power of our religion to be in its truth. I am willing to join them and say the truth of the Bible is ultimate. There cannot be a greater truth than "Thou shalt love the Lord thy God with all thy heart, with all thy soul, and with all thy might." Christ Himself gave to this the very highest excellence. The sages of antiquity knew a great deal of truth; indeed it has been contended for, that there is no new ethical truth in the world. But what of the ethics of Seneca or Tully? Seneca taught, and the world grew worse. Jesus taught, and the world grew better. Why I do not know, unless it is that our religion has the Holy Ghost in it. O, be

filled with the Spirit, and then it will be a living verity
to you, and you will praise God for the privilege of
loving Him with undivided affection.

It implies the *inclination to obey;* secondly, *ability to
obey;* and thirdly, *it will involve an unction of the Holy
One.*

What is unction? Is it pathos, or eloquence, or psychological power, or mental force? I apprehend it is
not these, though it may consist in part of one or all of
them. Unction is that subtle, mysterious, unaccount-
able, irresistible influence that proceeds from the Spirit,
to the individual filled with the Spirit—that seals instruction upon the heart and conscience of the person
receiving it; so that the unction tends to render a man
powerful and glorious in his life and history. That is
unction. That which sounds pleasant may not be unction; but that which, however feebly expressed, makes
an impression on your memory, and develops, until at
length it is a part of your existence, and becomes a great
power. This is unction. Lord, give us more of that
kind. (Many responses of "Amen.")

But some one may say that "to expect to be filled with
the Spirit is Utopian." But was not Jesus filled with
the Spirit? "Ay," say you; "but He was divine."
But was not Stephen and Barnabas? "Ay; but they
were inspired." But were not Wesley and Whitefield
filled with the Spirit? "Ay; but they were raised up
for a special purpose." But were not the saintly Summerfield, and the majestic Stephen Olin filled with the
Spirit? "Ay," say you; "but they were preachers."
But have not many persons, in this country and in the
Old World, been raised up and filled with the Spirit,

who have done more good than has resulted from many
pulpits? Precious friends, I conceive we are only on
the threshold of privilege. Be filled with the Spirit—
the eternal, wise, and holy Spirit. What a power
it would make us! O that God would make this
place another Jerusalem, and this day another Pentecost!

Come, Holy Ghost, with all Thy quickening power.
Will you bear with me while I tell you

HOW YOU MAY BE FILLED WITH THE SPIRIT.

There are three points.

In the first place *you must be emptied*. All those
sensual indulgences, all those prejudices that will not
bear the light of God's truth, all those obscene or un-
profitable words that would grieve the Holy Spirit, or
that unholy unbelief that would hinder the Spirit, must,
must, MUST be given up. The infinite Holy Spirit will
not come to abide in the heart of any one that connives
with sin or indulgence in any measure.

We must *go forward in the path of obedience*, for it
is in vain to think of having more of the Spirit, if we do
not use what He has given.

We must ask in the name of Christ to give us the Spirit.

I do not know, brethren, you do not know, Gabriel
does not know, how much more of grace the Holy Spirit
will give all those who ask Him, for " if ye abide in me
and my words abide in you, ye shall ask what ye will,
and it shall be done unto you." " When He ascended up
on high, he led captivity captive, and gave gifts unto
men," and the best gift is the blessed Holy Ghost. O
let us receive it to-day. Amen.

MR. McDONALD'S ADDRESS TO CLASS-LEADERS.

THE many devoted class-leaders who were present, were from time to time holding special services, and, on one of these occasions, Brother McDonald was appointed to deliver to them an address. The meeting was very well attended, and the remarks were listened to with evident interest and profit. In the meeting for testimony, which commenced immediately after the conclusion of the address, there were frequent favorable allusions to the speaker and the sentiments he advanced.

Brother McDonald said:—The class-leader comes closer to the members than do the ministers. When you desire your presiding elder to have some good preacher sent to your church, and he names one, you ask, "Is he a man of faith and of the Holy Ghost, and is he apt to teach?" The same questions should be asked by the minister of his class-leaders: "Is he apt to teach, and is he full of the Holy Ghost?" I have been more or less connected with class-leaders for twenty-six or twenty-seven years, and I have watched my class-leaders carefully, and asked what sort of men they were, and what influence they exerted upon the classes. I have seen some leaders, whose classes would invariably dwindle away under their direction. Shift them from one class to another, and the same result would follow. I believe most of those occupying the position could be successful if they would put themselves down to the work of heart culture and intellectual improvement. The first thing of all that I would recommend to a leader, is to

HAVE A HOLY HEART.

He may not be very learned, or indeed have but one talent, and scarcely that, and yet have a very pure heart. Though slow in communicating his thought, let that be red-hot from Jesus, and it will have an effect upon those with whom he comes in contact. The spirit of the man will attract others around him. You like to hear a minister talk right out of his heart, when his views seem hopeful and cheering. He may be defective in grammar or logic, or even in theology, but if he has a good heart, the people overlook his defects. They like the knowledge that comes from books, but it is more easily dispensed with, than to have in the soul an intimate acquaintance with God. A class-leader needs the baptism of the Holy Ghost to make him efficient, and if I were one, I would start out for this at the beginning. I would not rest until God had sanctified my soul, and thus prepared me to lead my class. But then sanctified leaders are not always successful. Therefore,

HOLD SHORT AND SPIRITED CLASS-MEETINGS.

You don't need a preacher for class-meeting, or any one to preach there. About one sermon at a service is all the people want ; and if they have to hear a sermon after each testimony, it is a little more frequent than they will be able to endure very long. You should put your class-meetings through with a zeal and readiness that will give everybody a love for it, and make them look forward with delightful anticipations for its return. When I, as a minister, go into a class-room, and the leader asks me to lead his class, I say "No, I want you to lead;" and if he has to give a long series of counsels, and relate what does not seem to be specially necessary, I conclude the people will soon think they cannot afford to go more than once in a month. I have seen others who would give a word of counsel or cheer, and sing occasionally one verse, and go through with a class of twenty members in an hour. Mr. Wesley said an hour was long enough for love-feast, and then the people would go right back again the next time. I believe the poorest class-leader in the land, if he would strike out in this way, and then be brief, might increase its attendance and power fifty per cent. in a little while. You say you "don't like long sermons," (responses of "yes," and "that's so.") Do not your class-members feel just so about long exhortations? I am not personally acquainted with any of you, but I rather suspect some of you are too lengthy in your exercises. Then again, as class-leaders, you should take special pains to

STORE YOUR MINDS WITH SUITABLE INFORMATION

to impart to your members. I do not believe you like your preacher to go into the pulpit, never having thought of what he is going to say until he gets there. If he should, pretty soon he would be running in the same channel, however large his stock of thought. You heard Bro. Boole the other day in his sermon, representing some class-meetings he had known of. Well, I have seen such, and you may find them frequently, and in various parts of the country, and in some places they occur every week. If a minister should go into the pulpit unprepared, he might do well for a few times, but not long, and neither can you without preparation in your department of the work. It is not enough for a leader to say to his members when they have spoken well, " Brother you have done pretty well, I hope you will get to heaven." To say that, to a poor soul that has not half enough religion to take it to heaven, is not sufficient. A class-leader cannot succeed without storing his mind with facts and Christian experience, and especially the sayings of the Bible, which has so much in it that is peculiarly adapted to Christians under a great variety of experience. You ought to read biography, history, systems of theology, experimental Christianity, in its various forms and developments, and get the very cream of it in your mind every week; and if you do that, your members will rally around you, and be sorry when you cannot be there.

Sometimes you require your ministers to build churches and parsonages, and thus you keep them going all the week, and then on Sunday they must go into the pulpit and preach to you a right down good sermon. Suppose your minister should say, " Brethren, you keep me so fully employed in secular labors, that I have not time to prepare good sermons," you would not be satisfied with that, but you would say, " Take the time." As sub-pastors of the church, and such you are, you see that the mind of the community about you is filled with false notions, and you ought to be prepared to correct them, or any erroneous views and impressions of theology And you ought to take time to prepare yourselves.

YOU OUGHT TO VISIT YOUR MEMBERS.

The discipline requires you to see them once a week.

I know many leaders say, " That was the rule when the number of members was limited to twelve ; but now we have twenty or thirty, and so cannot see them once a week." But because you cannot see them once a week, is it to say you should not see them once in a year ? and if you were to select two or three that were absent each week, and visit them, and take in as many others as you could, you can scarcely conceive the influence which it would exert. I appointed a man to be class-leader in the city of Boston, who was not much in sympathy with the rest of the Church, and at first it might have had the appearance of a mistake. He was much occupied, having a larger business than any other man in the Church, and yet he found time to visit his class. In the evening he would go through the lanes and streets, to find his members, make a short visit, pray with them, and invite them to the class ; in a few weeks it was running over, and people liked him, and said, " Why the leader came after me." It is as important for you to visit your class-members, as it is for the minister to visit the members of his flock. There is only now and then a minister who holds his congregation and fails to visit. It is not the case with the great mass of ministers. Let a pastor go to some poor souls who have not seen a minister in their houses for years, and next Sunday they will be out to hear him preach ; and it is just so with the classes ; and if you want to see them full, go to their houses. It will not be half as profitable to them, or advantageous to your class, to meet them on the street ; for then they would say, " He never took pains to visit me." This is the way it works with ministers, as well as class-leaders. I think there are not many leaders who visit as they should, yet some are faithful.   May God increase their number.

Brethren, *get your hearts filled with the Holy Ghost, your minds stored with good information; hold short and spirited class-meetings,* and then *faithfully visit your members,* and you will have good meetings, and be successful leaders.   O, do not leave this place without this olive branch of holiness in your lips.   If we can have holy ministers and class-leaders, we shall have holy churches.   I hope you will get your classes out of the old, stereotyped way of talking, since the theme is, Jesus and His infinite love.   On such a subject, it is quite too formal for them to say, "I am glad to meet you; though I have many temptations and trials, and make many crooked paths to my feet, I hope to get to heaven. Pray for me."   Get them where they can swing out of this little rut, where their feet may find "a broad place," and then they will prosper.   Instead of a long speech, suppose you should ask a brother, "Are you enjoying salvation, brother?   How many times in a day do you pray, my brother?   How often do you read the Scriptures?"   Urge these questions kindly, yet directly.   It is wonderful what good effect this will have, when done in Christian love, and from out of a heart all in sympathy with Christ and the good of souls.   When I have said, "Brother, how many times a day do you pray?" and he responds, "Well, I don't pray as often as I should."—"But, brother, that is not answering the question."   Then he may say, "Well, I suppose I should pray oftener."—"Well, brother, do you pray three times a day?"—"Well, no, I don't know that I do regularly."—"My brother, do you pray twice a day regularly?"—"Well, no, I don't know that I do." So, if you press the question, you will find sometimes that they have no regular seasons of prayer; and if they don't like these home-put questions, try to persuade them to the altar, to be prayed for again. We get into a kind of tread-mill process, if I may use the expression, when we should be shooting off heavenwards. You will agree with me, that a leader should understand the moral status of every member of his class; and then from a rich, deep, religious experience of his own, draw such illustrations and incidents as he may have treasured up, thus leading on his flock into the freshest and greenest pasturage. I take it you are all good class-leaders, or are longing, with God's blessing, to become so. O, stir up your classes, and through you and your members, may God kindle a fire that shall consume all sin.

CHAPTER XXV.

SERMON OF REV. WILLIAM REDDY, OF CENTRAL NEW YORK
CONFERENCE.—EXHORTATION OF REV. W. H. BOOLE, OF
NEW YORK EAST CONFERENCE.

MR. REDDY'S SERMON.

Gal. ii. 20.—*"I am crucified with Christ: nevertheless I live; yet not I, but Christ liveth in me: and the life which I now live in the flesh, I live by the faith of the Son of God, who loved me, and gave himself for me."*

THIS text is experimentally in keeping with the object and animus of this meeting, as I understand it. Paul tells his experience here, and there is always a mighty power in the rehearsal of experience. I have often noticed that the experience portion of sermons always takes well with the people, or produces a happy effect; and I think that one reason why the early preachers had so much power over their audiences, was their frequent use of anecdotes and experience. I rejoice that we have some of Paul's experience related by himself, to which we may turn and find profit.

This text is strangely paradoxical; I live, and I do not live; I am dead and yet I live. If you can understand that, I shall think that you have had some of the same experience. But here is a mystery: How can one being live in another? "Christ liveth in me," said the Apostle. There is a mystery about this which the world cannot understand, for only the Holy Spirit can enable the mind to comprehend this truth.

But there seems to be in the text also a kind of antagonism, and that antagonism seems to be between myself, or the Apostle's self, and Christ. "I am crucified with Christ: nevertheless I live; yet not I, but Christ liveth in me." There is always antagonism between self and Christ, so that to live for self, is to be at war with Christ; and to live for Christ, is to be dead to self. Christ and self are like the two scales of the balance; when one goes up the other must go down; and the Apostle plainly teaches that, in order to a true and acceptable exaltation of Christ, there must of necessity be the death of self. I must die in order that Jesus may live in me; for while self lives, it will always be crowding Christ out, as the two are at variance. The Apostle gives it as his experience that this self, which was at war with Christ, had not merely been overpowered and kept under, but slain, in order that by its death, Christ might live in his soul.

It is a strange fact that life should ever spring from death, and yet this is often true. Said our Lord: "Verily, verily, I say unto you, except a corn of wheat fall into the ground and die, it abideth alone: but if it die, it bringeth forth much fruit." In this He may, and doubtless did have in view, His own approaching death and resurrection, and He intended to teach, that unless He should die upon the cross, the fruits of His love could never appear to bless the earth, but that dying and rising there should come of this the fruit of life.

I think He meant also to apply these words to the carnal nature, and to teach that, unless this should die, the fruits of grace could never be produced upon the soil of the human heart, but that when this dies, then, springing from that death, will be seen these glorious fruits. Let us

ANALYZE THIS DEATH PROCESS.

Mark the transitions from the life of self to the death of self, and from the death of self to life in Christ. Paul designates it under the general figure of crucifixion, "I am crucified with Christ." There is here an allusion to the historical fact of the crucifixion of Christ, upon which hang all the hopes of humanity; and there is a question in my mind, whether there is not some analogy between the whole of the historical facts of Christ's life, death, resurrection, and ascension; and the processes of experience in the Christian who passes from sin to justification, and then to sanctification, and then to glorification. I shall not stop to examine this; but let us look at the fact and manner of the crucifixion, as an illustration of the death of the old nature. It is

PAINFUL AND IGNOMINIOUS.

There are two things in death by crucifixion, which make it peculiarly appropriate as an emblem of the death of the carnal mind, namely; it was painful, and ignominious, and these two ideas always attach themselves to the word cross whenever we use it; and yet, when we rightly understand it, we shall glory in the cross of Christ. Jesus commands us to take up the cross.

"If any man will come after me, let him deny himself and take up his cross, and follow me." We talk sometimes about taking up Christ's cross, but this is not what the Lord commands, and indeed this is beyond our power to bear. Christ bore His own cross, and we must bear our cross, and not His. In this cross, I think the idea of pain and ignominy are always present, and all they who expect to come from sin to righteousness without pain, will find themselves sadly mistaken in the end. Crucifixion is a painful death, and crucifixion of the old nature is painful, for connected with this death-struggle is such a denial of self as brings the keenest smart; and if any one thinks to glide out of self into life, as one would glide down a stream, he will awake one of these days to see his error. Many attempt to make religion fashionable and easy, so that the world can glide out of self into Christ without making any sacrifices, or bearing any crosses. How many efforts have been made thus to popularize religion, in order that its pain might be removed. But all these attempts have failed. No man dies to self without suffering the pangs of that death.

Why does Christ say, "If thy right eye offend thee, pluck it out; . . . and if thy right hand offend thee, cut it off"? Is it a painless operation to tear from its socket a right eye, or to sever a right hand? No, no. But Christ says this, because He knows a right hand and a right eye are so dear to us, that they are the last things with which we would part, and the parting with which, would give us intensest pain, and yet even this we are willingly to endure to gain Christ. With some the great pain will come from one source, and with others from

15

another. With the young man who came to Christ, it was in giving up his riches, and it was so keen he could not endure it; with others it is something else, but it is always present.

A CLEAN BUSINESS.

Some years ago, one of our preachers was holding a series of meetings in a region of country where there were many distilleries, and it was quite a business to buy corn and to sell to the distilleries, to be made into whiskey. At one of these meetings a brother came in who was in this business, and had, just before entering the meeting, been trying to close a trade for corn, to be distilled. During the meeting he was convicted for holiness, and went forward to the altar. While there, a voice seemed to ask him what he would do with the large quantity of corn he had on hand. Though he tried to do so, the Lord would not let him dismiss this question. He went away from the meeting without getting help, and did not appear again for two or three days. When he came back, he said to the minister that he might have thought it strange that he had not been there, "but," said he, "the Lord and I have been holding a protracted meeting around the corn cribs. I prayed long for a clean heart, but at last I seemed to hear God say to me, 'Give me a clean business, and I will give you a clean heart.' And then and there I said, 'Lord, I will give Thee a clean business;' and I settled it that the corn should rot in the crib, before I would sell it to be made into whiskey, and then the Lord poured salvation into my soul." Some of you here, perhaps, may have something to do with the hop business, or with signing applications for license to sell strong drinks. Let me say, you must have clean hands if you would have a clean heart. Let us look carefully to this, ministers as well as people, for, strange as it may seem, it is sometimes hard for us ministers to give up all things, so that we shall not murmur at poor appointments, or because we do not get all the good things. We must die to all ambitions that are not holy, and be willing to trust our appointments, our reputation, and our all to Jesus. Paul said: "I am less than the least of all saints." I used to wonder how John Fletcher could write such humbling things of himself, when I thought him about the saintliest man the earth has ever seen, next to Paul; but I see the reason now. He knew that the valley of humility is the valley of blessing. We must be little, if we would be exalted. We must first have death to self, and then a resurrection to the life of Christ.

How His enemies triumphed over Jesus, as they thought He was going down, and as He hung there upon the cross, they cried, in derision, "He saved others; himself He cannot save. If Thou be the Son of God, come down from the cross." But Christ only went down, that He might go up, He died, that He might deprive death of his victory. So we must die that we may live. We must die to every unholy feeling. Some of you may want a clean heart while you hold a grudge against your neighbor. You must die to this, and die to all of self. And we can tell pretty well when we are dead. I found it necessary in this death process, to lay wife and children, and all upon the altar.

Then came the question, "What if you die?"—"Well, then, let me die," I said. Then came the question, "What if you become superannuated and are poor, and are not permitted to die, what then?" This took me some time to overcome; but at last I put my fears upon the altar also, and then God saved me gloriously.

INSTANTANEOUS DEATH OF SELF.

Some object to the teaching that this work is instantaneous. Well, I know that it takes some of us a long time to die; but when at last we do die, it is in an instant. There is a moment when we are alive, and the next moment we are dead. So also, the making of us alive is instantaneous. God has but to speak, and the work is done. When you have come to the point when you can give all your heart to Christ, then you will soon die to self, and be made alive to God.

And now, in conclusion, let me tell you a little of my own

EXPERIENCE.

I was about nine months seeking the blessing of entire sanctification. I was brought up under Presbyterian influences, and was taught nothing of this doctrine; but when I came to read the works of Wesley and others, on perfect love, my soul coveted this blessing, and night and day I wrestled with God for it. My soul felt the import of the words—

> "I cannot rest till pure within,
> Till I am wholly lost in Thee."

But there were test-points from which I shrunk. They made me a class-leader when I was twenty-one years old. I procured the life of Hester Ann Rogers, and read it, and took it into my class and read it to the members, and then went home. My good Presbyterian mother had retired, and I took a candle in one hand, and my book in the other, and sat down to read, and when I came to the words, "reckon ye also yourselves to be dead indeed unto sin," the Lord enabled me to see it as I had not before, and I said, "Yes, I see it now; I see that this is true in the atonement, true in Christ, though it is not true in me, because of my unbelief." And so I began right there to reckon, and I said, "Yes, I am dead to sin; I have redemption in His blood;" and, brethren, it seemed to me that my orbit of the self life contracted till it was lost in nothingness; and I seemed to be as nothing; but O how the circle of glory that enshrouded my Saviour widened, till it came all around me. I went to bed, fearing that I might lose it, but I prayed God to keep me, and He did, and in the morning as I awoke, I began to reckon again, and in a moment I was free, though I had been so long seeking release from captivity.

THE TOBACCO TEST.

One of the tests which I constantly met was on the subject of tobacco. You may think that was a small matter, but it is sometimes the little foxes that spoil the vines. It takes but a single hair, or least particle of dirt, to derange the movements of a watch. If you get but a little dust in the eye, it causes a great deal of irritation and pain. It requires only a slight frost to kill all the beautiful flowers. I loved a good cigar, and every time I went upon my knees to seek perfect love,

this test would come before me. I begged God to indulge me in this, but He would not; so I would stop
sometimes for days and months together, and my appetite would sleep for a season under the power of my
will, and then it would awake and say, "Let us have
a good time now, for we have abstained so long."
Finally, after one of these lapses, as I had a cigar in
my mouth, and was thinking upon the subject, it seemed
as though God spoke to me and said, "If you don't let
those cigars alone I will let your conscience alone."
I was alarmed and said, "If it is so wrong, then I am
done with this indulgence." I looked to God for
help, threw away my cigar, and my appetite went
with it. I do not say that you will have to do this,
but I do say that you must die if you would live, and
that you will find death-struggles somewhere. And
I love this death because of the life, the glorious, spiritual life of love that comes afterwards, a life of symmetrical holiness, and of constant victory. In view of this the
Apostle cries out: "Who shall separate us from the love
of Christ? *shall* tribulation, or distress, or persecution,
or famine, or nakedness, or peril, or sword? As it is
written, For thy sake we are killed all the day long; we
are accounted as sheep for the slaughter. Nay, in all
these things we are more than conquerors through Him
that loved us. For I am persuaded that neither death,
nor life, nor angels, nor principalities, nor powers, nor
things present, nor things to come, nor height, nor
depth, nor any other creature, shall be able to separate
us from the love of God, which is in Christ Jesus our
Lord."

"More than conquerors!" Thank God, you may

outwit the devil every time, and be more than conqueror! And then comes glory, for glory always follows victory. You remember how, when General Taylor returned from his victories in Mexico, glory, like a cloud of incense, surrounded him. And when Grant, the victor, came from those struggles in the Wilderness, and around Richmond, what glory crowned his brow; and when, in olden time, Titus came home from his victories, you have read how the people rent the air with their shouts, as they ascribed glory to him. So, my brethren, you are conquerors, and the day of your coronation is coming, when, in the presence of the angels, who will delight to do you honor, you shall be crowned eternal victors. O, will not this be enough? And that life, which is born of this death to self, is an eternal life. Think, then, of this, when you shrink from the pain of the present strife, and press on—

"On! to the heights where the seraphim soar,
    On! to the bright hills of life evermore."

MR. BOOLE'S EXHORTATION.

This is a time and place for honest talk, and I propose to follow up in the same line of thought which our brother has brought to us. It is in the sixth chapter of Romans, I think, where we have brought before us the symbolical death of the soul to sin. Take, now, the passage: "Likewise reckon ye also yourselves to be dead indeed unto sin, but alive unto God through Jesus Christ our Lord." And let me add another from the same chapter: "For sin shall not have dominion over you: for ye are not under the law, but under grace."

There are two things stated here; *first*, the right of the Christian to declare his emancipation from under the power and dominion of sin; and, *second*, his ability, by the Divine assurance and Almighty help, to maintain that individual emancipation.

Sin presents itself to us in two forms—outward and inward. My arm may strike, but there is a will behind the arm, and my nature is behind my will. In our nature there is not only an evil disposition, but its heart, its spirit, its all, are evil; for "the carnal mind is enmity to God, is not subject to the law of God, neither indeed can be." And whether it be a wholly carnal mind, or partially purified, all that remains of the carnal, is in eternal enmity to God, whether it be found in my heart as a minister, or in yours as a layman. If, away down in the bottom of your heart, there is a sediment of evil, there is opposition to God; and it can ally to itself the hosts of hell, and can ally them in a moment. It is a maxim in military science, that a fortification is no stronger than its strength at the weakest point. So, a fort built on three sides of granite, and on the fourth with mud, is no stronger than if its four sides were built of mud; and he would be a poor general, who, in seeking to destroy such a work, would not direct his cannoniers to point their guns against the mud side of the fort. As between sin in the Church, and sin out of the Church, God has more trouble with that which is in the Church. Take sin from the Church, and you may write the millennial dawn in five years. (Great sensation.) Now, to find out where the weakness is, you must apply the Gospel test, which is to reckon ourselves "dead to sin." We find the Christian's right to reckon himself "dead indeed unto sin, but alive unto God through our Lord Jesus Christ," fully stated in God's word. Do you remember, when the proclamation of Emancipation was sent through the South, that our forces took them by hundreds of thousands, and scattered them all through that land? Now, that was a good instrument in itself, but there was just one thing lacking in it. That lack did not lie in the mind of the Executive who issued the proclamation, nor in the army that was to enforce its provisions, nor in the good-will of the Abolitionists, nor in its acceptance by the slave-owners; but in the mind of the slave himself. All else was of no avail, unless he chose to accept of its offers of emancipation. There were some slaves in Georgia who remained slaves, because· they chose to remain in that condition. There was power at Manheim, as there is here, but some souls have not yet felt it, though present at both meetings.

WE MUST DECLARE OURSELVES EMANCIPATED.

God does not do anything toward constraining us. He will show us the glory, and set before us the privilege and obligation ; but He never coerces the will. So He says, "Reckon ye also yourselves to be dead to sin." Have you ever thought that there was a power here, that could move heaven, and earth, and hell, and that God is waiting for you to exercise your authority, under this proclamation of God's independence, and say, "I am free from sin?" If not, the power of the proclamation cannot take effect.

Strange to say, human nature is always in friendship

17*

with sin. Man cannot see the good, and if he did he has no power to reach it. But if the power is tendered him by another, to be wise there is only one thing he can say, that is, "I will," and he can say that when he is dying. There is a great power in us, when we are backed by another strong enough to sweep away all resistance. When our officers, in the War of the Rebellion, went into the Southern States, they took with them the Emancipation Proclamation, and read it to the colored people. Suppose one of those black-faced men, more intelligent than the rest, should say, "How shall I know this is a fact? the laws of Georgia make me a slave; how shall I know I am free?" The officer replies, "You are no longer under the laws of Georgia, but under the general laws of the Union." "But," says the slave, "how may I know that I shall be sustained?" The officer points to the fixed bayonets, and says, "That is the power that will sustain you."

Honorable as you may deem your position in the church, and as good as you may be in some respects, yet on some one side of every unsanctified nature there is only that wall of mud. The passion that so often masters you has gone down, like the roots of the elm, that are down beneath the nether soil, until it sucks up the moisture of the springs. When you have resolved to refrain from its indulgence, you have succeeded for a while, and then you have fallen back into it again. It is one fault in one person, and a different one in another; and it is dishonest in us ministers to refuse to speak faithfully on this subject. We know that God has set us to show, to His praise, a church in clean garments, with sparkling eyes, clean hands, and a pure heart.

God has set us to raise up a church like this, and we have not done it. When a man knows the truth, and refuses to set it forth, it makes him less a man by so much—by such a course he does dishonor to his manhood. Satan enters on this weak side of the fort. All through the church of Christ there is weakness; in our conscience we know that there is weakness in the church, and we sometimes say we will leave the ministry, because we cannot rid our consciences of this burden in behalf of the church. They may say evil things about us, and that " He casteth out devils through the prince of the devils;" but they will have to say, he casteth out devils. " Holiness is power," and the soul that is armed with holiness is armed with power. How shall we obtain victory?

WE MUST JOIN OUR WILL WITH CHRIST'S.

We have the assurance of Christ that we shall be sustained, for " Sin shall not have dominion over you." God will do everything necessary, after your will has passed decision, and taken sides with holiness. But we must decide, you *must* decide and say, " I do here and now give myself to Christ, to be His, by his power."

But you say, " O this weakness." Didn't I tell you of the bayonets? I remember a scene of one of our gunboats. She lay out in the stream, in one of the Southern ports; and the slaves recognizing her as the means of their escape, hid themselves on the shore, and at a suitable time crept out from the grass, and entering the boats, rowed lustily for the gunboat. The rebels saw them and came down, and fired upon them. The gunboat seeing this, pulled up anchor and drew near , and ranging her guns just over the little boats containing the slaves, fired heavily, and the rebels fell back, and the slaves were soon liberated. Do you remember the time when the prophet and his servant saw the armies that were opposing Israel surrounding them, and the servant of the prophet was terrified?   There stood the trembling servant, and there stood the man of God so calm, so full of peace, and why? He would have his servant as calm as he, so he prayed, " Lord open his eyes," and he saw the armed hosts of God. You need not be afraid to claim the provision, and

DECLARE YOUR EMANCIPATION.

Yes, declare it now (many voices frequently responding, " Amen "), and if it requires that it should be done, God will open the heavens, and all this region shall be shaken before a saint of God shall lose his reward. You need sit no longer with granite on three sides and a mud wall on the other. Oh! that God may build you up of granite at all points, and on every side!

God is doing more than you are doing, and waiting to do still more. When those contrabands stepped, for the first time, on Freedom's side of the Potomac, they seemed to grow a foot higher. They had the same rags upon them, they lived still on corn bread and bacon, and thought that was good enough, for they always had it; they did not know that the government had rations for them, and that the soldiers in blue would distribute them; nor do you know where your reinforcements are to come from, but you, like them, may get on Freedom's side of religion, and then God will be your almoner. I remember one poor slave woman, just escaped to our forces, over whose shoulder I threw a blanket shawl, when she did not know she would be so provided for; and you don't know but the angels are coming down now to put white robes upon you. Yes, I believe they are coming. ("Hallelujah!") Now, the glory of the freedom of those contrabands all culminated in and proceeded from one thing. When they declared their emancipation they struck straight for the North Star. Now, mark. When you have said, "I will be free!" God marshals all His forces on your side. But without this declaration on your part, the proclamation of the Lord is of no effect, though He has planted the batteries, and put the angels in line to help you. And now He leaves it for you to *reckon.* He wants you to be freemen, and not to stay in bondage. God wants you to will—yes, He wants you to will. As Wesley said, God could no more do without good men than they could do without him. He wants men that will say, "I will!" "I will!" But, then, *you* must say it, and there must be no bartering, and no questioning.

I heard, from an authentic source, an item of history that transpired during the dark days of the Rebellion. You remember the attempt was made upon the part of Messrs. Stephens, Campbell, and Hunter, representatives of the South, in an interview with Secretary Seward and Mr. Lincoln, at Hampton Roads, to fix upon some terms of armistice, or cessation of hostilities, looking to the settlement of the national difficulties. As the rebel commissioners were receiving their instructions, Mr. Davis said that just as the respective armies stood at that time, so they should stand, and the line between them then, should be considered the dividing line between the contesting parties during the armistice, until some other solution could be reached. "But," said Mr. Campbell, "suppose they will not receive such a proposition?" "I know better; they will," said Mr. Davis. When the time of the interview came, Judge Campbell proposed such a line, and began to follow out, in his reasonings, the consequences of such a division. At this point Mr. Lincoln raised his hand, and just said—

"THE GOVERNMENT MUST HAVE ALL."

There was a pause, and he uttered it again, in his own emphatic way. No man from the other side answered a word, and there the conference ended. And God will not take less than all. Had they given all cheerfully it would have been a reasonable requirement, and then how many homes would have been blest with the return of husbands and sons. They refused to give all, and the government swept on and over their fair fields, and took all; and would have done so even against a more prolonged opposition. So God's government must stand. If we refuse, He will nevertheless have His will and way. God's government must have all. Sinner! you and I have seen years of rebellion against God, and, like the South, we persisted in it, and years more may be added, but the government of our God shall have all. And you, brother and sister, to you it is said, "The government must have all." Let us say, "Yea, Lord, life, property, honor, all;" and then He will give us power in His sovereignty. You may say, "I will put myself on the side of this government of Christ, that I may have power in the world;" or, you may refuse, but God will have all at last. Formalities in church-service, or names on church records, are no criterion. He will have all. All must come on the broad platform of this obedience to Christ, or we must suffer the consequences. Thank God that without further delay, loss, or war, we may have all. Let us surrender now, and receive the protection and aid of the Divine government.

CHAPTER XXVI.

SERMON OF REV. G. C. WELLS, OF TROY CONFERENCE.—RE-
MARKS OF REV. J. THOMPSON, OF PHILADELPHIA CON-
FERENCE.

MR. WELLS' SERMON.

1 *John*, i. ix.—"*He is faithful and just to forgive us our sins,
and to cleanse us from all unrighteousness.*"

JUSTIFICATION AS RELATED TO SANCTIFICATION.

IT is a common thing among many professed Christians, so to let down the Bible standard of religious
experience, as to take penitence for conversion, and conversion for holiness.

One of the greatest obstructions to the work of
Christian holiness is, that so many who profess it are
strangers to the experience. Under a defective system
of teaching, many are led to seek it from a wrong
stand-point. Either they were never converted, or they
are backsliders; and, from good convictions, they advance to seek for holiness of heart. As a result, they
are self-approved, and in their honest endeavors, find
comfort, and immediately profess to be saved fully. And
when the tests and the duties come, their experience
being defective, they are not able to meet them; and
the whole doctrine and experience of holiness is brought
into disrepute by multitudes professing it, who never

knew the experience, and who needed to have sought pardon first.

The text clearly makes distinction between justification and entire sanctification. We propose in this discourse to consider *the nature, extent, and duties of a justified state, as related to an entirely sanctified state.*

Justification and forgiveness of sin mean substantially the same thing. St. Paul clearly uses them synonymously. "Be it known unto you, therefore, men and brethren, that through this Man is preached unto you the forgiveness of sin, and by Him all that believe are justified from all things."

To be justified in an evangelical sense does not signify being made innocent, holy, or righteous, for this would confound it with regeneration and sanctification; but it is to be regarded and treated as such, in consideration of faith in Christ. It is to have sin pardoned, and its penalty remitted by a judicial act of God.

Justification is *full* and *complete*, and has no *degrees.* There are degrees in guilt, and degrees in condemnation, but justification admits of none. We mean by this that God does not pardon one sin to-day, and another to-morrow, till all are forgiven. He pardons no sin till there has been a thorough repentance, a complete consecration, and an unwavering faith; and when He pardons a sinner He pardons *all* his sins. "By Him all that believe are justified from *all* things." And this completeness is essential to constitute justification; for if we are not justified from *all* things, it is no privilege whatever, only as it may relate to the degree of punishment, to be justified from anything. For *one* sin unforgiven, would seal our just and eternal condemnation.

"'The wages of *sin*,' not of many sins, nor of great sins, but 'the wages of *sin*,' one sin, 'is death.'"

St. Paul is careful to assure us that justification is full and complete. "There is, therefore, now no condemnation to those who are in Christ Jesus." No condemnation to *any* who are in Christ Jesus in any sense. No, not to the merest babe in Christ. If he is in Christ Jesus, he is free from all condemnation. God has nothing against him, as he has nothing against God. "Therefore, being justified by faith, we have peace with God through our Lord Jesus Christ." There is not a feather's weight of guilt or condemnation on any forgiven soul. There is none from any source; there is none to any. There is no condemnation from God the Father: "It is God that justifieth. Who is he that condemneth?" There is none from the Son; "It is Christ who hath died for us; yea, rather who hath risen again; who also maketh intercession for us." There is none from the Holy Ghost; "The Spirit itself beareth witness with our spirit that we are the children of God." He has nothing to be condemned for, for every sin is pardoned. God has no condemned children; He has no guilty children; no wicked children. Condemnation and guilt pertain only to sinners, and pardon is a complete deliverance from them; so they may boldly throw down the challenge of the Apostle, concerning every forgiven soul: "Who shall lay anything to the charge of God's elect? It is God that justifieth. Who is he that condemneth?"

It is delightful to consider the completeness of this work as figuratively represented in the Scriptures. In the act of forgiveness, our sins are said to be covered—

covered by the righteousness of Christ, so that the eye of Omniscience even, does not behold them for our condemnation. "Blessed is the man whose transgression is forgiven, whose sin is covered." They are said to be hid—hid from the eye of justice, so that they can never be found for our punishment. God is said in the act of pardon to cast our sins, not upon the sea-shore, where they can be easily found and gathered up again, but, like Pharaoh and his host, into the depths of the sea. "Thou wilt cast all their sins into the depths of the sea." Moreover, God is said in this act to forget our sins. "I will forgive their iniquity, and I will remember their sins no more." Thus God is pleased in the strongest conceivable language, and in the most striking figures, to represent to us the completeness of justification; assuring us that all the sins we have committed, when we are forgiven, are covered, hid, buried, and forgotten, and even the record of them blotted out forever. "I, even I, am he that blotteth out thy transgressions for mine own sake, and will not remember thy sins." Connected with this divine act, and occurring at the same moment, is acceptance with God, adoption as children, a partial removal of the evil nature, and the witness of the Spirit; but we are not to speak of these now.

In regard to justification, there are two prevalent errors. One is the attributing too much to it, and the other too little. Those who attribute too much to it, claim that at justification the soul is entirely sanctified, so that, from that moment, there is nothing of attainable experience left, but simple growth and development.

We dismiss this point now, with the simple statement

that it has no authority from the word of God, and lacks the confirmation of experience.

The second error, of attributing too little to it, is a prevalent and practical one, and requires particular attention. This class undervalue a justified relation. They regard it as comparatively an insignificant blessing—a low religious state, and they look upon its duties as few and trivial. A very large proportion of the Church is included in this class. They imagine that as to the mode of life, and to duty, but little difference is required between them and the world—that they are allowed to live in the neglect of duty, and even to some extent in the violation of direct commands, because they profess nothing higher—that they are not required to obey the commandments, and to perform duty as one who is entirely sanctified, because their state of grace is professedly so low. The idea is, that they escape a vast amount of responsibility, because they do not profess holiness. Reprove them for wrong or neglect, or exhort them onward in Christian labor, and they fall back and take shelter under their low profession, and feel perfectly secure—and sometimes with an exultant air, they will tell you, " O, I do not profess holiness. I never made any flaming pretensions to religion," and seem to glory in their low profession as their stronghold. This is a most dangerous error. The truth is, that all the duties of the Christian, as they are written in the Bible, are just as binding on one who is justified, as on one who is entirely sanctified.

We are accustomed to say to the sinner, God has not given two codes of laws—one for the christian and another for the sinner. He does not say to the christian, " You keep this code of laws and live, and to the sinner, You keep this code and live." God's law is *one*, and is just as binding on the sinner as on the christian.

The profession of religion has no power to create or to annul, to increase or to diminish moral obligation; for, if it can create *one* obligation, it can twenty or one hundred, and thus the profession of religion, rather than the Bible, would become the standard of moral obligation. We say to him, those obligations are upon you, whether you realize it or not, and whether you admit it or not, and they are of the highest possible character, and cannot be increased or diminished. You have no more right to violate God's law, to kill, to steal, or to covet; you have no more right to withhold worship, or to restrain prayer, than the most devout christian on earth. Who has given you license to sin against God, or to be a violator or neglecter of His requirements? Now, all this applies with equal force to one who is justified. God has not two codes of laws—one for the sanctified, and another for the justified. He does not say to the sanctified, keep this code and live, and to the justified, keep this code and live. His law is *one*, and is just as binding on one who is justified merely, as on one who is entirely sanctified. Every sin that you commit, and every duty that you neglect, will just as surely bring upon you the displeasure of heaven as it will upon one who is entirely sanctified.

Will the commission of sin, result in a forfeiture of the blessing of holiness? The commission of sin, will just as certainly cause a forfeiture of the blessing of justification. Will the neglect of any known duty, cause the displeasure of God to rest upon one who enjoys entire holiness? The neglect of known duty will just as certainly bring the displeasure of God upon one who is justified. Neither the one nor the other, can commit sin or neglect duty, without standing condemned before God, and "There is therefore now no condemnation to them who are in Jesus Christ." The great difference between a justified and sanctified believer, is not so much in the outward walk, as in the inward experience. We say, then, that any professed christian, whether he professes much religion or little, who lives in the commission of sin, is a sinner. He is condemned before God, always observing the clear Bible distinction between sin remaining in the heart, but under the control of grace, and sin in the life, called in the Scriptures "committing sin." And we use the word sin, now, only in the sense of wickedness, not entering at all into those nice distinctions between sins in the abstract, sins of ignorance, inadvertent sins, &c.

We assert, then, on Bible authority, that he that is justified, if he commit known sin, is justified no longer, but is condemned, and, except he repents, will perish. Said the mild and loving John, "He that committeth sin is of the devil, for the devil sinneth from the beginning." What! this little sin make me a child of the devil? Just the indulging and exhibiting the pride of my heart,—just the allowing a rash and unholy temper? Just the speaking of angry words? This make me a child of the devil? It is not for me to vindicate the Almighty in the presence of His creatures. I give you His word, "He that committeth sin,"—not great sins, nor many sins, but "He that committeth sin is of the devil." But "I do not profess sanctification, I only

profess religion in the lower sense." The text does not
say he that professes sanctification and committeth sin,
but "He that committeth *sin*," no matter what his profession, "is of the devil." Oh, I do rejoice that religion
in its lowest sense, though it may admit of sin yet lurking in the heart, saves a man from committing sin ; that
the merest babe in Christ is saved from sinning, just
as long as he is a babe in Christ. This is the least that
salvation can do for any man, to save him from all his
past guilt, and keep him from committing sin.

But do you say, "I enjoy some religion—I am not
without acceptance with God, and a measure of religious comfort." "Hereby," saith the Apostle, "we
do know that we know Him, if we keep His commandments." "He that saith I know him, and keepeth not
His commandments, is a liar, and the truth is not in
him." If he does not keep the commandments he is not
to be regarded a Christian, even if he professes and
declares it. Said the Saviour, "He that hath my commandments and keepeth them, he it is that loveth me."
Obedience is the great test of discipleship. But do you
say, "I do keep the commandments as such. I only
transgress in some few things." "Whosoever shall keep
the whole law and yet offend in one point, he is guilty
of all,"—that is, he is as really guilty, though not to the
same degree, as if he had broken every command of the
Decalogue ; and if guilty, he is not justified, for guilt and
justification stand opposed to each other.

Here we begin to see that it means something to be a
Christian in the *lowest* sense. A justified state is a very
exalted one before God.

St. John descends to the manifest principles and

affections of the heart as a test of a justified relation, affirming that a man cannot hate his brother and be justified. "He that saith he is in the light, and hateth his brother, is in darkness even until now." "Whosoever hateth his brother is a murderer, and ye know that no murderer hath eternal life abiding in him." Hatred to a brother is the principle that takes life. It may not have attained that strength to develop itself in the overt act, but it is the principle that accomplishes murder, and God calls him a "murderer." In the light of this inspired saying, a man with his hands reeking with the blood of a dead brother, has just as good a hope of heaven as the man that hates his brother. We truthfully sing—

> "None who are truly born of God
>   Can live in enmity:
> Then let us love each other, Lord,
>   As we are lov'd by Thee."

There is no hatred among Christians of any grade. Never. Where hatred is allowed, religion dies. The very lowest type of a Christian is saved from indulging hatred, and enabled to cherish love.

LOVE OF THE WORLD.

We are assured also that a man cannot love the world and be justified. "Love not the world, neither the things that are in the world. If any man love the world, the love of the Father is not in him. For all that is in the world, the lust of the flesh, and the lust of the eyes, and the pride of life, is not of the Father, but is of the world." And furthermore, "Whosoever is born of God," not whosoever is sanctified, but "Whosoever is *born* of God," and thus becomes a *child* of God, "doth not commit sin." And "Whosoever abideth in Him sinneth not." Not whosoever is made holy, but "Whosoever abideth in Him," in any sense, "sinneth not." This is what the Scriptures teach, as pertaining to justification. This is the lowest type of a Christian freedom from guilt, and condemnation, and transgression.

I rejoice, and thank God, that to be a Christian in any sense, is to be so essentially different from the world, that even in a justified state the believer is saved from committing sin; and as long as he is justified, walks joyfully in the light of God's countenance, the Spirit witnessing with his spirit, that he is a child of God. O! blessed and exalted state. And yet it is to be observed, that as a matter of fact, the mass of professed Christians do not walk here. Look where you will, and you will find that the great majority professing to be in a justified relation are unstable and vacillating in their experience and walk. For a season they are in the light, and then they are groping in darkness. To-day they are justified, to-morrow condemned. Their course is one of sinning and repenting. O, how many have pursued this unsteady course, till they have become tired of themselves, disgusted with their vacillating service, and they have cried out in substance:

> " Now I repent, now sin again;
>   Now I revive, and now am slain —
>   Slain by the same malignant dart
>   Which, O! too often wounds thy heart."

This vacillating course is to be attributed chiefly to

16

two causes. First, it is an exceedingly difficult matter, to say the least, for a justified believer to reject such plain and positive commands of God as these: " Be ye holy, for I the Lord your God am holy :"—" Be ye therefore perfect, even as your Father in heaven is perfect : "— " Thou shalt love the Lord thy God with *all* thy heart, and thy neighbor as thyself," commands as direct and imperative as any in the Bible, and all the gracious provision and promises for the attainment of entire holiness, or be indifferent to them, and yet have God's approving smile.

And secondly, the inward traitors, yet lurking in the heart of one merely justified and born of God, sympathize with the foes of God without, and betray him into sin, and hence his frequent falls. And here we conceive, lies the great necessity for entire holiness, to cure this vacillating course, to *establish* believers in their christian walk, so that, every inward foe being destroyed by the great power of God, and all remaining unrighteousness washed away by the blood of Christ, they may walk steadily in the way of God's commandments, and be " mighty through God to the pulling down of strongholds."

But you will never walk thus with firm and steady tread, and be thus endowed with power, till you have a holy heart. And thanks be to God, the attainment of a holy heart is your *privilege*, the privilege of *all here*, and *now* look for it then with all your heart—look for it to-day, through faith in Jesus Christ. Give yourself to God in view of obtaining it.

And yet we must observe, that if you are now clearly justified and accepted, you will find nothing *new* to con-

secrate. You must be entirely consecrated to God to be justified. Only in seeking holiness of heart you renew the offering amid new measures of light, and new convictions, and in view of a new experience. Hasten, then, thus to make the offering, and lay hold upon Christ by faith, and my soul is a witness that you will succeed, and feel the power of the cleansing blood, and God will keep you amid duties and reproaches, and conflicts, and vicissitudes, and adversities, and bereavements ; keep you while you cling to the cross with a blessed consciousness of purity ; keep you steady and calm, and resigned, and secure, and you shall be a living example of one kept by the power of God through faith unto salvation.

* * *

REMARKS OF REV. J. THOMPSON, OF PHILADELPHIA CONFERENCE.

* *Delivered on Saturday Evening.*

In all the churches there are many members who cannot or do not say, that they are cleansed from all sin. If, now, such persons are to be found in such numbers, it becomes us to inquire why it is that they can bear no clearer testimony. Some would answer this question by saying that " they have never been converted." If this were granted, it would make sweeping work in all our churches. Others say that " these persons were once truly converted, but they are now backslidden." If this be so, then there are many more backsliders in the church than I have seen, or am willing to allow. Wesley, and Fletcher, and Watson, and every other writer of promise among our fathers, all wrote upon this subject ; and among them there was no difference, and they had another way of accounting for this fact. They assume that the trouble with such, is not that they have not been converted, nor that they have backslidden, but they have not gone on to perfection, and been saved from all sin.

Soon after my conversion I read Carvosso, and I wept over it, and rejoiced over it, and prayed over it. I turned to the account of his conversion, and I found it clear as the noon-day sun ; and no man has ever supposed that he was not converted, nor does any think that when he was groaning after more light and grace, he was backslidden. He says, though the work of grace had been progressive, he still found in him certain roots of bitterness, from which he prayed earnestly to be delivered ; and at a certain time he received a blessing that gave him complete deliverance, and he called it "holiness." If God gave these men—such as Wesley, and Clarke, and Watson, and Carvosso—this blessing, surely He can give it to us to-day, and this is what the church needs to enable her to give a clear testimony.

After I was converted, I found still in me some of these roots of bitterness ; and if there is a man here who has not felt these roots of bitterness since his conversion, I should like to hear that man's experience ; but such a man is not here. But now I know that God has taken all these roots, all the bitterness out of my soul. Brethren, you from Philadelphia who know me, you know that my conversion was clear. My brethren in the ministry, with whom I have long preached the Gospel, know this, and I might safely ask to-day, if, as I sat side by side with them in Conference, they ever suspected I was never converted, or that I had lost my religion? I do not believe they ever did. They surely never gave me reason to suppose so. They always gave me a warm grasp of the hand, and a hearty God speed. But yet the time came when, standing in the light of justification, I felt my need of entire sanctification, and I went to God, and He gave me the desire of my heart, and thank Him I have the victory now; and whenever the time comes that I am compelled to give up the idea that I was thus fully saved, then I must also give up the idea that I was ever converted, for the one was as clear as the other. But I know this, and if I ever backslide and go down to despair (I pray I may not), I will tell in hell, that once in time, the blood of Christ washed out all the stains of my heart, and removed all the roots of bitterness. I shall never be able to tell, with the language I now employ, how glad I am that I ever found my way among these "sanctified ones," as some call them; and I shall thank God to all eternity, that I ever found a people able to tell me this story of perfect love, and to put my feet into the right way. (Shouts of "Glory! Glory! Amen.") May God keep me steadfast! I never mean to give up this glorious hope, this blessed assuring grace. When I received this blessing, I did not stand still, nor have I since; but it is growing in me, and is better and better all the time. Oh that multitudes would seek this salvation to-night. If I had any influence with you, I would say, " *Come thou with us and we will do thee good.*"

CHAPTER XXVII.

SERMON OF REV. J. F. CHAPLAIN, OF PHILADELPHIA CONFERENCE—LOVE-FEAST, AND NATIONAL TESTIMONIES.

MR. CHAPLAIN'S SERMON.

Phil. iv. 6, 7.—*" Be careful for nothing; but in everything by prayer and supplication with thanksgiving let your requests be made known unto God. And the peace of God, which passeth all understanding, shall keep your hearts and minds through Christ Jesus."*

We are accustomed to think of happiness as a privilege. It is equally a duty. God does much in saying to man, " You *may* be happy—I *permit* it." But He does more. He says " You *must* be happy—I *command* it." No man attains the proper measure of either what God permits, or of christian obedience, if he is not happy.

Privilege and duty are as indissolubly blended in the Divine commands, as are light and heat in the sun's rays. There is much of christian privilege enjoyed, where little christian duty is performed, as the warmth of the solar rays is felt, where the light does not shine; but the privilege of such happiness as is worthy of a rational, immortal, redeemed creature like man, can only be realized by the faithful performance of duties such as he only can perform.

Many of us think of happiness as a rare exotic, which can only struggle into a dwarfed development by dint of the severest painstaking, and the costliest contrivances in a soil and clime as cold and uncongenial as this world of sin. This view of the case is correct, if you mean by it—christian happiness, indigenous to heaven, can only grow on earth in christian natures, as the result of all the costly appliances which the Gospel affords, and of the severe painstaking duties which the Gospel requires; but it is sadly at fault, if you get the notion 'that in a christian soil and in a christian climate, this heavenly exotic is not as much at home on earth as in heaven.

My text might, for aught we know, be as appropriate an utterance of our Heavenly Father to the elder children in heaven, as to the younger ones on earth. If one of us were called home to heaven this hour, could we conceive of any more comforting word that possibly could fall from the lips of our Lord, than this identical voice of the Spirit? Imagine yourself there in the presence of Jesus. Think of what now seem to you the best methods He might employ to inspire your fullest confidence, to stimulate you to the loftiest duty, and to give you a *home* feeling of the richest and purest enjoyment. Can you conceive of anything more effectual, more all-inclusive, more thoroughly to your taste, and more heaven-giving, than for Jesus to say to you, " My child, in this new world there is no room for an unhappy or disquieting thought. Dismiss all care. You can have your desires, and make your requests. This is a world of liberty, where all are free to be as good as they can, and as happy as they will. If you want anything, ask for it, and get it; and when you get it be grateful enough to return thanks for it. And the peace, the rapturous, infinite peace of God, which passeth all understanding, will keep your heart and mind through Christ Jesus." The full flood of the glory of the heavenly world would, in that moment, burst upon your soul, and, without a moment's pause of indecision and doubt, you would begin the eternally exultant experience—"I am happy! I cannot help but be happy!"

What Jesus will say to you and me in heaven, we must go there to find out. He will speak just such words as will make our enjoyment complete. What He says to us on earth, is what we are now concerned in; and if we experimentally listen to Him, we shall get a full enjoyment on earth, preparatory to our having larger faculties, for the fuller revelations of Christ-given happiness in heaven. The methods proper for heaven to use, in making each newly-arrived inhabitant a homogeneous part of heaven, we can trust with the God of heaven. A large part of the process is to take place on earth.

Jesus is on earth as really as He is in heaven. He is as much concerned for our welfare here, as He will be there. It would be impossible to conceive of any member of the family of God in heaven, as abandoned to a condition of precarious, doubtful, and stinted happiness. The conception is equally impossible, so far as it applies to any member of God's family on earth. That there are *duties* required in heaven, is unquestionable. Law enjoins duty, and heaven is a place where law has its fullest sway and amplest development. "And now *abideth* faith, hope, charity." And who will say that prayer any more than praise, will be obsolete in heaven? For if faith abides, and hope, which is the embodiment of desire, the only way to express our desires to God concerning the unseen, to which faith refers, is by prayer.

It is an imaginary spectacle, however, with which we have to do, in dealing with these words of the Spirit in their application to us. Something like them will be said presently when we get up higher,—perhaps inconceivably sweeter. I doubt not there will be; for God's word is a progressive thing, as well as His work and way. But here is a thing that *is* said, to prepare you and me to get up higher, to listen to the better things which are to be said. Oh! how glad I am that my Father has said to you and me, "Be careful for nothing." If He had given each of us a mountain of gold, it would have been poor in comparison with these words. Cherish them. Quote them till you remember them, so as never by any possibility to forget them. Rely on them and on Him who said them. Feed on them. Rejoice in them all the days of your life; and leave them as a legacy to your children and children's children, with the precious commentary of your happy life, as their living enforcement.

Duty and privilege are so closely blended, as to be difficult, if not impossible, to separate. "Be careful for nothing" is equally duty and privilege. You can put before it either "you *must*," or "you *may*;" and in everything by prayer and supplication "with thanksgiving let your requests be made known unto God," we can say the same thing. Thus with, "And the peace of God, which passeth all understanding, shall keep your hearts and minds through Christ Jesus." It may strike some that privilege is more prominent in this than duty, but it is very doubtful. The truth is,

16*

these two things are so bound together everywhere, that
duty is privilege, and privilege is duty. In this twofold
classification of blended duty and privilege, we see the
happy soul in a threefold posture, as *repellent, active,*
and *receptive.*

We are permitted and commanded to

REPEL CARE.

Care is a foe to happiness. When it enters a heart,
happiness departs. And as God permits and commands
happiness, he disallows and condemns whatever inter-
rupts it. But care has a good sense as well as a bad one.
The badness of the thing consists not so much in what it
is, as in the bad use made of it. A life free from care,
is not for that reason careless. A careless life is a sinful
one, for carelessness is sin.* In a certain sense we must
be careful. " This is a faithful saying, and these things
I will that thou affirm constantly, that they which have
believed in God might be careful to maintain good
works." The hymn has it, " Careful, yet without care
I am ; " and the sentiment is a very proper one.

One cannot be too careful, when the care is to be right
and to do right. And in this sense we may safely alter
the text and say, " Be careful in everything." But
when the case is a weight of anxiety, a burden that is
painful and distressing, we are commanded, as Christians, to have nothing to do with it. A burdensome
weight is not intended for any of us to carry. God
thinks too much of us for that, and we are not bond-scr-

---

* When Isaiah denounced wicked Babylon, he called her, " Thou
that art given to pleasure, that dwellest carelessly." And Zephaniah,
Nineveh, " This is the rejoicing city that dwelt carelessly."

vants bearing burdens. " Let us *lay aside* every *weight*."
And as care is one of the heaviest and most painful of
weights, we must especially lay it aside. " Cast thy burden on the Lord and he will sustain thee ; " not *it* only,
but "*thee*." " Casting all your care upon him ; for he
careth for you." What we cannot bear without pain,
Christ can bear for us, so as to make us light-hearted and
happy. Care, as a painful burden, comes from different
causes, and we are to take care to have none of it.
We break the law by taking it.

The most prolific source of care is *anxiety for the
future.* The man of care not only bears the evils of to-
day, but imports from the imaginary future, all sorts of
evils to increase his discomfort and distress. Jesus
says, " Sufficient unto the day is the evil thereof." Care
of the right sort, is actively engaged in being right and
doing right to-day—*now*, and while we do this, we can
very well afford to trust the future to God. He has
taken better care of the past, and secured better results
for the present, than we deserved ; why should He not
of the future ?

> " Ye fearful saints, fresh courage take ;
>   The clouds ye so much dread
> Are big with mercy, and shall break
>   In blessings on your head."

A burden of care is borne by many in the foolish
effort they make to shape, according to their notions,
the affairs of life, which are governed only by the All-
wise Sovereignty of Providence. After we have done
our best, (and things turn out differently from what we
had hoped), why should we sit like Niobe, in tears of

burdened grief which refuses relief, or, crouch like Atlas with a world of disappointment crushing us ? We have responsibility enough without bearing what does not belong to us ; and as God governed the world well, before we came into it, He will be at no loss to keep up good government, even if we keep at our own line of duty, and let Him have His own way ; and if we think our way so much better than God's, it is high time for us to meet with disappointment, to take such egotistic folly out of us.

And all sorts of burdens of care come from the selfish, avaricious, ambitious and covetous graspings and hoardings of life. The worldly desires of men are inordinate ; desire for dress, for show, for luxurious living, for social distinction, for admiration, for office, and for power. The absolute impossibility of satiating them, shows the emptiness of earth, to meet the wants of an immortal and redeemed nature like man's. But if a man will "mind high things," when God tells him not, he must pay the penalty. A burden of care comes. The cares of riches, of office, and of fashionable life, make the man a stranger to the joys of humbler people.

If, by the grace of God, the soul can be put so successfully into the repellent attitudes, as to rule out care, with all its attendant burdens, a long step is taken toward securing the privilege and achieving the duty of a permanent happiness.

THE SOUL'S ACTIVE POSTURE.

But freedom from care is not the only element of happiness. Happiness is a positive thing. It is more than the negative of disquietude and distress. And as God is the Infinite source of all goodness, so is He of all happiness. We get, therefore, the positive element of happiness by coming to God for it. The happy soul is not only to be in a repellent posture, warding off what will make it unhappy, but it must be in an active posture, putting it into contact with God, and bringing to bear all the joy-giving forces, which such vital contact secures.

The permission and the command, require what sort of activity? *Prayer and thanksgiving.* "But in everything by prayer and supplication with thanksgiving, let your requests be made known unto God."

Prayer makes our requests known unto God; supplication urges them with importunate entreaty; thanksgiving returns grateful and adoring praise for blessings received. These are active duties which bring the soul into direct contact with God; prayer and supplication, to ask for what we want; thanksgiving, to thank Him for what we get. When we consider who it is we come to, what it is we come for, the spirit of benignity on the part of God, which permits and commands our coming, and the spirit of filial confidence and gratitude in ourselves which is cultivated by it,—we see such active, joy-giving forces at work, that the man of true prayer and praise cannot help but be a man of joyous happiness. Whatever puts a man into company with God, makes him happy; for "in His presence is fulness of joy." As one cannot come to the fire without being warmed, he cannot come to God without being blessed. An impalpable spiritual influence goes out from almost all associations in life, which makes us catch the spirit of our associate. This is preëminently the case in our intercourse with God; and as He is the blessed God in himself, he becomes the blessing God to such as associate with Him. How is it then possible, my beloved, to find a greater argument for sending you and me often, yea, constantly, into such infinitely blessed intercourse?

But there is more than impalpable influence which goes out from this intercourse. We are to come to God with " requests." What requests? A request is expression of desire. And any desire which is holy and dutiful, can embody itself in request. The province of prayer is to offer up to God, in the name of Christ, our desires in the form of submissive and yet importunate request; for importunity is the work of " supplication," and supplication is that kind of prayer which stays for an answer, after request is made known.

" Prayer *and* supplication." What God hath joined together, let no man put asunder. Prayer without supplication, is the movement of too feeble a desire, of too weak a faith. It would be a strange spectacle to behold a man seeking an interview with the President, on business of great importance, after he had secured it, making so light of it as to wait for no answer, and expect no result. But is not much of our prayer of this sort? An answer is not waited for; a result is not expected. Supplication makes the petitioner plead, urge, wait, expect.

And this sort of prayer brings to the soul the positive part of happiness. If we could by any means, put into our own hearts and lives the same kind of holy and blissful ingredients, that enter into the heart and life of

God, would any doubt the efficacy of such an arrangement, or question the positive happiness thus implanted in human experience? And this is the very work that prayer does. The requests are to be made known unto God, that we may get the full benefit of all the infinities of the Divine nature, in the gratification or denial of them, in such a way as will give us better answers than our prayers called for.

So free from all disturbing influence, does our Father arrange for our happiness, that He will not allow us to have one particle of care. "Be careful for *nothing*." And so full of all that is joy-giving would He have us, that He requires us to come to Him with all our requests, touching all our affairs and interests.

No parent was ever so kind as to tell his child, "Come to me with everything." Constant coming with every little question, difficulty, trial, sorrow, duty, and lesson, would be insufferably wearisome. But this is the very thing which our Father commands all His children to do. "In *everything* by prayer and supplication with thanksgiving, let your requests be known unto God." We are to think nothing too trivial to bring to God in prayer. Anything important enough to go with life, will be important enough to go into the judgment; and what God deems important enough to bring to the throne of judgment, we must deem it important enough to bring to the throne of grace. And can you and I pray over "*everything*," and get the full benefit of the mind and power of God in it? How, then, can we be aught else than happy in everything, unless there be unhappiness which comes from God—which none of us believe at all possible?

This brings us to the third posture of the happy soul.
It must be

THE RECEPTIVE POSTURE.

Receptive of what? " And the *peace* of God, which
passeth all understanding, shall keep your hearts and
minds through Christ Jesus."

Peace is the great staple of happiness. Exultation
and rapture come with the experience at intervals.
But they tax the nature too severely for a constant experience. They would wear it out. But peace is
a healthful condition of the nature, which gives the
sort of joy for the practical purposes for which we are
put into a world like this. It flashes not like a meteor,
it shines like a star, with an even, steady, soft light,
which can be relied upon. Your flashing, exultant
Christians are very apt to be unsteady, unreliable,
and unavailable for the practical purposes which are before Christianity. In your astronomical maps there is
no place assigned a meteor. It flashes out with a light
which outshines the stars, and calls attention from them
to itself, but while you are looking it vanishes. Give
me the man of steady, sober, common-sense *peace*.
There is a place in your spiritual astronomical maps for
such milder luminaries.

So strong a thing is this *peace*, that it *keeps* the heart
and mind. It keeps the heart from all its wanderings.
It keeps the mind from all sinful judgments and unrighteous conclusions, elevating thought to the holy and
heavenly, and holding the whole man by the force of
truth as it is in Jesus Christ, to the reception of all the
communicable fulness of Christ. "Through Christ

Jesus." This peace "passeth all understanding." It is above the "understanding." But it is level with the experience of any one who will seek it aright, and it is much better to enjoy it than to understand it. Do you enjoy it? You see your calling, your privilege, and your duty. It is your blessed Father's will to make you blessed. Happy himself, He would have you happy. Be then so *repellent* as to allow no burden to rest upon you. Be so *active* in your constant communion with God as to bring everything to Him in prayer and praise. Be so *receptive* as to get "the peace of God, which passeth all understanding," and let it work so steadily as to keep your heart and mind through Christ Jesus. Then will the glorious ideal be realized of a happy Church on earth as well as in heaven, because there is a Holy One here, as well as there.

LOVE-FEAST TESTIMONIES.

Several remarkable Love Feasts were held. We attempted to report the exercises, but when three hundred and fifty persons stood up within an hour to speak, we can give but the merest shadow of what was said, and without fully separating the testimonies of different persons. At one of them Brother Inskip, admonishing brevity, opened the way by saying: "The Lord is my light and my salvation this morning."

Three persons were up in an instant, and we caught such expressions as the following: "For many years I was trying to keep Jesus; now Jesus keeps me. I am His. All within me says, 'Bless the Lord!' He satisfies my soul. God is the strength of my heart and my portion forever. I can say every thought has been brought into captivity to Christ. Now have I become a son of God. I hope to see Him as He is. Five years I have been a happy man. Christ is my righteousness and sanctification."

Then was sung—

"All hail the power of Jesus' name."

" Yes, my soul says, ' Crown Him Lord of all.' I thank God that I have strong confirmation of the power of Christ to save to the uttermost. The Father, Son, and Holy Ghost witnesseth that I am saved. I stand on the mountain top and feel the kindlings of Christ's love."

" These are my last days," said a very old man, "and I thank God they are my best days. Christ liveth in me. The kingdom of heaven suffereth violence, and I mean to take it. I am now trusting. It is thirty-six years since I embraced the doctrine of full salvation. God is still with me. I travelled three thousand miles to be here. I represent a great many people who are hungering and thirsting after full salvation. Although I crossed the ocean partly on business pursuits, I intended to ' seek first the kingdom of God,' and I rejoice to say my soul is free ! I was not argued into the acceptance and enjoyment of this grace, but *loved* into it. Pray for me, American christians, that I may *live* the doctrine of holiness wherever I go." Here there was great sensation, which was heightened by Mr. Inskip rising and taking the brother from England by the hand, and pledging him the sympathy and prayers of that vast congregation, who joined in an outburst of song—

> "Together let us sweetly live,
> Together let us die."

The speaking then continued :

"I was born, and born again in England, and in that land also found the pearl of perfect love. I travelled all the way to England lately to see some friends, and found them walking in the same light—we are one. I did not lease my heart to the Lord, but gave it to Him fully. Satan has no mortgage on it. I endeavor to dwell in God daily.".

"Read," said a sister, "read all of you the Life of Lady Maxwell, it will be a blessing to you." "I feel this perfect love shed abroad in my heart. So do I— and I—and I. Whether I live, I live unto the Lord." Then was sung—

> "O, how I love Jesus," &c.

"I feel very small; I have come down to the child state. This morning reminds me of the 'sea of glass,' and those who stand upon it. With me it is, 'Jesus, Jesus, all the way along it is Jesus.' Did not our hearts burn within us as He talked with us? I find that God's sanctifying grace makes things move sweetly at home. I feel as if floating along on this mighty tide of salvation, and around me are the everlasting arms." There was then sung a stanza of Mrs. Witenmyer's hymn—"The valley of Blessing." "Jesus saves me just now. I am permitted to see God. He has purified my heart. My experience is—

> "'Jesus paid it all—all the debt I owe.'"

The brother sung this, and the chorus was taken up by

the multitude. "I have been to one hundred and ninety-nine Camp-meetings, and if God spares me will go to as many more." (This was said by "Happy John Allen," of Maine.) "I have moved out of Grumbling alley, and live now in Thanksgiving street. Jesus satisfies my soul fully. This tide of Gospel holiness reached me beyond the Mississippi river. His name is *Jesus*. Yes, His name is *Jesus*, and He is mine. I feel in the presence of so many of God's witnesses, that I am less than the least of all. By the grace of God, I am what I am. I want to say, ' Glory to God '—(say it, brother) —Amen. I am very hungry for more of this grace. Jesus is the bread of life. I began to love holiness forty years ago. I rejoice to see this day. It is the nearest heaven I ever experienced before. I had my first birth in Canada, among Catholics ; my second in Massachusetts, among Methodists ; and on this ground, last night, I laid all on the altar, and shall henceforth be all the Lord's. My heart is constantly crying : ' Nearer, my God, to Thee, nearer to Thee.' " (This was then sung.)

" There is not much of me, but the Lord has it all. At all times and everywhere I try to confess Him. Never more powerfully and sweetly saved than now. All is well—Jesus satisfies."

A preacher rose singing—

" My all to Christ I've given," &c.

and said, "This is my experience."

Here Rev. B. Pomeroy, Author of " Shocks from the Battery," rose, saying :

" I don't know how much a minute is, when measured

by sweet emotion. I like this meeting very much—I like the singing. It has been held up to the 'Old Hundred' cadence—good, weighty, and sublime. I like the countenance of this Israel—I feel proud of these faces. I see in these a guarantee against fanaticism. This is a wonderful meeting. Do we—can we comprehend the vast results of these days? It seems I could afford to stay out of Heaven for this! This meeting has rolled the world *a hundred years toward millennium!* We are coming into Isaiah's holy visions. I see the multitude of camels are coming—the dromedaries of Midian and Ephah, with the flocks of Kedar, are coming up on God's altar, and Holiness is to be written on the bells of the horses. This is the out-flow of heavenly influence—God's great river Amazon, that is to flow around the globe. Let the nations make way for the coming of God—my time is out, but I am not."

NATIONAL TESTIMONIES.

At this point, and at another time during the Camp-Meeting, the States, and some of the neighboring Provinces and Nations were called for testimony, and as the leader called from the stand the names of the States, responses were made. The following are some of them :—

MAINE.—" Full of faith and of the Holy Ghost."

NEW HAMPSHIRE.—" New Hampshire is suffering for the want of a holy ministry."

VERMONT.—" Vermont has the evergreen of perfect love. Our banner is up, and we mean to keep it flying."

MASSACHUSETTS.—" God is there at ' the hub of the

universe,' and this work is reviving; and I believe God will carry it on."

RHODE ISLAND.—" A Congregationalist responded. 'We have the Lord with us there, but we are going to carry back a mightier flame from this Camp-Meeting.'"

CONNECTICUT.—" The Lord is marching on. We are in for the beauty of holiness."

NEW YORK —(A Brother) " I hail from Albany, the place of corrupt legislation, the centre of Romish intrigue, and various abominations; but we expect to conquer all by the *power of holiness.*" [Here there was a general shout of " Amen," " Lord, help ! "]

Dr. Lore, speaking for Central New York, announced —" The official press advocates holiness." [" Bless the Lord ! "]

NEW JERSEY.—" In this State was held the first National Camp-Meeting. We expect to fight it out on this line. We claim the State for the Lord Jesus."

PENNSYLVANIA.—" We are going home to write 'HOLINESS' upon the keystone of the arch. Then shall the inhabitants of the rock sing, and the dwellers in the vales catch the flying joy."

MARYLAND.—" Baltimore is catching the holy fire." . . " Many at the last, shall appear among the blood-washed from old Maryland."

DELAWARE.—" The Governor in his last Thanksgiving Proclamation, told the citizens to praise God for a *full* salvation, and didn't we do it though ? " The Governor's class-leader also responded.

VIRGINIA.—" We are reconstructing Virginia upon the basis of holiness."

WEST VA.—" The work of full salvation is begun,

and the holy fire is spreading; and we pray the work may go on till it fills all her valleys and covers all her mountain tops."

OHIO.—"We have one hundred thousand members, and six hundred ministers in Ohio, who need this baptism."

INDIANA.—"Thousands there pant after holiness."

ILLINOIS.—"The standard of holiness is being lifted up in the Prairie State, and we look that upon her very prairies 'Holiness to the Lord' may be written."

MICHIGAN.—"The fire is there, and I want to return and help to spread the holy flame." "God has a holy people there."

IOWA.—"We have 'touched the altar.' Allusion was made to Mrs. Bishop Hamline, and prayer was offered."

WISCONSIN.—A preacher said: "We have emblazoned on our State Arms the word 'Forward'—that is also the motto of the Church."

"A mighty effort has been made to destroy our Sabbath and raze our religious institutions. Pray that the Dutch and the devil may not succeed."

MINNESOTA.—"We have strong helpers there, and are standing up for holiness."

NORTH CAROLINA.—"This wilderness will yet bloom with the beauty of holiness."

SOUTH CAROLINA.—"We want to be anointed afresh with the Spirit of holiness."

LOUISIANA.—Mr. Baldwin rose and said, "I bless God, we have a little leaven there."

KENTUCKY.—"We are doing what we can. The meaning of Kentucky is the dark and bloody ground,

but we are trying to get the people there to wash
their robes and make them white in the blood of the
Lamb."

ALABAMA.—"Our theological standards are the Bible,
the Methodist Catechism, and Hymn-book, and we find
holiness in them all. By God's grace we will hold up
this standard more faithfully hereafter."

CALIFORNIA was represented by Dr. Peck, who said
"much harm had come to the doctrine of holiness, by
extravagance and pretended revelations, but there was
a returning to the old theory."

COLORADO.—Reference was made to meetings being
held under the charge of Rev. P. Peterson for the promotion of holiness.

OREGON.—"Methodism is accomplishing its mission
and leading thousands to Christ and Heaven."

DISTRICT OF COLUMBIA.—"In nearly all the churches
in the city of Washington there are held weekly meetings for the promotion of holiness. Also in the daily
prayer-meetings of the Young Men's Christian Association this doctrine is being held up, and God is blessing us."

KANSAS.—"In Baker University there are young men
who stand up for holiness."

CANADA.—"Give us an International Camp-Meeting
for holiness." . . . "I bless God that I go back to
Canada with a heart cleansed."

GREAT BRITAIN.—Mr. Morgan, who came from Lon-
don in part to attend this meeting, said: "I will speak for
England, the home of Wesley and Fletcher, God bless
her. I wish I could tell a better story as to this theme
of holiness, but I believe many in England are waking
up to its importance, and a goodly number are enjoying

its comfort, and expect that number will be greatly multiplied."

The time allotted to this exercise having expired, it was closed, though voices were heard in various directions asking that other States and "Ireland" and that testimonies from men of the Sea might be called.

17

CHAPTER XXVIII.

SERMONS OF REV. W. H. BOOLE, OF NEW YORK EAST CON-
FERENCE, AND REV. A. LONGACRE, OF NEW YORK CON-
FERENCE.

SERMON OF MR. BOOLE.

Hebrews, 5th chapter, 12th, 13th, 14th verses, and 6th chapter, 1st, 2d, and 3d verses.—"*For when for the time ye ought to be teachers, ye have need that one teach you again which be the first principles of the oracles of God; and are become such as have need of milk, and not of strong meat.*

"*For every one that useth milk, is unskilful in the word of righteousness: for he is a babe.*

"*But strong meat belongeth to them that are of full age, even those who by reason of use have their senses exercised to discern both good and evil.*"

"*Therefore leaving the principles of the doctrine of Christ, let us go on unto perfection; not laying again the foundation of repentance from dead works, and of faith toward God.*

"*Of the doctrine of baptisms, and of laying on of hands, and of resurrection of the dead, and of eternal judgment.*

"*And this will we do, if God permit.*"

THIS sounds to me like the language of a wise schoolmaster, giving instruction to tardy, delinquent, and dull scholars, who have remained too long in the elementary principles, when they should have gone on to the graduation of teachers. I presume there is not much difference between the disciples of the present day, and those of the Apostles' days. Customs and manners have changed radically, but the general laws of our nature are the same. By the same principles we are brought to the knowledge of Christ through all the generations of men. In the beginning it was said: "While the earth remaineth, seed-time and harvest, and cold and heat, and summer and winter, and day and night, shall not cease." And therefore we see this succession. So in divine things we are instructed to "stand in the ways, and see, and ask for the old paths, where *is* the good way, and walk therein, and ye shall find rest for your souls."

CHRISTIAN CLASSIFICATION.

I presume, as far as classification of character is concerned, the Apostle's discourse is as applicable to Christians now as ever. There are, if I may divide them so, *adult* Christians; those who believe in Christ under all circumstances, whatever may be their feelings or condition and surroundings; living constantly in the favor of God; not stirred by each tempest or overcome by a tumult; they have come where, by the power of God, they stand. Then there are the *ready-to-halt* Christians, who love God more than the world, but they do love that some; they have faith, but it is neutralized by chronic unbelief, just as a sour condition of the system may cause good food to turn. They trust when on the mountain top, but in the valley fail; they walk as on the sea, but look upon the dark waters and begin to sink, and they are not saved by faith when sinking, as was not Peter. There are many things which neutralize their faith.

Then there are *babes* in Christ. They are babes, first, because they have just been born into the family of God. Through the Holy Ghost given unto them, they are stirred to desire, yea they are panting, to know more of God; yet they are babes, and desire the sincere milk of the Word.

Others are babes, secondly, because they are not grown, though fifteen, twenty, or twenty-five years since they were born. They have been mistaken both as to growth, and adult knowledge in Christ. Chronic unbelief has not hindered them, but they have missed the right road to God, and their ignorance of that way has brought them into labyrinths and by-ways. They are weak and become uneasy, and, I was about to say, tormented; they are the little Tom Thumbs and Minnie Warrens of the Christian family. May God wake them up to see a better way.

I find in the text some radical truths. The *first* is—

THE CHRISTIAN'S LIFE IS A GROWTH.

Growth is by a positive and unalterable law, and when we cease to grow we begin to die.

The *second* is—

Growth is by an absolute standard which defines the point unto which we are to arrive. We are to go on to something.

I. Growth, progress, and development are the woof and warp of Christian nature and life. If it be not so, our Christianity is fatally unlike everything in nature. Everything that has life, so far as I know, goes on in a steady increase, ay, and fulfils in itself the purpose of the Divine power. All over the world, among the fishes of the sea, the plants of the garden, and the trees of the forest, this is the case. And shall there not be growth in this Christian faith, this heaven-born new man, if I may so speak of it ; shall it not grow and develop; and shall it not also have its point of perfection, as God also has in himself, where it is relieved of the presence of the " old man " in which it was born, so it can begin to develop itself into the fulness of life ? O, how straight the word goes to the mark, when Jesus commands, " Be ye therefore perfect, even as your Father which is in heaven is perfect." The Apostle, taking up as it were the command of his captain, gives us the order, " Go on unto perfection."

By various figures and illustrations, the Gospel gives us growth in this life as the Christian's privilege and duty. Now we have the leaven that works until the whole lump is leavened. Then we have the corn, the blade, the ear, then the full corn in the ear. Then the grain of mustard seed, which grows until it becomes a tree, and the fowls of the air lodge in it. All these figures indicate a state of growth, and ultimate maturity, a maturity necessary to accomplish the processes of its existence, and without which they would fail of the end of their creation. Corn is very beautiful when seen waving in the wind, but the purpose is in its becoming full corn in the ear. If the leaven stops when the loaf is only half finished, the one-half spoils, and the other part soon falls.

If the leaven of grace in the human heart stops short of leavening the entire nature, it corrupts the first part, and overflows and spoils the other part. Steady

growth, and maturity in growth, growth for the purpose of maturity, that it may reach the result and
object of its creation, whatever that may be, is one of
the unalterable laws of God.

IMPERFECT CHRISTIANS.

This half-leavened experience is very common in the
Church of Christ, and this is attested by your wonder
at the oft-repeated exhibitions of inconsistency. I cannot deny they are Christians, nay, I acknowledge them;
for sometimes these wrongs are more apparent than
real, though at other times they are in appearance just
as they are in the heart, and the world asks what mean
all these inconsistencies? Here is a man in the Church
who is undoubtedly earnest in a certain way; is a class-
leader, and prays and labors for the church; but, being
wealthy, ask him for money to aid the cause, and he
immediately denies you. Now the old man of avarice
has not been taken out of him, and so he clings to
money, but oh, how many other things he will give to
God! Here is an excellent class-leader; he has grace,
and is lavish of his means, always ready to help the
cause of God; but, should a few cross words be spoken
to him in business, he is angry in a moment, and he is
half leavened, and spoiling in the other half. God said
that Ephraim was a cake unturned,—that is, not done,
and, alas! that this should represent so many Christians.
Paul says: " And I, brethren, could not speak unto you
as unto spiritual, but unto carnal, *even* as unto babes in
Christ. I have fed you with milk, and not with meat:
for hitherto ye were not able *to bear it*, neither yet now
are ye able." Then babes in Christ are carnal

"There is much of the old man in the new," says an old writer. The Apostle is addressing the Corinthian Church. They were half saved. You may justify this class of Christians as you please, you have not taken out all the old man. They favor the old man, and are betrayed by him oftentimes into open sin. You have gone into orchards at some time, and noticed a tree having leaves and fruit on one side, with a smooth trunk, and affording delightful shade; but on the other side the trunk is rough, the leaves dried, and the fruit is very scarce,—perhaps only one old apple hangs there, the growth of a year ago. Yet it is the same tree, having the same trunk and root. If you get on the good side of some Christians, they are real good; their prayers are fervent, and their faith is strong, and if you could stay on this side all the time, it would be pleasant; or if some ministers could but stay in the pulpit; if you could only see us on the class-meeting or the prayer-meeting side, when our hearts were open, and we had something for others, you would love us. But when you get on the home side—where it ought to be best, on the business side—where it ought to be good and true and patient—oh, how gentle it should be, but how different you find it! Yet it is the same tree, and they have not let God's truth go down and separate the two parts, so they should only have the good. All the process of education is to go from one acquisition to another, until it is complete, and from its beginning to conclusion, means that the scholar shall accomplish something in life. Progression is the law everywhere; and yet is a Christian to go backwards and forwards like a weaver's shuttle? There is a foundation of repentance from dead works, and of faith toward God, that we are not to lay the second time. Some Christians are always talking about faith, forgetting that the first lesson after their conversion, was faith in Christ. Some are speaking much of baptism, or the judgment, or resurrection from the dead, and keep in these elementary principles. What would you think of a builder who has to complete a house by a certain time, and having prepared for his foundation, draws his line, and builds up one course after another through the whole day? As he looks over it, here and there are kinks and irregularities, so it has to come down, course by course; and so it goes on day after day, building and pulling down. A superior mechanic seeing this folly, says: " Here is a line and plummet to build by, why don't you use them, and at first carry up your wall aright?" Here is a Christian who has the Gospel plummet, and yet you see the bunches and hollows in his work; and stretching the line, he sees them and repents, and goes on to repeat this sad workmanship. Is it any wonder, with so much tearing down, you can never get any farther than the ground-work, so you will never be able to show the handiwork of God? When will the angels rejoice, and God be satisfied with these beautiful temples, made after the pattern shown us in the Mount? The science of astronomy has made progress, and, with the greatly improved and powerful instruments of astronomers, they have pierced the heavens, and resolved the nebulous mass, and shown it composed of bright particular stars; and so they have gone on from height to height, soaring untiringly, their minds in a glow, and the wings of imagination all spread to make discoveries. Yet there are more sublime things than these,—the relations of this world to the world to come, that lie beyond the powerful glass of the astronomer, the soaring from height to height in the things of Christ. Our lives should encourage others to stretch away to know more of these things; we should have a telescope that can resolve the nebulous map of promise into joyful experiences. There is something more for us all, than these first principles. Imagine an old astronomer, with a small and imperfect glass, having no acquaintance with the later discoveries, beginning to tell you about the planets that are in our system. I fancy you would say, "Old man, you are but a child; this glass belongs to an old age; take it away." What shall I say to those old christians who are trying to lay the structure of first principles? Leave them, O leave them, and g, on unto perfection.

ILLUSTRATION OF CLASS-MEETINGS.

O the developments of this elementary life! Let us hold a class-meeting. "Tell us your experience, my brother," says the leader, after a formal opening of the meeting.

"God converted my soul fifteen years ago; I have been trying to get to heaven over this stormy sea of life. Pray for me." Leader says: "Go on, brother." "Next:"—"I thank God it is as well with me as it is. I, too, have made many crooked paths, but pray for me." Then they sing:—

> "Prone to wander, Lord, I feel it,
> Prone to leave the God I love."

17*

("Too true," was repeated by many voices.)

A sister gets up :—" I've been striving to get to heaven for a long time, but meet with many crosses ; I do the things I should not, and leave undone the things I ought to do."   Class sings :—

> "Look how we grovel here below,
>   Fond of these earthly toys;
> Our souls, how heavily they go
>   To reach eternal joys."

A sister speaks, turning her face to the wall, and away from the leader. Leader says: "Well, sister, I did not hear all you said, but it will be a happy time when we all get to heaven ; " and now they sing :—

> " Come on, my partners in distress,
>   My comrades through this wilderness,
>   Who still your bodies feel."

But who are these men and women of this class? Are they simpletons; have they no knowledge; or are they children in knowledge? Nothing of the kind. They are business men of great capacity, as sharp in business as can be found. Those women are as able as any of the women who are on the platforms of the day, advocating women's rights. They are neat, clean house-keepers, and real helpmeets for their husbands. The men are strong, when national questions are being settled. They have definite and settled purposes, and will not be moved from what they think is right. They can tell about affairs in Europe, and determine the chances of success in Cuba. In the world they are men and women, but in the church only babes. It is a shame on christianity. Cultivating the religious side of our natures, does not make us imbecile. To have been fifteen years or more, an attendant on class-meeting does not make you insipid. To be so, is an insult to your intelligence, an insult to your manhood, and womanhood; it is a libel on your christianity. If nothing more were done by the National Camp-Meeting, than lifting the Church on to a right platform, I believe that result would be better than the conversion of a thousand souls without securing such a position; I speak it reverently. Give us class-leaders who will say, "Come on, I can point you to the citadel of strength; I have power to call on God, and the gates shall fly open and let you in." Give us these men and women filled with the Holy Ghost, and then let them stand in the class-room, with their faces shining as though they had seen God; give us these, and we will take the world. ("Yes, and Amen.")

See what the Methodist Church made herself by her outspoken way in the late great national struggle. Do you remember how she volunteered her sons by thousands and thousands, until from the President down to the lowest officer they said: "Thank God for the Methodist church?" O! if we were filled with the same loyalty to Christ, as to give life and all we have, how soon we would be done with this baby talk in the class; and then we would say to all the other denominations, "Come on, we have left these low grounds, and taken flight for a nobler work."

Take a cog out of one wheel, and the power is gone; just snap one thread while the shuttle is flying, and see how it will snarl all the rest. Now, do you look at your weakness? God will take a worm to thrash a mountain; and all through the ages, God has shown that he does not care what He uses to do His will. Our strength is in Him.

"GO ON UNTO PERFECTION."

These are the words of the Holy Spirit, and we cannot afford to fritter them away by any subsequent explanations.

I find the word "justification," or that which is the same in meaning, twenty-eight times; and I find "sanctification," or that which is put for it, two hundred times in the Word of God. "Perfect" is one of the most commonly used words. When men look at things they like, they say, "That is a perfect thing." If a thing answers the end for which it was made, it is perfect. I describe a circle six inches in diameter, and it is perfect. I now describe another circle two feet in diameter, and it also is perfect. Though one is smaller than the other, it is just as perfect. Instruments of music differ, but a particular piano or violin may be perfect of its kind. But do you say "You can rasp away on your violin notions of perfection, but you will never find perfection in this world." But there it is in the Word of God. Suppose a man wants to weigh off a hundred pounds, he puts it on a scale that will weigh but one hundred pounds, but does that exactly. Along comes another man, desiring to weigh his articles that are two hundred pounds in weight, and, because the scales will not weigh his amount, he calls them "poor, miserable things that are good for nothing." You answer, "No, sir, they are perfect; the maker only designed them for one hundred pounds."

Now, when you pack your prejudices up, and make them weigh more than ever God intended, then you say " The scales are good for nothing." But they were not made for your weights.

Perfection in the Gospel is an absolute word. God puts it there, and you can find, " Thou shalt love the Lord thy God with all thy heart, and with all thy soul, and with all thy might, and with all thy strength." Can you answer to that? If you can, you are perfect. Show me a statute in the Bible, that sets up or requires any other standard. It is not there. " He that loveth, hath fulfilled the law."

IT IS ATTAINABLE NOW.

This perfection is attainable, for if there is a standard that is unattainable, that is an imperfect standard. I find in this world, a perfection that is an attainable grace. With this in your heart, you can grow as never before. I need not refer you to the familiar illustration of weeds pulled from the soil of a garden. " But how can you grow, when you are perfect?" I answer, you don't want to grow in some things; that's the trouble: some people want to grow on in little things that belong to children. Suppose a room is filled with heat, and your thermometer indicates one hundred and forty degrees, and there is no cold air in the room. Now go to the engineer, and ask him to turn on the heat, and go to the room again, and there is no difference in the appearance of the room, but the thermometer shows two hundred and forty degrees; put on the heat again, and you have two hundred and fifty. You say it was filled at each successive stage. God can fill us, and then add more, and more, to all eternity; and so you can grow. Prove to me that a thing cannot grow, and you prove it is an imperfect thing. We must grow here in the graces of the Spirit, and there in the glory.

Christ always comes down to the plane of our present condition, and never requires us to move out of it, in order to be saved.

> " Just as I am, and waiting not
>   To rid my soul of one dark blot."

Now, do you need the grace? Now, then, you may have it. How long would it take, if you had the rubbish of a field collected, to burn it all up? How long would it take for us to be lifted up into a state of perfection, where we can begin to grow, by the arm Omnipotent? Are you ready for this? You say, " That inbred sin has been a torment to me." The very weakest of our passions are too strong for you and me. Would you come over entirely to the Lord? Would you be made "complete in him?" It is for you now. Why not by one blessed stride, by one desperate leap of faith, " Go on unto perfection?" Reach it now! Reach it by faith through Jesus Christ!

SERMON OF MR. LONGACRE.

Isaiah, 26th ch., 3d verse.—" *Thou wilt keep him in perfect peace, whose mind is stayed on thee: because he trusteth in thee.*"

IT may not be brave, but it is a great comfort, in a time like this, to take a text which is able to preach its own sermon. My text is such a one. I do not know that I ever read it, without stopping to read it again. I think any one who would pick up the Bible to find what he could admire, would pause, struck with the beauty and harmony of the language—so clear, so simple, so transparently disclosing the Divine thought. And as we read it over slowly, think—will keep him in perfect peace, whose mind is stayed on thee. It seems to me it distils peace—it breathes an atmosphere of peace. I think a hasty, angry man would feel quieted to read it. But when we stop to think about it, looking at it again when that first delightful impression is over—keep him in perfect peace—I should not wonder if we were to doubt, and ask, "Can it be? Is there such a thing? Can man in this poor world, with all he has to do, with his public disturbances, and private troubles, and little frets, can a man be kept in perfect peace?" I do not know but some such doubting one is here. I have prayed God to help me put this in some such heart. I feel as if God had given it to me, to give to you afresh, and that it is God's present. Of course it is true, or it would not be here.

Without attempting to give any extensive characteristics of this peace, I would like you to get hold of the thought, what peace is, just enough to hold and keep it as we go on. You know peace is not having quarrels and disturbances—the absence of war and strife. It calms and composes, and the man of the world deems it good breeding to assume it, if he has it not. The Heavenly Father knows how vain is the peace of unhappy souls, though with pleasant outward circumstances but with inward wrath, distress, and clamor; and how many who think they have a perfect peace, are not quite so sure of the thing. It is a reality. The soul satisfied, and at rest. It has gotten past the discontent—is out of the clamor of dissatisfied desire. It is not wavering, like a wave of the sea driven and tossed, but like the sea when the Master says, "Peace, be still," and the great waves are hushed, and they come down and down, under God's mighty word, all the way down.

It is called "perfect," for it is all-pervading in its nature. It keeps the heart and mind and the whole man, and all that makes the man, all that's sensitive, and living, and sharp, and quick, and energetic in him; the whole man is at peace, the whole human nature comes into this Sabbath stillness. He is balanced. You remember the beautiful words of the old Moravian to Wesley: "Repose in the blood of Christ." The highest tranquillity and serenity of mind, is meant by perfect peace. It is not fitful and transient, but a life; at all times, everywhere, and under all circumstances fulfilling that prayer, "Now the Lord of peace himself give you peace always by all means. The Lord be with you all." Have you ever thought that He is making everything fit us for the reception of peace, turning hindrances, and what was to our inner destruction, into the nourishment of the peace of God? Hence we sing:

> "These surface troubles come and go,
>   Like ripples on the sea;
> The deeper depth is out of reach
>   To all, my God, but thee."

I believe the text is the key to the attainment, and the permanent possession of a perfect peace. I believe it because of what it says of itself. It is not only a beautiful device, but it also exhibits all its skeleton work. It shows us how it is built up. "Thou wilt keep him in perfect peace whose mind is stayed on thee, because he trusteth in thee." It is a mind that is stayed on God, that is kept in perfect peace. It is because man trusts in God, that he is kept perfect. I do not know that I can show better what this means, than by asking you: WHAT ARE THE THINGS THAT ORDINARILY DISTURB PEACE?

And, WHAT ARE THE THINGS THAT SUBDUE THEM?

I think we can arrange these troublesome things under these heads: *Sin, temptation, affliction,* and *anxiety.* Now ask yourself how trust in God can overcome these? Take the first:—

SIN.

The Bible says there is no peace to the wicked, and we have all experienced that. Whether our sins are many or few, there is no peace in sin, and no peace where it is. There are people here who are impressed by Satan, and who would like to die to get rid of their impressment, but dying will only push you face to face with it. O poor abashed soul, trying to shut away the hell of your own mortification, if you only understood how God loved you, and how He had provided a pardon for just such as you, and how His ample provision can take away every burden, and that you have only to come to Jesus, and let Him cancel your sin, then you might sing in faith—

"Jesus paid it all, all the debt I owe."

TEMPTATION.

A man may be delivered from his sins, without being delivered from temptation. This cannot be, until the servant be higher than his Lord. When we are past such trials, we are the better for them; but temptation is not sin. The devil only wants us to consent to come down and wrestle with him; and there is no man that can afford to accept his challenge. The text teaches us, as we counsel our children: Do not go with bad boys to keep their company; and, returning from school, they sometimes tell us of their troubles with these wicked children, and then they say to the parent, "Suppose you come with me; then your presence will keep them away:" so the Psalmist says, "I have set the Lord always before me, therefore I shall not be moved." To have Him with us who shall keep us, no matter how fierce the tempter may be, is to forearm ourselves with peace.

AFFLICTIONS

cannot be prevented, and God does not always deliver His people from them. Whether losses, or trials, or many difficulties of various kinds, these all come upon his saints. What then? I had a brother whose only son came to his death by a sad accident, and it seemed as if the accident might have been averted. That thought was a very bitter one to the father, and he was inconsolable, though many friends used their loving skill to soothe, and to reconcile him to the providence. It happened that the minister who attended at the funeral, as he arose to officiate, said: "We have come here, dear friends, not by any command of man, but by the direction of God;" then this brother said, "It's all right." I pity the man who looks at the instrument, and circumstances, and surroundings, and does not think of the hand that deals them out. And these trials, sent by Him, are good, for the Lord does not like to give to any of His children, that which is only second best. Not that you may not take this now, and afterward you shall have something better; but to-day, child, this is the very best for you.

ANXIETY.

I believe there are many christians who can get over their sins and temptations, and can bear up under trials, who cannot endure *anxiety*. It may be anxiety about little things—household affairs, daily troubles, or anxiety for things of moment, or what seem so to us. God does not exempt His children from cares; there is nothing in the Bible to show that. Cares may come through the deceitfulness of riches; and we have to meet with men who have their influence, and who propose a course we do not think wise; and we have our influence, and that entails a sort of strife; and the man of thought, decision, and energy, must inevitably run against a great many other men; and when that comes, and when we have worked for the best results, we are not sure we have done it right, or with the purest spirit; and these are sources of anxiety. I do not think there is any lot in life, but enough anxieties are associated with it to eat out peace of mind, save as we get and keep it, according to the direction of the text. Have not you read the Bible, to see how the Infinite and Almighty heart beats for you, and have you not seen how He

brings the assurance of His care right down to us? The
lilies of the field He cares for, and you are of more
value than they; and the birds of the air, and you are
better than they; and your hairs are all numbered.
His is ceaseless and perfect care—infinite, tender, loving, and reaching over every possible necessity. Has
He not a right to say, "Cast thy burden on the Lord,
and He shall sustain thee." There may be cares growing out of church responsibilities, or from the imper-
fections of christians. Mr. Wesley spoke of two christian women who lived in the same house, and as he said
to them he thought their home must be a little heaven,
they replied, with tears in their eyes, that it took all
their religion, to bear each other's burdens. Oh, instead
of bearing all the troubles and anxieties, to lay them all
on Christ, and to realize how blessed it is when He
giveth quiet, and there is sweetest peace!

Have you ever tried to pray in secret, when the mind
has flown off in fibres and tendrils? Have you ever
felt, when you have passed through temptation, a desire
to be able to keep the presence of God always before
you, and then have you brought your inability in contact with the promise? "The peace of God, which passeth all understanding, shall keep your hearts and minds
through Christ Jesus." But here it is, through Christ
Jesus, and of or by ourselves, never. What you cannot effect, let the Almighty doer accomplish. The
Apostle said: "For though ye have ten thousand instruc-
tors in Christ, yet have ye not many fathers;" and
there is a fatherhood of the soul, that is sweeter and
more tender than any other relationship in the world;
and this Infinite Father cares for His children.

I have longed that the life of peace might be the inheritance of God's dear children. Shall it be so? When I was told by a friend that I had left my mark for good on a certain gentleman, I thought, "My mark! What business have I to stamp him, and leave my mark upon him?" Souls should only have one mark, and that Christ's; and I feel like flying to Him— to sweep out everything but what He does. I beseech you, take hold of that life of Christ, which shall give you perfect, permanent peace. I have not set this text forth theologically, and I did not mean to do so. And now, finally, remember there is a life of strugglings to keep the heart right and in peace; but it is not, cannot be peace, though we may think it is. There is another life—the life of Christ in the soul—letting Him watch over and keep us, and through His indwelling, helping us to abide in Him. This is peace, perfect peace. May God grant you to enter upon it. Amen!

CHAPTER XXIX.

SERMON OF REV. L. R. DUNN, OF NEWARK CONFERENCE.— TESTIMONIES AND EXPERIENCES.

MR. DUNN'S SERMON.

"1 *John* i. 7.—*And the blood of Jesus Christ His Son cleanseth us from all sin.*"

I THINK I am safe in saying that this is the most wonderful utterance that ever was made. It is, at once, occasion of rejoicing to the white-robed in heaven, and to the purified saints on earth. It presents before us, the foundation of the hope of pardon and salvation, purity and victory, and eternal life for a lost race. It reveals to us the only way to God. The consciousness of guilt presses heavily upon the great heart of the world, and all along the ages, man has been crying out under that mighty pressure, "Oh, wretched man that I am, who shall deliver me from the body of this death?" In the midst of this universal unrest and misery, God proclaims this, His great evangel, "The blood of Jesus Christ His Son cleanseth us from all sin." Oh, how sweetly does this fall upon the ear of a dying man, for it is just what the world wants, and it is the burden of all the songs of heaven; and while we are here to-day talking about the blood, all heaven is vocal with songs of the blood.

I wish to call attention at this time to two points in the text, viz.:

1st. To the blood of Jesus Christ, the Son of God.

2d. To its cleansing power.

THE BLOOD.

Among all nations blood has ever been regarded as of peculiar and even of sacred value. The foundation of all mythology is laid in the fact, that blood was considered sacred to the gods. In the very infancy of time we hear the blood of Abel assuming a voice, and crying to God for vengeance. In the grant which God gave Noah, that he and his descendants might eat the flesh of certain animals, there was a prohibition of blood. "But flesh, with the life thereof, which is the blood thereof, shall ye not eat." This law was afterward re-enacted upon Sinai, and thus made binding upon all the Jewish people.

The question may arise, Why this prohibition? Some have answered, "Because the eating of blood makes men and nations more ferocious and sanguinary;" but it is by no means certain that this is so. The true reason, I apprehend, is that God designed that blood should forever be sacred, and that it should ever be the representative of the sacrificial offering of His Son.

As we come down the stream of time, we see blood chosen as the token which the destroying angel, in passing over the land of Egypt upon his mission of death, was to regard. You remember the account, how the Israelites were directed to slay a lamb, and sprinkle the blood upon the posts of the doors, and the angel, beholding this sprinkled blood, was to pass over and leave there the first-born unharmed. The idea was, that the blood of the lamb was substituted for the first-born of Israel, and because it was shed, they were spared.

Again: We find this great principle recognized in the law of blood for blood, and life for life. "At the hand of man, at the hand of every man's brother will I require the life of man." The reason of this is also plainly given. "Whoso sheddeth man's blood, by man shall his blood be shed: *for in the image of God made he man.*" This great law is almost as old as the world, dating back centuries before the origin of the Jewish nation, and, in my opinion, cannot be interfered with, without serious peril.

Further: Under the law, the blood of the slain victims was recognized as an atonement for sin. God says of it, "I have given it to you upon the altar to make an atonement for your souls." Remember this, if there be a Unitarian or "Liberal Christian" here, God says, that the blood maketh atonement for the soul. And for this reason blood was kept streaming upon the Jewish altars. There is a remarkable utterance of the Apostle in regard to this. He says: "Whereupon neither the first *testament* was dedicated without blood. For when Moses had spoken every precept to all the people according to the law, he took the blood of calves and of goats, with water, and scarlet wool, and hyssop, and sprinkled both the book, and all the people, saying, This *is* the blood of the testament which God hath enjoined unto you. Moreover he sprinkled with blood both the tabernacle, and all the vessels of the ministry. And almost all things are by the law purged with blood: and without shedding of blood is no remission." Thus blood for sacrifices was not peculiar to one dispensation or people; but necessary to all. All nations, nearly, have had bloody sacrifices, and often human sacrifices have been made to the gods. Human sacrifices were only abolished in Rome a short time before the coming of Christ; and on this continent, but comparatively a little time ago, in Mexico, among the Aztecs, in the great temple of the Sun, human blood flowed from sacrificial altars.

The question arises, Whence this universal idea of bloody sacrifices? I answer: It comes from a common source, as the God-ordained way of approach to God.

I advance now to the proposition that

THE BLOOD OF JESUS

was shed for the express purpose of making an offering for sin, and that it has been proclaimed by God as the only ground upon which sin can be pardoned.

The Lord Jesus understood well what He was going to do, in and by His sacrificial death; and when, at the Last Supper, He took the cup and said: "This is my blood of the new testament, which is shed for many for the remission of sins," He plainly declared that the blood He was about to shed, was to be the sacrifice for sin, and the only ground of pardon. He gives us to understand, also, that this was necessary, and not a plan of mere expediency.

Behold the Son of God for a moment in the garden of

GETHSEMANE.

And before He goes there, hear what He says to the Father: "I know that Thou hearest me always." Now

18

He goes to the garden, and, away from the disciples; He kneels down, and Oh, how He prays : " Father, if it be possible, let this cup pass from me ! " Listen ! Is there any response ? No ; the throne of God is silent. He goes back and prays again, using the same words. Is there any response now ? Does the Father say, " This is my beloved Son ? " No ! the throne of God is silent—the universe is silent. Again He returns, and again He prays. His agony is increasing, till now He is sweating great drops of blood falling down to the ground ; and Oh, how the prayer is wrung from His heart : " If it be possible, Oh, Father, let this cup pass from me ! " Is there a response now ? No ! the throne of God is silent ! And what does Jesus understand by this ? " Why, that He must tread the wine-press alone, and that of the people there should be none with Him ; " and that there is no other way by which sinners can be saved. And after He had passed through death and risen again, He opened the eyes of the disciples, and showed them that it was necessary that He should die, that repentance and remission of sins might be preached to all men. The great redemption, then, is in the shed blood of Christ. It is not by His teachings, or His doctrine, or His example, or His holy life, that men are redeemed, but by His blood, and by His blood alone. Hear what Krummacher says, that lion-hearted preacher at Berlin, whose mighty soul has lately gone up to God. After noticing some of the objections of rationalism, he proceeds in an imaginary dialogue with the objector : --

" What avails the blood of Christ ? It avails what mountains of good works, heaped up by us—what columns of the incense of prayer, curling up from our

lips toward heaven—and what streams of tears of penitence, gushing from our eye-lids—never could avail:
" The blood of Jesus Christ His Son cleanseth us from
all sin."

"Helps us to cleanse ourselves, perhaps?" No;
cleanseth us.

"Furnishes the *motive* and the obligation for us to
cleanse ourselves?" No; it *cleanseth* us.

"Cleanseth us from the *desire* to sin?" No; cleanseth
us from *sin* itself.

"Cleanseth us from the sin of *inactivity* in the work
of personal improvement?" No; from *all* sin.

"But did you say the *blood* does this?" Yes, the
blood.

"The *doctrine* of Christ you must mean?" No, his
blood.

"His *example* it is?" No, *his blood, his blood.*

That is it; that is the Gospel. This sacrificial offering was ordained by the Father, and is now proclaimed as the only ground of pardon and salvation,
"Whom God hath set forth to be a propitiation through
faith in His blood." This God ordained, and He has
recognized it also. Do you ask how? I answer: My
blessed Saviour died and went down into the grave, as
the inspired prophets had foretold. And then His enemies said, "Let us make sure that He is kept in the
grave, and thus show that He is an impostor." And so
they asked and were given a Roman guard. and they
placed the guard at the sepulchre. Very well: tramp,
tramp, tramp went the sentinels before that sepulchre,
watching a dead man, as they supposed. All the rest
of Friday, and through the night, and all day Saturday

and Saturday night, they kept their watch; but early on the morning of the first day of the week, down came two angels, and one of them touches the seal with his finger, and it is broken; and then they roll away the stone; and now I see Jesus come up, breaking the bond of death. Not hastily does He arise, but deliberately; and carefully folding up the linen clothes, He sternly takes His way out of the sepulchre. I never think of those clothes, so carefully folded, without thinking of the majesty of that resurrection. Now, in all this, God proclaimed to the universe that the sacrifice of His Son was acknowledged and accepted by Him, as the one offering for sin.

But why is the blood regarded as of such

EFFICACY AND AVAIL?

It is more than the blood of a saint or the blood of a man. The Apostle says, "It speaketh better things than the blood of Abel." This is the blood of Jesus Christ the Son of God, and that is what makes it of such avail. Human sacrifices were forbidden by God; but here is a human sacrifice ordained by God, for God was pleased to bruise Him. How are we to reconcile these things? I answer: There is a new principle here which explains this, and that is, that this life was voluntarily given up. Jesus could have prevented His death, for He says: "No man taketh it from me, but I lay it down of myself. I have power to lay it down, and I have power to take it again." And yet God required that blood, and was pleased with it, when Christ voluntarily poured it out for the sins of men. But I think I hear it asked, "What connection is there between the blood and the cleansing?" I do not know that I can philosophically answer this, and yet I may, perhaps, illustrate it; and right here is a battle we shall have to fight, for there are many and bitter enemies to the Scriptural idea of cleansing by blood. Just for a moment let me show you how they talk about the blood of Christ. A writer in *The Liberal Christian* of May 27th last, in noticing a new Baptist Hymn-book, says: " We like everything about the book but the theology, which is stuffed into the hymns in all possible ways, and which sticks out in the most offensive forms, even where we least expect it. Scores of hymns are so saturated with 'the blood of Christ,' that the sanguineous currents seem to drip from every line." And what hymn do you suppose they especially object to? Why, it is that glorious one commencing—

> " There is a fountain filled with blood,
> Drawn from Immanuel's veins."

That is a specimen of what is coming out in the nineteenth century, and we shall have to meet them; but we shall overcome them " by the blood of the Lamb and by the word of our testimony." These are our weapons, and they are trusty and sure.

These very men will get up in public meeting on the Fourth of July, and tell us that it has been the fate of all nations that have succeeded in reaching places of greatness, to be baptized in blood; and that our liberties were bought with blood; that the soil of America is consecrated by the blood of her sons; and that it cost the blood of three hundred thousand of our sons and brothers, to wipe out the great sin of slavery. Look at

the consistency of these men. If blood bought our
national liberties, why may not the blood of Christ buy
our souls' pardon ? If blood consecrated the soil of our
country, why may not the blood of Christ consecrate
us ? If blood washed away the foul blot of slavery,
why may not the blood of Jesus wash away sin from
our souls ?

But the Word of God makes this plain, and tells
us clearly that the blood has power to cleanse us from
all unrighteousness. From the Bible we learn that
there is seven-fold value in the blood of Christ. Seven,
you know, is a sacred number used in the Bible, to
express an idea of completion or perfection, and seven-
fold efficacy is attributed to this blood.

First, we have redemption in His blood; *Second*, we
are "justified" by His blood; *Third*, we are "washed
from our sins" in His blood; *Fourth*, we are "made
right" by His blood; *Fifth*, Christ "made peace" by
His blood; *Sixth*, we are "sanctified" through His
blood; *Seventh*, the Saints "overcame" by the blood.
This is the seven-fold value we find in His blood, and
no wonder the Saints rejoice and triumph by it. O,
the precious blood of Jesus! I can never tire of talking
of the blood. While the infidel and skeptic hate it, I
love it more and more.

What does this blood do ? I answer :

IT CLEANSETH FROM ALL SIN.

Sin exists in various forms. There is original sin,
and actual sin; there are presumptuous sins, and ag-
gravated sins, sins of ignorance, and secret sins. So
there are various degrees of sin, as represented by the

unrighteous, the wicked, and the ungodly. There are the outbreakingly wicked, and those who are outwardly correct, while they are inwardly unholy. How various the forms and degrees of sin. In the light of the holy law even our infirmities are sins. From sin, from all sin, the blood of Jesus cleanseth. If it had said from sin, we might have said, " it may cleanse others who have not been so bad as I:" but it does not say so; it says from *all* sin, hence we may each confidently say, " I have redemption in His blood." We repeat, this provision is for all sin, and to cleanse at once. After the believer is justified, he feels the remains of sin in his heart. Pride will rise up and struggle for independence, and the old passions stir within him. They do not reign, but they struggle; and how many tears, and headaches, and heartaches have they cost us. But there is a cure for all this; there is an unfailing panacea for all these ills. It is the blood of Jesus. There are many who try to do this work for themselves. They say, " I will not be angry any more." They are like the woman in Scotland of whom I have read, whom they called Hell-Fire. When they asked her if she was going to sign and keep the pledge, she turned fiercely upon them and said, "When I say I will, *I will!*" So they think they *will*, but soon they find themselves suddenly tripped, and they fall. But "the blood of Christ cleanseth us from all sin." It does not say it will save us from every mistake, or infirmity, or imperfection, but it does say "it *cleanseth* us from all *sin*." Glory to God! Jesus is the Lamb of God, "slain from the foundation of the world," and He is our great and perfect Saviour.

Some say, "one drop of that blood can cleanse my soul from sin." No, no! This is a mistake. There is a whole atonement for each one of us. Just like the sun; my eyes are all filled up with the light, but that does not take away any light from any other. So the blood that cleanses me, leaves none the less for my neighbor. There is a whole atonement for each. Bless the Lord! The redeemed in heaven, the multitudes who have washed their robes and made them white, had each this whole atonement, and now they sing the praises of the Lamb forever. They "have washed their robes and made them white in the blood of the Lamb, *therefore* are they before the throne."

This salvation in the blood of the Lamb is within the reach of all; it is right here for every one to-day, now. This moment you may believe in Jesus; believe that His blood can cleanse from all sin, that it does cleanse from all sin, and you are saved—saved now, cleansed in the blood. This is what we need. Many of us have it to-day. All may have it now. This Scripture, if there were no other, is enough. It is said that a missionary once crossing the desert, observed at a place where they had stopped to rest, a man, a native, apart from the rest, and dying. He went to him, and whispering in his ear, asked him how it was with him? "The blood of Jesus Christ His Son cleanseth us from all sin," he replied. How is this, thought the missionary, that this heathen man knows of this Saviour? But after he was dead they found, clenched tightly in his hand, a little scrap of paper, and on it this text. It was probably the only Scripture he ever possessed, and it had saved him. Every one may be cleansed from all sin now, in the blood of Jesus. God help us to come to it, and trust its power.

TESTIMONIES AND EXPERIENCES.

A BROTHER.—"I want to go to heaven, if for nothing else, to get time to speak, for I have not had an opportunity here. The formalists of the day are not mighty enough, nor good enough for me. I found out long ago that I could not grow into religion, and when I was converted, I found I could not grow into the rest of religion. I was not like Topsy, who was not born, but '*growed.*' Look out for these religious Topsies that are growing into sanctification, as the corn grows, they tell us. It took God's old-fashioned regeneration to save me."

A BROTHER.—"Some years ago the Lord brought me into the light of perfect love, but after a time I lost it ; I lost it by neglecting duty, and I see now that neglect of known duty, is as really sin, as outward transgression. I came to this meeting hungering for the bread of life, and longing for a clean heart, and I bless the Lord that He has met me, and cleansed me, and filled me with love; and now my soul says, ' Glory be to His name for ever.' "

A MINISTER.—" It is a very great pity that any who have had the blessing of perfect love, should be compelled to say that they have lost it, but I am nevertheless in very deep sympathy with such. Many years of coasting near the shores of the sea of perfect love, and often getting aground, brought me into sympathy with this class. There are two ways in which we can be kept in this blessing. One is, not to harbor for a mo-

ment the idea of coasting, but to turn your vessel's prow
from the shore, and stand right out boldly to sea—out
into the broad, deep sea, where there are no rocks, or, if
there are, they are so far down in the depths, that we
ride safely far above them. The other way is, whenever the least suspicion of doubt arises, to go at once
to the blood, and after it is clear to you, that you are
all the Lord's, then look around you, and ask how you
came into such danger, if you will, but never till you
have first found the Spirit fully assures you that you
are all the Lord's again."

A MINISTER.—" God sent me four thousand miles to
find this blessing. A little while ago I was preaching
in London. Something strongly impressed me that I
should go to America, and by a strange succession of
events I came to this country. I believe the Lord
sent me here, that I might see a Camp-Meeting. I
did not like Camp-Meetings, and I came here resolved
that I would not be affected by anything I might see or
hear, but I could not rest. In the great tent, while
Brother Inskip was talking, I went over my consecration again, and laid all anew upon the altar, and it
remains there. I have had no mighty demonstrations
of the Divine power, but I feel that the Lord is mine
and I am His, *all* His."

A MINISTER.—" Yesterday I told you I came to this
ground the weariest man you ever saw. Last night a
sister wrote on a card, and handed to me these words :
'Are you rested?' I feel to-day that I am rested; I
rest in the blood of Jesus. One of the happiest times
of my life was, when I lay sick and apparently near to
death, in a rebel prison, among five hundred prisoners,

and covered with vermin. O such rapturous visions of glory as arose before my soul, as I lay there in my weakness; and when the question came to my mind if I would be willing to stay, and preach Jesus to my fellow-prisoners, if God should raise me up, I said: 'O yes; I would rather stay here and preach Jesus, than go home to see my wife and children.' The trouble with me was not in consecration, but in getting rid of the shame of my past life of sin; but this morning a crimson veil seemed to come down, and hide all my life of sin from my eyes, and I now have rest in Jesus—satisfying rest."

A BROTHER.—"I feel I am one of the family, and hardly need an introduction. From a child I have known the Scriptures. Forty years ago God converted me, and in connection with my regeneration, I sought and found this baptism; and I have since received, baptism after baptism, and my soul now rejoices in Christ's salvation. I have always thought that this doctrine and experience of holiness is our greatest glory as a Church."

A MINISTER.—"I want just to tell my brethren in the ministry, how I came to be in my present relation to the great subject of holiness. I had been for about twenty years in a religion of combats; of terrible conflicts. In these battles I was generally a conqueror, but I labored under a great disadvantage, because the conflicts were mostly within.

"The first thing which led me to special thought upon this subject, was that I received a letter from a good brother, in which he most affectionately inquired after my experience in the matter of personal consecration and holiness,

"The next thing was that I received a letter from Stephen Allen of Maine, a man who, perhaps, knew me better than any other, in which occurred this passage: 'Seekest thou great things for thyself? Seek them not.' That passage rang loud in my ears, and appealed mightily to my heart.

"The next voice that came to me was this : I was then teaching, and had a student, a brilliant, promising young man, who became a raving maniac. I went to see him in the asylum, where he was in a strait-jacket. He fixed his bright, glassy eye upon me, and said, 'Great big ——,' calling me by name, 'You preach Jesus Christ ? No! You preach great big ——,' repeating my name. That was the third voice to me.

"The fourth thing was this : At the session of Conference, I went out of the Conference room where my character was under examination, as was common in those days. Soon a brother came and told me I could go in. I asked him if my character had passed, and he said it had. I asked him if they said anything against me ; he said they did not, but they thought I needed a little more religion. Did they say so, inquired I. No, said he, but they *thought* so.

"The next thing that stirred me was, that some one put it into the minds of the trustees and faculty of a college to give me the degree of Doctor of Divinity. I thought, and said to myself, This is a great thing, that I should be made a doctor of divinity. I was so young, and it was uncommon, I was told, to bestow the honor upon one so young.

"I went to bed thinking of it, when suddenly I sprang up saying, 'what a foolish doctor of divinity I am, to be pleased with this poor toy;' and I besought God to deliver me in some way from this folly. I went to Middletown with these five voices ringing in my ears.

"I came back to Watervliet to Camp-Meeting, resolved to seek and find deliverance. When upon the ground, a simple-hearted brother was preaching an unpretending sermon, but he said things that went through me. After the service, I went out upon the ground, and soon met a good sister, and she said to me, ' Brother, how long since you professed the blessing of holiness?' I had to confess that I had never experienced it, and I shall never forget her reply, 'Why,' said she, 'how can you preach a gospel of holiness and not enjoy it yourself?'

" Soon after I found myself in a kind of class-meeting in brother J. Hillman's tent, and I prayed God to break my heart, that I might have tears to weep; very soon my heart was melted, and I found the tears pouring from my eyes, and in the straw upon the tent floor, I continued to struggle for liberty. In the midst of my praying, there came this voice to my spirit ear : ' RENOUNCE THE WORLD!' I cried out to myself at once, I do renounce it. Then the thought came, ' this is sincere—surely I do renounce the world;' and then there flashed through my mind the thought 'it has been done,' and immediately there seemed to me something like the moving away from me of a great cloud, and it kept going away further and further, and I thought ' let it go, farewell to it, and adieu to the world; I have renounced it forever.' Then I rose, and I said to myself, ' Now I have got nothing left, all is gone;' and I wondered how I should get everything, and I knew it must be from Jesus. While

I was meditating thus, this Scripture came to me, 'For we have not an high priest which cannot be touched with the feeling of our infirmities.' Then I tried to think of the Greek word which is translated 'touched,' and as near as I could remember, it meant *sympathize*, and I got a new view of the sympathy of Jesus, which enabled me to 'come boldly to the throne of grace;' and when my faith took hold upon a sympathizing Jesus, my soul was as though it had been held under a current of blood, till it was washed whiter than snow. And I gladly stand here to-day, a witness to the power of Jesus' blood to cleanse from all sin."

CHAPTER XXX.

SERMON OF REV. WM. BUTLER, D.D., AND ADDRESS OF REV
WM. M°DONALD, BOTH OF NEW ENGLAND CONFERENCE.

Job xix. 25.—*" I know that my Redeemer liveth."*

THIS is, all things considered, the grandest utterance
of human faith.   In one sad day calamity had come upon this man's home, and property, and family, and even
his character was endangered; and down from the depths
of a misery such as no man besides has ever felt, he
lifts up his voice and says: " I know that my Redeemer
liveth."   It is evident that there fell on him light and
confidence from heaven, which enabled him to utter these
memorable words, and those of the context, the whole of
which are : " Oh that my words were now written ! oh
that they were printed in a book ! That they were graven
with an iron pen and lead in the rock for ever !   For I
know that my Redeemer liveth, and that he shall stand
at the latter day upon the earth : and though after my
skin worms shall destroy this body, yet in my flesh shall
I see God : Whom I shall see for myself, and mine eyes
shall behold, and not another; though my reins be consumed within me."

I shall attempt to-day, *first*, to define the word Redeemer ; *second*, to illustrate the attribute of immortal

life which is attributed to Him; and *third*, to show that all men, who like Job, have this living Redeemer as theirs, are conscious of this fact.

I. What, then, is the meaning of this term Redeemer?

We sometimes satisfy ourselves with the superficial meaning of this term by saying, our Redeemer is He who has bought us with His blood—that glorious person who, having bought us, saves us from our sins. But O, how far does this fall below the truth! Look at some of the terms adopted in the New Testament from the Old, and trace them back to their original use, and you will find new light shining upon the page; for, after all, the legal and ceremonial is oftentimes the true key to the spiritual. This is true of this term; and to know what the Redeemer was under the old dispensation, will give us an idea of what Christ is under the Gospel.

1st. Under the law, the redeemer must be a kinsman of the redeemed, as brother, or sustaining other blood relationship, and the nearest in kinsmanship was always the redeemer. The offices which this redeemer had to fill were four.

1st. He was a *vindicator*.

When a man had slain another, accidentally or otherwise, he might fly to the city of refuge, but if the vindicator overtakes him before he reaches the city, he may take his life, and he is counted blameless; but if the man-slayer reached the asylum, he was protected until inquiry was made whether he intended the crime, and if it was found he did, he was judicially delivered to the avenger; but if not, he must dwell in the city of refuge till the death of the high priest, when he might return in safety to his home.

2d. The redeemer was a *liberator*.

If a man became poor, he might sell his service till the coming of the year of jubilee, or the obligation became intolerable. In the interval, he had the right to appeal to the leader of his clan or family, and it became his duty to do all in his power to secure his emancipation.

3d. This was equally so in regard to the family inheritance, and he was under the same obligation to restore the inheritance, as to secure the freedom of his kinsman, so that the lands should not accumulate in the hands of the few, and an aristocracy arise upon labor, but so that the land should be returned in the hands of each tribe and family, as it had been divided between them.

4th. The last office of the redeemer was, that when a man died childless, his brother was to marry his wife, and raise up seed to his brother; and the first male child of the marriage, was to receive the name and take the inheritance of his deceased uncle.

Let us now apply these thoughts to Christ, and see how they illustrate the character of our blessed Redeemer.

OUR BROTHER.

1st. The Saviour of mankind is the brother of man. "Both he that sanctifieth and they who are sanctified are all of one," which means that they are all of the nature or blood of humanity; "for which cause He is not ashamed to call them brethren." He passed by the nature of angels, and took upon Him the nature of man, as Paul says: "Forasmuch then as the children are partakers of flesh and blood, He also Himself likewise took part of the same; that through death He might destroy him that had the power of death, that is, the devil. And deliver them who, through fear of death, were all their lifetime subject to bondage. For verily He took not on Him the nature of angels; but He took on Him the seed of Abraham. Wherefore in all things it behoved Him to be made like unto His brethren, that He might be a merciful and faithful High-Priest in things pertaining to God, to make reconciliation for the sins of the people." So our Redeemer was born of a woman, and could say, " I have the right to redeem man because I am his brother, the brother of his life." As Methodists, we have preached, when it was more difficult to do so than it is at the present day, that Jesus Christ, in the same extent, and with the same intention, died for every man ; that there are no exceptions or partialities in the Divine mercy; that none are unconditionally reprobated to perdition : but, from the cradle to the grave, all are within the power of the cross, and hence within reach of salvation. Our theology has taught us this, but the true ground for it is in the fact of Christ's perfect humanity; for because of this we share in His death upon the cross. Whoever you are, your blood, as it flows through your veins, is " part of the same" blood that flowed through the veins of your Redeemer, and was shed for you and for every man ; so that you cannot separate the man from God, as a redeemed human being ; for He, our God has said, that Jesus Christ has "tasted death for every man."

Here, then, is the foundation for our faith in the Redeemer. He is the brother of your life ; and shining as He does now, far above all principality and power crowned, and enthroned, and adored, He is still not ashamed to acknowledge you as His brother. He is your near kinsman, the very brother of your heart.

Your Redeemer is your relative, your near kinsman

OFFICES OF THE REDEEMER.

2d. What are the offices He sustains?

First.—He is our Vindicator. As such He says to the christian, " You must have no anxiety about your possessions, your character, or your future, while you obey God." You may act as John Wesley did when one of the public prints assailed him, as he was about to leave the city upon one of his tours of labor. His brother Charles remonstrated with him, and wished him to remain and answer the article. "No," said John ; " when I gave myself to God I did not reserve my reputation, and I will let God vindicate me now, as He has before." Job, when in the midst of afflictions, and when his friends were trying to impugn him as a hypocrite, cried out, " Though he slay me, yet will I trust in him." And my soul remember thou, that though the grave is yawning for thee, yet out of that dust thy Redeemer shall bring forth thy righteousness as the light, and thy judgment as the noonday. He may have to slay me, yet in the day when the secrets of all hearts shall be made known, God, my Redeemer, will stand by me. We may leave our cause and character entirely in the hands of God, for He has told you, as your Redeemer, " He that toucheth you, toucheth the apple of His eye." "No weapon formed against you shall prosper." "Vengeance is mine, saith the Lord, and I will repay." Ay, when death itself shall come, and when the last enemy of man shall stand by your bedside, the doctrine of the Redeemer's power shall be your comfort, for He will vindicate your body as well as your character, and bring your body up where legions of angels could not detain you; and in your identical humanity you shall see God.

Second. He is our Liberator.

We have forfeited our liberty, and by nature and practice are the slaves of sin; and there is no tyranny like that of Satan's. The iron enters into the very soul, and yet we consent to be led captive by him at his will, though for this service we are paid with the wages of sin—eternal death. There is One who goes before him, who is mightier than the strong man armed. Your cry has reached the ear of your Divine Redeemer, and your chains shall be knocked off, and the prison-doors fly open at His presence, and you go forth at His bidding. We have bartered our liberty and sold our inheritance, and are not only slaves, but paupers, having no inheritance in heaven or on earth. In the midst of this wretched state of poverty, Jesus comes and offers to us riches and life, and accepting this by the act of our faith, the Holy Spirit comes and seals us as the purchased property of Christ. Thus Paul says: "In whom also after that ye believed, ye were sealed with that Holy Spirit of promise, which is the earnest of our inheritance, until the redemption of the purchased possession unto the praise of His glory." But Jesus has a personal affection for, and intimate relation to, every holy human soul. He might have stood afar off and vindicated us, and given or sent back to us the blessings which by sin we had forfeited and lost, and held our human heart at an eternal distance from him, but He has Himself a human heart, full of purity and sympathy and love, and He wishes to ally that heart to us, and make the bond so dear and strong, that it shall never be broken, so that though earthly friends may pass away, Jesus shall ever remain. Admit Him and He makes you His bosom friend, and He becomes the brother, the friend, and the husband of your soul. Fairer than all the earth-born race, the chiefest among ten thousand, and the One altogether lovely—this is our friend—Jesus, the lover of our souls, who gave Himself for us, and to whom we are to give ourselves, in a gift never to be forgotten or revoked, to remain perpetually and entirely His, that He may wash and cleanse us in His own blood, and present us to Himself without spot or wrinkle, or any such thing; and that standing before the hosts of heaven you may feel secure, for He that sitteth upon the throne is yours—yours forever and ever. Such are some of the thoughts which the Holy Spirit gives us in the text.

IMMORTAL LIFE.

Again, our Redeemer is described as possessing immortal life. "I know that my Redeemer liveth." That was spoken more than thirty centuries ago. He was living then, and He is living now. It has been my lot to stand at the shrines of many of the heathen religions. Standing there, I might have asked the Hindoo worshipper, "Where is Menu?" and he would have said, "He is dead, and for thirty-five hundred years he has been in the grave." I have stood in the Mohammedan mosque, and asked the devout Moslem as he came to offer his prayers, "Where is Mohammed, your Prophet?" and the answer has been, "He is dead, and his body lies buried in the Mecca." In the Buddhist temples the same question meets the same answer, for Gatama Buddha is dead, and seven-and-twenty centuries have passed away since, according to their own faith: the flame of contemplation, bursting from the breast of the corpse, consumed their god. So Zoroaster is dead, and all the heathen deities are dead, and all the founders of the various religions of men are dead. But it is our glory, and the glory of our holy religion, that its Founder, our Redeemer, lives, and is the only Immortal founder of a living faith that the world has ever seen; for, though as a man He was slain, yet we can, with joy, sing of him—

> "He lives! He lives! who once was dead;
> He lives! my everlasting Head!"

These heathen religions are religions of death; ours is a religion of life. These religions of death have dead founders, but our religion of life has a living Redeemer, and He has a living Church. He loved us and gave Himself for us; and though He died a shameful death upon the Cross, thereby manifesting His love for us while He redeemed us, yet, He has risen from the dead and ascended on high, and to-day we may say with all confidence, "I know that my Redeemer liveth!"

TIGRANES.

Herodotus tells us that when the victorious Cyrus was pushing his conquests toward India, the various princes of the country resisted him, and that among them was one, Tigranes by name, who gave him more trouble than all the others together. But at last Ti granes was overcome; and in the evening of the day of the battle, Cyrus, seated upon a throne in a large pavilion, received the captives, and looked upon the trophies of his victory as they passed before him; at last came the royal family of Tigranes, consisting of himself and wife, and his father and mother. There they stood, and the royal conqueror upon the throne looked at them, and asked Tigranes with what he would redeem his father and mother. He offered for them all his remaining treasure, and they were ordered to stand aside. Then there came another question: "Tigranes, with what will you redeem your wife?" A look of horror is said to have passed over that manly face, as he thought that all was gone, and nothing had been reserved, nothing with which to redeem the wife of his love. He knew that according to Oriental usage she was doomed, and so absorbed was he in the misery of the moment, that the question was thrice repeated before he was aroused. At last, lifting his head, he said, "O Cyrus, I will redeem her; I will die for her, if you will restore her liberty!" Such an answer could have but one effect upon a noble mind, and Cyrus ordered their immediate and unconditional release. In the evening of that day, as they were conversing together on its eventful scenes, Tigranes turned to his wife, and asked her if she was not struck with the noble appearance of Cyrus. A second time was the question asked, before she seemed to notice it, and then she answered, "No; I was not looking at Cyrus."—"To whom, then," said the surprised Tigranes, "may I ask, were you looking?" That question filled her heart, and, with hands pressed upon her bosom, and eyes streaming with tears, she answered, " I was looking at the man who offered to redeem me with his life." What to her heart was the splendor of Cyrus, and the magnificence of the circumstances in the midst of which she stood? Her husband's love, stronger than death, she saw, as vastly more glorious than all the pomp and array of armies or thrones.

Now, my friends, you and I expect, by and by, to go up to yonder world of immortal bliss, and whatever heaven may be, there will be one object upon which you and I will look with greater interest than upon all others combined, and that will be our blessed Redeemer. And there, as you stand before Him, you may say to the seraph that stands by your side, " There is the Man who redeemed me ; not a man who in a moment of magnanimity was *willing* to redeem me, but One who, when I was in sin and misery, came down and took upon himself my nature, and for three-and-thirty years wore my flesh and tasted my grief; and who, despising the shame, endured the cross, and bled upon it for me. That face, now radiant with glory, was once suffused with tears and blood ; that brow, now encircled with the kingly crown, was once pierced with thorns. That is my Redeemer ; the Man who died for me!" You can then understand John Fletcher's remark, when his wife asked him if he supposed they should know and love each other in heaven? "Oh, Polly," said he, "when I get to heaven, I do not know as I shall see you for ever so long, for I shall be so taken up with gazing on my Redeemer."

Suppose that Cyrus had said to Tigranes, " Yes, I accept your offer," and the order had gone forth to prepare the block and the axe, and lead the loving husband forth to execution. And suppose now, that this husband had remained true and firm to his purpose. He takes the fond last look at his wife, he lays his head upon the block, and the axe falls, and the mutilated body is borne away and buried. If you had been there, in the morning you would have seen that wife, whose life had been redeemed by the life she loved, bending in tears and grief over that new-made grave, while no truth like that of the text, " I know that my Redeemer liveth," would have cheered her heart. No, no ; but with tears she must have said, " My redeemer is dead." But thank God our Redeemer liveth ; this world does not contain the grave of Jesus Christ. Search the world, and you find it not.

When Christ had been taken down from the cross, and his body embalmed and laid away in the sepulchre, after a sleepless night, Mary, her eyes wet with tears, came in the early morning to the sepulchre, and finding not the body, she said to one whom she supposed to be the gardener, " Oh, sir, if thou have borne him hence, tell me where thou hast laid him." She was weeping a dead Redeemer, but when that sweet voice told her she had a living Redeemer, and bade her "go tell my brethren," with what joy did she depart, and became the first preacher of a risen Redeemer.

John, who was privileged when Jesus was on earth to lay his head upon His bosom, in after years, when his hairs had become gray with age, saw the living Christ upon Patmos, and when he saw Him he fell at His feet as dead! So glorious was the sight, that he could not see Him as he was, without fainting. But he tells us that

"He laid His right hand upon me, saying, 'Fear not, I am the first and the last; I am He that liveth and was dead; and behold, I am alive for ever more, Amen; and have the keys of hell and of death.'" He liveth, and because He lives we shall live also.

WE KNOW OUR REDEEMER LIVETH.

Lastly.—Every one who has this living Redeemer knows it, and every believer can lay his hand on his heart, and amid all his sorrows and tears, say with Job, "I *know* that my Redeemer liveth." This is the crowning glory of our Christianity. God has not left us to reason out our salvation, or our knowledge of it, but has provided for every redeemed and saved man a witness, even His own Spirit, which attests our salvation; so that we teach that we may know of the remission of our sins, and the sanctification of our soul.

To show forth this truth was one of the great designs of God in raising up the Methodist church. I shall never forget my surprise when, more than thirty years ago, I first heard that there was a people who believed and taught, that men may know that their sins were forgiven, and that it was the duty of all to be consciously saved. I fear there is still too much doubt upon this subject. This is the testimony we all ought to bear, and much more depends upon it, I apprehend, than we are accustomed to think. Brethren, let us bear this testimony! It is higher and better than any and all doctrine can be without it.

HOW DO WE KNOW?

But how do we know that our Redeemer liveth? We

have already indicated the answer to this question, and the Apostle Paul clearly answers it in the second chapter of 1st Corinthians, where he says: "But as it is written, Eye hath not seen, nor ear heard, neither have entered into the heart of man, the things which God hath prepared for them that love him. But God hath revealed them unto us by his Spirit; for the Spirit searcheth all things, yea, the deep things of God. For what man knoweth the things of a man, save the spirit of man which is in him? Even so the things of God knoweth no man, but the Spirit of God. Now we have received, not the spirit of the world, but the Spirit which is of God."

That is, God has suspended this upon the exercise of our personal faith; and when we come and apply to Him for pardon and purity, and the act of mercy passes the Divine mind, there is only one Spirit in the universe that knows of it, and that is the Spirit of God. Then the Holy Spirit is sent as God's authorized and competent agent to attest it to our soul, and thus we know it, not by an audible voice from heaven, nor is it written upon the sky, but by the testimony of the Holy Ghost to our hearts. He delights to take the things of God and show them unto us, and to bring into our souls the love, and joy, and peace and light; and all that can benefit us, is thus freely given of God.

And then if He is pleased to take us from this world by death, we know that we shall be received to the joys of heaven, shall go where our loving Jesus, our living Redeemer is, and shall look upon Him as He is. Oh, let us be jealous of this truth that brings to us the knowledge of a living Redeemer, and bless God for

a religion which we may know by the testimony of the
Divine Spirit. I believe this is one of the truths that is
to be a mighty agency in converting the world. When
we have argued with the Brahmish priests upon the
banks of the Ganges, one thing has never failed to
silence their cavillings. These men will argue with you
by the hour, and urge their metaphysical questions and
learned sophisms, but when the moment of candor has
come, and we have told them of our living Redeemer,
and what He has done for our own soul, and testified
that we know Jesus to be a present Saviour, and then
have asked, " Brahm, what has the Shasta to offer you,
and what has Brahma done for you ? " he has stood
there without an answer. The sense of sin is universal,
but the sense of salvation is a peculiarity of evangelical
Christianity in the pardon of sin, and the purity of
heart which our Redeemer confers. In God's name,
then, let us be zealous for our Redeemer. Let us press
forward the conquests of the Cross, till Jesus shall be
proclaimed King of kings, and Lord of lords.

ADDRESS OF REV. W. McDONALD.*

The people generally believe in holiness. They believe it a possible attainment—believe they ought to
seek it here, and at once ; and they are here for that
purpose. The doctrinal questions they have settled, and
the only remaining question of interest to them is, *How*
shall I seek it ? Show me the way to the Cross. Point

* On Friday Evening, July 9, in the large tent.

out the steps which bring me to this fountain of cleansing.

FAITH THE CONDITION.

Faith is the condition of entire holiness, as it is of
regeneration. But, how shall I believe? We shall find
that the difficulty is not so much in believing, as in a
preparation for believing, or the removal of hindrances
to faith.

We should carefully examine the motives which
prompt us to seek this grace. We may be greatly hindered here. If, as ministers, we seek this blessing that
we may be able to preach more acceptably, or be more
popular, or have the reputation of being more eloquent;
if these be the motives, we shall miss our way. It is
not found on this line, for this is selfishness. Brother
Cookman, in his sermon, spoke of human and divine
unction. The difference between the two, I conceive to
be this: human unction attracts men to us, while divine
unction drives them to Jesus. With one, it is the minister; with the other, it is Jesus. It is said that those
who listened to Cicero's orations retired complimenting
the orator—his musical voice, his faultless gestures, his
chaste and eloquent language. It was all Cicero. But
those who heard Demosthenes, went forth exclaiming,
"Let us fight Philip." When I hear a congregation, on
leaving the church, eulogizing only the minister, I suspect there has been a display of human unction; but
when a congregation leaves the holy temple, stirred by
the burning words of the minister, exclaiming, "Let us
conquer the world for Jesus," I suspect that a divine
unction has fallen upon the man of God.

We are unwilling to be *nothing* for Christ, and
Wesley's idea of being "little and unknown" cannot
be accepted or submitted to. Then those other words
trouble us: "To be, or not to be, to do, or not to do, I
leave to thee." We are very willing "to be," but unwilling, "not to be." We consent "to do," but dissent
"not to do." This, however, is the point to be gained.
The idea is, that honor, position, influence, reputation,
and apparent usefulness, we hand over to God, and
allow Him to dispose of it for His glory.

If our chief object in seeking this grace is to be
happy, we make a mistake. Holiness, not happiness, is
the object to be sought.

BELIEVE WITHOUT STRUGGLING.

We must remember that faith is not exercised by
struggling, or by trying to believe. We never try to
believe. Whatever we believe, is done without a struggle, without trying. We say we have renounced all—
have made a full consecration—have even given ourselves to Christ, and we are *trying to believe.* Trying
to believe what? Trying to believe that God will do as
He says He will? Are we trying to believe that God
does not lie? He says, "I will receive you;" and are
we trying to believe it? Do we treat the promise of a
friend thus? Should my friend promise me a thousand
dollars to-morrow, and assure me that at a given time,
if I will call at his place of business, I shall receive it;
what would be thought, if, near the time, I should get
into an agony over it; and when asked the cause of my
agony, I should say, I am trying to believe that the
promise will be fulfilled, and that my friend will supply

my needs? The whole proceeding would be a reflection on my friend's veracity. Think you that God regards such a course with more favor?

If we would receive Christ, it must be as a crucified Christ. It is not as a *king*, a *ruler*, but as the Man of the garden and the cross, that He is to be received. This road leads through the garden, and by the way of the cross. We are very willing to be *exalted* with Christ; but *crucifixion* hurts us. It is, nevertheless, true, this way of death is the only way to full salvation. Are we ready to die with Christ; to be killed, so that *we* shall live no more? If so, so far, all is well.

BELIEVE WITHOUT REGARD TO EMOTION.

We must receive this grace on God's blessed word of promise, without regard to our emotions. My emotions may deceive me; my faith in God's promise, never.

> "Faith, mighty faith, the promise sees,
> And looks to that alone."

It swings off, and says, "If God does not save me, all is gone." We must

RECEIVE THIS GRACE NOW.

It must be now, if ever. Our faith is that He "doeth it." He is doing it while I believe. Do you thus feel? Now, have you given all to Christ? You say you have. Very well. Having done so, do you believe God? Can you say now that you believe Him? Mark! He says, "I will receive you." Do you believe that? Do you believe it now? What, just as you are? That is what Jesus requires. But you say,

"I DO NTO FEEL IT."

That may be; but do you *believe?* I did not ask you how you *felt*, but whether or not you believed. It is *faith*, not *feeling*, we are after now. If feeling is the evidence you seek, how can it come before the blessing, of which it is the evidence? Many would like the evidence first, the blessing next, and then the faith, which is the condition of all. God's order is, first *believe*, then *receive*, and then comes the witness. Faith only has to do with the promise. Will you trust Him then? Will you trust Him now?

CHAPTER XXXI.

SERMON BY REV. M. SIMPSON, D.D., BISHOP OF THE METHO-
DIST EPISCOPAL CHURCH.

Romans, 12th chap., 1st v.—"*I beseech you therefore, brethren, by
the mercies of God, that ye present your bodies a living sacrifice,
holy, acceptable unto God, which is your reasonable service.*"

IN this grand epistle, written to the church in the
then capital of the world, the Apostle has discussed some
of the grandest questions of which the human intellect
can take cognizance—the gift of God and His dwelling
with men. He shows that God, from time to time, has
raised up men of certain families or nations, for the
purpose of carrying out His great work among men, and
as these failed to perform their duty in the great work,
He became displeased and called others to take their
places. Taking a survey of the nations of the earth,
and of God's purpose to save humanity, and remembering that all these callings and gifts are but a part and
parcel of one grand system, he cries, "O, the depth of
the riches, both of the wisdom and knowledge of God!"
Showing that all these plans are God's alone, and that
there is no counsellor with Him, and none to give Him
aid, he says, preceding our text, "For of Him and
through Him and to Him, are all things; to whom be
glory forever;" and then turning from the survey of
the purposes of God, and His plans for the government

19*

of men, all pointing to their salvation, he makes this personal and practical appeal: "I beseech you therefore, brethren, by the mercies of God, that ye present your bodies a living sacrifice, holy, acceptable unto God, which is your reasonable service." That is, in view of all God has done for you, by His abounding goodness and His readiness to save you, by all He gives you, socially, civilly, personally; I beseech you therefore, that ye present your bodies a living sacrifice.

MAN NATURALLY A WORSHIPPER.

In discussing these words, let me ask your attention, as a preliminary thought, to the fact that we are all naturally inclined to some worship,—and the word service in this passage, means that form of service known as worship. We may not all worship alike, but the human mind in all ages has sought some object to venerate, and whether men have found it in the sun, or moon, or stars, the winds, or the waves, in animals, or in idols graven with art and man's device, still it has been with the conviction that the human mind must adore something.

I think this arises from two convictions of the mind. First, a consciousness of our own weakness, and that we need help; and second, the feeling that there is an invisible world around us and near us, in which we have some certain interest, and to which we sustain certain relations.

Revelation gives us the knowledge of the only true object of worship, and tells us how we should worship God, and how we may gain His favor. Among all the religions of humanity, Christianity stands before the world as pre-eminently a reasonable service, while all others are unreasonable.

DIVISIONS.

I pass to notice, First, THE DUTY ENJOINED IN THE TEXT, what it is we are to do in our worship; then to SHOW HOW THIS IS A REASONABLE SERVICE, and afterward to NOTICE THE EXHORTATION OF THE APOSTLE.

NO IMPOSSIBILITY REQUIRED.

We remark first, that this worship or service required, is the "presentation of our bodies a living sacrifice to God."

The first thing to be noticed in this worship is that God does not require of us anything which we cannot perform. However our minds may be wandering this morning, we have this only gospel to preach, that " The word is nigh thee, even in thy mouth and in thy heart," and God does not require anything of any one that there is not power to perform. Anciently God required men to offer sacrifices, but the sacrifice was always within the possibilities of the offerer. They were to go to the flock and take a lamb and offer it to God, and though there was no necessary connection between the lamb and the blessing, yet if they offered it they were always blessed, if it was offered aright. But if they had no lamb they might buy one, or, if too poor to offer a lamb, then they might bring a dove, or, if too poor to bring a dove, then they might bring a handful of fine flour and a little oil. So God brought the sacrifice within the reach of all, even the poorest and weakest. The offering must cost the offerer something, and yet the poorest might bring one that should be acceptable.

The sacrifice now required consists of but two things— our bodies and our souls, and these God has given us in this world joined together, and we cannot be where we have not the sacrifice with us, and where we may not offer it. The offering is always within our possibilities.

WE MUST OWN THE OFFERING.

Again, we must own, in the sense of possessing, this offering which we are required to bring. So it was with the offerer anciently ; if the lamb or the dove was not his own, he must make it so by purchase before he could offer it, and no man can ever possess the right to offer what is not his own. The Jew owned the lamb or the dove, or the flour which he brought to offer, but the moment he offered it, it became the Lord's. So with us. When the offering is made, it passes over from us to God, and we have no more claim upon it as ours. It has become separated from us and consecrated to God, and this is the very essence of sacrifice, that we take what was ours and give it to God. In this sense the Christian is called upon to make a sacrifice of that which he truly possesses, and which is in an important sense his own, his body. This he is to bring and give to the Lord.

The term body is employed here not because it is the whole of man, nor the chief part, but because it is that which alone we can visibly offer to God, and being this, it embraces the whole of man in the meaning of the Apostle.

THE CHRISTIAN NOT HIS OWN.

After thus offering himself to God, I have said the christian is God's and no longer his own, just as the Jew's sacrifice, when it touched the altar was no longer his, but the Lord's. In what sense, let us inquire, is the christian thus the Lord's and not his own? I answer: He gives himself to God, and yet he lives, and living as God's servant, he is His, in that all His powers and faculties are to be devoted to the work which God gives him to do. No new duty may be enjoined, but he *feels* now that he is all the Lord's, and His for any and all duty.

And if we present ourselves thus to God, being then His in the sense that we have voluntarily made the offering, we may never take ourselves away again. How strange would have been the conduct of the Jew, if, after bringing his gift, he had taken it, or sought to take it from the altar; and how would that act have been regarded as the grossest sacrilege! So the christian, when he makes the consecration of his powers and himself, is to feel from that moment that he belongs irrevocably to the Lord, and that henceforth his will, and purposes, and actions, and *all* are to be the Lord's, and that at home and abroad, and everywhere, all he can do and all he can be, and all he is, and all he hopes for, are to be for ever in harmony with the Divine will. If it was sin and sacrilege for the Jew to take his slaughtered sacrifice from the altar, how much more for the Christian to take back his living offering! Such is the sacrifice we are all required to make, and you and I are able to do this here and now. Where we sit in this congregation this morning, we may now say, "All I have and all I am—head, eyes, tongue, hands, feet, all, everything—I here and now give to God, to be His forever." And if you make that sacrifice you have performed the service which God requires of you.

A LIVING SACRIFICE.

Let us now notice some of the peculiarities of the christian's sacrifice.

1st. It is a *living* sacrifice. In the order of the words of the text we have this : that your sacrifice may be living, holy, acceptable, reasonable.

It *must be* then a living sacrifice; not a dead offering, to be consumed by the fire, and taken out of the way and perish. But God breathes upon it His own heavenly life, and these bodies not only retain all the life that is in them now, but we receive also the life of God in the soul. In this consecration to God there is nothing which God has given that is taken away from us. We live on, the same beings that God made us. God takes away our sin and guilt and makes us His own, and cleanses us in Jesus' blood ; but He cleanses and saves us, not some one else, but us personally, OUR soul, and spirit, and we go on with the same heart and impulses as before, the same beings as before, and though changed, there is nothing but wickedness removed, and this being taken away, we are now separated to God, yet retain fully our individuality. We have the same language and impulses as yesterday ; yet having given them to God, they now go out to Him and He comes to us, and dwells with us.

CONTROLLING INFLUENCE.

And now let me touch upon a subject which has to me a great and fearful significance, but which I cannot fully comprehend. That is, while God gives us bodies subject to these souls of ours, and subject to no other souls primarily or chiefly, yet we are so constituted that there always seems to be room for some other power to get into these bodies, and dwell there along with these souls, and help or take part in the control of ourselves. I can imagine a being so made that no other soul could influence him, so that no other power but himself could act upon him; but that is not humanity. In childhood we are under parental authority and direction, and the thoughts of father and mother, and those around us do somehow come into our hearts, and help to direct and control us.

And just here comes in the danger of the submission of our hearts to wrong influences, for there is in us a susceptibility to such influences. And just beside these spirits of ours, is what is called the spirit of the age, or of public opinion, or the spirit of the world, and these are not good to control us. Hence the Apostle says: " Be not conformed to this world; but be ye transformed by the renewing of your mind, that ye may prove what is that good, and acceptable, and perfect will of God." As much as to say, " Now, as ye are, ye are governed by the worldly spirit; the spirit of the times is with you, as the controlling spirit; but this should not be so, wherefore be not conformed to this spirit, cast it out and let God's Spirit come in, and then you shall prove what is the power of God dwelling in the heart; you shall have then, the will that comes from God, and not from the world; you shall *prove* what is that good, and acceptable, and perfect will of God.

The thought is to me a fearful one, that just beside my heart in this body, there may come to sit down some foreign spirit. It may be a spirit from the society around me; it may be a good spirit from the bright world of light; or it may be an evil spirit from yon dark pit, and then ill-will rankles in my bosom, anger gets possession of my soul; lust and passion clamor in me, and how far that evil spirit may get the mastery over me, I do not know. At first the evil spirit may seem to us like an angel of light; but soon it casts off that shape and becomes a spirit of darkness, and when I thus see it, I may first loathe; but how often, alas, do men scorn, pity, and then embrace, and their souls so come under the dominion of this power, that they are driven down till the pit of darkness engulfs them. So on the other hand, if I have given myself to God; if I do present myself to Him fully, so that He comes and abides with me and dwells in me, I do not know to what extent He may fill my glad heart, until my soul, made strong by His soul, shall rise in her chariot of fire, till the moon seems under my feet, and the song of rejoicing is in my heart and on my lips; until Christ dwells in me in all the fulness of the Godhead bodily, and I go on rising, *rising*, RISING until I shall hardly know the change when I pass through the gates into the New Jerusalem, and it will be only a little transformation I shall experience, when I go to the bosom of Jesus. And Oh, this moment, had we the power to look within, what is the spirit which we should behold

beside your soul and mine? What are the spirits that
are controlling us? What are the influences going out
from us? I have no doubt that beside many of you, I
should see a pure spirit from between the cherubim;
but with others, I fear there would be seen a spirit of
darkness blinding you, manacling you, charming you,
leading you to darkness, and preparing you for an eternal abode with the damned in hell. ("Lord save!")

CONSECRATION WILL NOT CHANGE OUR PECULIARITIES.

Now we go on in our life, if we are Christians, a constant living sacrifice, living as we did before. I wish
to call particular attention to this point, for it is right
here so many hesitate. When you give yourself to
God, making a *perfect* presentation of yourself to
Him, you are not to be like anybody else, but only like
yourself, as before. God does not change the color of
your eyes or hair, or the tone of your voice, nor the
form of your features, nor the talents of your intellect,
nor your æsthetical culture, nor your peculiar sensibilities, when He saves you. He made you just as you are,
because He needed a being just like you, for His great
work of the salvation of the universe; and not one of
you all could be struck out of being, without showing a
flaw in God's work. He made you just as you are, with
all your peculiarities, that He might show the universe
how He could save a man just like you. He gave you
that very peculiarity that it seems so difficult to save,
for the purpose of magnifying His grace, in showing
how grace can save just such a being as you are, with
all your peculiarities, and difficulties, and temptations.
These peculiarities He does not change. You are to re-

main just as before. But you say, " I ought to lose
something which I have, for I am passionate ; I have
quick impulses that sometimes bear me away, and these
must surely be removed." No, not so at all, my brother!
God has made you quick, to take fire as the tinder under
the spark, and He is not going now to change you into
a phlegmatic being, with no more sensibility than a
snail, but your peculiarities and your impulses, quick
as the electric spark though they be, are to be sanctified,
that you may employ all these in God's work.

THE CHARIOT OF IMPULSE.

I have sometimes used a simple illustration of this
point, and have often applied it with great comfort to
my own heart. I have fancied myself sitting in a carriage drawn by wild, furious horses, myself holding the
reins. The steeds are young and full of mettle, and
taking the bits in their teeth, prancing and neighing,
they bear me on, and I have not power to control them ;
but just as I am in my extremity, and am about to be
run away with, I feel a sensation as though a strong man
had come into the chariot behind me, and encircling me
in his arms, had stretched out his strong hands and taken
the lines, and was controlling my impetuous steeds.
He does not take the fire out of them, but he guides
them and makes them go, and I am safe, though flying
like the wind, while this mighty charioteer is with me.
Let me have, then, all the powers God has put in me; let
me have all the fire He has given me, but let all these be
controlled and directed of God, and I am safe—I shall go
on, though sanctified, living and breathing, but doing
this and using all my powers for God, and for Him alone.

THE MOSAIC OF HUMANITY.

When I have looked at humanity, I have sometimes thought of it as a great picture. These thousands of faces here to-day, all upturned while you listen to the Word, constitute a grand picture, but I think, as I look upon it, what shall be God's great picture of humanity in the last great day, when angels and seraphim and cherubim shall gather around, and perhaps beings from some distant part of the universe look on, as God shall hold it up before their astonished sight, and show how He has arranged, and polished, and perfected it, taking some from Europe and some from America, and some from Asia and some from Africa, some from the rich and some from the poor, some from the learned and some from the ignorant, some from the valleys and some from the mountain-tops, and wrought them all into His great picture of humanity, to show forth His glory.

In some of the great halls of Europe, may be seen pictures not painted with the brush, but mosaics, which are made up of small pieces of stone, and glass, and other material. The artist takes these little pieces of material, some of which are individually so small, as to be almost invisible to the naked eye, and polishing and arranging them, he forms them into the grand and beautiful picture. Each individual part of the picture, may be a little worthless piece of glass or marble, or shell, but with each in its place, the whole constitutes the masterpiece of art. So I think it will be with humanity in the hands of the Great Artist. God is picking up these little worthless pieces of stone and brass, that might be trodden under foot unnoticed, and is making of them His great masterpiece, and if you and I are in His hands, we shall each have our place in that great mosaic, and shall shine there forever to the glory of God; and insignificant as we may be, not one of us could be taken out of the picture without marring it. Then, though you and I may be the smallest of all, if God will so save us, as to make us a part of his great picture, it shall be enough. It seems to me that if the little pieces of stone, metal, and glass were endowed with consciousness, each would bring itself, and lay itself on the artist's table, and say, " Here am I, use me any- where, but let me form some part of the picture." So should we bring ourselves to God the great artist, each willing and anxious to occupy his own place, and none other. And thus coming, God will use us each in our own sphere, and according to our individual peculiarities. I do not know what your place or work may be. You may be a singer; if so, then sing for Jesus; or you may have an eloquent tongue; then use that for God. God has put you, it may be, in a family; then be a true father, a faithful mother, a kind brother or sister, an obedient child. Do not be anxious about the place you are put into. Do well the duties of the hour and of your place, and then you will be happy and useful.

But the great trouble is, we want to be somewhere else than where we are, or somebody else than God has made us, and that mars the picture. Oh, make this resolution here this hour, that henceforth you will be where and what God wants you to be; that you will be a good father, or mother, or child, or citizen; a good and faith- ful physician, or attorney, or poet, or laborer; that just where God has put you, you will do the very best for

Him and for yourself that you can. Thus will you be always the Lord's, and always about the Lord's work, and answering God's order, and you cannot fail to be happy.

THE ALTAR RENDERS THE SACRIFICE HOLY.

In the next place, I remark, this sacrifice is to be holy. Here many trouble themselves because they know their bodies and souls are not holy, and they try to make themselves so, before they come to God. What was it that made the Jews' sacrifice holy? It was this, that *it was put upon the altar.* Yonder were a thousand lambs skipping and gambolling in their innocence, but no one of them was holier than another, but when one of these was taken and consecrated to God, and touched the altar, it became a holy sacrifice, and in the very act of consecration, God considered and reckoned it holy and acceptable. So now, we come with our offering and put it upon the altar, our offering of body and soul, to be a living sacrifice, and the offering of it makes it holy, for the altar sanctifieth the gift. If you wait, before you present yourself to God, till you are holy, you will never come to him.

> "If you tarry till you're better,
> You will never come at all."

And then, it is not that better somebody that God wants, but it is you just as you are, and with all your infirmities, and your errors, and your peculiarities—you are the very person God calls for, and He asks you to make the sacrifice of yourself to Him, and to make it now. And when you do this, the offering becomes holy.

And oh, if He can take so poor an offering and use it in His great work, so much the more does it honor Him ; if he can take a poor old pen, which is almost worthless, and write a beautiful hand with it, how much more is this to His glory.   Your duty is to come to Him just as you are.   Do not wait to make yourself right, but come to God and let Him make you right.   I thank God that He has a place for one like me, and that as I come this very moment, I know that He looks upon me through the Son of His love, and calls me a holy sacrifice.

Oh, then, is it not possible to make a great many holy sacrifices to God without further delay ?   Bring yourselves just as you are, unholy though you be, and He will accept and make you holy.   Come, man of business and man of pleasure ; and come all ye sons of men, and God will breathe upon the offering which you bring, and make it live in holiness.   Oh, blessed be God, if you are even like the dry bones of Ezekiel's vision, at the bidding of the Almighty, bone shall come to bone, and the breath of the Lord shall raise you up a living and mighty army, to the praise of His grace.   This, too, is

AN ACCEPTABLE SACRIFICE.

I wonder when I think that God the Infinite should accept the poor offering which we have to bring, and yet this is so.   He could get along very well without us, and yet whenever any come to Him, the sacrifice is acceptable and well pleasing in His sight.   God looks down upon our poor tribute and says, " It is all he could do," or, " she hath done what she could," and He receives us.

How such sacrifices are pleasing to Him, I shall not fully attempt to answer, nor how He makes manifest the fact of their acceptance. I shall only say, God has, and always has had, some way to make it manifest. Abel and Enoch, and all the old worthies, always knew that their sacrifices were accepted.

What a moment of suspense is it, when the offerings of the Israelites are to be made. There is the priest and the victim. The sins of the people have been confessed, the victim is slain and the blood sprinkled; and now, while the smoke fills the temple, the priest goes into the Holy of Holies, and is lost to the sight of the people. Does God accept the sacrifice ? The people, with bowed heads and throbbing hearts, are waiting in silence without. It is a moment of most intense anxiety; but see, the priest raises the curtain and comes out with his face all radiant with Divine Glory ! God has accepted the sacrifice, and the nation is free; and O ! what a glad shout goes up from the lips of the waiting thousands.

Look at the worshippers of Baal ! they cry to their God, but no answer comes. But now Elijah builds the old altar, and preaches the old theology. He brings his sacrifice and lays it upon the altar, and bids them build a trench about it, and pour water over it, till it fills all the trench. He waits till after three o'clock in the afternoon, when the sun had passed his meridian heat, and then he looks up and prays calmly, that God may accept his sacrifice and honor His own name, and his faith seems to fasten itself to the throne; down comes the fire of God and consumes the sacrifice, and burnt up the wood, and the stones, and the dust, and licked up the water that was in the trench, and the people cried out, " The Lord He is God ! the Lord He is God ! "

In these latter days there is no outward fire to consume,

but there is a way by which God makes it manifest that the sacrifice is acceptable.

Jesus says : " I will manifest myself to him, I will come in to him." How this is we may not fully know ; but when the sacrifice is acceptable to God, there comes somehow into the soul, the sweet consciousness that we are the Lord's. There is no audible voice. There may be no sudden shock as of electricity ; the man may be as calm and quiet as a summer evening hour, but he can lift up his eyes and call God his Father. The light has entered in, and he knows his sacrifice is accepted. I do not care how it is God does this ; that does not concern me. If I put myself upon the altar, I am content to leave the sacrifice there, till God shall accept and take it. And this is

A REASONABLE SACRIFICE.

Men sometimes say, when we urge them to entire devotion, that there is something unreasonable about it. But, are we not in this, simply giving back to God what belongs to Him already ? He has made us, and has He not a right to us ?

If I should build a machine, and it could speak, ought it not confess me as its maker ? I might not have made the spring, or the weight, or the power which moves it, and yet, having made the machine, if it could be conscious, it ought to recognize my right to it. Now, here is a machine which God has made—one that can talk and think, and feel ; nay, that is more than a machine, for it can act. And ought not this to recognize God as its author, as its proprietor ? Is it not reasonable that it should speak the praises of its Maker ? O yes ! Let me bear the mark of my Father, and give myself entirely to Him, that I may show forth His praise. If I might, I should rejoice to tell the angels that God is my Father, and publish to man and seraphs that I am His child. And I thank God we may call Him Father. That the little child, with the gray grand-sire, may say, "Our Father, who art in Heaven." The tallest seraph, as he burns before the throne, can do no more; the patriarchs and the sainted in glory can do no more; and I thank God, that my little child has the same blessed privilege.

And now, God having given me these powers which I possess, is there anything unreasonable in my using them, and using them *all* for God? Can you imagine greater treachery, than for a man who has been intrusted with the command of the armies of his country, to deliver them to the enemy? God has given us certain powers, differing with different men, and yet to all some, and is it not unreasonable, nay, treasonable, to give these powers, or any of them, to Satan? Look at that young person to whom God has given a beautiful voice, using it only for wicked and profane songs. O, how wrong this is. These powers are given us for our good, and God would control, regulate them for our good. If He gets into the chariot with us, it is not to drive us over a precipice into ruin; if He comes into the boat, it is not to drive it out to sea in the storm, or upon the breakers to engulf it. All God does for us is to help us, and all He does with us, is best for us. And yet there is a feeling sometimes, that if we receive God into our hearts and give ourselves to Him, we lose something valuable. Yes, you do lose something! You lose the companionship of wicked men and devils.

20

You lose the corruption of sin. You lose the prostitution of your noblest powers, but you gain the holiness of God.

We are put here, in this world, to work for God, and for this work we need preparation. Take an iron tool that has become rusty, and it is unfit for use. You must remove the rust, and it will be ready to use. So God would take us and burn up the dross of sin, and cleanse us by the blood of Jesus, and then we are ready to work for Him. God polishes us till we become like mirrors, and men look upon us, and see Jesus reflected in us; and as the moon must shine when the sun shines upon it, so when God shines upon us we must shine upon men, for the light of God will shine in our very faces.

I firmly believe that there is power enough on this camp-ground to-day, to secure the salvation of all that are here, if that power were all consecrated to God, and working together for this end. What we want is power, to get these forces all to work for God, and to keep all the people employed together in this work. But we often move in the wrong direction; we move too much against each other. What we want is God's holy love and constraining power, that shall give us such a concentration of the influences of the Spirit, as shall enable us to labor all as one man, while we all exalt Jesus, and Him alone—no minister saying or thinking anything against another, and no member saying or thinking anything against another, but all helping each other. And this would be a reasonable service, and would give power to the Church, and promote the glory of God. What a glorious world this would be, if all were just right. I would scarcely wish then to go to heaven, though I would like to be there; but if I could see the prospect of this, and God would let me live to be as old as Methuselah, I would gird myself for the work, and gladly live till the day of the final conflagration, if I might aid in bringing in the millennial glory.

THE APOSTOLIC EXHORTATION.

"I beseech you by the mercies of God." So Paul besought the Romans. What shall I say to this congregation? "Brethren, I beseech *you* by the mercies of God that ye present your bodies a living sacrifice, holy, acceptable unto God."

Look at the glorious land God has given us! O let us try to save it! See the glorious Church of Christ with which God has united us. O let us work for the church. God has given us children and friends to be saved. You have come, many of you, to attend this meeting. O I beseech you by the mercies of God, make the sacrifice complete to-day. Do it now, just as you are. All heaven is ready; God the Father is ready; Jesus the Saviour is ready; God the Holy Ghost is ready; angels are ready, clad in white robes, and with their harps in their hands, waiting for you, to strike the key-note. In God's name strike it to-day, and now.

When will you make this reasonable sacrifice? Heaven is above you, the church is around you, all things are ready. O when will you make the consecration? (A voice, "Now!") Now? Is that it? That word is variously understood and used. Sometimes we mean by it just a little ahead. That is not its true meaning. It means *just now, before you can have another thought, or speak another word.* Now! I may say, and you may say, not irreverently, " A body hast thou prepared for me," and I give my body to thee, O God. I give myself and you give yourself now to God. Does it require an effort ? Yes, but it is worth the making. If I had to carry the Lamb from Galilee to Jerusalem on my shoulders, I would do it to make my sacrifice. If I had to make a weary pilgrimage to save my soul, I would make it, but I need not. God is here, and *here* may I have salvation. Let not one, then, leave this congregation without offering himself to God. In this altar, up and down these aisles, and all over these grounds make the offering, and make it now. Do just what you can, and you have done enough; God will do all the rest ;—and now, just as the sun has shone out from behind the clouds, may God shine with his glorious light upon this congregation. Are we not a part of His great family ? Yes. Thank God, we are His sons and daughters. God is our Father, our everlasting Father, and He does not cast us away, though we have wandered from Him, but is ready to receive us as we return to Him, and throw His arms of love around us. By the very kindness then, that does not cast us away, I want to be made a better son, so that I can say, " I do always those thin rs i at please Him" in the place He has given me. At home, abroad, everywhere, all is done with an eye single to His glory."

> " I want the witness, Lord,
>   That all I do is right,
>   According to Thy will and word—
>   Well-pleasing in Thy sight."

CHAPTER XXXII.

EXPLANATIONS—SPECIAL MEETINGS, &C.—SACRAMENT—
NATIONAL COMMITTEE—APPREHENSIONS AND PREJUDI-
CES—RESULTS—CLOSING.

To the children of God assembled at Round Lake National Camp-Meeting, the days passed swiftly and de-
lightfully, and soon were numbered among the things
that were. Through ages yet unborn, that hallowed spot,
as well as Vineland and Manheim, will be remembered,
and the glorified may recount the gracious victories
there achieved. So, too, dear reader, have we come to
the concluding chapter of " PENUEL." We would
gladly have given more particulars of Vineland, Manheim, and Round Lake, but the limits of our space forbade. We have been compelled to omit several excellent sermons and exhortations given at the Round Lake
meeting, as well as similar efficient services of other
brethren at the preceding National Camps. And here
we may ask the indulgence of the reader, for the editorial
department of " PENUEL," as our preparations for the
press were necessarily hurried. Various favorable articles have appeared in the religious periodicals, of the
three National Camp-meetings, and we have observed
that our commendations fall below the standard of others;
this is not because we think theirs are at all overdrawn,
but because we have preferred that the results themselves,
should most fully commend the meetings. And now,

with some incidents and impressions, and a few words relating to services of which we have thus far given no account, we will close this book and bid adieu to the reader.

SPECIAL MEETINGS.

Not the least among the interesting features of the Round Lake meeting, were the special services held for the *young people, the class-leaders, the preachers' wives, the children, and the ministers' experience meeting.*

THE MINISTERS' EXPERIENCE MEETING

was held each evening from six to seven o'clock. Here the ministers who were upon the ground (and there were hundreds of them) delighted to assemble, to familiarly recount their experience, and to uncover their hearts to each other and to God, and together to look for a Pentecostal blessing ; and here many a preacher received a baptism which, we apprehend, will make itself felt upon his church and upon the world in the time to come. The Great Head of the Church was present, commissioning anew His messengers, and anointing them with fire and with the Holy Ghost. The meeting for ministers' wives, which was held daily, was also fruitful of good results, which, we doubt not, will be seen in the day of the Lord.

YOUNG PEOPLE.

The young people's meetings were held daily in the large Congress Street tent, and were scenes of remarkable interest and power. Hundreds of the young men and women of the Church here entered into a depth of experience which must be felt through all their lives, and which, we pray God, may lead many more of the dear youth, all over the land, to an entire consecration to Jesus.

CLASS-LEADERS.

Interesting meetings of the class-leaders on the ground, were held at intervals, where the men and women of God present—to whom the Church has committed the interests of her members, as to sub-pastors—came together to counsel and to pray with one another, and find, as they did not fail to do, new strength and wisdom for their important duties.

Last, though not least, of these special gatherings was

THE CHILDREN'S MEETING.

Two ladies, Mrs. James and Mrs. Wittenmyer, were appointed by the National Committee to take charge of and conduct them, and their duties were performed most efficiently. Each day, at 1.15 o'clock, P.M., in the large tent, the "lambs of the flock" gathered to be instructed in the things of the kingdom.

At one of these meetings a brother most beautifully and forcibly illustrated, by means of a magnet and iron spikes and nails, how the attractive power of the Gospel fails, more and more, to influence the heart and life as men grow older. A large spike represented the aged sinner, and smaller spikes and nails those of less age, till the children found their illustration in the small iron tacks. When the magnet was applied to the large spike (the aged sinner) it failed to move it; when put in contact with a smaller one, representing a sinner past middle age, it lifted it slightly; but when applied carefully, directly to the head of the spike, it raised it; showing that the Gospel meets the assent of the intellect of such, but does not move the heart. When applied to the smaller spikes and nails, representing early life and youth, the magnet raised them with comparative ease; but when put among the tacks (the children), it lifted them in multitudes, and represented them as clinging to each other, even to be lifted, though all could not touch the magnet.

Besides those above mentioned, several brothers and sisters addressed the children at these meetings, among whom was Bishop Simpson, who most earnestly and affectionately pointed the little ones to the Lamb of God.

A gentleman from the South, expressing a deep interest in these meetings, inquired concerning their origin, and remarked : "It is a most beautiful feature of this Camp-meeting, and entirely new to me"—never having heard of a children's meeting in connection with a Camp-meeting—" and now," he added, "I shall report them for our Southern papers, and I hope our people will take the hint and introduce them at our Campmeetings." Amen!

As showing the effect of the meeting upon the children, the following incident may be mentioned :

One evening a lady, hearing a child's voice in prayer, peeped into the tent whence the sound proceeded, and saw eight little girls kneeling in prayer, and one leading in a very devout and earnest manner, in which the others joined with great fervor and sincerity. How touchingly beautiful and instructive a lesson to those of larger growth.

PRAYER MEETINGS.

These were numerous and full of interest; indeed, they were the great centres whence radiated the wondrous fervor which attended all the exercises of the Camp, and which was so manifestly present everywhere, that all, even the most careless or wicked who came upon the ground, felt, and were compelled to confess its influence. The following, in reference to one of the many prayer meetings in the tents, is from the pen of a scoffing and hardened skeptic, who was upon the ground as the correspondent of one of the most irreligious of the New York dailies, and is the more valuable a testimony because of its source.

"To one of these tents I was attracted by a woman's voice of singular pathos and sweetness. I looked in over the shoulders of two rough countrymen. Within, there was a numerous company of men and women on their knees, and in the centre there was turned up one sweet white face, whose whole tearful expression was so unspeakably sad and soft, heightened, too, by the supplicating hands held together as we see children perform their devotions, that I myself was startled at the picture. She was praying. The tears were streaming down her face. I listened; it was no repetition of Biblical phrases, no glib offering of platitudes. The voice was singularly sweet in its mildness; it seemed wet with inward tears. She was appealing to a beneficent Father, with all the ingenuous directness of a child and all the boundless love of a mother. And it was for men everywhere! She could see no converts for her tears. She was really praying for her race. Something of the woman's uni-

versal solicitude seemed to enchain the listeners.   She
asked for pardon, for light, for mercy, and there must
have been presented to her mind a world of misery, hy-
pocrisy, and folly, for whom she was quite as willing to
work as to pray.   I noticed that the crowd here were
awed by the majesty of this woman's weak voice.   If
they could not understand her, they felt that sovereign
influence which is exerted by a pity, competent to grasp
the whole of mankind.   When I looked about upon the
faces of the listeners, peering in with curiosity at this
exhibition of a woman's nature, it seemed to me at the
moment like sacrilege."

THE SACRAMENTAL SERVICE.

The following account is from the pen of the Rev. A.
Wallace, of the *Methodist Home Journal :*

This was one of the most impressive and memorable
scenes of these ten extraordinary days.   On the platform
sat the aged ministers ; conspicuous among them the
venerable and excellent Father Reynolds, of Brooklyn ;
Coleman, of Troy Conference ; De Vinne, of New York,
and others.   The Bishop sat on one side of the table,
covered with snow-white cloth, and Mr. Inskip on the
other.   Within an extensive circle formed by settees all
round the elevated stand, were gathered the preachers,
and without and beyond, to the farther limits of the
canvas, sat the people.

CONSECRATION OF THE ELEMENTS.

Rev. Dr. Lore, Editor of the *Northern Christian
Advocate*, read the Scriptures ; a sacramental hymn was
sung with melting emotion, and Rev. Dr. Wright, of

Cincinnati, led the bowed and fervent throng up to the "midst of the throne," and into the presence of Him "who was dead but is alive for evermore." O what a prayer! and while yet pleading the answer came—sweetly, powerfully to the waiting heart.

After some earnest words from the Bishop, he proceeded with the ritual service, in due form, and consecrated the bread and the wine. Around the table, kneeling with him, we noticed Rev. S. V. Leech, of Baltimore; Dunn, of Jersey City; Dr. Peck, of Albany; Wells, Pomeroy, of Troy; Clemm, Riddle, of Delaware; Bristow, of Kentucky; Adams, of Brooklyn, and others, who, after partaking "with thanksgiving," administered the emblems of dying love to all the ministers present. Then the laity came up and knelt around the circle in successive hundreds until nearly two thousand had commemorated Calvary.

PARTITIONS BROKEN DOWN.

It will hardly be credited, but it is a fact that there, side by side with the ardent Methodist, knelt the hitherto close communion Baptist, the Churchman, the Congregationalist, the Friend, and some who, twenty-four hours previously, were unawakened and unconverted—but now rejoicing in the new-found joy of Jesus' pardoning love.

THE BLOOD CLEANSETH.

As each table was dismissed, one of the ministers officiating delivered a brief address. The Bishop taking his part, and rising into a realm of eloquent thought and utterance, such as we have never observed before, except on one occasion at a conference of colored preachers. He was at white heat and imbued with extraordinary unction from "the Holy One." At the close, he said, "Dear ministers of Jesus, if there is anything you have not given up, now is the time to consecrate fully your all to Christ. You need, and may have a fresh anointing just now. O Holy Ghost, come now upon us all! We see no visible tongue descending, but the *fire is here!* The refining flame is in our hearts. Brethren, there never was a day when we needed more power than now. We are called to meet, in this land, the tide of heathenism rolling in upon our shores. Infidelity is making its fiercest onset. We need and must have apostolic power. O Lord, clothe us with salvation! Help us to preach Christ as we never preached before —a present, a full, and precious Saviour. Let us have Him in our hearts, in all the glory of His name, and ever realize that He saves—that His blood cleanseth, *cleanseth*, CLEANSETH."—("Me," shouted many voices.) "Yes," continued the Bishop, "the blood of Jesus cleanseth *us from all* sin!"

A LIVING MONUMENT.

Addressing the people, who at this awful moment were being thrilled through and through with Divine power, and whose faces were wet with streaming tears —he beautifully said, "We raise a monument to the living Jesus. When our friends die we erect a tombstone, and inscribe their name, and our love there; but our Lord and Master needs no tombstone! He is not here. The grave could not hold Him. He has ascended up on high! Let our monument be, believing hearts, sanctified hearts, united in one, built up in Him. The base on this earth, but the top reaching to the heaven of heavens!"

THE NATIONAL CAMP-MEETING COMMITTEE.

In the selection of ministers, good and true, for this Committee, the hand of Providence may be seen—men of one mind, one heart, and one work—who felt they were in the true Wesleyan succession, by intensely desiring, and constantly endeavoring to spread Scriptural holiness over all lands. They asked nothing for themselves, but everything for their Divine Master. Perhaps a company of men never more fully realized their need of special aid from on high. Therefore, they were much given to prayer, especially during the progress of Camp-meeting. There was no self-seeking, and no spirit of favoritism. From the first they acted as though they were conscious the most holy of all causes was committed to them, and yet they possessed that freedom from solicitude, which only can result from an implicit trust in Christ. Brothers they were and are, the most of whom had been tried by fire, and through whom, we humbly trust, God has ordained great good to His Church and the world.

APPREHENSIONS AND PREJUDICES.

That the more praise may be given to God for His safe conduct of the National Camp-Meeting through the formative and critical part of its history (as men may look upon it), we give the following from a Presiding Elder in New Jersey Conference.

The disapproval expressed by some of the church

authorities against holding the Vineland Camp-meeting, was expressed in the gentlest forms, which made it still more of a cross to resist.

It was based upon the fear, that it would introduce division among the members of our beloved church, by creating a caste. It is difficult to resist the opinions of a man you love, and whose head and heart you revere, and so it was in this case. It is proper to add, that no bishop has ever apparently loved or regarded me less because of my identification with this God-blessed effort to revive Scriptural holiness. Some of the oldest and most prominent members of the Conference, however, did not accept my action in as gentle a light, and I received official notifications several times that my character would be called in question at the Conference, under the form of a regular complaint. I tried to be kind and loving in my replies, without, however, conceding in any manner, that the course pursued in reference to the Vineland Camp-Meeting was one that needed apology. It was certain to me that our brethren would cease to speak against this way, when they once learned that it was simply the old Methodism of the fathers, pressed into immediate experience, and it is probable that they became convinced that we were not schismatics, and did not bring their complaint. It is pleasant to add, that no friend has been permanently alienated from me by my advocacy of the doctrine; a number of my friends have passed with me into its permanent experience and profession, and, above all, my power with man has largely increased since the precious gift of a *full salvation* has been realized in daily experience. God has sweetly removed the apprehensions of a multitude of the lovers of our Zion.

RESULTS.

We opine this is one of the great movements that, from time, to time, have taken place in the world, and which have left behind them, far wider and more abiding results, than the original actors could have conceived or understood. If God but continue His smile upon the effort, it certainly will be left for future historians, each in succession, to chronicle still wider and more precious results. A veteran editor has said, " This meeting has already grown to mammoth proportions. It now wields a powerful influence in the Methodist Episcopal Church. No one present at the late gathering at Round Lake, could for one moment doubt this ; representatives were present from almost every State in the Union, and they returned by the hundred and by the thousand, carrying with them the spirit and influence, and peculiarities of this meeting, for it was a meeting of shaping and of moulding power."

We have now to speak of the more immediate fruit of these meetings, and first as to *Vineland*. A brother, who did not attend the Camp-meeting, visited the place fully six months after its close, and found the different denominations all on fire, and they spoke of the National Camp in the most reverent manner, as "that great light;" while others thought it was the commencement of the millennium.

In a little church near Vineland, which had lost its pastor, a preacher was obtained to minister to them who had been baptized by the Spirit at Vineland. He found them uninstructed in the first principles of Scripture. One of the deacons had, at Vineland, entered into the experience of entire consecration to Christ, and victory over sin. At first, strong appeals were made to the unconverted without apparent fruit, save in two instances. One of these, was that of a young man who had, for a bet, impiously pretended to pray among the christians at Vineland Camp. On his conversion he said, " I felt, but half an hour ago, as if the very ground would open and engulf me, my sin was so great ; but now I am placed in the very heart of God."

After considerable discouragement on the part of this church, by thorough prostration of spirit, and earnest pleading with God, the answer came. Dead souls heard the voice of the Son of God, and were quickened into life. Large numbers asked, " What shall I do to be saved ? " After these were converted, they were led right on to the Canaan of Perfect Love, and our esteemed brother, who, we judge, was one of the laborers in that harvest, says, " Sinners continue to receive the pardon of their sins, and saints the sanctification they need, and the meeting seems to yet grow in numbers and power."

We cannot think there were less than from one hundred, to one hundred and fifty conversions at Vineland, and a still larger number fully sanctified. The demonstrations of the Holy Spirit's outpouring, were so manifest and glorious, that without a question, God settled the point that there should be, the next year, another such national meeting held, for the same special purpose—nay, Vineland Camp-meeting may be said to have determined the point, that national camp-meetings, for the promotion of Christian holiness, should become an institution in the Methodist Church, and one of vast magnitude and proportions, and very great moulding power. In short, that its work should be, to keep the Church to the Wesleyan and Scriptural doctrine of holiness of heart and life, and to kindle a fire that should burn more and more intensely, until "the earth shall be filled with the knowledge of the glory of the Lord, as the waters cover the sea."

Of Manheim, it is said by all who were present, that the general results were even more glorious, than at Vineland. Many love to dwell upon the special display of the power of God on Monday night. The following description is by a devoted servant of Jesus, a member of another denomination:—

"On Monday evening, after preaching by a man full of faith and of the Holy Ghost, a season was set apart for silent prayer by the vast congregation. While thus engaged in deep stillness, a wonderful sense of the presence and power of the Holy Ghost came over the meeting, so marked that almost the whole company of christians fell on their knees without a word, and unconverted men fled from the scene. A minister tried to pray, but failed; having a strong voice, he tried to raise it to break the silence, but again failed. Expressions of the overwhelming feeling, seemed like intrusion. There was that vast assemblage upon their knees, with upturned faces, in anxiety and dread, or in wonder and joy, and not knowing what next to expect. It seemed as though the visible presence of Jesus was there, and as though we should all be swept up into heaven. I almost hesitate to describe this, to those who have not seen or experienced the like; but a similar experience of the presence and wondrous power of the Holy Ghost, a year ago at Vineland, was the means of giving me such wondrous views of the reality of the scene on Calvary, and of leading me to such implicit dependence on the guidance and power of the Spirit, that I am compelled to acknowledge it as a special grace, to meet the need of God's children. I have not known either scene succeeded by any acts of fanaticism or excitement, and by every scriptural and evangelical test of its fruits, I must own it to be indeed of God. It was not the result of over-wrought feeling in excitement, but came while God's people were in silent, earnest prayer before Him for His presence, and it was simultaneous over the assembly. Many conversions appeared to follow it."

Another speaks of the same occasion on this wise: " Wave after wave of sacred influence seemed to roll in upon the people, until the entire audience was prostrate before the Lord. The discourse which preceded this visitation was on ' Hindrances to Holiness,' by Rev. John Thompson, of Philadelphia, followed by Rev. Mr. Inskip, in an earthquake exhortation, pressing home the claims of God on every conscience, and urging to an immediate effort for full salvation. Then such cries, such groaning, wrestling, mighty, grasping faith, as was engaged in, cannot be described. The power came. The people fell. It was a baptism of the Holy Ghost and of fire; victory and glory rested on all. The sensation continued far into the night, and shouts of holy triumph resounded on every hand."

One of the old soldiers of Jesus, whose locks are white, alluding to this special season, said he left the stand to see if the same power was resting on any of the people who might be in their tents. He found it was, and returning to the stand, he looked upon the ministers there, and he could not tell whether his eyes deceived him or not, but every face was shining, and the hair of every one seemed as white as his own, and they all seemed to have come "face to face with God."

Of *Round Lake*, we can only speak in very general terms, except to give a few illustrative incidents. Of the generally unknown, and officially unacknowledged works of God in the conversion of sinners, take the following:—

"The presence and power of the Holy Ghost were not only in the public and private meetings, but there seemed diffused throughout the grounds a solemn awe that forbade trifling; and efforts to reach souls privately, found a peculiar response, even among those who came upon the ground careless and unawakened.

"As an instance of this, a Congregationalist, a wealthy merchant, came with his wife and daughter, to spend two days. The whole scene was new to them, but soon the influences of the Spirit not only led the parents to entire consecration to Christ, but their daughter, a sweet child of fifteen, was awakened from her carelessness to seek forgiveness of sins. She did not attend many meetings, but the Spirit of God did its work in her heart. Finding her thus awakened, we pressed her to an immediate act of faith in the blood of Jesus, and as we kneeled, smiles of joy soon burst through the tears that covered her face. While we were giving thanks for the great salvation, a young woman of about eighteen, an entire stranger, looked into the tent and asked permission to kneel with us. She too was under deep conviction for sin, all ready for the message of grace to sinners. We told her of what the Lord had just done for the child kneeling beside us, and soon she also came to the cross with all her sins, and left the tent with us, now a saved sinner."

A newly baptized and eloquent ambassador of Jesus, from Philadelphia, says :—

" By the grace of God, I have been at the third National Camp-Meeting, at Round Lake, in the State of New York. I expect to thank God for it through the everlasting ages.

*   *   *   *   *   *

" The effects of the meeting were Pentecostal. And who but an infidel will wonder at it ? Wherever there is pentecostal prayer, pentecostal faith, pentecostal unity of aim and effort, pentecostal directness, pentecostal entreaty and expectation, that 'the promise of the Father' will be fulfilled in the name, and by the authority of Jesus, there *must* be pentecostal effects, in the munificent gift of the Holy Ghost. The Holy Ghost fell on that vast assemblage, time and again, in such marvellous and evident revealings of the glory of God as were, perhaps, in advance of the previous experience of the oldest and most favored children of God, who witnessed and felt these heart-cleansing and life-giving shocks of love, and joy, and power. No one went wild. Only one lost sense or consciousness. There was no case of trance. At times, emotion became so uncontrollable, as to make a pentecostal shout like the voice of many waters. But evidently God was there in such felt majesty and love that it was hallowed ground. Every one seemed to feel it. Never have I seen such uniform decorum and propriety of behavior."

A veteran minister speaks in this wise :—

" At Round Lake, as at Manheim and Vineland, it was shown that a solemn, earnest, positive committal of souls before the congregation, was a decisive action. Several times, especially amid the stillness of the night, the altar, containing hundreds, was filled with seekers, and then the ministers were driven from their beautiful stand, and that was made an altar. Oh! my soul, thou wilt never forget the solemn tramping of immortal ones up those steps to the consecrated stand, as if climbing up the ladder Jacob saw—climbing up to glory, immortality, and eternal life. And then, when this body of earnest seekers was thus gathered to one spot for mighty knee-work, how the power came! Gray-headed ministers, young ministers, with the brightness of promise upon their brow—veteran members, and young soldiers of the Cross—all in solemn, living consecration. And how, by scores, they rose to testify of the cleansing blood, or the conscious witness of justification! Those were ' *night-scenes* ' sublime—indescribable. Angelic hosts, hovering over the scene, were entranced by the wonders of redeeming love."

We take the following from the *Guide to Holiness :*

The personal appearance, conversation, public exercises, and conference standing of the many ministers present at Round Lake, gave fullest assurance that they were men of no ordinary calibre, and whether they went to the meeting fully in sympathy with its object or not, we believe it to be entirely true, that none of those ambassadors for Jesus left that hallowed spot, without stronger convictions of the truth of this old Bible doctrine, and thanking God that our fathers, and our Church, so fully espoused it. Indeed, the impression made upon these ministers was, perhaps, the most marked feature of the whole meeting. They listened to preaching and experience with the closest attention, and, jealous for Zion, watched for anything that might develop into hurtful tendencies. Yet, with wonderful unanimity, they were delighted with, and profited by, the sermons, and were so charmed with the humility, zeal, and love of both preachers and people professing entire sanctification, that criticism was disarmed, all objections were speedily removed, and they, with the rest, were intently anxious to be borne far out on the sea of perfect love.

But we must leave the further statement of results, to the many witnesses for Jesus scattered through the land, and the revelations of the day of eternity.

CLOSING EXERCISES OF THIRD NATIONAL CAMP-MEETING.

On Friday, July 16th, at 8 o'clock, A.M., the bell summoned the people to the stand for the closing exercises. The hymn commencing—

> " Blest be the tie that binds
> Our hearts in kindred love,"

was announced and sung, followed by a most impressive and comprehensive prayer. Rev. Mr. Inskip then addressed the audience, giving appropriate counsel to those about to take their departure. He thought a change for the better was coming over everything. The church was growing better. He loved it more, and never had he loved his brethren of the ministry so well, as since his heart had been wholly sanctified to God. "Don't be censorious," he said, appealing to those who professed the blessing of holiness; over five hundred ministers, he remarked, had visited the Camp, and he did not hear an unkind word uttered by one of them. All met and mingled in the sweetest harmony, and leaving, would take " Christ formed within," as their glorious personal Saviour. The effect of the Round Lake Camp-Meeting would, perhaps, be most powerful, as instanced in the profession and ministrations of so many ambassadors of Jesus, who had their souls newly baptized and consecrated here.

BISHOP SIMPSON'S CLOSING ADDRESS.

After Mr. Inskip sat down, Bishop Simpson, who, with his family, has attended all the National Camp-Meetings, rose and said:—

Did the time permit, there are many things I should like to say, but the closing moments are upon us, and our words must be few.

In the first place, I wish to say that I have been exceedingly pleased with this Camp-Meeting. Standing as I have, apart from its management, that being in the hands of the Committee, I could note carefully its general working, and I have been highly pleased with it, and with the oversight and general arrangements. Indeed, I do not know that anything more could have been done than has been, to promote harmony, and add to the efficiency and spiritual results of the meeting. I have been specially pleased with two things. *First*, with the deep earnestness and piety which has prevailed, united with so much intelligent christian action. It is almost impossible in so large a concourse, but that some things should be said or done, by one or another, that a good judgment could not approve ; but I must say that I never before saw a Camp-meeting where there was so much earnestness, with so little extravagance.

Second. I have been much pleased with the earnest *calmness* displayed here.   There has been much of calm waiting on God, and trusting in the atoning merits of the Lord Jesus Christ.   It has been earnest calmness, and calm earnestness, and I pray that this may be diffused throughout the church.

As you scatter to the north, east, south, and west, I know you intend to work for Jesus with new zeal. While I sympathize most fully, with all that can be said about the deeper baptism, the baptism of fire and of the Holy Ghost, of latter years, and indeed throughout my life, I have had the impression that God gives wondrous baptisms of blessing, not so much for the sake of the recipient of them, as for the benefit of the community where he resides, and the world at large.   When Jesus blessed His disciples, He said, " Receive ye the Holy Ghost ; " and I am inclined to think, that in that upper chamber, they did receive the sanctifying influence of the Holy Spirit ; and Christ said to them, " Tarry ye in Jerusalem till ye be endued with power."   And prepared by this, they did tarry, and with one accord, in one place, till the power of the Spirit came down, and the tongues of fire rested upon them.   This prepared them to preach Jesus, and its first effect was to set them all to proclaiming Christ, and with wonderful results, for three thousand were converted in a single day.   In this there seems to me to be a voice saying, that in giving a wonderful baptism, God has a wonderful work for that person or people to do.   I have never myself enjoyed a great baptism, without finding one of two things to follow. Either great trials have come, in which my faith has been severely tried, or a great work has been set before me, for which the special baptism has specially prepared me. And I would say to each one of you here who has received this baptism, look that God will try you, or suffer great temptation to come upon you, or give you some greater work to do, than you have before done. I have no doubt that now, at this closing meeting, Satan would fain have you that he might sift you as wheat. Jesus said to Peter, "Simon, Simon, behold, Satan hath desired to have you, that he may sift you as wheat. But I have prayed for thee, that thy faith fail not; and when thou art converted, strengthen thy brethren."

So you may be tried, but Jesus will stand by you and strengthen you, and then, when you are saved, go out to strengthen your brethren, and go from this place with the conviction that God hath baptized you for special work, or special trial.

In 1857, I was on a bed of sickness, and when friends came and told me of the wondrous revival influences that were all abroad through the land, they would sometimes ask me what it meant. I remarked, that it was to prepare the people of our nation, either for a great work or a great struggle; but I never saw the fulfilment of this, till the great and terrible conflict of the rebellion came on; then I understood it.

We have now a great and increasing work to do. God is sending the heathen to our shores. Already we have the Chinese with their temples and heathen worship, and soon this will be spread all over the land.

What we need, is the highest type of Christianity to bring to Jesus those whom God sends to us. I fear the faith of the Church is not mighty enough, and especially do I fear, that we who live in the cities, have not faith enough in the power of God to convert all classes. Some of you are going to New York. Don't be afraid to do business there for Jesus. Some of you will go to Philadelphia. Do not hesitate to go into the worst places with the Gospel. Some go to the country. Go there, and everywhere, resolved to do more than ever before for Christ. If you all do this, I shall look for a mighty revival that will spread all over the land. But brethren, if you let this power evaporate, you will be shorn of your strength. You must show all, that you have been with Jesus, and if you do this, and work in His spirit, you will have success. You must have, and exhibit this power in your homes, and in your business, and everywhere. O, may God's grace be with us; and if we never meet in another Camp-meeting, may we meet in that better gathering, where we shall join in ceaseless ascriptions of praise unto God and the Lamb forever.

After the doxology was sung, and the Bishop pronounced the benediction, a procession was formed, the ministers walking arm in arm, headed by Bishop Simpson and Mr. Inskip, and followed by "a great multitude," male and female, singing of "the Lamb." They compassed the Camp circle three times, and then deployed in front of the large altar railings, the clergy standing in line, and the laity shaking hands with them all, as they moved on and dispersed over the grounds, rejoicing in conscious favor with the Holy Trinity, and in perfect peace and good-will to each other.

Let us, dear reader, lift our prayers that this book, like the meetings of which it is an imperfect embodiment, may be blessed of God, to the conversion and sanctification of many souls; and with the holy Apostle we say to all who are in Christ Jesus :—

"Now unto Him that is able to keep you from falling, and to present you faultless before the presence of His glory with exeeding joy,

"To the only wise God our Saviour, be glory and majesty, dominion and power, both now and ever. Amen."

TITLES in THIS SERIES

geles, 1925), *AROUND THE WORLD BY FAITH, WITH SIX WEEKS IN THE HOLY LAND* (Los Angeles, n. d.), *TWO YEARS MISSION WORK IN EUROPE JUST BEFORE THE WORLD WAR, 1912-14* (Los Angeles, [1926])

6. Boardman, W. E., *THE HIGHER CHRISTIAN LIFE* (Boston, 1858)

7. Girvin, E. A., *PHINEAS F. BRESEE: A PRINCE IN ISRAEL* (Kansas City, Mo., [1916])

8. Brooks, John P., *THE DIVINE CHURCH* (Columbia, Mo., 1891)

9. RUSSELL KELSO CARTER ON "FAITH HEALING." R. Kelso Carter, *THE ATONEMENT FOR SIN AND SICKNESS* (Boston, 1884) *"FAITH HEALING" REVIEWED AFTER TWENTY YEARS* (Boston, 1897)

10. Daniels, W. H., *DR. CULLIS AND HIS WORK* (Boston, [1885])

11. HOLINESS TRACTS DEFENDING THE MINISTRY OF WOMEN. Luther Lee, *"WOMAN'S RIGHT TO PREACH THE GOSPEL; A SERMON, AT THE ORDINATION OF REV. MISS ANTOINETTE L. BROWN, AT SOUTH BUTLER, WAYNE COUNTY, N. Y., SEPT. 15, 1853"* (Syracuse, 1853) *bound with* B. T. Roberts, *ORDAINING WOMEN* (Rochester, 1891) *bound with* Catherine (Mumford) Booth, *"FEMALE MINISTRY; OR, WOMAN'S RIGHT TO PREACH THE GOSPEL . . ."* (London, n. d.) *bound with* Fannie (McDowell) Hunter, *WOMEN PREACHERS* (Dallas, 1905)

12. LATE NINETEENTH CENTURY REVIVALIST TEACHINGS ON THE HOLY SPIRIT. D. L. Moody, *SECRET POWER OR THE SECRET OF SUCCESS IN CHRISTIAN LIFE AND*

WORK (New York, [1881]) *bound with* J. Wilbur Chapman, *RECEIVED YE THE HOLY GHOST?* (New York, [1894]) *bound with* R. A. Torrey, *THE BAPTISM WITH THE HOLY SPIRIT* (New York, 1895 & 1897)

13. SEVEN "JESUS ONLY" TRACTS. Andrew D. Urshan, *THE DOCTRINE OF THE NEW BIRTH, OR, THE PERFECT WAY TO ETERNAL LIFE* (Cochrane, Wis., 1921) *bound with* Andrew Urshan, *THE ALMIGHTY GOD IN THE LORD JESUS CHRIST* (Los Angeles, 1919) *bound with* Frank J. Ewart, *THE REVELATION OF JESUS CHRIST* (St. Louis, n. d.) *bound with* G. T. Haywood, *THE BIRTH OF THE SPIRIT IN THE DAYS OF THE APOSTLES* (Indianapolis, n. d.) *DIVINE NAMES AND TITLES OF JEHOVAH* (Indianapolis, n. d.) *THE FINEST OF THE WHEAT* (Indianapolis, n. d.) *THE VICTIM OF THE FLAMING SWORD* (Indianapolis, n. d.)

14. THREE EARLY PENTECOSTAL TRACTS. D. Wesley Myland, *THE LATTER RAIN COVENANT AND PENTECOSTAL POWER* (Chicago, 1910) *bound with* G. F. Taylor, *THE SPIRIT AND THE BRIDE* (n. p., [1907?]) *bound with* B. F. Laurence, *THE APOSTOLIC FAITH RESTORED* (St. Louis, 1916)

15. Fairchild, James H., *OBERLIN: THE COLONY AND THE COLLEGE, 1833-1883* (Oberlin, 1883)

16. Figgis, John B., *KESWICK FROM WITHIN* (London, [1914])

17. Finney, Charles G., *LECTURES TO PROFESSING CHRISTIANS* (New York, 1837)

18. Fleisch, Paul, *DIE MODERNE GEMEINSCHAFTS-BEWEGUNG IN DEUTSCHLAND* (Leipzig, 1912)

19. SIX TRACTS BY W. B. GODBEY. *SPIRITUAL GIFTS AND GRACES* (Cincinnati, [1895]) *THE RETURN OF JESUS* (Cincinnati, [1899?]) *WORK OF THE HOLY SPIRIT* (Louisville, [1902]) *CHURCH—BRIDE—KINGDOM* (Cincinnati, [1905]) *DIVINE HEALING* (Greensboro, [1909]) *TONGUE MOVEMENT, SATANIC* (Zarephath, N. J., 1918)

20. Gordon, Earnest B., *ADONIRAM JUDSON GORDON* (New York, [1896])

21. Hills, A. M., *HOLINESS AND POWER FOR THE CHURCH AND THE MINISTRY* (Cincinnati, [1897])

22. Horner, Ralph C., *FROM THE ALTAR TO THE UPPER ROOM* (Toronto, [1891])

23. McDonald, William and John E. Searles, *THE LIFE OF REV. JOHN S. INSKIP* (Boston, [1885])

24. LaBerge, Agnes N. O., *WHAT GOD HATH WROUGHT* (Chicago, n. d.)

25. Lee, Luther, *AUTOBIOGRAPHY OF THE REV. LUTHER LEE* (New York, 1882)

26. McLean, A. and J. W. Easton, *PENUEL; OR, FACE TO FACE WITH GOD* (New York, 1869)

27. McPherson, Aimee Semple, *THIS IS THAT: PERSONAL EXPERIENCES SERMONS AND WRITINGS* (Los Angeles, [1919])

28. Mahan, Asa, *OUT OF DARKNESS INTO LIGHT* (London, 1877)

29. THE LIFE AND TEACHING OF CARRIE JUDD MONTGOMERY Carrie Judd Montgomery, *"UNDER HIS WINGS": THE STORY OF MY LIFE* (Oakland,

[1936]) Carrie F. Judd, *THE PRAYER OF FAITH* (New York, 1880)

30. THE DEVOTIONAL WRITINGS OF PHOEBE PALMER Phoebe Palmer, *THE WAY OF HOLINESS* (52nd ed., New York, 1867) *FAITH AND ITS EFFECTS* (27th ed., New York, n. d., orig. pub. 1854)

31. Wheatley, Richard, *THE LIFE AND LETTERS OF MRS. PHOEBE PALMER* (New York, 1881)

32. Palmer, Phoebe, ed., *PIONEER EXPERIENCES* (New York, 1868)

33. Palmer, Phoebe, *THE PROMISE OF THE FATHER* (Boston, 1859)

34. Pardington, G. P., *TWENTY-FIVE WONDERFUL YEARS, 1889-1914: A POPULAR SKETCH OF THE CHRISTIAN AND MISSIONARY ALLIANCE* (New York, [1914])

35. Parham, Sarah E., *THE LIFE OF CHARLES F. PARHAM, FOUNDER OF THE APOSTOLIC FAITH MOVEMENT* (Joplin, [1930])

36. THE SERMONS OF CHARLES F. PARHAM. Charles F. Parham, *A VOICE CRYING IN THE WILDERNESS* (4th ed., Baxter Springs, Kan., 1944, orig. pub. 1902) *THE EVERLASTING GOSPEL* (n.p., n.d., orig. pub. 1911)

37. Pierson, Arthur Tappan, *FORWARD MOVEMENTS OF THE LAST HALF CENTURY* (New York, 1905)

38. *PROCEEDINGS OF HOLINESS CONFERENCES, HELD AT CINCINNATI, NOVEMBER 26TH, 1877, AND AT NEW YORK, DECEMBER 17TH, 1877* (Philadelphia, 1878)

39. *RECORD OF THE CONVENTION FOR THE PROMOTION OF*

Scriptural Holiness Held at Brighton, May 29th, to June 7th, 1875 (Brighton, [1896?])

40. Rees, Seth Cook, *Miracles in the Slums* (Chicago, [1905?])

41. Roberts, B. T., *Why Another Sect* (Rochester, 1879)

42. Shaw, S. B., ed., *Echoes of the General Holiness Assembly* (Chicago, [1901])

43. The Devotional Writings of Robert Pearsall Smith and Hannah Whitall Smith. [R]obert [P]earsall [S]mith, *Holiness Through Faith: Light on the Way of Holiness* (New York, [1870]) [H]annah [W]hitall [S]mith, *The Christian's Secret of a Happy Life,* (Boston and Chicago, [1885])

44. [S]mith, [H]annah [W]hitall, *The Unselfishness of God and How I Discovered It* (New York, [1903])

45. Steele, Daniel, *A Substitute for Holiness; or, Antinomianism Revived* (Chicago and Boston, [1899])

46. Tomlinson, A. J., *The Last Great Conflict* (Cleveland, 1913)

47. Upham, Thomas C., *The Life of Faith* (Boston, 1845)

48. Washburn, Josephine M., *History and Reminiscences of the Holiness Church Work in Southern California and Arizona* (South Pasadena, [1912?])